1991

D1714772

TEXTUAL CRITICISM AND SCHOLARLY EDITING

Textual Criticism
and
Scholarly Editing

G. THOMAS TANSELLE

PUBLISHED FOR THE
BIBLIOGRAPHICAL SOCIETY OF THE UNIVERSITY OF VIRGINIA
BY THE UNIVERSITY PRESS OF VIRGINIA
CHARLOTTESVILLE AND LONDON

THE UNIVERSITY PRESS OF VIRGINIA
Copyright © 1990 by the Rector and Visitors
of the University of Virginia

First published 1990

Library of Congress Cataloging-in-Publication Data

Tanselle, G. Thomas (George Thomas), 1934–
    Textual criticism and scholarly editing / G. Thomas Tanselle.
        p. cm.
    Includes index.
    Contents: Texts of documents and texts of works—The editorial
problem of final authorial intention—External fact as an
editorial problem—Some principles for editorial apparatus—
Problems and accomplishments in the editing of the novel—The
editing of historical documents—Classical, Biblical, and medieval
textual criticism and modern editing—Textual study and literary
judgment.
    ISBN 0-8139-1303-9
    1. Criticism, Textual.   2. Editing.   I. Title.
PN81.T319   1990
801'.959—dc20   90-37487
                                                           CIP

Printed in the United States of America

FOR

Jed, Susan, and Jack

Contents

Preface   ix

PROLOGUE

Texts of Documents and Texts of Works (1981)   3

I

The Editorial Problem of Final Authorial
    Intention (1976)   27

External Fact as an Editorial Problem (1979)   72

Some Principles for Editorial Apparatus (1972)   119

II

Problems and Accomplishments in the Editing
    of the Novel (1975)   179

The Editing of Historical Documents (1978)   218

Classical, Biblical, and Medieval Textual
    Criticism and Modern Editing (1983)   274

EPILOGUE

Textual Study and Literary Judgment (1971)   325

Index   341

Preface

This volume brings together eight essays on textual criticism and scholarly editing that I published between 1971 and 1983. It is intended to complement my two recently published volumes, *Textual Criticism since Greg* (1987) and *A Rationale of Textual Criticism* (1989), by making more conveniently accessible a series of discussions that amplify some of the arguments of those volumes. The 1989 book (consisting of my three Rosenbach Lectures of 1987) attempted to be a basic statement about the nature of texts in the various arts and about the task of preserving and editing verbal texts. The 1987 book reprinted three of my essays from *Studies in Bibliography*, those that survey and analyze the debates on editorial theory (mostly in English and mostly on post-medieval literature) since 1950. And the present volume deals with the same issues by focusing at greater length (and with additional examples) on particular problems or areas. Aside from the more general opening and closing pieces, the contents fall into two parts: the first takes up three basic questions that editors often face (how to assess authorial intention, how to handle factual errors, and how to present textual evidence); the second looks critically at editorial traditions in three disparate fields (fiction, historical documents, and writings that antedate the invention of printing).

These essays have played some role in the ongoing debates, and I am therefore letting them stand as they were originally published. (The five from *Studies in Bibliography*—abbreviated *SB* in footnotes—are reproduced photographically from copies of the published volumes, and the others are reset in the same typographic style and with the same form of documentation.) I do not find, in any case, that my views on these matters have changed in any major respects, though at a number of places I would now express those views in somewhat different language. The changes I would now make, if I were revising these pieces, are largely stylistic; but there are some statements that I would rewrite entirely, not to alter their fundamental points but to eliminate their possible ambiguities by taking into account certain concerns that have become prominent in subsequent discussion.

One example of a class of such statements will, I think, be instructive to mention here. The opening sentence of "The Editorial Problem of Final Authorial Intention" (1976) reads as follows: "Scholarly editors may disagree about many things, but they are in general agreement that their goal is to discover exactly what an author wrote and to determine what form of his work he wished the public to have." To write that statement now would certainly be incautious, given the many recent discussions of editorial goals other than authorial intention. But the source of the carelessness in my statement is not what it may at first appear to be, for I have never regarded authorial intention as the only aspect of textual history that an editor could legitimately focus on. The real problem is that I was using the term "scholarly editing" far too loosely to mean "critical editing"—to mean, that is, the kind of editing in which critical judgment is employed to make alterations in received texts so as to try to reconstruct some historical form of a work that is not accurately represented in any surviving printed or written document.

Obviously critical editing can be directed toward the reconstruction of texts other than those intended by authors. But my position, then and now, is that critical editing is in general most usefully employed for reconstructing authorially intended texts, whereas an interest in the public forms of texts as intended by authors' friends, or by scribes, or by publishers' editors, is likely to be better accommodated by unaltered transcriptions or facsimiles than by critical editions. The texts that are present in written and printed documents are of course not necessarily in every respect what the producers of those documents intended, but they are nevertheless what reached an audience as the result of the collaborative process of production and dissemination. My 1976 sentence, and several other similar ones, were not meant to disparage the study of documentary texts as social or collaborative products; they were meant only to assert that, if one were undertaking a critical edition, the most appropriate goal would seem to be the reconstruction of an authorially intended text (leaving other goals to other kinds of editions).

Debating this point (and clearly it is debatable) is a very different matter from debating whether authorial intention is the only legitimate or sensible goal of editing. The former is a potentially fruitful topic; the latter is not, for no aspect of the past can be ruled out as a subject for historical investigation. One can choose, according to one's temperament, to focus on verbal works as the creations of individual minds, or as the collaborative products of given intellectual milieux, or as touchstones for the measurement of readers' responses at different times. All these studies together are required to encompass the life history of a work. In the theoretical debates of recent decades, those arguing for a particular position have too often felt it necessary to attack other positions, as if discrediting another's view adds legitimacy to one's own. Many approaches to editing, as to everything else, are possible, and the validity of each one depends on the rigor of the arguments that are adduced to support it.

Nevertheless, the recent discussions have been healthful and invigorating for the field of textual studies, helping to show the inextricability of textual criticism and literary criticism. But the well-established, if irrational, barrier between these areas has not yet by any means been broken down. Although many recent literary theorists have been concerned with exploring the nature of verbal communication, they have scarcely acknowledged the insight that has underlain more than two millennia of textual criticism: that language is an intangible medium and that words on paper are therefore not verbal works themselves but only guides to the reconstitution of such works. If this point were more widely recognized, there would be greater understanding of the inseparability of textual and literary criticism: the act of reading entails the questioning not simply of the meanings of works but of the makeup of the texts of those works. Distinguishing between the texts of documents and the texts of works—which is the essence of textual criticism—is crucial to an appreciation not only of verbal works but of all other works (such as musical ones) that employ intangible media. The essays in this volume do not always explicitly use this formulation of the nature of verbal texts and their problematic status in relation to works (a formulation that I developed in *A Rationale of Textual Criticism*), but it is implicit in all of them, as it is, I believe, in the idea of textual criticism itself.

*   *   *

A few comments are in order on each of the essays that follow. This is not the place, however, to list subsequent treatments of the same subjects—which in any case are taken up in *Textual Criticism since Greg* and in a further survey essay now in preparation.

The opening essay, "Texts of Documents and Texts of Works," was originally published under the title "Literary Editing" in *Literary & Historical Editing*, edited by George L. Vogt and John Bush Jones (Lawrence: University of Kansas Libraries, 1981), pp. 35–56. This is the only essay in the present volume for which I have supplied a new title. The original title, "Literary Editing," reflects the fact that "literary editing" was the topic assigned to me at the Conference on Literary and Historical Editing held at the University of Kansas, 25–27 September 1978, from which the papers for the Kansas volume were derived. But the original title would be misleading if retained now because the essay argues that the editing of literature is not essentially different from the editing of other writings and that the significant distinction between kinds of editing is quite another one (as indicated by the new title). Indeed, I consider the entire present collection of essays to deal with issues relevant to the textual study of writings in all fields and from all periods, even when the examples are drawn from literary works of the last century or two.

"The Editorial Problem of Final Authorial Intention" was first published in *Studies in Bibliography*, 29 (1976), 167–211. In the years since then, aspects of intention—both its definition and its place in editing—have received a great deal of attention, and I have commented on many of these discussions in the second and third essays in *Textual Criticism since Greg*. In a footnote (81) to the third essay in that volume, I responded to the view, expressed by a few writers, that my 1976 piece does not place intention within the *process* of verbal composition: "All I can say is that I meant for it to: when I spoke, for example, of 'the intention of the author to have particular words and marks of punctuation constitute his text' (p. 182), I was assuming that such intention manifests itself continuously throughout the writing of a work (and often shifts, producing revisions—a problem I took up in the later parts of the essay). (I am aware of the irony: this situation illustrates the fact that a writer's statement of intention does not always match what readers find in the work.)"

"External Fact as an Editorial Problem" originally appeared in *Studies in Bibliography*, 32 (1979), 1–47. The principal body of examples in it emerged from my work on *Moby-Dick* as one of the editors of the Northwestern-Newberry Edition of Melville; the NN *Moby-Dick* has since appeared (1988), and its section of "Discussions of Adopted Readings" contains many further discussions illustrative of the approach to "external fact" set forth in this essay.

"Some Principles for Editorial Apparatus," first published in *Studies in Bibliography*, 25 (1972), 41–88, is here provided with an appendix, "Editorial Apparatus for Radiating Texts," that was published later (*Library*, 5th ser., 29 [1974], 330–337) and was intended as a supplement to the earlier essay. In reprinting the earlier essay, I should perhaps repeat a point made in it: that my concern is not to prescribe specific forms for editorial apparatuses but to explore the considerations that should underlie, and be accommodated by, any apparatus. In reprinting the supplementary piece on radiating texts, I should like to add an observation: that the idea of editing without a copy-text, set forth briefly here in relation to one particular kind of situation, has further applications that ought to be explored.

"Problems and Accomplishments in the Editing of the Novel" was published in *Studies in the Novel*, 7 (1975), 323–360, as the introductory essay to a special issue (dated Fall 1975) on "Textual Studies in the Novel." Because I was not given the opportunity to read proof, I am taking this occasion to correct some dozen and a half errors that appeared in the periodical text; I have not incorporated any new revisions in the essay but have simply restored some readings from my typescript that were incorrectly set in type.

"The Editing of Historical Documents" first appeared in *Studies in Bibliography*, 31 (1978), 1–56, and was made available as a pamphlet in time for the September 1978 Kansas conference (mentioned above). There has been much discussion of documentary editing since 1978, partly as a result of the formation of the Association for Documentary Editing, and I have commented on some of this discussion in the third of the essays in *Textual Criticism since Greg*, pp. 112–121.

"Classical, Biblical, and Medieval Textual Criticism and Modern Editing," published in *Studies in Bibliography*, 36 (1983), 21–68, is my attempt to examine concisely the main traditions of textual criticism that preceded the period dealt with in more detail in *Textual Criticism since Greg*.

"Textual Study and Literary Judgment" was delivered in Denver on 28 December 1969, at the annual meeting of the Modern Language Association of America (Bibliographical Evidence Group), and was published in *Papers of the Bibliographical Society of America*, 65 (1971), 109–122. The earliest piece in this book, it presents the view that editing is an art, not a science, a view that underlies all the other essays as well.

For permission to republish these essays here, I wish to thank the editors of the *Library*, *Papers of the Bibliographical Society of America*, *Studies in Bibliography*, *Studies in the Novel*, and the University of Kansas Library Series. My indebtedness to Fredson Bowers for his hospitality to my essays in *Studies in Bibliography* was suggested by the dedication to him of an earlier collection of my essays, drawn entirely from *Studies in Bibliography*; I wish here to repeat my gratitude to him for his unfailing helpfulness and loyal support over many years.

* * *

The two terms that form the title of this book are the traditional terms for the two intertwined concerns that are the subject of these essays. Textual criticism is the evaluation of the correctness (according to some specified standard) of surviving texts, based on an examination of the physical evidence present in the documents conveying the texts—including the variant readings in them—as well as on historical knowledge and literary judgment. Scholarly editing is the use of the insights provided by textual criticism to produce new documents, either editions containing photographic facsimiles and literal transcriptions of individual documentary texts or editions containing critically constructed texts that draw readings from any relevant documents and from the editors' own thinking. When the two terms, "textual criticism" and "scholarly editing," are used together, these traditional meanings are still likely to be the ones generally understood. But when "textual criticism" is used alone, one can no longer be confident that it will be taken in this sense. Many literary critics of the last several decades have habitually used "text" to mean "work," and to them and their readers "textual criticism" means "literary criticism." This equation might be greeted as a positive sign if it indicated a recognition that the critical reading of works made of words includes the examination of the makeup of every text of those works, and vice versa. But in fact it only means that the basic distinction between texts and works has been ignored and that textual criticism in the traditional sense is still not regarded as an activity of literary criticism. My joining of "textual criticism" and "scholarly editing" in the title is meant to indicate that I use "textual criticism" in its traditional sense and not as the equivalent of "literary criticism." But every essay in the volume is grounded in the belief that the study of textual histories and the production of editions rely on critical judgment and that the interpretation of works cannot be divorced from the questioning of texts.

New York, March 1990   G.T.T.

Prologue

Texts of Documents and
Texts of Works

WHEN JOHN PASSMORE RECENTLY REVIEWED THREE VOLUMES OF the new Harvard edition of William James, he complained about the attention that had been devoted in them to recording variant readings and punctuation. Having spent some time, he said, on the textual study of the Jacobean drama, he was able to see the value of such information for those "devoted to the study of James's rhetoric, or to changes in punctuation and spelling in the earlier years of the century." But "as an edition for philosophers," he maintained, "one cannot but wish that the editorial energies devoted to its preparation had been rather differently distributed." Philosophers, he had stated earlier, "go to James because they are interested in, let us say, truth or meaning or experience and they suppose that James might have something to teach them." As a result, he asserts, "The function of an edition of a philosopher is in this respect quite different from the function of an edition of a novelist."[1]

The idea that scholarly editions of literary works should somehow be different in approach or emphasis from those of philosophical, historical, scientific, or other writings is a curiously widespread one, and Passmore's remarks are characteristic of this point of view. But the form his remarks take also makes clear, to any thoughtful reader, how untenable the position is. He assumes, first, that stylistic and formal matters are distinct from the content of a piece of writing and, second, that students of literature concentrate on the style of literary works, whereas philosophers are concerned with the content of philosophical works. Obviously, however, writings generally referred to as "literature" have truths and insights to convey, and literary scholars examine nuances of style as the means by which ideas are communicated with

1. "A Philosopher of the Particulars," *Times Literary Supplement,* 24 June 1977, pp. 746–747.

precision; similarly, one is not in a position to get the most out of a piece of "philosophic" writing without looking closely at its form of expression. As Frederick Burkhardt said in his letter replying to Passmore's review, "It is difficult to understand why the writings of our leading thinkers do not merit the same scrupulous editorial attention given to literary figures, unless it is assumed that a philosopher's thought can somehow be seriously studied in isolation from the style which conveys it and the process by which he developed his final text."[2] A careful reading of any piece of writing, whatever its content or approach must—by definition one would have thought—involve consideration of the manner of expression, which is indeed an inextricable part of the content.

That so-called "literary" works should not be accorded different editorial treatment from other kinds of writing is evident when one considers that no distinct boundary lines exist separating one type of writing from another. Many efforts have been made to define "literature"; and while some of them provide illuminating insights into the nature of the literary experience or of communication in general, they have not resulted in any established or accepted method for distinguishing "literary" works from other types of communication. Even if the literary or imaginative or creative aspects of communication could be effectively segregated from the more directly factual or expository, one would still have no practical basis for classifying whole works, since they would so frequently be found to contain both kinds of communication. Novels can contain factually accurate expository passages, and philosophical or historical treatises can utilize passages of metaphorical statement. The nature of each work as an entity may be equally mixed: "histories," for instance, are often read as literary works, whereas works that superficially appear to be novels may actually be historical accounts. Stanley Edgar Hyman's book *The Tangled Bank* (1962) effectively illustrates how the works of Darwin, Marx, Frazer, and Freud can be taken as imaginative writing. Any approach to editing that attempts to justify differing treatment for "literature" and for other works is thus built on an insecure foundation, for the simple reason that "literature" is not a fixed body of material and what constitutes "literature" is a matter of judgment.[3]

2. *Times Literary Supplement*, 5 August 1977, p. 962. Further criticism of Passmore's review appears in Fredson Bowers, "Editing a Philosopher: The Works of William James," *Analytical & Enumerative Bibliography*, 4 (1980), 3–36 (esp. pp. 7–10, which include a quotation from the present paper).

3. For some additional discussion of this point, and references to other discussions, see G. T. Tanselle, "The Problem of Final Authorial Intention," *Studies in Bibliography*,

But there is an even more important, and basic, reason. Whether a work is "creative" or "nonfictional," it is made up of an arrangement of words and punctuation marks; it is a piece of verbal communication, whatever else it may be. And while one may argue that literary communication is different from other communication, the fact is that both utilize words and language; one must therefore know precisely what arrangement of words and marks is involved before one has any basis for deciding that a particular text is "literary." A writer may claim to be writing a novel or a history, but that claim does not determine what the finished product turns out to be; one can venture an opinion on what the work is only after examining it. Serious readers will wish to know that the texts in front of them are reliable ones, and they will wish to have available for each work a textual record indicating its textual history and listing the variant readings that have been present in significant texts of it. The task of the scholarly editor is to prepare such editions, placing before readers the evidence necessary for an intelligent approach to each work. To believe that philosophers can expect to extract the "truth" from a philosophic work without being concerned with its means of expression and without wishing to know at particular points what textual variants there may be is to believe that philosophers are careless readers. Of course, some of them are, just as some literary scholars are: there are irresponsible people in every field. But surely all serious students, regardless of their fields, are concerned to have at their disposal as much information as possible about the contents of the documents that preserve their heritage. They cannot hope to understand what those documents say without examining their style and form. The inseparability of form and content in historical writing has been well put by Savoie Lottinville, who recognizes that "the search for historical reality is only half the game, the search for historical meaning, captured in writing style, is the other half."[4] The same point could be extended to any other kind of writing: attention to the details of expression is not unique to the study of literature but is in fact a prerequisite for understanding any verbal communication.

The useful distinction to be made is not between literary editing and other kinds of editing but instead between the kinds of documents that editors —regardless of their fields—have to deal with. Two broad classes of documents, calling for different editorial treatment, do exist: documents preserving writings of the kind normally intended for publication and those preserving

29 (1976), esp. pp. 176–177 and note 19; and Tanselle, "External Fact as an Editorial Problem," *SB*, 32 (1979), 1–47.
    4. *The Rhetoric of History* (1976), p. 51.

writings of the kind not normally intended for publication. Historians more often find themselves editing the latter kind of writing, and as a result they have not had as much experience editing the former as have literary scholars; and literary scholars, in turn, have had somewhat less occasion for editing private documents. This situation no doubt accounts for some of the lack of understanding that has existed between editors of NHPRC editions and those of CEAA and CSE editions.[5] But historians do at times have to edit the texts of published books, and literary scholars frequently are called upon to edit diaries, notebooks, and letters, and their methods in these cases are often different from those of their colleagues in the other field. There is no reason, however, why a diary should be edited one way if its author was a statesman and another way if its author was a novelist, or why the text of a published work should be approached differently according to whether it was written by a "historical" or a "literary" figure. The promotion of better understanding among editors in different fields is greatly to be desired, but progress in assessing common problems can be made only if the problems are indeed seen to be common: little is to be gained by comparing an NHRPC volume of letters with a CEAA volume of a novel. In making a few comments on "literary editing," therefore, I wish to look first at writings not intended for publication and then at those intended for publication—for these categories extend beyond the bounds of "literature." In other words, I am dealing with "literary editing" only in the sense that the rationale and approaches set forth below are those that seem to me to represent the best practices on the part of recent editors of the writings of "literary" figures; but I do not wish to imply that those approaches are somehow more appropriate for "literary" writings, since in fact I believe that they are equally applicable to virtually all writing.

I

Writings not intended for publication are fundamentally different in character from those intended to be published, by virtue of the fact that, as private documents, there are no constraints placed on their idiosyncrasy. What one writes in a diary, private notebook, or journal for one's own purposes has no obligation to meet any public conventions of decorum or even of intelligibility. One may write a diary in a private shorthand, like Pepys; or when in a notebook one inserts an alternative wording for a phrase there is no necessity

5. Some of the literature that has grown up around the National Historical Publications and Records Commission, the Center for Editions of American Authors, and the Center for Scholarly Editions is referred to in *SB*, 31 (1978), notes to pp. 4–7, and in the survey of textual scholarship in *The Center for Scholarly Editions: An Introductory Statement* (1977), pp. 4–15 (also printed in *PMLA*, 92 [1977], 583–597; see pp. 586–597).

to make a final choice between the two versions. Even letters, though they are intended to be read by someone else (usually an audience of one), are not normally written for the public at large, and they can be just as eccentric in manner of presentation as other private papers. False starts, excised words, slips of the pen, peculiar abbreviations, and unusual punctuation are among the characteristic features of all kinds of private documents. These elements constitute part of the evidence that such documents preserve and can often be important clues to the writer's psychology and personality. They are, in other words, integral parts of the content of the documents, whether or not they were consciously intended by the persons who wrote them. The writers' intention is not an issue here, because what one is interested in is the historical evidence that the documents present as they stand. Whatver form a letter was in when it was sent or whatever form a journal was in when its author died is by definition the "intended" form of such documents (that is, with all canceled or alternative readings as integral parts of the text); they were constructed to serve a private function, which is inevitably subverted by any attempt to alter the precise form present in the documents.[6] However rough these documents may seem, they cannot be regarded as rough drafts: they are finished products, not preliminary stages of uncompleted works, and the roughness is simply one of the usual characteristics of this kind of writing.[7]

Many editors would be in essential agreement with this view, but they would not necessarily draw from it the same inferences about the nature of the published text that should result. Some would argue that, for purposes of serious study, there is no substitute for the original documents and that therefore little useful purpose is served, and much effort wasted, by many of the attempts to be meticulous in transferring to print the characteristics of manuscripts. A more effective argument, however, would stress the advantages of having conveniently accessible a text that has had the benefit of a specialist's attention and would point out how frequently a carefully prepared text can in fact serve scholars more effectively than the original documents. It is true, of course, that such features of an original as the paper

6. These remarks obviously apply only to original documents. When originals do not survive and the texts are preserved only in scribal copies or in printed forms, the editor faces the same kinds of problems of textual transmission that are encountered by editors of published works, and the approach described in Part II below would therefore be appropriate.

7. Of course, there can be rough drafts of letters, or earlier versions of journal entries that are later written out by their authors in fair copies and altered in the process, and other similar documents, but each of these qualifies as a document of interest in its own right; and any slips, cancellations, and so on in the texts of any of these documents—even in the apparently "final" version—are integral elements of those texts.

and the inks, the formation of the letters, the positions of the words and lines in relation to each other and to the piece of paper, the method of crossing out words, and so on furnish evidence about the writer's habits and state of mind, and any form of publication of a document entails a loss of evidence to some degree. But the effects of the compromise can often be mitigated by editorial commentary, discussing the aspects of the document not recoverable in the published version, and certainly the editor's transcription of the text of the document, providing readers with an expert assessment of what each mark on the paper signifies, can be a great boon to further scholarly work.

If there is no doubt about the desirability of publishing the texts of significant documents,[8] the editorial question becomes the determination, in each case, of what degree of compromise—of alteration of the original—can be considered appropriate. Some form of photographic reproduction naturally entails the least sacrifice of detail, and when accompanied by a transcription it offers an ideal means for making a document widely available. The expense of publishing documents in this fashion,[9] however, prevents it from becoming the method employed routinely for all sorts of documents. Type facsimiles are also too expensive for general use: *Shelley and His Circle*[10] is a great example of the detailed representation in print of handwritten documents, with careted insertions, for instance, placed above the line in smaller type, but the method employed in it is obviously not feasible economically in most situations. And a practical problem not solved by photographic or type facsimiles is the difficulty of quoting from the texts they present; each quoter must in effect become an editor, determining how the quoted passage is to be rendered in ordinary typography. For practical purposes, then, discussion of the editorial treatment of writings not intended for publication comes down to a consideration of what alterations need to be made in the *text* of a document before it is published in printed form. One can take for granted that such physical features of the document as the paper, the ink(s), the margins, the spacing of the lines, and so on will be sacrificed and will have to be covered by the editor's description. What remains to be transferred to print is the actual writing, and the question is how faithful the transcription ought to be to the *textual* (as opposed to the spatial or

8. Deciding what documents are significant is not a problem unique to editors: all scholars must decide what they wish to spend their time on, and general agreement on the significance of given documents is unlikely.

9. Not merely the expense of the photography but that entailed by the bulkiness of the resulting production.

10. Edited by Kenneth Neill Cameron and, later, by Donald H. Reiman (1961–   ).

physical) features of the original. Should unconventional practices, such as the use of dashes for periods and lower-case letters for sentence openings, be normalized? Should canceled words or false starts be reproduced? Should interlinear insertions be labeled as such? In discussing these questions, many editors—though by no means all—have adduced "the reader's convenience" and argued on that basis that some normalization is appropriate. Their position involves two curious assumptions: first, that the reader's convenience sometimes takes precedence over textual accuracy; second, that certain aspects of punctuation and spelling are not significant parts of the original and can therefore be altered without affecting a reader's understanding of the text. These two interrelated points deserve to be examind, because any rationale for editing materials not intended for publication will rest on the stand taken in regard to them.

When the reader's convenience is spoken of, one assumes that it is the welfare of the "general" reader, not the specialist or scholarly reader, that is being considered (although many editions of documents would seem not to have much of a potential audience other than scholars)—for surely no serious scholar would feel "inconvenienced" by having to adjust to idiosyncratic punctuation and spelling, if those were characteristics of the text of the document. But just how much is the general or nonspecialist reader really put off by such features of a text? The answer would appear to be that they are not bothered nearly so much as many editors seem to think. In fact, when editors argue that various alterations must be made if certain sentences are to be readily comprehensible to the reader, they often succeed only in showing their over-zealousness and condescension. To tell readers that the text has been smoothed out by placing periods at the ends of sentences and capital letters at the beginnings (this situation is a very common one) is bound to be an insult to their intelligence and is certain to make them wonder why the editor has gone to such unnecessary trouble. When the punctuation at a particular point in a manuscript produces a true ambiguity, the matter can always be discussed in a note; but to eliminate such problems by repunctuation is to alter the nature of the text, and in most instances of unconventional punctuation there is no real lack of clarity anyway. Readers will generally have little more difficulty with such texts than with some letters from their friends—indeed, they expect raggedness as a characteristic of texts not intended for publication. Serious readers—whether scholars or not—do not consult texts because they are easy to read and will not abandon them merely because they offer some difficulties; but such readers have cause for complaint when they are presented with texts containing editorial alterations made for the ostensible purpose of helping them to follow those texts. To place the reader's ease of reading above fidelity to the original text is doubly misguided: in the first place, the assistance rendered the reader is generally superfluous; in the second, the reader's convenience is surely better served by the availability of a text as close to the original as possible.

A more serious issue than the reader's convenience is the role which idiosyncratic punctuation and spelling, canceled words, apparently superseded but uncanceled readings, and the like play in the text of a document. Even if the retention of such features caused readers some difficulty (which in general it does not), there would be strong reason for retaining them. After all, the point of editing a document not intended for publication is to make more widely available the evidence it contains, and every mark on it is a part of that evidence, including canceled words, slips of the pen, and dashes for periods. A few editors have regarded close attention to these details as pedantic and have felt that the exact reproduction of the spelling and punctuation of a documentary text stresses quaintness over content. But anyone who can dismiss as "pedantic" a concern with the totality of textual evidence available or who cannot see more than quaintness in the characteristics of a given period or writer is surely taking a superficial view of what it means to read and study a document from the past. Responsible scholars and serious readers will not wish to be deprived of any of the evidence that can be transmitted through the medium of print, for they will understand that the punctuation and spelling, the errors and cancellations, and so on, are part of the texture, and thus ultimately of the meaning, of the text of a document. Sentences joined with dashes or punctuated sparsely produce a different effect from those regularly ending in full stops or those that are heavily punctuated, and knowing what word a writer put down before altering it to another word can often give one a fuller understanding of what is being said; all such details help one to assess a writer's frame of mind and method of working. Normalizing, or smoothing out, a text does not necessarily have the same aims as modernizing, but in practice it becomes a form of modernizing, for it moves one some distance away from the surviving text and forces the text to yield to an alien regularity. Modernizing the spelling and punctuation of a text not intended for publication is clearly inappropriate because it conceals some of the evidence that constitutes the reason for looking at the document in the first place; one can hardly improve on Clarence E. Carter's statement—made in particular reference to historical documents—that modernization "tends to obscure rather than to clarify."[11] Any attempt at nor-

11. *The Territorial Papers of the United States*, 22 (1956), ix.

malizing can be objected to on the same grounds. The best course to follow, therefore, in bringing into print the text of a document not intended for publication is to do as little to that text as possible.

Although one can naturally find many editions of the letters and journals of literary figures that do not follow this advice, it is also true that there is a strong tradition among literary editors of preserving all the textual features of these documents with scrupulous care. Gordon N. Ray, in his edition of *The Letters and Private Papers of William Makepeace Thackeray* (1945–46), recognized that not to reproduce the peculiarities of the manuscripts would be "to falsify the tone and blur the meaning" (I, lxxiii). R. W. Chapman, in *The Letters of Samuel Johnson* (1952), similarly followed the manuscripts "as closely as typography admits," preserving Johnson's "inadvertences" because they "furnish some indication of his state of health or his state of mind" and "show the sort of error to which he was prone" (I, viii). Leslie A. Marchand, in the first volume of his edition of Byron's letters and journals (*"In my hot youth"*, 1973), pointed out that one cannot be sure, from the punctuation of the originals, whether Byron "recognized the sentence as a unit of expression" and that an attempt to normalize his punctuation "may often arbitrarily impose a meaning or an emphasis not intended by the writer"; Marchand concluded that "there is less danger of distortion if the reader may see exactly how he punctuated and then determine whether a phrase between commas or dashes belongs to one sentence or another" (p. 28). Other effective statements and demonstrations of the intelligence of this policy can be found in Paget Toynbee and Leonard Whibley's *Correspondence of Thomas Gray* (1935), Ralph L. Rusk's *The Letters of Ralph Waldo Emerson* (1939), Hyder Edward Rollins's *The Letters of John Keats* (1958), Thomas H. Johnson's *The Letters of Emily Dickinson* (1958), Henry Nash Smith and William M. Gibson's *Mark Twain–Howells Letters* (1960), the edition of Washington Irving's *Journals and Notebooks* (1969–) produced by Henry R. Pochmann *et al.* (and containing a particularly detailed discussion of the matter), Herbert M. Schueller and Robert L. Peters's *The Letters of John Addington Symonds* (1967–69), and Elvan Kintner's *The Letters of Robert Browning and Elizabeth Barrett Barrett, 1845–1846* (1969)—to name only a few excellent editions of the past forty years or so.

It should be clear that the editor's task, viewed in this light, does not become simply a mechanical one. The fact that editors pledge themselves to report all textual details of the documents does not mean that no judgment is involved. Some manuscripts are of course clearer, and offer fewer difficulties, than others, but it is a rare case in which the editor's judgment is not called upon to determine exactly what the author wrote at particular points. The editor, as an expert in the handwriting of a given author and period, is in a better position than most other people to read that handwriting accurately, and one of the great contributions of an editor's transcription is the authority it represents in the deciphering of the hand. But the fact remains that subjective decisions are required, and no two qualified editors would be likely to come up with precisely the same transcription of a manuscript—at least, if it contains any difficult spots at all. For this reason, one can scarcely be too meticulous in describing the evidence and discussing any debatable readings. Even though an editor is undertaking no emendations—no alterations to correct or normalize the text of the document—there are still textual decisions to be reported: printing as "these" a word that could possibly be "those," for example, or deciding that what looks like "brng" is actually a careless rendering of "bring" and not an abbreviated form or a misspelling. One edition that deals thoroughly with this kind of problem is Merrell R. Davis and William H. Gilman's *The Letters of Herman Melville* (1960); a perusal of the textual notes to this edition illustrates how editors must often differentiate between careless handwriting (where a word may be regarded as spelled correctly, though some of its letters are indistinctly formed) and actual misspellings or nonce abbreviations (which would not be corrected or expanded in a printed *literatim* text). Transcribing the text of a document thus requires editorial expertise and judgment—directed toward the determination of what is actually in the text, not what one may believe ought to be in it.

There is also another way in which editorial judgment enters into preparing an edition of a text not intended for publication: one must decide which details can be incorporated within the text itself and which are to be relegated to textual notes. This decision involves more than a question of form, for whenever a characteristic of the text (such as a canceled word or the fact that a particular word was inserted above the line) is reported in a note rather than in the body of the edited text, the resulting text is a step farther from the original than would otherwise be the case. Some editors, however, may feel that this additional compromise is justified in certain situations. The incorporation into the text of cancellations and information about insertions requires a number of symbols, and in the case of complicated manuscripts an editor may decide that the symbols become inefficiently cumbersome and that the information can be more conveniently conveyed through a set of appended notes or tables. Although practical considerations may sometimes dictate this procedure, one must recognize that it in effect involves editorial emendation, for certain elements integral to the original text are deleted or altered; having them available in the notes is of course essential but not quite the same thing as being able to see directly the role they play in the texture of the original. Several admirable editions, whose editors thoroughly understand the necessity of preserving the texture of writings not intended for publication, manage effectively to combine the idea of retaining most of the irregularities of the documents with that of emending a few particularly troublesome ones. For instance, both *The Journals and Miscellaneous Notebooks of Ralph Waldo Emerson* (ed. William H. Gilman *et al.*, 1960–) and Mark Twain's *Notebooks & Journals* (ed. Frederick Anderson *et al.*, 1975–) offer careful texts containing cancellations, insertions, and so on, but each also contains at the end a list of certain editorial alterations not labeled in the text. The point to be emphasized about these editions is not that they incorporate some emendations which might not be universally agreed upon but that they put on record any editorial changes made, recognizing the crucial importance of informing the reader of all textual details of the original.

Varying circumstances may naturally lead to varying treatments: material by prominent writers likely to be widely read and quoted, for example, may sometimes call for somewhat different handling from documents of a more limited appeal. But such adjustments are concessions to practical exigencies and do not affect the theoretical position; their result may be that the textual evidence is reported in a different fashion but should not be that any of it is concealed through silent emendations. The most satisfactory editing of documents not intended for publication has been founded on the principle that all the irregularities and roughnesses of the texts of such documents are inextricable parts of what those texts communicate; editors following this principle have therefore aimed to reproduce in print as many of these features of texts as possible, and when they have decided that certain alterations should be made they have provided a complete record of the changes and the original readings. One is interested in these texts as their authors left them, not as they might conceivably have been revised if their authors had had further opportunity; and no detail of these texts is so small that it can safely be regarded as an inconsequential, and thus expendable, part of the preserved evidence.[12]

II

What this reasoning asserts about the importance of the formal features of texts not intended for publication is equally applicable to texts intended

12. The point of view expressed here about editing materials not intended for publication is set forth more fully, and with more illustrations and references, in "The Editing of Historical Documents," *SB*, 31 (1978), 1–56.

for publication; but in the latter case there is an additional factor—the author's intention—to be taken into account. Authors writing for the public have preferences and intentions regarding the words and punctuation that are to appear in their texts in print, but there can normally be no guarantee that any one of the surviving printed or manuscript texts contains all these desired features and thus corresponds exactly to its author's intentions. Editors who wish to establish the most authoritative form of a text, the form that represents the author's desires as fully as surviving evidence permits, must therefore take an eclectic approach and incorporate into their text evidence derived from various sources. They cannot have as their goal the faithful reproduction of any single document, for no one document can be confidently relied upon to reflect the author's intentions in every respect; in occasional instances, of course, it may happen that an editor judges no emendation to be called for in a particular text, but the resulting edited text is still the product of critical evaluation and not of a policy requiring the blanket acceptance of all the details of a given text. An edition of this kind is generally called a "critical edition" because its text is prepared through a process relying on the editor's judgment and critical insight: the editor, after an assessment of all relevant evidence, may decide that certain readings from one text should be combined with those from another text or may believe that certain readings are corrupt in all texts and require editorial substitution. This type of editing is what is frequently thought of as "literary editing," because fiction, drama, and poetry have been accorded this treatment more often perhaps than any other genres of writing. But clearly all kinds of writing intended for public distribution—histories, scientific treatises, expository and analytical essays of all sorts—are equally amenable to this approach. It is true, nevertheless, that editors of "literary" works have had the most experience in thinking about and putting into practice the concept of critical editing.

One of the first points they would make about the nature of their work is that the emendation of a text does not involve any lack of respect for historical evidence. Indeed, scholarly critical editors will always insist on including some form of editorial apparatus to make clear exactly what changes they have made in a particular basic text and what other variants exist in other relevant texts. They wish to place before the reader, in other words, the evidence that underlies their textual decisions. Their emendations, when responsibly made, are not merely officious tamperings but attempts to produce a text nearer its author's wishes than any preserved document happens to be; though these editors are specialists, their decisions still involve subjective judgments that are legitimately open to debate, and they recognize that readers need to have available the original readings of the emended text, as well as any other readings that constituted part of the fund of information on which the editorial decisions were based. There is no question, then, in critical editing, of any concealment or distortion of historical evidence: by consulting the notes a reader can always reconstruct the textual features of the relevant documents.

One might ask why the reader should be put to this bother and what is gained by incorporating the editor's emendations into the text rather than printing them in notes. The answer involves both theoretical and practical considerations. On the theoretical side, one must recognize that a work intended for publication should somewhere be given an appearance in print that as fully as possible realizes its author's wishes. To offer suggested emendations only in notes would be to present the materials for a finished text but not the finished text itself; and there is a great difference between being able to read and respond to a coherent text and having to construct that text as one goes along. Just as works not intended for publication should be printed so as to show the roughness characteristic of the original, works intended for publication should be printed so as to reflect their authors' intentions. The fact that these intentions can rarely be known with complete certainty and that some of the editors' decisions are thus open to question does not invalidate the attempt: one is willing to accept some degree of uncertainty in return for the benefits of texts incorporating specialists' judgments regarding the authors' intentions. From a practical point of view, there is the question of what text will be used in future reprintings and editions. Many works intended for publication (and not only those in belles lettres) have become classics that circulate more or less widely among the general public, and it is unrealistic to think that the editions in which they appear will normally contain lists of variant readings or that the persons who prepare those editions will generally give careful attention to such lists in scholarly editions. Scholarly critical editors will therefore be contributing to the widespread dissemination of texts in the forms intended by their authors if they publish those texts in such a way as to encourage reprinting. The simpler it is for a reprint publisher to lease and reproduce by photo-offset a reliably edited text the more often such reproduction will occur. It is true that publishing a critical text without its accompanying textual apparatus conceals some textual evidence, but that evidence is available in print in the original scholarly edition

—and surely it is better for a text to receive wide distribution in a form representing its author's intentions, insofar as scholarship can determine them, than in a form known to contain errors or superseded readings.

None of this is meant to suggest that there is not also a place for editions of unemended texts of individual documents. Many manuscripts or drafts of works intended for publication are complex enough or of enough significance for literary history that it is appropriate to have exact transcriptions of them available in published form. Such editions, one must clearly recognize, are no different from editions of writings not intended for publication: in both cases the interest is in the features present in a particular document. The fact that a document contains a draft of a work intended for publication does not mean that one cannot treat it as an end in itself; in this sense it is a private document, not intended for publication in precisely its present form,[13] and students of the author have a legitimate interest in the evidence displayed in the document. The central point, however, is that in the case of writings intended for publication the matter does not end here, as it must for private writings. There is nothing further to do to writings not intended for publication; but any work intended for a public audience demands an additional operation, which attempts to evaluate the documentary text or texts: first assessing how closely each of them conforms to what the author intended the audience to see, and then producing, if required, an eclectic and emended text that does conform more closely with those intentions. Only in this way can justice be done to a work as a finished intellectual production; justice can be done to a document as a repository of physical evidence by reproducing that evidence faithfully, but if the work embodied in the document is one intended for publication, the act of transcription does not fulfill the scholarly obligations toward the text of the *work* (as opposed to that of the *document*). This point is well illustrated by the treatment accorded Melville's *Billy Budd* manuscript by Harrison Hayford and Merton M. Sealts, Jr. (in their 1962 edition). At the time of his death, Melville had not put this manuscript in final shape; indeed, it is a very difficult manuscript, full of cancellations and revisions, but it is the only source of the text of this work. Because of its importance as a document in American literary history, Hayford and Sealts present it in a "genetic" transcription, indicating with the help of symbols the textual features of the manuscript and the stages of revision involved. If the text of this document had been made up of journal or diary

13. Even an authorial fair-copy manuscript is a pre-publication (or private) document, and it cannot be assumed to represent its author's intention in every respect (it may well contain unintended slips, for example).

entries, they could have stopped at that point; but because it consists of a work of fiction, a work of a kind normally intended for publication, they go on and produce a "reading text," a text free of editorial symbols and composed of Melville's final readings, along with any further emendations that they judge to be necessary to rectify authorial slips. The reading text is thus concerned with a work of American literature, the genetic text with a document of American literary history. Providing authoritative reading texts is the ultimate editorial goal in connection with works intended for publication; and because the information supplied by genetic transcriptions can (with greater or lesser efficiency, depending on the complexity of the situation) be appended, in the form of textual apparatus, to reading texts, those transcriptions are not likely to be separately published except in the case of the most important documents. Subordinating this information to a finished reading text is not meant to belittle its importance—for it is clearly important—but simply reflects the fact that transcription is not the final stage of the scholarly editorial process for certain kinds of writing.

Just how one can tell when a piece of writing was intended for publication—or how one settles any other question of authorial intention—is naturally a difficult matter. Generally one can operate on the principle that works of the kind normally intended for publication—novels, poems, essays, and so on—should be treated as intended for publication, whether or not their authors actually published them. But there are borderline cases: deciding, for instance, whether the manuscript of an unpublished novel is finished enough to serve as the basis for a critical edition or whether it is so rough and fragmentary that it must be regarded as a private paper. Similarly, with writings not normally intended for publication, like letters and diaries, there will be instances in which external and internal evidence convinces the editor that the writers of these documents were indeed writing for the public and that the texts should be edited accordingly.[14] Another problem of intention that requires the exercise of editorial judgment is defining what intention to focus on in preparing a critical text. Certainly one cannot accept at face value statements that writers may make about their own intentions: such statements may be at odds with what is evident in the writings themselves, and, even when the discrepancy is not so obvious, the mixture of motivations

14. The fact that a writer would probably have wished to make alterations in letters or diaries before they were published does not, of course, mean that the editor should try to guess what those alterations would have been: the documents remain private ones, and the editor, in bringing them into print, is not changing their nature. But when writers publish, or prepare for publication, some of their own letters or diaries, they are thereby converting these materials into writings intended for publication.

that may underlie those statements makes them an untrustworthy guide. Although all available evidence, including authors' statements, should be taken into account, editors must ultimately rely on the characteristics of each piece of writing in determining what its author intended to say; the editor is concerned not with what writers intend in advance to do, or think afterward that they have done, but with their intention in the act of writing, their intention to have one particular word follow another. The only primary evidence for that intention, therefore, is the writing itself: the editor, armed with knowledge of the author's habits, contemporary customs, and other historical information, decides whether or not to emend at a given point (that is, decides what the author intended at that point) by an informed assessment of the context of the disputed reading.[15]

Authors' intentions change over time, however; and although the apparatus of a critical text can record the readings that reflect such changes, the critical text itself can only represent the author's intention as it stood at one particular time. Determining which stage of intention is to take precedence over the others and be incorporated into the main text is another difficult question of judgment that the critical editor faces. When an author publishes successive revised editions of a work, it often happens that whatever authorial revisions are present in the last edition supersede the corresponding readings of the earlier editions—they are indications, that is, of the author's final intention. But in some cases an author's revisions result from external pressure —a publisher's demands, for instance—and do not therefore point to a new authorial intention. Furthermore, revisions are sometimes so radical that they alter the nature or conception of a work and in effect produce a new work; in such cases it is probable that the earlier version and the later one are best treated as two separate works, each worthy of a critical edition. Classic examples of this sort of revision are Henry James's rewriting of his earlier novels for his New York Edition of 1907–09 and Walt Whitman's changes in each new edition of *Leaves of Grass*. Although these authors believed that their last revisions superseded earlier versions, critics need not feel that the earlier versions (or "works") are superseded aesthetically and may indeed find them superior; at any rate those versions represented their authors' "final" intentions at the time of publication and may still be worthy of study as literary works, not simply as literary documents. Deciding whether a particular set of revisions can be regarded as producing a new work or whether it merely refines and adjusts the original conception is a crucial

15. This review of intention and its relation to editing is expressed in more detail in "The Editorial Problem of Final Authorial Intention," *SB*, 29 (1976), 167–211.

question for the critical editor, since the eclectic process of critical editing works well in the latter case but not in the former except as applied to the two distinct versions separately. Some editors have suggested—as a way of dealing with works that appeared in several revised editions—the exact reproduction of the text of one of them (generally either the first or the last), with an appended apparatus setting forth the variant readings of the remaining texts. This approach is of course perfectly acceptable as an efficient way of producing a historical record. But one should have no illusions that such a text could render a critical text unnecessary: the main text would have been selected largely on the basis of its convenience for keying the variant readings to, not because it is a text (particularly when unemended) that deserves to be broadly circulated as representing the author's intentions. It would have been treated, in other words, as a document and not as a work.[16] A critical edition, on the other hand, could equally well display in apparatus the historical record of variants and simultaneously offer a reading text that would embody the results of an informed scholar's decisions regarding what the author intended at a particular time.

The choice of copy-text—that text judged to have presumptive authority, the one to be followed at points where no emendations are made—is therefore the central decision for the critical editor to make. If all choices among variant readings could be rationally arrived at and if all errors in the extant texts could be detected by analysis, there would be no need for the concept of copy-text. But inevitably there will be points at which the editor has insufficient evidence for making reasoned textual decisions and must fall back on the readings of a text judged to have presumptive authority. The text chosen as copy-text thus has a considerable bearing on the characteristics of the critical text as finally edited, for a conservative editorial policy will dictate that the copy-text be followed at all points except those where a convincing case can be made for emendation. Of the various approaches to the selection of copy-text that are conceivable, the rationale that has had the greatest influence in the last quarter-century—indeed, has shaped the modern editing of literary works—is the one formulated in 1949 by W. W. Greg.[17]

16. Sometimes one encounters an illogical mixture of aims, when an editor objects to any eclectic procedure as an unjustified mixing of discrete historical documents and yet is willing to make editorial alterations in individual texts (apparently not recognizing that the incorporation of one's own corrections produces an eclectic text and that reference to other texts might call attention to further "corrections" no different in kind from those already contemplated by the editor).

17. "The Rationale of Copy-Text," *SB*, 3 (1950–51), 19–36; reprinted in Greg's *Collected Papers*, ed. J. C. Maxwell (1966), pp. 374–391.

His suggested rationale has been the subject of extensive, and sometimes heated, discussion,[18] but those objecting to it have generally failed to grasp its essential nature and have taken it to be a much more prescriptive and arbitrary method than it actually is. Greg recognized that editors normally have a firmer basis for reasoning about the intended words of a text (what he called its "substantives") than about the intended punctuation and spelling (or other formal features—what he called its "accidentals"); and he observed that texts usually become more and more corrupt as they descend through successive editions—particularly in punctuation and spelling, which have often been regarded by printers and publishers as within their prerogative to alter. As a result, he argued that textual authority may often be divided, the most authoritative accidentals tending to be in the author's fair-copy manuscript or in the first edition (the edition closest to the manuscript) and the most authoritative substantives often tending to be in the last edition supervised by the author. His distinction between substantives and accidentals, however, was meant only as a practical guide, based on the characteristic practices of writers and printers, not as a philosophical observation about the nature of literary communication; and nothing in his position was intended to restrict the freedom of editors to employ their informed judgment. Whenever editors have convincing reason to believe, for instance, that certain alterations in punctuation are authorial—or, indeed, to believe that the punctuation of a particular late edition was more likely to have resulted from the accurate reproduction of authorial revisions than from the introduction of errors or alterations by the compositors[19]—they are of course free to follow where their evidence leads them; but when they have no other basis for deciding, Greg would argue that his rationale offers them a way of increasing the likelihood that they will choose authorial readings rather than nonauthorial ones.[20] His approach, emerging from his work on Elizabethan drama, has shown its flexibility by being usefully employed in the editing of a wide variety of materials from different centuries, ranging from sixteenth-

18. This discussion has been surveyed in G. T. Tanselle, "Greg's Theory of Copy-Text and the Editing of American Literature," *SB*, 28 (1975), 167–229, and "Recent Editorial Discussion and the Central Questions of Editing," *SB*, 34 (1981), 23–65.

19. This possibility is among those considered by Fredson Bowers in his important recent analysis of Greg's position, "Greg's 'Rationale of Copy-Text' Revisited," *SB*, 31 (1978), 90–161.

20. It is true that in preferring early to late readings they may be eliminating some authorial alterations but at least are not importing into the text what are likely to be a larger number of nonauthorial ones; and the readings taken from the early edition can be plausibly argued to have a better chance of representing an author's practice (even if not, in every instance, that author's final preference).

and seventeenth-century drama (Dekker, Dryden) to eighteenth- and nine-teenth-century fiction (Fielding, Stephen Crane) and nineteenth- and twen-tieth-century nonfiction (Thoreau, John Dewey), including cases where extant manuscripts can serve as copy-text (e.g., Hawthorne's *The House of the Seven Gables*) and those where they cannot (e.g., Howells's *Their Wedding Journey*), and instances where serialization (as in Howells) or transatlantic editions (as in Melville) complicate the chronology of variant readings.[21]

One essential element of any editing where printed texts are involved is illustrated in all these editions: the necessity of understanding the processes of printing and book production in the period concerned and of examining multiple copies of each relevant edition. It is surprising how often scholars who are otherwise experienced in the critical examination of evidence will naïvely accept what they find on a printed page as "the text" of a work or at least of that edition of the work, without focusing on the fact that other copies of the edition may be different. Presumably most scholars are aware, from the great attention which the editing of Shakespeare and other Eliza-bethan and Jacobean dramatists has received, that textual variants are likely to exist among copies of sixteenth- and seventeenth-century editions. But what is not always recognized is that the advent of machine printing and stereotyping did not eliminate the possibility of variation among copies and that variations in fact do often exist in editions down to the present time. Elizabethan proofreading practices, which resulted in sheets representing varying combinations of uncorrected and corrected type-formes, were not the practices of later periods; but the making and the correcting of error exist in all human activity and have from time to time in all periods necessitated textual alterations during press runs, after press runs but before publication, after the distribution of some but not all copies, and between press runs from the same typesetting. Knowledge of printing and publishing conditions in a given period enables one to see the range of variations possible, and an informed analysis of the physical evidence present in the printed book—which has come to be called "analytical bibliography"—must underlie any attempt to establish a text for which printed materials are authoritative

21. See the edition of Dekker edited by Fredson Bowers (1953–61); Dryden, ed. Bowers (1967); Fielding, ed. W. B. Coley, Bowers, Martin C. Battestin, *et al.* (1967–   ); Crane, ed. Bowers (1969–76); Thoreau, ed. William L. Howarth *et al.* (1971–   ); Dewey, ed. Jo Ann Boydston (1967–   ); Hawthorne, text ed. Bowers (1962–   ); Howells, ed. Edwin H. Cady, Don L. Cook, Ronald Gottesman, David J. Nordloh, *et al.* (1968–   ); and Melville, ed. Har-rison Hayford, Hershel Parker, and G. T. Tanselle (1968–   ). More detailed identification of these and other editions that utilize Greg can be found in *The Center for Scholarly Editions* (see note 5 above), esp. pp. 5–6 (or *PMLA*, 92 [1977], 587–588).

documents. Just as in working with manuscripts one cannot finally be content with photocopies but must see the physical evidence directly, so with printed pieces one must examine the evidence at first hand; because a printed item, however, is not normally unique, but is a part of an edition of a certain number of copies, the evidence consists of the totality of that edition. Although it is not feasible in many instances to examine every copy of an edition, a responsible editor must examine a large enough number of copies of every printing of an edition to have some confidence that all the evidence bearing on the text has been uncovered; just what percentage is sufficient will of course vary with the situation, but the day is long past when a scholarly editor can use a single copy of a book, even a nineteenth- or twentieth-century book.[22] Recognition of the great contribution that analytical bibliography can make to solving textual problems has been one of the principal factors that have altered the character of scholarly editing in this century.

The point of view I have been outlining here is, in its essentials, simple to state. It begins with the premise that the serious study of a text depends on access to the documentary evidence (whether the documents are manuscripts or printed) and that the process of editing therefore should not be one that conceals such evidence. It moves on to recognize that for writings not intended for publication the surviving documents are the end products, which should be reproduced with as much fidelity as possible; for writings intended for publication, on the other hand, it recognizes that none of the surviving documents may be a faithful representation of the intended end product and that an eclectic text, based on an editor's informed judgment, is called for in an attempt to establish such a representation. Although any given text of a work intended for publication can usefully be reproduced as a document for study, the editorial process for such a work cannot be regarded as completed until there exists a text incorporating a specialist scholar's view as to what readings the author wished to be present. For scholarly purposes, this kind of edited text must naturally be documented, but the apparatus should intrude as little as possible into the text itself, in order not to detract from the effect of the text as a finished work (and incidentally to encourage the broad dissemination of the text by photoreproduction). An eclectic or critical approach—when it involves editorial judg-

22. The bibliographical literature is full of examples of the dangers of failing to examine enough copies; one recently reported by Jeanne A. Roberts, in *SB*, 31 (1978), 203–208, involves a reading in *The Tempest*: most copies of the First Folio appear to have "wise" (with long "s") at IV.i.124, but further checking shows that a few copies do contain the evidence for seeing that the word is really "wife" (the "f" became damaged in the process of printing so that it looked like a long "s").

ment directed toward establishing what the author wished, not merely what the editor prefers, and when it entails the recording of the evidence (variant readings, emendations) for assessing that judgment—at once shows respect for the historical record and for the work as a completed intellectual production. Decisions about such matters as the choice of copy-text or whether regularizing spelling and punctuation amounts to modernizing are extremely important, but varying answers to these questions can be defended under differing circumstances; what is crucial is that they be discussed within a framework of the kind suggested here. Not all editors of literary materials, I must recognize, would support this framework—and neither would all editors from other fields necessarily oppose it. Indeed, there is more divergence of opinion about editing within the literary field and within the historical field than there is between certain literary editors and certain editors of the works of statesmen and philosophers: the lines of debate do not coincide with disciplinary boundaries. As editors from various fields come increasingly to recognize this fact, there will be greater progress in what is ultimately a common enterprise.

I

The Editorial Problem of
Final Authorial Intention

CHOLARLY EDITORS MAY DISAGREE ABOUT MANY THINGS, BUT THEY
are in general agreement that their goal is to discover exactly
what an author wrote and to determine what form of his work
he wished the public to have. There may be some difference
of opinion about the best way of achieving that goal; but if the edition
is to be a work of scholarship—a historical reconstruction—the goal
itself must involve the author's "intention." The centrality of that
concept to scholarly editing can be illustrated by W. W. Greg's "The
Rationale of Copy-Text,"[1] which, in the quarter century since it first
appeared, has established itself as the most influential document in
modern editorial theory. What Greg succeeded in accomplishing was
to provide a rationale for selecting, and then emending, a basic text
in those cases in which the choice was not made obvious by the histori-

An earlier version of this essay was
written in the spring of 1968 for the first
volume of *Bibliographia*, a journal then
proposed for publication by Oliver & Boyd
of Edinburgh. The plans for that journal
have now been canceled by Oliver & Boyd,
who have ceased the publication of works
of this nature; and I am publishing the
essay here, considerably revised. I mention
this background only because I have
alluded in print to an article with this
title as "forthcoming in *Bibliographia*";
such citations should now be taken to refer
to the article printed here.

1. *SB*, 3 (1950-51), 19-36; reprinted, with
a few revisions, in Greg's *Collected Papers*,
ed. J. C. Maxwell (1966), pp. 374-391. Cf.
Fredson Bowers, "Current Theories of
Copy-Text," *Modern Philology*, 48 (1950-
51), 12-20; and "McKerrow's Editorial
Principles for Shakespeare Reconsidered,"
Shakespeare Quarterly, 6 (1955), 309-324.
For a detailed examination of Greg's position and of the commentators upon it, see
G. T. Tanselle, "Greg's Theory of Copy-
Text and the Editing of American Literature," *SB*, 28 (1975), 167-229. The Center
for Editions of American Authors of the
Modern Language Association of America
has published a manual based on Greg's
approach, *Statement of Editorial Principles
and Procedures* (rev. ed., 1972); an appended essay, "Relevant Textual Scholarship," pp. 17-25, conveniently draws together references to many of the discussions of Greg's theory or of editions based
on it.

cal, biographical, bibliographical, and linguistic evidence available. In such instances, an editor requires some guiding principle by means of which he can maximize the chances of adopting what the author wrote and minimize the chances of incorporating unauthorized readings into his text. Greg's now celebrated solution rests on the position that, if a finished manuscript of a text does not survive, the copy-text for a scholarly edition should normally be the text of the earliest extant printed edition based on the missing manuscript, for it can be expected to reproduce more of the characteristics of the manuscript than any edition further removed; variants from later editions which are convincingly shown to be revisions by the author can then be incorporated into this copy-text. Because authors who revise their work do not always give as much attention to what Greg calls "accidentals" (matters of spelling and punctuation) as to "substantives" (the words themselves)—and because such attention is in any event extremely difficult to determine—the copy-text usually remains the authority for accidentals; and if an editor adopts as authorial certain substantive variants in a later edition, he need not adopt all the other variants in that edition. Following this plan, the editor has a rational means for deciding among indifferent variants (he retains the copy-text readings); and the resulting critical text should be closer to the author's intention than any individual surviving form of the text.

Although Greg did not address himself to the question of a precise definition of "author's intention," it is clear from such a summary that he considered the goal of an edition—and he was speaking of an "old-spelling critical edition"—to be the reconstruction of a text representing the author's final wishes about the version of his work to be presented to the public. In Fredson Bowers's words, the task is "to approximate as nearly as possible an inferential authorial fair copy, or other ultimately authoritative document";[2] or, as he put it another time, following Greg's theory will produce "the nearest approximation in every respect of the author's final intentions."[3] If an author can be shown to have gone over his work with scrupulous care for a revised edition, examining accidentals as well as substantives, the revised edition (as the closest edition to an "ultimately authoritative document") would become the copy-text. Such a situation does not arise in most

2. "Textual Criticism," in *The Aims and Methods of Scholarship in Modern Languages and Literatures*, ed. James Thorpe (rev. ed., 1970), p. 33. Cf. his *Textual and Literary Criticism* (1959), p. 120: a critical edition attempts "to approach as nearly as may be to the ideal of the authorial fair copy."

3. "Some Principles for Scholarly Editions of Nineteenth-Century American Authors," *SB*, 17 (1964), 227.

instances, but Greg recognized its importance: "The fact is," he said,
"that cases of revision differ so greatly in circumstances and character
that it seems impossible to lay down any hard and fast rule as to when
an editor should take the original edition as his copy-text and when
the revised reprint" (p. 390). In other words, an editor cannot avoid
making judgments about the author's intention on the basis of the
available evidence; the strength of those judgments, in turn, will
depend on his historical knowledge and his literary sensitivity.[4] The
job of a scholarly editor, therefore, can be stated as the exercise of
critical thinking in an effort to determine the final intention of an
author with respect to a particular text.[5]

Just what is meant by "author's final intention," however, has not
been made entirely clear, although at first glance the concept may
seem so self-evident as not to require formal definition. Its use in
connection with editing suggests that an editor's task is not to
"improve" upon an author's decisions, even when he believes that the
author made an unwise revision, and that an editor's judgment is
directed toward the recovery of what the author wrote, not toward an
evaluation of the effectiveness of the author's revisions.[6] Furthermore,
the concept, as a goal of editing, would seem clearly to imply that,
when an editor has strong reason to attribute a revision to the
author, he will accept that revision as "final" on the grounds that,
coming second, it represents the author's considered and more mature
judgment. Greg suggests that this procedure is equally valid for dealing with wholesale revision when he writes, "If a work has been
entirely rewritten, and is printed from a new manuscript, . . . the
revised edition will be a substantive one, and as such will presumably
be chosen by the editor as his copy-text" (p. 389).

It is true that, in many instances, the simple interpretation of

---

4. I have made further comments on the role of judgment in editing in "Textual Study and Literary Judgment," *PBSA*, 65 (1971), 109-122.

5. It is convenient to use the word "author" in such statements as this. But nothing said here or elsewhere in this essay is meant to imply that scholarly editing is not also appropriate for anonymous works or works which are the product of an oral tradition. One can infer an "author" who created a given work even if a particular name is not attached to him or if "author" has to be defined as encom-

passing a number of people; in such cases, it is still meaningful to set as a goal the historical reconstruction of the text which reflects the intention (as defined below) of its creator (s) at a particular time. Cf. note 68 below.

6. Sometimes the literary effectiveness of a variant reading is used as an argument that the revision is authorial; but it is fallacious to assume that an author's revisions will always result in improvements (as judged by the editor or present-day scholars) and that no one else was capable of making such improvements.

"final intention" to mean that intention reflected in the last alterations made or proposed by the author is workable enough and results
in no ambiguity as to the aim of the editorial process. Nevertheless,
such an interpretation does not answer certain theoretical questions
which can assume practical importance in the remaining instances.
Two basic kinds of situations particularly require further consideration: cases where the editor must distinguish authorial alterations
from alterations made by someone else and must decide what constitutes "authorial intention" at such times; and cases where the editor
faces alterations unquestionably made by the author but must still
decide which readings represent the author's "final intention." In what
follows I shall offer some preliminary comments on these two situations. But it is necessary to begin with at least a brief consideration of
the meaning of "intention" for this purpose and with some recognition
of the critical implications of attempting to discover "authorial intention."

I

The question of the meaning of "intention," both in general
terms and in relation to works of art, involves many complex philosophical issues and has been widely debated.[7] Probably the best-known
and most influential discussion of this subject in relation to literary
works is W. K. Wimsatt and Monroe C. Beardsley's 1946 essay, "The
Intentional Fallacy," which takes the point of view that the author's
intention is irrelevant to the process of literary interpretation and
evaluation.[8] Although the essay is not as clear as it might be in dis-

7. Many of the general philosophical discussions do not take up the specific case of
intention in literature (or in art generally), but such discussions may nevertheless provide some useful background by
showing ways of approaching the subject.
Two well-known works of this kind are G.
E. M. Anscombe, *Intention* (1957; 2nd ed.,
1963) ; and Jack W. Meiland, *The Nature
of Intention* (1970), which includes a
checklist of related studies on pp. 131-134.
A general treatment of the theoretical basis
for connecting intention and art is provided in Anthony Savile's "The Place of
Intention in the Concept of Art," *Proceedings of the Aristotelian Society*, 69 (1968-
69), 101-124.

8. *Sewanee Review*, 54 (1946), 468-488;

reprinted in Wimsatt's *The Verbal Icon*
(1954), pp. 3-18. They first set forth their
position in the article on "Intention" in
Dictionary of World Literature, ed. Joseph
T. Shipley (1943), pp. 326-329; the criticism of this article by Ananda K. Coomaraswamy in "Intention," *American Book-
man*, 1, no. 1 (Winter 1944), 41-48, was
in part responsible for their elaborating
their argument in the now famous essay.
Since that time, each has restated and
offered further comments upon the position. Beardsley began his *Aesthetics* (1958)
with a section on "The Artist's Intention,"
pp. 17-29, 66-69; and more recently he has
published *The Possibility of Criticism*
(1970). And Wimsatt has made a "reentry
into the debate" with "Genesis: A Fallacy
Revisited," in *The Disciplines of Criticism*,

tinguishing among kinds of intention, it has become a classic statement of the position that the critic should not be influenced in his examination of the literary work itself by any information relating to what the author thought he was saying in that work. Other writers have argued the opposing view—notably E. D. Hirsch, Jr., whose *Validity in Interpretation* (1967) supports the position that the meaning of a work is the meaning put there by the author.[9] Discussions of this kind, however, regularly take the text as given and focus on the activity of the critic as he faces that text; they do not raise the question of the authority of the text itself, apparently assuming that the text in each case is the text as the author wished it to be.[10] Of course, a

ed. Peter Demetz, Thomas Greene, and Lowry Nelson, Jr. (1968), pp. 193-225. A great many discussions of the Wimsatt-Beardsley view have been published. Among the adverse criticisms, valuable essays are Eliseo Vivas's review of *Verbal Icon*, "Mr. Wimsatt on the Theory of Literature," *Comparative Literature*, 7 (1955), 344-361; William H. Capitan's examination of Beardsley's *Aesthetics*, "The Artist's Intention," *Revue internationale de philosophie*, 18 (1964), 323-334; and Michael Hancher's review of *The Possibility of Criticism* in *Journal of Aesthetics and Art Criticism* [*JAAC*], 30 (1971-72), 391-394. Leslie Fiedler's "Archetype and Signature: A Study of the Relationship between Biography and Poetry," *Sewanee Review*, 60 (1952), 253-273, which takes a view opposed to Wimsatt and Beardsley, led to the discussion of both essays by Emilio Roma III, "The Scope of the Intentional Fallacy," *Monist*, 50 (1966), 250-266; and Frank Cioffi's "Intention and Interpretation in Criticism," *Proceedings of the Aristotelian Society*, 64 (1963-64) 84-106, brought a rejoinder from Beardsley in a review in *JAAC*, 26 (1967-68), 144-146. Generally favorable responses are R. Jack Smith, "Intention in an Organic Theory of Poetry," *Sewanee Review*, 56 (1948), 625-633; and Rosemarie Maier, "'The Intentional Fallacy' and the Logic of Literary Criticism," *College English*, 32 (1970-71), 135-145 (with comments by Michael Hancher and Maier in the following volume, pp. 343-348).

9. Hirsch's argument had earlier appeared in "Objective Interpretation," *PMLA*, 75 (1960), 463-479, an essay included as an appendix in his book, pp. 209-244. The book, as an important and thoughtful statement of a position which has been unpopular since the advent of the New Criticism, has naturally been the subject of a great deal of discussion. Among the important reviews of the book are those by George Dickie, *JAAC*, 26 (1967-68), 550-552, and Robert Scholes, *Philological Quarterly*, 47 (1968), 280-283. The July 1968 number of *Genre* (1: 169-255) was devoted to "A Symposium" on the book, with contributions by Monroe C. Beardsley, George Dickie, Morse Peckham, Gale H. Carrithers, Jr., Leo Rockas, Arthur Efron, Merle E. Brown, and John Huntley. The following March Hirsch replied with "The Norms of Interpretation—A Brief Response," *Genre*, 2 (1969), 57-62; and he has recently offered a further elaboration of some of his ideas in "Three Dimensions of Hermeneutics," *New Literary History*, 3 (1971-72), 245-261. Morse Peckham discusses both the Wimsatt-Beardsley essay and Hirsch's book in "The Intentional? Fallacy?", *New Orleans Review*, 1 (1968-69), 116-124, reprinted in *The Triumph of Romanticism* (1970), pp. 421-444.

10. For instance, Wimsatt, recognizing that the contents of a work may be used to learn something about the author, says, "For whatever does get into a poem presumably is put there by the poet and reflects *something* in the poet's personality

corrupt text could equally well be the subject of critical analysis;[11] but the question of the bearing of authorial intention on interpretation would hardly arise unless the text is assumed to be what its author wished.

One might at first conclude, therefore, that such discussions of intention are irrelevant to editorial work, conceived of as operating at an anterior stage and providing the material for the critic to analyze. If, in other words, one could assert that the editor's task does not involve critical decisions but only the recovery of factual information about what word or mark of punctuation the author wanted to have at each point in his text, one could then say that any effort to understand or assess the "meaning" of the text is an entirely separate matter and that the possibility of an "intentional fallacy" applies only to this interpretive and evaluative activity.[12] It is immediately apparent, however, that the job of the editor cannot be so regarded. If the aim of the editor is to establish the text as the author wished to have it presented to the public (and we shall postpone any consideration of other possible editorial aims), he cannot divorce himself from the "meaning" of the text, for, however much documentary evidence he may have, he can never have enough to relieve himself of the neces-

---

and life" ("Genesis: A Fallacy Revisited," p. 199). But the role of the editor is precisely to try to remove that "presumably" and to present a text consisting of what was in fact put there by the author. Similarly, Marcia Muelder Eaton, in "Good and Correct Interpretations of Literature," *JAAC*, 29 (1970-71), 227-233, remarks, "For purposes of simplicity I am assuming that the speaker uttered the words he meant to utter, i.e., that there were no slips of the tongue. This is certainly not too much to assume, since our main interest here is literature, and we certainly make such assumptions with respect to literary works" (p. 230). But slips of the author's pen or the compositor's hand, not later caught by the author, are the equivalent of "slips of the tongue" and certainly do occur in printed matter.

11. Throughout this essay I use "critical" in the common sense of "entailing judgment"—the sense which the word carries in the term "critical edition." I am not, that is to say, using "criticism" in the spe-

cial sense which Hirsch (*Validity in Interpretation*, pp. 210-211) gives to it in his distinction between "interpretation" and "criticism," where the first means "the construction of textual meaning as such" ("the *meaning* of the text") and the second "builds on the results of interpretation," confronting "textual meaning not as such, but as a component within a larger context" ("the *significance* of the text"). I do not discuss here (except briefly near the end of section III) editions which are not critical—editions, that is, which present exact transcriptions of particular texts and which do not involve the editor's judgment in emending those texts.

12. This view is expressed by Rosemarie Maier (see note 8 above): "it is extremely unlikely that the determination of a text to criticize is actually literary criticism; textual decisions, unless they are the result of criticism of each version as an individual poem, are actually pre-critical decisions" (p. 144).

sity of reading critically. Suppose, for example, that the only extant text of a work is a fair-copy manuscript in the author's hand. The editor in such a case cannot simply reproduce the text mechanically, without thinking about its meaning: there is always the possibility that the author, through an oversight or slip of the pen, did not write down what he meant to write, and the editor who is reading critically may be able to detect and correct such errors, or at least some of them. It is an act of criticism, however elementary, for an editor to recognize that where the author wrote "the the" he actually meant "to the." In other instances it may be equally obvious that the author cannot have meant what he wrote, and yet it may be impossible to say with certainty which of several possible corrections conforms with what he had in mind. Yet the editor will probably find it necessary to make *some* correction, since the reading of the manuscript is plainly wrong. When two or more texts of a work exist and there are differences between them, there may be no conclusive evidence to show which differences are the result of the author's revisions and which are not. Yet the editor must decide which of the readings to accept at each point of variation. These decisions are based both on whatever external evidence is available and on the editor's judgment as to how the author was most likely to have expressed himself at any given point. This judgment in turn is based on the editor's familiarity with and sensitivity to the whole corpus of the author's work and on his understanding of the individual work involved. He may be specifically concerned only with the author's intended meaning in one sentence, or even one phrase, but the interpretation of that sentence or phrase may depend upon the author's intended meaning in the work as a whole.

It is clear, then, as soon as one starts to talk about "intention," that various kinds of intention need to be distinguished, and many of the recent discussions of intention in literature do attempt to subdivide the concept. Thus T. M. Gang differentiates between "practical intention" (intention "to achieve a certain result") and "literary intention" (intention to convey "a certain significance"); John Kemp distinguishes between "immediate intention" (that which a man "intends, or sets himself, to do") and "ulterior intention" ("that which he intends or hopes to achieve as a result of doing what he does"); Morse Peckham discriminates between "mediated intention" ("a statement or other sign") and "immediate intention" ("metaphorical extension of mediated intention into the area of 'mind' "); and Quentin Skinner, borrowing terms from J. L. Austin's *How to Do*

Things with Words (1962),[13] speaks of "illocutionary intention" (what a writer "may have been intending to do *in* writing what he wrote") and "perlocutionary intention" ("what he may have intended to do *by* writing in a certain way"), as well as of "intention to do x" (a writer's "plan or design to a create a certain type of work").[14]

Of such classifications of intention, one of the clearest and most useful has been set forth by Michael Hancher.[15] In his view, "author's intentions" can be divided into three types: (1) "programmatic intention"—"the author's intention to make something or other"; (2) "active intention"—"the author's intention to be (understood as) acting in some way or other"; and (3) "final intention"—"the author's intention to cause something or other to happen." The first refers to the author's general plan to write a sonnet, say, or a realistic novel;

13. This influential treatment of meaning (edited by J. O. Urmson from Austin's notes for the 1955 William James Lectures) provides a useful terminology for discussing speech acts. A "locutionary" act involves only the "performance of an act of saying something"; an "illocutionary" act involves the "performance of an act *in* saying something" (p. 99); and a "perlocutionary" act involves "what we bring about or achieve *by* saying something" (p. 109). Another important account of meaning, taking an intentionalist approach (based on the idea that language consists of "nonnatural" signs which are given an "occasion-meaning" by a speaker), is H. P. Grice's "Meaning," *Philosophical Review*, 66 (1957), 377-388, supplemented by his "Utterer's Meaning and Intentions," *Philosophical Review*, 78 (1969), 147-177. There have been a considerable number of papers which build upon or analyze Austin's and Grice's contributions. Austin has been used by, among others, William P. Alston in *Philosophy of Language* (1964), esp. pp. 34-49 (cf. his "Linguistic Acts," *American Philosophical Quarterly*, 1 [1964], 138-146), and John R. Searle in *Speech Acts* (1969), esp. pp. 54-71; and Michael Hancher has illustrated the usefulness of the concept of illocutionary acts in analyzing literature in "Understanding Poetic Speech Acts," *College English*, 36 (1974-75), 632-639. A "largely destructive criticism" of Grice which is of particular interest to students of literature is Max Black's "Meaning and Intention: An Examination of Grice's Views," *New Literary History*, 4 (1972-73), 257-279 (which also contains a listing of many of the previous commentaries on Grice). Marcia Eaton has contributed a checklist of material on speech-act theory to *Centrum*, 2, no. 2 (Fall 1974).

14. The essays referred to are Gang, "Intention," *Essays in Criticism*, 7 (1957), 175-186; Kemp, "The Work of Art and the Artist's Intentions," *British Journal of Aesthetics*, 4 (1964), 146-154; Peckham, "Reflections on the Foundations of Modern Textual Editing," *Proof*, 1 (1971), 122-155 (see p. 152; Peckham discusses these matters at greater length, but does not use these particular terms, in "The Intentional? Fallacy?", cited in note 9 above); Skinner, "Motives, Intentions and the Interpretation of Texts," *New Literary History*, 3 (1971-72), 393-408. See also Richard Kuhns, "Criticism and the Problem of Intention," *Journal of Philosophy*, 57 (1960), 5-23, which distinguishes "intention as aiming at a result" from "intention as the conveying of a meaning." George Whalley prefers to use the term "intension" (which he defines as "the impulsive orientation of the person [author] in a moment of awareness"), because "intention" implies "a disguised attempt to explain the contemplative in terms of the technical" (*Poetic Process* [1953], p. xxvii).

15. "Three Kinds of Intention," *Modern Language Notes*, 87 (1972), 827-851.

the third refers to his hope that his work will change the reader's viewpoint, say, or bring wealth to himself. The second is the one which concerns the meanings embodied in the work: "Active intentions characterize the actions that the author, at the time he finishes his text, understands himself to be performing in that text" (p. 830).[16] Hancher's argument is that the first and third kinds of intention—programmatic and final—are indeed irrelevant to the interpretation of a literary work but that the second—active intention—must be taken into account in the interpretation (and evaluation) of the work.

Before pursuing the implications of that argument, we should pause long enough to note that what editors in the tradition of Greg are likely to call "final intention" does not correspond to what Hancher here calls "final intention." Rather, the intention with which editors are concerned is Hancher's "active intention," the intention that the work "*mean* (and be taken to mean) something or other" (p. 831). The fact that an editor, as briefly suggested above, must examine both the author's intention to use a particular word and the author's intention to mean a particular thing in the work as a whole—indeed, must make decisions about the first in the light of the second—is adequately accommodated in Hancher's concept of "active intention." Hancher's initial illustration of the concept includes comment on Hopkins's intention in using "buckle" in "The Windhover" as well as on his intention for the meaning of "the whole action of that poem." Because an intention regarding the meaning of a work as a whole may not always seem distinct from a programmatic intention, Hancher later recognizes that a programmatic intention may "involve a kind of active intention" (p. 836) but distinguishes between such "*projected* active intention" and the "active intention that ultimately defines the meaning of the completed text" (p. 837). Therefore "active intention," as he defines it, does cover the authorial intentions with which an editor has to deal. Accordingly, whenever I speak of "intention," unless otherwise specified, I am referring to the kind of intention included in Hancher's concept of "active intention"; even when I use the term "final intention," in conformity with the common practice of editors, the word "intention" still refers to the same concept (and not to what Hancher calls "final intention")—though just what "final" may mean in the phrase remains to be examined later.

It can readily be inferred from what I have already said about Hancher's conclusion that he does not belong to that group of critics

16. Active intention thus corresponds to Austin's illocutionary act and to most of the locutionary act (Hancher, pp. 841-842).

who believe in "semantic autonomy" (to use Hirsch's phrase)—the idea that a verbal construction carries its own inherent determinate meaning regardless of what meaning was intended by the author. As Beardsley puts the idea, "texts acquire determinate meaning through the interactions of their words without the intervention of an authorial will."[17] Hancher's argument for the relevance of active intention to literary interpretation shows that he defines "the" meaning of a work as the meaning intended by its author.[18] It is difficult to refute such an argument without taking the position that the language of a literary work operates in a different way from the language of ordinary discourse; yet that position cannot convincingly be taken so long as it is impossible to draw a distinct line between works which are literary and works which are not.[19] Language, after all, consists of

17. *The Possibility of Criticism*, p. 30.

18. His emphasis on "the" in several key statements (e.g., p. 851) implies that other definitions of meaning are possible; indeed, he goes on to make explicit the point that "we may entertain other meanings that seem valuable."

19. Richard Ohmann has attempted to draw such a line in "Speech Acts and the Definition of Literature," *Philosophy and Rhetoric*, 4 (1971), 1-19; and "Speech, Literature, and the Space Between," *New Literary History*, 4 (1972-73), 47-63. His definition of a literary work as "a discourse whose sentences lack the illocutionary forces that would normally attach to them. Its illocutionary force is *mimetic*" (1971, p. 14). He insists that his dividing line is a firm one, but the result is that some utterances not usually regarded as literature (jokes, "ironic rejoinders," "fables within political speeches") fall on the literature side. "Let me simply record my belief," he replies, "that the definition is not severely at fault in admitting the wrong discourses to the category of literature" (p. 16). Cf. his earlier "Speech, Action, and Style," in *Literary Style: A Symposium*, ed. Seymour Chatman (1971), pp. 241-259: "literature can be accurately *defined* as discourse in which the seeming acts are hypothetical" (p. 254). Beardsley takes a similar approach but seems to concede that his dividing line is more sugges-

tive than precise. Literature, he says, is characterized by "its exploitation to a high degree of the illocutionary-act potential of its verbal ingredients"; it is "the complex imitation of a compound illocutionary act" (*The Possibility of Criticism*, p. 61). But he admits that what this amounts to is that a literary work has "richness and complexity of meaning"—or, earlier, that it "directs attention to itself as an object of rewarding scrutiny" (p. 60). More recently he has refined his definition, partly in response to Colin A. Lyas, who (in "The Semantic Definition of Literature," *Journal of Philosophy*, 66 [1969], 81-95) had criticized his previous definition of literature (*Aesthetics*, pp. 126-128) as "a discourse in which an important part of the meaning is implicit." Beardsley now defines "literary discourse" as "discourse that is either an imitation illocutionary act or distinctly above the norm in its ratio of implicit to explicit meaning" (both help to make a discourse "an object of attention in its own right")—see pp. 37-38 of "The Concept of Literature," in *Literary Theory and Structure: Essays in Honor of William K. Wimsatt*, ed. Frank Brady, John Palmer, and Martin Price (1973), pp. 23-39. This kind of definition, it seems to me, does not solve the problem but only shifts the terms in which it is expressed: one still has the problem of distinguishing between real illocutionary acts and imitations of illocutionary acts. Moreover, Marcia Muelder Eaton has shown that the author's inten-

symbols, which must be invested with meanings if they are to mean anything. At the same time, a reader does not have access to an author's mind, and, if he understands a text to mean something, it is (at least to begin with) as a result of certain conventions of language which both are following.[20] Yet texts (or utterances) do not have to be complex in order for the conventions involved to be capable of more than one interpretation. The possibility is raised, therefore, that the meaning or meanings a reader finds in a text do not correspond to the meaning or meanings which the author intended.[21] To reject "semantic autonomy" (or "immanent meaning") is not to deny that texts are capable of multiple interpretations. Indeed, the fact that multiple interpretations are possible is a refutation of the idea that a text embodies a determinate meaning.

How, then, is the author's intended meaning to be discovered? In answering that question, one is inevitably drawn back to the work itself as the most reliable documentary evidence as to what the author intended. If he made no statement setting forth his intention, one has

---

tion has just as direct a bearing on such imitations of illocutionary acts as on illocutionary acts themselves; she proposes (in an extension of Austin's terminology) that these imitations be called "translocutionary" acts. See "Art, Artifacts, and Intentions," *American Philosophical Quarterly*, 6 (1969), 165-169; and "Good and Correct Interpretations of Literature" (see note 10 above). E. D. Hirsch, in "Some Aims of Criticism" (in the Wimsatt festschrift, pp. 41-62), argues that literature has "no independent essence": "It is an arbitrary classification of linguistic works which do not exhibit common distinctive traits, and which cannot be defined as an Aristotelian species. . . . The idea of literature is not an essentialistic idea" (p. 52). Cf. also *College English*, 36 (1974-75), 453.

20. As Quentin Skinner puts it, "an understanding of conventions, however implicit, must remain a necessary condition for an understanding of all types of speech act." See p. 135 of his "Conventions and the Understanding of Speech Acts," *Philosophical Quarterly*, 20 (1970), 118-138. He later (in the article cited in note 14 above) makes a focus on conventions one of his two rules (along with focus on "the writer's mental world") for recovering in-

tention (pp. 406-407). The role of conventions in understanding is one of the concerns of Karl Aschenbrenner, in "Intention and Understanding," *University of California Publications in Philosophy*, 25 (1950), 229-270. Saussure's distinction between "langue" and "parole," summarized by Hirsch in *Validity in Interpretation*, pp. 231-235 (cf. pp. 69-71, leading into his discussion of "genre"), offers an approach to the relation between the "system of linguistic possibilities" which a language provides ("langue") and an individual utterance made in that language ("parole"). Theories of language are discussed by Morris Weitz in connection with multiple interpretations of a literary work in *Hamlet and the Philosophy of Literary Criticism* (1964), pp. 215-227. See also P. F. Strawson, "Intention and Convention in Speech Acts," *Philosophical Review*, 73 (1964), 439-460, and other discussions of Grice alluded to in note 13 above.

21. Geoffrey Payzant expresses this idea in broader terms: "Of the shapes that are imposed through skill upon stuff . . . some are devised by the maker and some are not." See p. 157 of "Intention and the Achievement of the Artist," *Dialogue*, 3 (1964-65), 153-159.

nowhere else to go for direct evidence (though of course one can take into account various historical and biographical circumstances); and if he did make a statement, it may, for a great variety of reasons, not be accurate. As Morse Peckham has pointed out, any attempt, by the author or someone else, to explain the intention of a work ("an utterance") constitutes an inference about an event which took place in the past; the author's account carries greater weight "only because he is likely to have more information for framing his historical construct, *not* because he generated the utterance."[22] Furthermore, as William H. Capitan has noted, "what an artist gives us as his intention is subject to the artist's limitations in putting his intention into words."[23] The position has been well stated by Quentin Skinner:

> To discount a writer's own statements is not to say that we have lost interest in gaining a correct statement about his intentions in our attempt to interpret his works. It is only to make the (perhaps rather dramatic, but certainly conceivable) claim that the writer himself may have been self-deceiving about recognizing his intentions, or incompetent at stating them. And this seems to be perennially possible in the case of any complex human action.[24]

Hirsch, who does not recognize as "meanings" any meanings other than the author's, decides what Wordsworth "probably" meant in "A slumber did my spirit seal" by turning to "everything we know of Wordsworth's typical attitudes during the period in which he composed the poem" (p. 239). Contemporary statements about these attitudes may of course be useful, but are not Wordsworth's poems the chief source of information about his attitudes? And if a given body of writings can provide such evidence, is it not possible that a smaller body of writings—or even the single poem—could provide it? As Hirsch

22. "The Intentional? Fallacy?" (see note 9 above), p. 441. Cf. Sidney Gendin, "The Artist's Intentions," *JAAC*, 23 (1964-65), 193-196: "We do expect, much of the time, that authorship or discovery will carry with it expert knowledge. But in such cases it is the knowledge itself which becomes the ground for being the authority; the authorship is not the ground. . . . If an artist has some peculiar knowledge of his work, it is not obvious that this is so merely because he is its creator. We must have some independent means of establishing his expertness" (p. 194). René Wellek says that an author's statements "might not even represent an accurate commentary on his work, and at their best

are not more than such a commentary," in his and Austin Warren's *Theory of Literature* (2nd ed., 1956), p. 137.

23. "The Artist's Intention" (see note 8 above), p. 328.

24. "Motives, Intentions . . ." (see note 14 above), p. 405. Of course, authors' statements may be deliberately deceiving rather than "self-deceiving." Beardsley points out that artists "are often inclined to the most whimsical and bizarre statements [about their work], and seem to enjoy being deliberately misleading"; see p. 292 of his "On the Creation of Art," *JAAC*, 23 (1964-65), 291-304.

admits, "A poet's typical attitudes do not always apply to a particular poem" (p. 240); so one is inevitably thrown back on the poem itself. I do not think it necessary to review here the various arguments for or against "semantic autonomy"[25] in order to make my point: all I am suggesting is that a rejection of the notion of "semantic autonomy" is not incompatible with the position that the work itself provides the best evidence of the author's intended meaning.

The bearing of these ideas on the task of the editor is worth making explicit. At the start, the editor has settled one important question through his definition of his goal: he is concerned with establishing the text as intended by the author, and thus he has no doubts about the relevance of the author's intention to his undertaking. But then he recognizes that the most reliable source of information about the author's intention in a given work is that work itself. He will take other information into account, but he must always measure it finally against the very text which is the subject of his inquiry. The editor may at first feel that his job is different from the critic's in that he is concerned with establishing intended *wording*, not with explicating intended *meaning*. That is, he may think (in Austin's terms) that he is dealing only with the author's locutionary act, not his illocutionary act. But he soon realizes that his discovery of textual errors or his choice among textual variants involves his understanding of the intended meaning of the text. For if either of two alternative words makes sense at a given point, the determination of which the author intended clearly involves more than his locutionary act.[26] Greg's

25. Such as that supporting the idea offered by Beardsley in *The Possibility of Criticism*, pp. 16-37; or those opposing it presented by Hirsch in *Validity in Interpretation*, pp. 10-14, by Peckham in "The Intentional? Fallacy?" (see note 9 above), and by Hancher in "Three Kinds of Intention" (see note 15 above).

26. Coomaraswamy (see note 8 above) makes a similar point: "one can so identify oneself with a subject and point of view that one can foresee what will be said next. . . . If, in fact, one cannot do this, textual emendation would be possible only on grammatical or metrical grounds" (p. 46). Isabel C. Hungerland, too, comments on this matter: "The way in which we interpret (explain and see) a whole literary work may determine our understanding of words (e.g., where there are ambi- guous words), of sentences (e.g., where ironic meanings are possible), or allusions"; see p. 742 of "The Concept of Intention in Art Criticism," *Journal of Philosophy*, 52 (1955), 733-742. Hans Zeller, in "A New Approach to the Critical Constitution of Literary Texts," *SB*, 28 (1975), 231-264, takes the "predictability" of a text as an argument against the use of the text as a key to its author's intention: "To edit the text according to the intention of the author, when the singularities of his intention are known to us only through this text, can be achieved only if the text is in a certain sense redundant, that is to say, predictable. But this condition is fulfilled, as experiments have shown, only in the case of utilitarian texts (e.g., newspaper articles), and not in the case of poetic texts" (p. 259). But this position surely takes "predictability" in too narrow a

rationale tells an editor what to do when he is at an impasse, but it does not eliminate the need for judgments; indeed, it relies on them. So the editor finds himself in the position of the critic after all. Merely because he has already decided that his concern is with the author's intention does not mean that the issue of "semantic autonomy" is irrelevant to him, for he, too, will be turning to the text itself as his primary evidence.

The key to the use of the work as evidence of its author's intended meaning must lie in the approach which the critic (editor) takes.[27] One critic may believe that he has found through internal evidence the most satisfactory explication of a work and may not be interested in whether or not this meaning was intended by the author.[28] Another critic, who wishes to find the author's intended meaning, will read the work in the light of all the historical and biographical evidence he can locate and may thereby eliminate certain meanings as ones which the author could not have intended;[29] his interpretation of the text is thus limited by certain external information, but his positive evidence still comes from the text itself. If I hastily dash off a message for someone and the recipient finds it ambiguous, he will attempt to rule out certain meanings on the basis of what he knows of me and of the circumstances which occasioned the message; what he finally concludes to be my intended meaning, however, cannot be based merely on what the external evidence suggests I would be likely to say in that situation but must rest on the words I actually did use. Furthermore,

---

sense: the fact that "artistic structures . . . themselves transgress the rules or codes which they have set up in the text" does not mean that the critical editor is prevented from seeing when such a transgression is taking place.

27. Henry David Aiken puts the matter this way: "The aesthetic relevance of a particular interpretation . . . can be established only with respect to a certain mode of appreciation, a certain way of approaching and handling the work of art." See p. 748 of "The Aesthetic Relevance of Artists' Intentions," *Journal of Philosophy*, 52 (1955), 742-753.

28. Hirsch admits, "The text sometimes seems so much better if we ignore the author's probable intention or what he probably wrote. Every interpreter has a touch of the medieval commentator look-

ing for the best meaning, and every editor has a drop of Bentley's blood. It is not rare that anachronistic meaning on *some* ground or other is undoubtedly the best meaning" ("Three Dimensions of Hermeneutics" [see note 9 above], p. 259).

29. As Cioffi (see note 8 above) says, "biographical facts act as a kind of sieve which exclude certain possibilities" (p. 90); "They can serve the eliminative function of showing that certain interpretations of a work are based on mistaken beliefs about the author's state of knowledge" (p. 92). Similarly, Huw Morris Jones, in "The Relevance of the Artist's Intentions," *British Journal of Aesthetics*, 4 (1964), 138-145, comments, "We can eliminate some interpretations as being such that an artist at a certain period in a certain society could never have intended such meanings" (p. 140).

if I mistakenly wrote one word while intending another, it may be that the external evidence would cast doubt on my use of that word, but any correction of the error would have to be justified by the context. The work itself is the controlling factor in statements made about its meaning, whether or not those statements aim at elucidating the author's intended meaning.

The scholarly editor is in the same position as the critic who is concerned with the author's intended meaning. Regardless of how many meanings he finds in the text, the scholarly editor makes corrections or emendations on the basis of the one he judges most likely to have been the author's intended meaning. Hancher speaks of a *science* of interpretation, in which the critic's aim is to determine the "authorized" or intended meaning, and an *art* of interpretation, in which the critic's aim is to find the most satisfying meaning according to his own "norms of value."[30] Some critics would protest that all meanings are part of an intended complex combination of meanings, intended in the sense that the author, whether consciously or unconsciously, created a structure in which they could be discovered. But this appeal to "subconscious intention," as T. M. Gang has indicated,[31] implies a universal set of relationships between consciously produced patterns and their subconscious origins—relationships which, if they are always in operation, cannot be specifically intended and are always available for anyone to discern. One need not deny that such meanings can be found in the work and that they may be valuable (and offer revealing insights into the author's personality and motivation) in order to believe that "intention" cannot be a useful concept if it is made so broad as to cover all potentially discoverable meanings. It is certainly true that neither the author nor anyone else can construct an explanatory paraphrase which is the exact equivalent of the work itself; but

30. "The Science of Interpretation and the Art of Interpretation," *Modern Language Notes*, 85 (1970), 791-802. The first, he says, involves questions of validity, the second questions of value. A similar distinction is made by Eaton in "Good and Correct Interpretations of Literature" (see note 10 above).

31. "Intention" (see note 14 above), pp. 184-186. Hirsch's principal discussion of "Unconscious and Symptomatic Meanings," on pp. 51-57 of *Validity in Interpretation*, tries to distinguish between those unconscious meanings that are "coherent with the consciously willed type which defines the meaning as a whole" (p. 54) and those that are "symptomatic" of the author's personality, attitudes, and the like. The latter, while interesting and even important, are not part of the "verbal meaning" of a work, whereas the former are a part of it, since they are locatable in a specific "linguistic sign." This dichotomy is of course an application of Hirsch's larger distinction between meaning and significance, but it also serves to illustrate that one cannot escape the primacy of the text itself as a guide to intended meaning. Some criticism of this part of Hirsch's discussion occurs in Beardsley's *The Possibility of Criticism*, pp. 20-21.

it does not follow that the *intended* meanings of the work are inexhaustible.

An editor could, of course, emend a text so that it would, in his view, be a more successful expression of that meaning which he finds most valuable in it; but his activity would have nothing to do with the author. In Hancher's terms, he would be engaging in the "art" of interpretation—or, rather, editing on the basis of that kind of interpretation. A scholarly editor sets as his goal the reconstruction of the text intended by the author. In Hancher's terms, he is engaging in the "science," not the art, of interpretation—but it is still *interpretation* and entails critical thinking. His defined approach is what controls the use he makes of what he finds in the work. He will probably find more than one meaning there, but his specialized knowledge places him in a privileged position for assessing which of them can most reasonably be regarded as the author's.[32] The text he produces can, like any other text, be the subject of critical speculation by those who have no interest in the author's intention; but it can also serve the needs of those critics who are concerned with the work as the product of a particular mind. That an interpretation by one of the former turns out to seem more satisfying to many readers than an interpretation by one of the latter has no bearing on the importance or desirability of the task which the scholarly editor has set himself.

These considerations suggest, first of all, that editing is a critical activity and that the scholarly editor cannot avoid coming to terms with the critical problem of authorial intention. Second, there is a specific and clearly defined aspect of the broad concept of "intention" which is the appropriate concern of the scholarly editor—the intention of the author to have particular words and marks of punctuation constitute his text and the intention that such a text carry a particular

---

32. Theodore Redpath is making roughly the same point when he says that "the probable intention of the poet does at least sometimes afford a criterion by which to judge whether a certain meaning which is attributed to a poem is probably correct or not." See p. 366 of "Some Problems of Modern Aesthetics," in *British Philosophy in the Mid-Century*, ed. C. A. Mace (1957), pp. 361-390. In other words, the primary emphasis is on what one finds in the poem; one can then try to determine whether it is a possible, and even a probable, meaning for the author, given the circumstances he was in at the time, to have intended. Similarly, Savile (see note 7 above) remarks, "At least in the context of art we know that the temporal and geographical point of origin of the text, the documents accessible to the artist, and the cultural climate of his time are all of first importance in assessing what interpretation of his text is the best in the circumstances of its production. . . . With the aid of hindsight we may get closer to the best possible contemporary reading than any contemporary did. We may be helped in this by later works, or by theories of behaviour that make explicit to us what the artist only dimly intuited" (pp. 122-123).

meaning or meanings. Finally, the scholarly editor will amass all the evidence he can find bearing on each textual decision; but, whenever the factual evidence is less than incontrovertible, his judgment about each element will ultimately rest on his interpretation of the author's intended meaning as he discovers it in the whole of the text itself. What controls the editor's freedom of interpretation is his self-imposed limitation: he is concerned only with that intention which his knowledge of the author and the period allows him to attribute to the author.

II

An editor who has given some attention to such preliminary questions has at least begun to reach an understanding of "authorial intention." But there are a number of further questions which arise as he attempts to make judgments in the light of this conception of intention. Perhaps the most common editorial situation is that in which the editor must decide whether a given variant reading is a revision by the author or an alteration (conscious or inadvertent) by someone else. In these cases, at least one intermediate stage of documentary evidence is lacking, and the editor is trying to determine from the surviving material those changes which the author made in that now missing document. He must also face the question whether it is ever possible to think of changes not made by the author as nevertheless fulfilling, or contributing to, the author's intention.

The basic situation can be illustrated by Sherwood Anderson's *A Story Teller's Story* (1924). The only surviving prepublication text of this work is the typescript printer's copy, which bears revisions by three people: Anderson himself, Paul Rosenfeld, and E. T. Booth, the publisher's editor. One has direct evidence, therefore, for assigning the responsibility for each of these alterations; but the first printing of the book (Huebsch, 1924) contains additional changes, not marked on the surviving typescript and presumably entered on the now lost proofs. Deciding which of these changes were made by Anderson is the central task in editing this book.[33] What the editor has to do is to familiarize himself with all the available relevant evidence—bibliographical, historical, biographical. He may then find that some of it is

<hr />

33. Ray Lewis White's edition (1968), though it is called a "critical text," fails to make these decisions, for it includes in brackets in the text both the passages marked for deletion on the typescript and the further passages deleted in the printed text. I have commented on the shortcomings of this volume and the other volumes in this edition in "The Case Western Reserve Edition of Sherwood Anderson: A Review Article," *Proof*, 4 (1974), 183-209.

convincing enough to dictate certain decisions. For example, on (or just before) 28 October 1924 Anderson wrote to Rosenfeld explaining why he had cut out some material about Waldo Frank.[34] Since several paragraphs about Frank are present in the typescript but not present in the first impression, one can conlude that this is the deletion referred to and that it was made by Anderson on the proofs. But for most of the alterations in the first impression there is no such compelling evidence; most of the editor's decisions must finally be critical judgments, resulting from an evaluation of what evidence there is, from an understanding of Anderson's habits of revision, and from a familiarity with and sensitivity to his style and ideas. Even the deleted Waldo Frank passage leads the editor to a related judgment, for that deletion is only a part of a considerably longer deletion made in the first impression. Because the entire passage concerns Anderson's reactions to various writers, one may conclude that he probably eliminated all of it, and not merely the part about Frank which he happened to mention to Rosenfeld. But that conclusion is a judgment, supported by a critical argument, not by verifiable facts.

The same observations can be made about situations involving variants between printed editions. In these cases the missing documents are the author's marked copy of the earlier edition (or its proofs, or whatever served as printer's copy for the edition set later) and the marked proofs of the later edition. If no document survives which antedates the proofs of the earliest setting of the text, then of course one is dealing wth texts which have already been subjected to the routine of the printing- or publishing-house. Thus the essential difference between this situation and the one described above is that here the editor is working at a greater remove from the author's fair-copy manuscript or typescript; but his approach to the problem remains the same. For instance, neither the manuscript of *The Rise of Silas Lapham* nor the proofs set from it survive; and the history of the early printed texts, which vary from one another substantively at a number of points, is such that one text might contain the later readings in one part of the book and another the later readings in a different part. So for any given variant, the editor must first try to determine the order of the readings and then decide whether the later one could be an authorial revision or correction. At one point in Chapter 19 Irene's complexion is described as "snow-white" in the serialized magazine text and as "colourless" in the first book edition

34. See Walter B. Rideout's review of   in *English Language Notes*, 7 (1969-70),
White's edition of *A Story Teller's Story*   70-73.

(set from proofs of the magazine text); since the publication schedule for the book made it highly unlikely that the book proofs of the last part (Chapters 19-27) were given a proofreading by anyone outside the printer's or publisher's offices and since there was an opportunity for second magazine proofs of this part to be gone over later, one can reasonably conclude (barring the unlikely possibility that "colourless" is simply a compositorial error or that the book publisher's editor engaged in this kind of revision) that the magazine reading "snow-white" is the later reading here. Deciding that it was in fact Howells's alteration is of course a matter of judgment, but a judgment made within the limits imposed by the factual evidence.[35] In the case of *Moby-Dick*, those limits are wider, because it is known that the publisher's reader for the English edition made numerous substantive alterations and that Melville also had the opportunity to make revisions for that edition; distinguishing the two categories can result only from critical judgments as to which kinds of changes are likely to have been made by a somewhat pedantic reader concerned with expurgation and which are more characteristic of Melville.[36] Fredson Bowers makes the same point in connection with Fielding's *Miscellanies*, where some parts of the first edition were set from marked copies (not extant) of printed periodical texts: "This is a critical process almost exclusively, with only occasional bibliographical guidance, in which the editor shoulders his proper responsibility to separate the author's intended alterations from the verbal corruption that inevitably accompanies the transmission of a text."[37] Sometimes a statistical analysis of internal evidence can be of material assistance in making a critical choice among variants: tabulating the pattern of recurrences of unusual spellings and other features in Shakespearean texts can help to determine which characteristics of those texts derive from the compositors' preferences and which from the printer's copy itself;[38] or examining each variant in the syndicated appearances of Stephen

35. For further details, see *The Rise of Silas Lapham*, ed. Walter J. Meserve and David J. Nordloh (Selected Edition of William Dean Howells, 1971), pp. 373-388.

36. The relationship between the readings of the American and English editions is explored in detail in the "Note on the Text" to the forthcoming *Moby-Dick* volume in the Northwestern-Newberry Edition of *The Writings of Herman Melville*.

37. "Textual Introduction," in *Miscella-nies by Henry Fielding, Esq; Volume One*, ed. Henry Knight Miller (Wesleyan Edition, 1972), pp. lii-liii.

38. Most of these techniques of bibliographical analysis are conveniently illustrated in Charlton Hinman's *The Printing and Proof-Reading of the First Folio of Shakespeare* (1963); the principles underlying the use of the techniques are explored in Fredson Bowers's *Bibliography and Textual Criticism* (1964).

Crane's stories and dispatches in the light of the quantitative evidence (how many times each reading turns up) can help to establish the reading of the syndicate's master proof. Such evidence must then be subjected to critical scrutiny: the fact that only one out of six newspaper texts of Crane's "The Pace of Youth" reads "clinched" at a point where all the others read "clenched" does not in itself dictate "clenched" as the authorial reading, for Crane invariably wrote "clinched."[39]

Once the editor has made his judgments as to which variants are attributable to the author and which to someone else, he must consider the exact status of the latter group. Are all variants for which someone other than the author is responsible to be rejected outright, or is it conceivable that the author's intention may sometimes be fulfilled by other persons? It is not only conceivable but unquestionably true that others can and do sometimes correct an author's writing and in the process fulfill his intention. An author may write down one word but be thinking of a different one, or in reading proofs he may fail to notice a printer's error which creates a new word. When these erroneous words are plausible in their contexts, they may never be recognized by anyone as erroneous; but when one of them does not make sense, and when the correct word is obvious, anyone who makes the correction is carrying out the author's intention. Frequently an editor may believe that a particular word cannot have been intended but is not certain just what the intended word should be; only his critical assessment of the whole matter can determine whether it is preferable in that case to let the questionable word stand and call attention to the problem in a note or to substitute a word which catches the apparent intended sense (again, of course, with an explanation), even though that word may not be the exact one which the author had in mind. In the typescript of *A Story Teller's Story*, then, alterations in the hand of E. T. Booth cannot simply be dismissed; they must be inspected carefully, because Booth may have noticed places where the typescript reading certainly (or almost certainly) cannot have been Anderson's intended reading, and there is always the chance that an editor might otherwise fail to detect some of them.

An examination of Booth's revisions, however, leads to a more difficult question. Since Booth was the editor for the publisher, can one

---

39. This example is discussed by Fredson Bowers in his edition of Crane's *Tales of Adventure* (University of Virginia Edition of *The Works of Stephen Crane*, 1970), p. 198. He takes up the general problem of "radiating texts"—the situation in which two or more extant texts are equally close to the lost manuscript, with no intervening texts surviving—in "Multiple Authority: New Problems and Concepts of Copy-Text," *Library*, 5th ser., 27 (1972), 81-115.

argue that, because Anderson expected his book to be gone over in the publisher's offices, the changes made by Booth become a part of Anderson's intended wording? Or, to put the question in more general terms: can one argue that changes made (or thought to have been made) by the publisher and passed (or presumably passed) by the author in proof constitute changes intended by the author? This question is very different from asking about an editor's alteration of obvious errors. The correction of a reading which the author cannot have intended amounts to a restoration of what was in his mind but not on paper, or of what was in his now lost manuscript but not in print. It does not involve any change of the author's intention. But revisions, as opposed to corrections of outright errors, were not previously intended by the author; if the author then explicity endorses them, he is changing his intention. He is free to do so, of course, just as he may have shifted his intention several times before his manuscript ever left his hands. What is at issue, however, is whether he can delegate someone else to carry out his intention, or part of it. If he says that he expects changes, or certain kinds of changes, to be made in the publisher's offices, can the results be regarded as representing his intention, without shifting the definition of "intention"? One might argue, for instance, that Anderson—aware of some of the shortcomings, by conventional standards, of his spelling, punctuation, and sentence structure—did not "intend" for his writings to be published exactly as he wrote them but "intended" for them to be made to conform with conventional practice. But one might also argue, on the other side, that Anderson's writing as it came from him reflects his intention more accurately than it does after being standardized, and that any intention he may have held regarding publishers' alterations amounted only to his realistic understanding of what had to be done in order to get published (and thus was not part of his active intention in the text).[40]

40. Anderson's editor, Ray Lewis White, seems to take both sides of the question. In his edition of *Tar* (1969), he says that "Anderson's loose punctuation, meant to reproduce for the reader a flowing, simple style, was standardized and 'stiffened' by the Boni and Liveright editors" (p. xvii); in *Marching Men* (1972), he reports that Anderson "learned to apologize for his untutored prose" and "continued all his life entrusting to his publishers final preparation of his writing" (pp. xxiv-xxv). Cf. note 33 above. For the view of a publisher's editor, defending publishing-house alterations as part of an author's intention, see Albert Erskine, "Authors and Editors: William Faulkner at Random House," in *The William Faulkner Collection at West Point and the Faulkner Concordances*, ed. Jack L. Capps (1974), pp. 14-19. Simon Nowell-Smith has provided a survey of author-publisher relations in respect both to punctuation and to censorship in "Authors, Editors, and Publishers," in *Editor, Author, and Publisher*, ed. William J. Howard (1969), esp. pp. 8-16.

The importance, for editorial practice, of settling this question in general terms is evident. When an editor faces a choice for copy-text between a fair-copy manuscript (or printer's copy) and a first impression, he needs to have—in the absence of convincing evidence—a general policy to fall back on, a policy based on the inherent probabilities in such situations. Of course, if the editor has convincing evidence—not merely the author's statements but detailed information about the author's methods of going over proofs—he can make his decision on that basis. But, as is more likely to be the case, if the evidence is not sufficient for making a competent decision, the editor must have further guidance. Greg's rationale, pointing out the usual deterioration of a text (particularly its accidentals) from one manuscript or edition to another, leads the editor back to the fair-copy manuscript or the earliest extant text which follows it. There has been some disagreement with this position, however, based on the view that the author's intention encompasses the actvities which take place in the step from manuscript (or typescript) to print and that the intention is not "final" until the text conforms to the standards which will make it publishable. Philip Gaskell concludes that "in most cases the editor will choose as copy-text an early printed edition, not the manuscript"; the accidentals of the manuscript, he says, "the author would himself have been prepared—or might have preferred—to discard."[41] James Thorpe agrees:

In many cases, probably in most cases, he [the author] expected the printer to perfect his accidentals; and thus the changes introduced by the printer can be properly thought of as fulfilling the writer's intentions. To return to the accidentals of the author's manuscript would, in these cases, be a puristic recovery of a text which the author himself thought of as incomplete or unperfected: thus, following his own manuscript would result in subverting his intentions.[42]

41. *A New Introduction to Bibliography* (1972), pp. 340, 339.

42. *Principles of Textual Criticism* (1972), p. 165. Paul Baender similarly believes that the Center for Editions of American Authors (following Greg's principles) "has not sufficiently recognized that a writer's acquiescence in his publisher's alterations may also be construed as self-expression"; see p. 141 of "Reflections upon the CEAA by a Departing Editor," *Resources for American Literary Study*, 4 (1974), 131-144. Zeller (see note 26 above) goes farther and says that whatever an author passes in preparing the copy for an edition (with the exception of a strictly defined category of "faults") should be regarded as authorized, regardless of its source, for the author in passing it is reacting to a different version of his work in which it plays a role: "it does not matter whether the variants are original or extraneous, misprints (as we shall see, there are misprints and misprints) or variants introduced by a publisher's editor. . . . The necessary condition for our establishment of text is only that he [the author] should have registered the

In support of his view, Thorpe offers examples of a number of writers over the years who have expressed their indifference to matters of spelling and punctuation or have asked for help in making their spelling and punctuation conform to an acceptable standard.

Such arguments for preferring the first edition to the manuscript seem to me misguided. While it is true that most authors have the intention of getting published, such an intention is of a different order from their intention to have certain words and punctuation, resulting in a certain meaning, in their text. The intention of writing something publishable is what Hancher would call a "programmatic intention"; what the editor is properly concerned with, as we have seen, is the author's "active intention" manifested in the work. There is no reason why in some instances an author's active intention might not conflict with his programmatic intention. That an author may submit to various publishing-house alterations as a routine procedure in the process of publication does not amount to his changing his active intention about what his writing is to consist of. To say that he "expects" or is prepared to have certain changes made by the printer or publisher is not the same as to say that he prefers or wishes to have them made; to take his implicit approval of these changes on the proofs (or the printer's copy) as a sign that he is now more satisfied with his text is to ignore the many external factors (Melville's "Time, Strength, Cash, and Patience") which at this stage might prevent him from restoring readings that he actively desired. It is of little help to survey what writers in the past have said on the subject of publishers' alterations of their spelling and punctuation, even if there were a valid statistical basis for concluding, as Thorpe does, that most are "of the indifferent persuasion" (p. 151). Indifference is far from suggesting intention; and the motivation for the indifference would in each case have to be examined in order to know how to interpret the statements. But if the attitudes of writers toward this question cannot be fairly generalized about, the views and practices of printers and publishers can. Printers' manuals, after all, are normative and instructional statements, offering a far more trustworthy basis for generalization than individual authors' expressions of their own attitudes. Thorpe himself, after quoting from various manuals, recognizes that, for most of the period with which he is concerned, "it has been the printers (particularly the compositors and proofreaders) who have

readings in question" (p. 256). Examining the author's motivation in passing certain readings which did not originate with him is futile, Zeller argues, because "the magnetic needle of the author's wishes is quivering in the field of non-aesthetic forces" (p. 245; see also note 52 below).

mainly exercised this control over the text in the process of transmitting it" (p. 152). And Gaskell admits that "printers seldom gave
authors much choice in the matter" (p. 339). If printers and publishers can be assumed as a general rule to have made alterations in
the accidentals of the texts which passed through their hands, and if
the attitudes of authors toward those changes have been complex and
uncertain, it would seem that, in the absence of additional evidence,
an author's manuscript could be taken as a safer guide than the
printed text to his intentions regarding accidentals.[43]

Whether there is sufficient evidence in a given case to justify
taking the first edition rather than the manuscript as copy-text is a
matter of judgment. What the editor must attempt to assess is whether
the author genuinely preferred the changes made by the publisher's
reader or whether he merely acquiesced in them. The idea that an
author can actively intend in his work a revision made by someone
else depends in effect on the extent to which the two can be regarded
as voluntary collaborators. Since collaboration implies shared responsibility, the "author's intention" in a collaborative effort results from
a merging of the separate intentions of the individual authors; the
final result is thus intended by each of the authors. A work need not
be signed with more than one name, of course, for it to be a collaboration. Nor is it necessary for the authors involved to perform equal
shares of the work; indeed, two people may collaborate only on
certain aspects of a work, and their joint intention would apply only
to the words or elements involved. The facsimile edition of the revised
manuscript-typescript of *The Waste Land* offers a rare opportunity
to observe some of the collaboration which can underlie a great work.
In certain passages Pound's revisions (such as "demobbed" in line
139) or deletions (as in "Death by Water") actually constitute collaboration, though there are other places where Eliot rejects Pound's
suggestions (as in the lines on Saint Mary Woolnoth, lines 67-68).
That the work is to some extent collaborative is implied by Valerie
Eliot's comment, in her description of "Editorial Policy," that "It has
been difficult to decide who cancelled certain lines, especially when
both Eliot and Pound have worked on them together."[44] A study of
this facsimile does not suggest that an editor should incorporate into
the text of the poem the lines which Pound rejected and Eliot did not
restore; one can argue that at those points Eliot's intention merged

43. I have offered a more detailed and
direct criticism of Thorpe's and Gaskell's
position in *SB*, 28 (1975), 222-227.

44. *The Waste Land: A Facsimile and
Transcript of the Original Drafts Including
the Annotations of Ezra Pound*, ed. Valerie
Eliot (1971), p. xxxii.

with Pound's intention, even though Pound's markings are what survive on paper. The fact that Pound went over the poem as a friend and not as a publisher's editor does not alter the essential point: in either case it is possible for someone other than the "author" to make alterations which are identical with the intention of the "author," when the relationship partakes of the spirit of collaboration.

The question, posed earlier, of whether it makes sense to believe that an author can ask someone else to carry out his intention in some respect may now be answered in the negative. By definition, an author's active intention cannot include projected activity and cannot include activity of which he is not in control. The ultimate example of delegated intention in writing would be for a person to ask someone else to write an entire work for him; if he then announced that it represented his "intention," he could only mean his intention to write a certain kind of work (his programmatic intention), for his active intention would not be involved. The same is true regardless of what portion or aspect of a work is at issue, as long as the element contributed by someone other than the author must be described with such expressions as "It is what the author expected to have done" or "It is what the author would have done if he had found time." However, if an author accepts what someone else has done not in a spirit of acquiescence but of active collaboration, the result does represent his active intention. Since the scholarly editor, in establishing a text, is concerned with an author's active intention in that text, he can accept into the text what he knows (or strongly believes) to be initially the work of someone else only when it can be regarded as having been accepted by the primary author as a true collaboration. This approach does not alter the crucial role which the editor's judgment plays in evaluating evidence, but it may provide a useful framework into which that evidence can be placed. It also suggests the relative infrequency with which publishers' alterations can be taken to supersede an author's known practice in a prepublication stage of his work.

III

After the editor has separated authorial from nonauthorial alterations and has decided how to treat the nonauthorial ones, he still faces the question of how to define "final" with respect to the authorial variants. Normally, of course, when there are two authorial readings at a given point and their sequence can be determined, the later one is taken to represent the author's "final intention." However, there are in general two kinds of situations in which this view of "final

intention" will prove unsatisfactory: (1) when the nature or extent
of the revisions is such that the result seems, in effect, a new work,
rather than a "final version" of an old work;[45] and (2) when the
author allows several alternative readings to stand in his manuscript
or vacillates among them in successive editions. In the first case, one
may say that there is more than one "final" intention; in the second,
that there is no final intention at all.

The editorial problem in both cases usually reduces itself to quantitative terms: when the authorial variants are few in number, it
makes little practical difference if an editor selects one group of readings as "final" and incorporates them into his text, since the reader
will be able without much difficulty to analyze the variants for himself
and come to his own conclusions about the way in which these variants
alter the total effect of the work; but when the number of variants is
great, the system of presenting one final text with variant readings in
notes is less satisfactory, and the only practical solution is to produce
more than one text (perhaps arranged in parallel columns), each representing a different "intention."[46] That the recognition of more than
one valid text of a given work is often forced on an editor by the
practical exigencies of recording variant readings should not obscure
the fact that the theoretical problem of determining "final" authorial
intention has no necessary connection with the quantity of variants.

Turning to the first of the two categories—in which an author's
revisions produce, in a manner of speaking, a new work—one can
idenitfy several patterns. The most clear-cut involves those situations
in which the author's revisions reflect motives which make it impossible for an editor to accept the later version of a work as truly representing the author's intention, even though, in temporal terms, this version
is "final." If, for instance, an author deletes passages for the purpose
of producing a condensation or simplifies the language to make the
work appropriate for younger readers, the special motives in each case
prevent the resulting revisions from being definitive. The revised version, in such cases, does not represent a refinement of the work as
previously "completed" but a new work conceived for different pur-

45. One must use such qualifiers as "in
effect" when calling this kind of version a
"new work," since obviously there must be
something similar about the two versions
or they would not be regarded as "versions
of a work" in the first place. At the same
time, there is the implication that not
every difference produces, for the practical
purposes of editing, a "new work." Cf. note

54 below.

46. Bowers, in his essay "Textual Criticism" in the Thorpe pamphlet (see note 2
above), briefly refers to such cases in which
"the rewriting is so extensive as to make
ridiculous any attempt at synthesis of the
two forms in one critical text" (p. 47; see
also his footnote 32).

poses; if the new version has merit, it is as an independent work to be edited separately. This is not to deny that the author might make in the process some revisions which an editor would adopt as emendations in his copy-text, but in order to qualify for adoption they would have to be revisions unconnected with the aim of condensation or simplification.[47] In other words, two types of revision must be distinguished: that which aims at altering the purpose, direction, or character of a work, thus attempting to make a different sort of work out of it; and that which aims at intensifying, refining, or improving the work as then conceived (whether or not it succeeds in doing so), thus altering the work in degree but not in kind. If one may think of a work in terms of a spatial metaphor, the first might be labeled "vertical revision," because it moves the work to a different plane, and the second "horizontal revision," because it involves alterations within the same plane. Both produce local changes in active intention; but revisions of the first type appear to be in fulfillment of an altered programmatic intention or to reflect an altered active intention in the work as a whole, whereas those of the second do not.

A similar situation occurs when an author makes revisions, not because he wishes to, but because he is asked or compelled to. Herman Melville, after the publication of *Typee* (1846), was asked by his American publisher, Wiley & Putnam, to soften his criticism of the missionaries in the South Seas for a revised edition, and in July 1846 he complied by deleting about thirty-six pages of material and revising other passages. These changes alter the tone of the book and are not in keeping with the spirit of the original version. There is no question that Melville is responsible for the changes, and in this sense they are "final"; but they represent not so much his intention as his acquiescence. Under these circumstances, an editor is justified in rejecting the revisions and adopting the original readings as best reflecting the author's "final intention"; in fact, to accept the readings which are final in chronological terms would distort that intention. But again the two types of revision must be separated, for Melville made some revisions in July 1846 which had no connection with the expurgation of political, religious, and sexual references—and these an editor would

---

47. Of course, a revision which does not actually implement the aim of, say, simplification may have been made by the author in the belief that it does. It may be impossible for an editor to distinguish between such revisions and those which genuinely were unconnected with the motive of simplification. All he can do is to judge, on the basis of the texts in front of him and his knowledge of the author, which revisions the author can reasonably be thought to have considered simplifications (whether or not they seem such to the editor himself).

adopt.[48] In other words, the "vertical" revisions are rejected, and the "horizontal" revisions are accepted.[49] Just as accidental and substantive variants are, in Greg's rationale, to be treated separately, so, too, known authorial revisions must be divided into categories for editorial decision according to the motives or conceptions they reflect.

A further related problem—the weight to be attached to an author's statement about his revisions—can also be illustrated by the *Typee* case. After removing the passages on the missionaries from the American edition, Melville wrote to John Murray, his English publisher, "Such passages are altogether foreign to the adventure, & altho' they may possess a temporary interest *now*, to some, yet so far as the wide & permanent popularity of the work is conserned [*sic*], their exclusion will certainly be beneficial." One could argue that Melville is simply making the best of the situation, that he is rationalizing the changes and trying to convince himself that they are for the better; on the other side, one could say that here is a strong statement from the author about his "intention" and that the author's wishes, so stated, must be respected. However, in the same way that an author may make revisions which do not reflect his ultimate wishes about his work, he may also make statements which, for various reasons, are less than completely candid. In the end, one cannot automatically accept such statements at face value; as in any historical research, statements can only be interpreted by placing them in their context, by reconstructing as fully as possible the course of events which led up to them. The publisher, in the case of *Typee*, and not the author, initiated the revisions, and there is no evidence, internal or external, to suggest that they are the kinds of changes Melville would have made without pressure from someone else; even his statement implies that the revised work is in a sense a different work, stemming from a different set of programmatic intentions—aimed at producing a permanently popular work, not dated by discussions of current issues. After these considerations, an editor need not feel that Melville's statement makes the case for rejecting the expurgations any less strong.[50] Such state-

---

48. For a more detailed discussion of these revisions and the editorial problems they pose, see *Typee*, ed. Harrison Hayford, Hershel Parker, and G. Thomas Tanselle (Northwestern-Newberry Edition, 1968), pp. 288-291, 315-318.

49. Whether or not one might wish to produce a separate text incorporating vertical revisions generally depends on how

much historical or aesthetic interest such a text would have. In the case of revisions made because of outside pressure to expurgate, there would presumably be little interest in having a separately edited text of such a version.

50. Further examples of Melville's revisions of *Typee*, along with a discussion of the possibility of editorial rejection of

ments by authors should always be carefully evaluated, like any other evidence, but they cannot be binding on an editor. Only the circumstances of each case can dictate the weight to be accorded to these statements, just as the author's actual revisions cannot be indiscriminately adopted without reference to the entire historical situation surrounding them.

This treatment of authors' statements has certain further implications. The essential issue, stated baldly, is whether an editor can presume to reverse an author's decision. Even if Melville did not want to revise *Typee*, the fact remains that he did so and even asserted decisively that the result was an improvement. Is it not the author's prerogative to determine the ultimate form of his work? Suppose that Melville meant what he said and that, even though he would not have made the revisions without external influence, he was sincerely convinced that he had done the right thing. Most editors would disagree with him, but they would also say that it is not an editor's place to determine what the author *should* have done. If the author has a lapse in taste, the argument goes, that lapse is a historical fact which scholarly research cannot undertake to repair. There is no answer to this argument, of course, so long as the revision was definitely an attempt to improve the work in terms of its original conception (horizontal revision). But when the revision shifts that conception and thereby produces a different work (vertical revision), the editor may only confuse matters by presenting the revised version as the basic text: if he finds the original version a more faithful representation of the author's vision, he is not abdicating his scholarly responsibility in favor of an undisciplined subjectivity if he edits that version on its own terms as a separate work (and goes on to include the variant readings of the revised edition in notes). It is one thing for an editor to impose his taste upon an author's work by choosing among variant readings solely on the basis of their appeal to him; it is quite another for him to put that taste to the service of historical understanding by allowing it to guide him in distinguishing among the levels of authorial revision and discriminating among the various artistic conceptions they represent.

The most familiar situation in which more than one "final" intention can be said to exist occurs when an author, at a later stage in his career, extensively revises a work completed years before—not because

---

authorial revisions in this and other works of Melville, are given by Hershel Parker in "Melville and the Concept of 'Author's Final Intentions,'" *Proof,* 1 (1971), 156-168.

he is compelled to, nor because he wants to condense it, expand it, or adjust it to a different audience, but because he feels he can improve it artistically. The classic case of such revision is the New York Edition (1907-09) of Henry James. It seems to be generally agreed that an attempt to record in textual notes the variant readings between the original and revised versions of the novels and stories included in that edition would be of questionable utility, since the revisions are so pervasive that they create substantially new works. Both versions of a given work deserve to be read in their own right, and an essay generalizing upon and categorizing the differences between them may be more useful than a list of variants appended to one of the texts. Many essays of this kind have appeared, and a fairly recent one, on "Pandora," sums up the situation: "the net result is neither striking improvement nor fatal tampering. The story is better in some ways, worse in others. But it is different—one cannot assert that the changes really add up to nothing."[51] The revised version, because it is essentially "different," manifests a "final intention" which does not supersede the "final intention" of the earlier version. Merely because the revision came at the end of a long career, when James's artistry and insight were presumably more mature, it cannot invalidate the intrinsic merits of the original version. The two are discrete works.

If this point of view has been readily accepted in extreme cases of revision, it has scarcely been considered at all in instances of slight revision. But why should the *quantity* of alterations affect one's theoretical position? If one treats a heavily revised text as an independent work simply because the difficulties of handling the variants in any other way are overwhelming and then edits a less heavily revised work as a single text with notes because it is possible to do so, the theoretical basis of the whole operation is questionable. The idea that a revised version can be considered a separate work is sometimes said to rest on the concept of organic form—the view that form and content in a work of art are so integrated that any alteration produces a new entity. Of course, it is not necessary to adduce this concept in order to make the point: changing a word in any utterance results technically in a different utterance. Although the change of one word in a novel

51. Charles Vandersee, "James's 'Pandora': The Mixed Consequences of Revision," SB, 21 (1968), 93-108 (see p. 107). The same kind of comment can be made in regard to revisions in a lyric poem. Thomas Clayton, for instance, writing on "Some Versions, Texts, and Readings of 'To Althea, from Prison,'" in PBSA, 68 (1974), 225-235, says of two readings that "it is pointless to argue which is 'better'; the readings are different, and the versions of the poem are significantly different depending upon the presence of 'birds' or 'gods,' respectively: the dialectic of the whole depends upon the part" (p. 234).

makes less practical difference than the change of one word in a brief lyric poem, strictly speaking each version (both of the novel and of the poem) is a "separate work." Maintaining this position would not quite put an end to all scholarly editing, because editors would still have the task of detecting nonauthorial readings (emendations of publishers' readers, compositors' errors, and the like) and purifying the text of them;[52] but they could not choose among authorial variants, for they would have to consider each group of them, for each successive impression or edition, as resulting in a new work to be edited separately.[53] Clearly such a situation would be intolerable from a practical point of view; in the majority of instances editorial choice among authorial variants does not deprive readers of the opportunity for reconstructing other forms of the text on the basis of the material presented in the apparatus, and a list of variants has the positive advantage of drawing together the evidence from various versions into a form where it is conveniently comparable.

52. Even a nonauthorial variant, of course, produces a separate work which could be made the subject of critical analysis, but the scholarly editor's aim, as it has been defined, is to reconstruct the text (or texts) in conformity with the author's intention. As to whether his aim should be so defined, see below in section IV. Zeller (see note 26 above) does hold the position that "a new version comes into existence through a single variant," because "a text, as text, does not in fact consist of elements but of the relationships between them" and therefore "variation at one point has an effect on invariant sections of the text" (p. 241). He believes that each authorized text has an integrity of its own and that the editor's duty is to intervene in a text only to correct "textual faults" (readings which contradict "the internal text structure" [p. 260] and which are confirmed as corrupt by bibliographical analysis). To judge variants individually and to emend one text with authorial variants from another is, in his view, to produce a "contaminated" text. Zeller has focused clearly on the problem, and certain parts of his discussion are similar to what I am saying here. The central difference between his position and the one I set forth below is that for him a "new version implies a new intention" (p. 241), whereas I believe that a critical distinction can be made between versions resulting from different intentions for the work as a whole and those resulting from the same intention. Furthermore, Zeller does not think that intention can be defined to exclude the nonliterary forces which affect authorial decisions: "What is termed the intention of the author is an undetachable part of these forces. . . . Only the textual history is within the editor's reach" (p. 244). But if it makes sense to speak of artistic and nonartistic elements in intention (that is, to speak of active intention and certain programmatic intentions), then there is surely a dividing line between them (however concealed) which critical intelligence can attempt to discover. Zeller's procedure does produce what can be called a critical text, because errors are corrected; but emendations of authorial variants are ruled out, and the issue finally becomes the question of the value of a critical approach to editing.

53. If they considered the variants singly rather than in groups, even a relatively small number of variants would result in an astronomical number of separate works; it is true, however, that any group of authorial revisions may contain some which seem to move in a different direction from the others and which thus demand separate consideration.

If, in practice, editors are not going to regard each version as necessarily a separate work, then some rationale is required for distinguishing those instances of revision which are to be edited as separate works from those which are not. A quantitative dividing line is not logical: it would be impossible to set up a particular number of revisions, or words involved in revisions, as the test for defining a separate work in this sense.[54] What is more meaningful than the extent of the revisions is their nature. One author might make 3000 changes in his selection of adjectives and adverbs, for instance—and perhaps improve his book stylistically—without altering his original conception of the work at all; another might make only ten revisions in key passages and change the whole direction of the book. Whether or not two versions of a book are treated by an editor as independent works should depend on a qualitative, not quantitative, distinction. If revisions do not spring from the same conception of an organic whole as the original version manifested (what I have called vertical revisions), then they produce a new work, even though the actual number of new readings is small; if revisions are attempts to develop and improve the original conception (what I have called horizontal revisions), then they do not produce a separate work for practical purposes, regardless of the number of changes involved.[55] Generally, large numbers of alterations do follow from a changed conception or programmatic intention, but the point is that there is no necessary connection between the two.

In making decisions about authorial intention, an editor may be inclined to take into account a related factor, the timing of the changes. When an author, late in his life, makes revisions in an early work, one could argue that the result will almost surely constitute an effectively different work, since it is unlikely that the author will have the same conception of his work in mind as he had during the process of its original composition. James's revisions are a case in point, but the argument can be applied to other instances in which neither the extent of the changes nor the shift in intent is so pronounced. When

54. From here on I use "separate work"—as I trust the context indicates—in the practical sense of "a work to be edited separately."

55. Richard Kuhns (see note 14 above) is getting at this same question when he says, "Within limits changes can be made without altering the basic organization and fundamental meaning of the work; but if we go outside those limits the work is seriously affected. . . . There is a difference between the values of the parts of a work which if changed would not alter the over-all effect of the work, and the values of the elements of a work which if changed would alter the over-all effect of the work" (p. 18). The key, in his terms, is whether or not the "style" is affected, "style" being defined as "a kind of organization of elements capable of sustaining a constant 'focal effect.'"

Arthur Stedman edited *Typee* in 1892, he claimed to have made alterations "by written direction of the author" (who died in 1891). The only presently known evidence of any authorial direction is a note in Mrs. Melville's hand listing four changes which her husband requested.[56] Even assuming that this note accurately represents Melville's final wishes, how much weight is to be given to a few isolated changes suggested nearly fifty years after the original composition of the work? Two of the changes represent the same kind of expurgation which Melville was required to make for the earlier revised edition and are not consistent with the spirit of the work. These revisions are different from James's not merely in quantity but in the fact that they are not part of a sustained and coherent reshaping of an early work. Instead, they are simply instances of sporadic tinkering; such tinkering, when performed during or soon after the composition of a work, can be expected to fit the general tone and spirit of the whole, but when it occurs much later the results may well seem out of place. A systematic job of revision, even if it does not result in many changes, may have a coherence of its own, but isolated changes frequently clash with the larger context. Nevertheless, it is obviously possible for authors to make consistent sporadic revisions late in life, and the timing of revisions is therefore not in itself the key. Just as a quantitative measure of revision will not serve to distinguish what versions are to be edited as separate works, so a time limit is similarly unrealistic: one cannot say that all revisions made within a week, or a month, or a year of the original composition are to be accepted as part of the same conception, while those made after that time either result in different works or represent random thoughts not consistent with any coherent plan. What is important, once again, is the nature of the changes, and no mechanical rule—about their extent or their timing—can produce meaningful distinctions among them with respect to underlying conceptions or motives.

The role which these considerations play in editing and the critical nature of the decisions they imply are well illustrated in Bowers's edition of Stephen Crane's *Maggie*.[57] Crane's book was first printed privately in 1893; three years later, in order to secure publication by D. Appleton & Co., he agreed to make revisions, particularly the elimination of profanity. But, as Bowers points out, Crane's alterations were not limited to bowdlerizing: "It is clear from many examples

56. For a fuller discussion of this document and its editorial implications, see *Typee* (cited in note 48 above), pp. 312-313.

57. In *Bowery Tales* (University of Virginia Edition, 1969).

that he took the opportunity to make stylistic revisions as well as literary improvements" (p. lxviii). As in the case of *Typee*, an editor will reject the enforced expurgations and will accept the stylistic revisions made at the same time. But *Maggie* offers in addition a difficult intermediate category: the removal of various sordid details, culminating in the cancellation of a 96-word paragraph describing a "huge fat man," which had appeared in the 1893 edition at a strategic point, just before Maggie's death at the end of Chapter 17. The first critical question is obviously to decide whether these alterations were among those which Crane made under duress or whether he made them independently, judging them to be artistic improvements. Answering that question, as Bowers recognizes, involves literary judgment, and he provides a long interpretive discussion (pp. lxxvii-xci) of the implications of the removal of that paragraph, concluding with the view that Crane did delete it for artisic reasons. Once that decision is made, there is a second critical question to be faced: does this revision (and the scattered lesser ones similar to it) produce an essentially different work? Bowers clearly states the possibiliy:

> In some literary works it is generally recognized that a revision may be so thoroughgoing—so motivated throughout by the author's altered political, social, or artistic concepts—as to require complete acceptance on its own terms as the final intention in every respect both of accidentals and of substantives. . . . Under such conditions there is nothing for it but to treat the early and late texts as quite independent units and to establish each separately, perhaps in parallel form, with no attempt to merge the two in terms of the divided authority of accidentals and substantives. Divided authority does not exist and no synthetic text is possible for the early and revised editions of such works as Jonson's *Every Man in His Humour*, Wordsworth's *Prelude*, or Whitman's *Leaves of Grass*. (pp. xciii-xciv)

He then concludes that "*Maggie* does not bear comparison with these examples," arguing that Crane "was operating from a strong literary conviction about the integrity of a text once written and published" (p. xcv). It is possible, then, by incorporating the 1896 revisions which Crane "made for his own purposes and satisfaction" (p. xcvii), to produce a single " 'ideal' text of *Maggie* as a literary fact, not a limited 'ideal' text either of the 1893 or of the 1896 edition" (p. xcv). Obviously this conclusion is reached through critical analysis, and another editor might analyze the situation differently and come to the opposing view—that there are two distinct *Maggies* which it would be improper to merge.[58] No incontrovertible answer is to be expected to a question like this, dependent on judgment; but every editor in his own work must recognize that the question exists and reach an answer to it.[59]

With some authors the possibility of multiple "final" intentions is further intensified. Instead of making one systematic revision of a work at some point later in life, they revise their work continually throughout their careers. An extreme example of this method, referred to by Bowers in the passage quoted above, is Whitman's *Leaves of Grass*, which was extensively revised eight times between 1855 and 1892. When an author works in this way, successive editions constitute a printed record of a developing mind. The fact that Whitman said of his final "deathbed" edition (1891-92) that any future edition should be "a copy and facsimile, indeed, of the text of these . . . pages" does not mean that critics and scholars must reject all earlier editions as works in their own right.[60] Even if Whitman came to think of the earlier editions as preliminary drafts for his final version, each of those editions was published and at the time of its publication represented a final version that he was willing to present to the public and thus his final intention as of that moment.[61] If one decides that the revisions at each stage are the kind which spring from an altered conception of the whole, one can argue that each edition of *Leaves* is a separate work with its own final intention. (The situation would differ from that of Henry James only in the greater number of separate works, resulting from the greater number of stages of revision.) In that case, Whitman's last text is not—as an intended work—any more "final" than his earlier texts; it merely comes later. To one taking this position, Whitman's own judgment should of course be no embarrassment; it is only a critical pronouncement about his work, not an element within the work.

58. I have discussed this case in connection with Greg's theory, on pp. 221-223 of "The New Editions of Hawthorne and Crane," *Book Collector*, 23 (1974), 214-229.

59. Bowers has made further comments on the relationships between editions offering "eclectic" texts and those offering texts of particular stages of revision, in "Remarks on Eclectic Texts," *Proof*, 4 (1974), 31-76.

60. Some of the earlier versions have been edited separately: see, for example, *Whitman's Manuscripts: Leaves of Grass (1860)*, ed. Fredson Bowers (1955), which prints as parallel texts the manuscript versions of

certain poems and their first published versions (in 1860); and *Leaves of Grass: The First (1855) Edition*, ed. Malcolm Cowley (1959). Cf. Bowers, "The Walt Whitman Manuscripts of 'Leaves of Grass' (1860)," in his *Textual and Literary Criticism* (1959), pp. 35-65.

61. As John Kemp (see note 14 above) says, "a published work of art has been, as it were, detached from the artist, and he has sent it out into the world, with the result that later versions do not necessarily cancel earlier published ones as later cancel earlier in the working-out stage before publication" (p. 152).

These issues are raised in an acute form in connection with the poetry of W. H. Auden. Joseph Warren Beach, in *The Making of the Auden Canon* (1957), describes in great detail the way in which Auden continually omitted or revised passages to bring his poems into conformity with his current ideological preoccupations. In 1945, for example, he gave the poems from "In Time of War," in Beach's words, "a more distinctively religious cast than they had when first written in 1938 and published in 1939" (p. 10). Throughout his career, according to Beach, Auden displayed a faculty for "domesticating, within the frame of mind that at any moment possesses him, work conceived in some quite different frame of mind" (p. 15). In preparing a collected edition, he not only revised poems to make them "reasonably acceptable to him at a time when he was concerned that his work should be as edifying spiritually as it was imaginatively arresting" (p. 242); he also arranged the poems in alphabetical order so that their connections with previous volumes or particular stages in his career would be obscured. The situation is reminiscent of Whitman's preparation of an authorized final edition, but in Auden's case the emphasis is more clearly on ideological content than on artistic form. As with Whitman, Auden's final text can be regarded as only another text, reflecting a different conception of his work.

Beach's analysis presents, in effect, the apparatus for a critical edition in essay form—a method which, for this kind of author, is perhaps more useful than a list of variant readings, since such a list tends to suggest that the versions compared are essentially the same work. At the end of his book Beach takes up—in one of the few discussions of the subject in print—some of the editorial implications of multiple authorial intention. One can concur with his feeling of dissatisfaction about Auden's collected text and yet find a curious logic in his conclusion:

[Auden's] alternative would have been to range his poems in chronological order and leave them, as far as was consistent with his artistic standards, just as they were originally written. We should then be able to read them in their original context and to follow the course of an interesting mind in its progress through successive periods in the pursuit of truth. This manner of presentation would have done better justice to many fine poems as intelligible and organic creations of poetic art. It would have involved the candid admission on the author's part that, by his present lights, he had occasionally been subject to error and confusion. But such candor would only have reflected credit on the poet, and it could not in the end have been a disservice to the truth as he later came to see it. (p. 243)

In these comments Beach is explaining what he wishes Auden had done but in the process confuses the roles of author and scholarly editor. The particular revision and arrangement which Auden decided upon for his collected poems represent, in themselves, one of the "successive periods" in the "course of an interesting mind." The fact that he did not arrange his poems in chronological order or leave them unaltered does not prevent the editor from making the earlier texts available. Many of Auden's decisions may not please an editor, but, whatever they are, they constitute the only material the editor has to work with. One can criticize an author's lapses, but one cannot expect him to treat his own work as if he were a scholarly editor.

Pursuing the nature of Auden's "identity," Beach sensibly asks, "And how . . . can we question the right of an author to be his own judge as to the intent of a piece of writing, or to make it over so as to give it a new direction?" (p. 251). This, after all, is the central issue. But the answer again proves troublesome: "What I have suggested is that such a making over of a work of literary art is not to be accomplished by cutting out a few offensive passages, or by merely hanging the work in a different gallery in different company; and that it is vain to suppose that now it means something essentially different from what it did." In other words, as he goes on to say, a work of art should have "a wholeness, or integrality, that underlies all the diverse and even conflicting elements" (p. 253). It is precisely because of its "integrality," however, that any adjustments made in a work of art may turn it into a different, if no less integral, work. To say that an author's last version of a work means the same thing as his earliest is to abandon all criticism; but to find that a late version fails to supersede an early one is not to deny the author's right to do with his work as he pleases. In the end, whenever there are authorial revisions, an editor is not fulfilling his responsibility to the work of literature if he does not assess the nature of those revisions, in order to determine whether he is really dealing with only a single work.

Before glancing at the argument that this approach to editing gives the editor too much freedom to be eclectic, let us turn to the second major category in which "final intention" is problematical—those instances in which there is literally no final intention, either because the author never prepared his manuscript for publication or because he wavered in his revisions for successive printings.[62] Perhaps the most

62. If finality is defined in terms of publication, one could say that the latter case involves multiple intentions. The whole pattern of revisions in such a case, however, separates it from the usual instances of continual revision and suggests that the author had not really come to a decision when he was forced to select one reading or the other for publication at a particular time.

common instances of this situation occur in the editing of letters. Although letters, generally full of abbreviations and elliptical remarks, can be described as manuscripts not prepared for publication, they have one peculiar feature: they were not (in most cases) intended for publication. Whatever form the manuscript is in, therefore, if the letter was sent, represents "final intention"; the posting of a letter is equivalent to the publication of a literary work, for each activity serves as the means by which a particular kind of communication is directed to its audience. When letters are published, do they automatically become a different genre, subject to different conventions, or is their intention distorted if they are not reproduced exactly as they arrived in the recipient's hands? If the author prepares his own letters for publication, he will almost certainly alter them (at least with respect to accidentals, but possibly also to substantives), and he will probably expect them to be subjected to the same processes of copy-editing and house-styling as any other work. But when letters are published posthumously, does the fact that the author would have expected them to be adjusted to conform with the conventions of published writing justify an editor's attempt to perform those adjustments? Clearly it does not, because, as we have seen, what an author expects is different from what he actively intends. In any case, an editor cannot possibly put himself in the frame of mind of a publisher's house-stylist of some previous period, and the changes he would introduce, however knowledgeable he may be, could carry no authority. Additionally, the abbreviations and other unconventional features of a letter may be its most revealing characteristics; if they are removed or normalized, the substance of the letter and the nuances conveyed to the recipient may be obscured, if not substantially altered. Naturally, some adjustments are inevitable, since complete fidelity to the original would mean photographic reproduction on the same quality of paper. But alterations—even in such matters as the misspelling of words—should be made with extreme caution if the effect of a letter as a private document is to be retained. This procedure comes closer to the author's intention, as revealed in the finished text of each letter, than following any directions the author may have pronounced when he was thinking of his letters more as literary property than as private expression.[63]

A similar situation exists in connection with journals, notebooks, and other personal papers, except that for these classes of material

63. For a fuller discussion of these problems (with somewhat different conclusions), see Robert Halsband, "Editing the Letters of Letter-Writers," *SB*, 11 (1958), 25-37; and Simon Nowell-Smith (see note 40 above), esp. pp. 16-27.

there is not even that degree of finality accorded to letters by the act of posting. If the writer made no final selection among alternative words or phrases, an editor has no basis—nor justification—for doing so; to prepare a "clear text" which reads smoothly is to change the essential nature of the document. Such works, though they may turn out to be literature, form a special genre in which the necessity for final choice (forced upon an author in the case of published works by the act of publication) does not apply. From a practical point of view, some of these works gain little from the preservation of their formal texture, and it may be that the group of readers who will be turning to a particular document may find the loss of such fidelity a price worth paying for a conveniently readable text. The nature of the document and the uses to which it may be put will in each instance determine the degree of compromise which can be tolerated. In some cases a full transcription may be accompanied by a separate "reading text."[64] But the theoretical point remains: altering private papers to conform to conventional standards of publication makes different works of them and thus is bound to distort their meaning.

When writers leave unfinished, or unprepared for publication, literary works of other genres—those which are normally circulated in published form—the problem is somewhat different. In these cases the rejected readings, false starts, and uncanceled variants are of interest in showing the writer's manner of working and stylistic development, just as they are when found in the surviving manuscripts of a published work; but they do not reflect the essential nature of the work itself, as they do in a letter or a journal. An editor who completes the author's job by preparing such works for conventional publication (correcting errors, choosing among uncanceled variants, and the like) is not obscuring the final effect or meaning of the work but rather clarifying it. When a poem, left in manuscript, is posthumously published in the form of an exact transcript, it is being treated like a his-

64. A good example of this method is the Harvard University Press edition of *The Journals and Miscellaneous Notebooks of Ralph Waldo Emerson*, ed. William H. Gilman *et al.* (1960-   ). The volumes of detailed transcription currently in progress are to be followed by selections in clear text. Whenever a text is likely to be quoted or reprinted frequently in standard typographical contexts where symbols and multiple readings seem (by tradition) out of place, it becomes particularly important to provide such additional clear texts, despite the theoretical difficulties they entail. For a discussion of some of the problems of editing journals, see William H. Gilman, "How Should Journals Be Edited?", *Early American Literature*, 6 (1971), 73-83. Cf. also G. T. Tanselle, "Some Principles for Editorial Apparatus," *SB*, 25 (1972), 41-88 (esp. pp. 46-47); and Eleanor D. Kewer, "Case Histories in the Craft of the Publisher's Editor, Culminating in a Justification of Barbed Wire," in *Editor, Author, and Publisher*, ed. William J. Howard (1969), pp. 65-73.

torical document; when it is published in a clear reading text, it is being treated like a work of literary art. Both forms may have their uses, but only the second can represent (or attempt to represent) the author's intention.[65]

The poems of Emily Dickinson present a special situation: they are clearly poems (not journal entries or letters), but they were not intended for publication. They contain both eccentric punctuation (often impossible to reproduce in type) and uncanceled alternative readings. If an editor decides to publish as exact transcriptions as possible of these poems (or even photographs of the manuscripts), he is doing what normally is most sensible for works not intended for publication. But in this case he would be doing less than full justice to the material, which belongs to a genre conventionally circulated in some kind of published form and with decisions among alternative readings already made. The fact that Emily Dickinson did not "intend" publication does not alter the basic nature of the material and automatically convert into notebook jottings what would have been called poetry if published. Her distrust of publication does not obligate an editor to leave her poems unpublished (or to edit them as if they were private papers) any more than an author's "deathbed" edition obligates an editor to regard previous editions as superseded. In either case the work has an existence distinct from the wishes (expressed or implied) of its creator, and "intention" regarding publication is different from the active intention embodied in the work. Whether or not Emily Dickinson's manuscripts were specifically "intended" for publication is really beside the point; the important matter is that they are manuscripts of poems not prepared for publication. Although an editor will rightly feel an obligation to present as fully as possible the evidence available in those manuscripts (as documents in the history of American literature), he should feel equally obliged to make decisions among the author's alternative readings and produce a clear text of the poems (as literature).[66] An editor who

---

65. E. A. J. Honigmann, in *The Stability of Shakespeare's Text* (1965), argues that Shakespeare perhaps made revisions in the process of copying, so that some of the variants we now have may represent authorial "second thoughts." The editor, therefore, must "screw his courage to the sticking place and choose between each pair of variants"; what he is doing is "to attempt a feat left undone by Shakespeare, to finalise an unfinalised text" (p. 168).

66. Thomas H. Johnson's Harvard edition of Emily Dickinson's poems (1955) presents a clear text, with variant readings in notes; but the decisions as to which readings were to be included in the main text were not generally made on the basis of literary judgment. Cf. Johnson's "Establishing a Text: The Emily Dickinson Papers," *SB*, 5 (1952-53), 21-32.

thus "completes" unfinished poems is not being presumptuous but is simply facing his responsibility. One editor's choice among alternatives may of course differ from another's, but the excellence of any critical edition—whether based on unprepared manuscripts or not—is directly related to the critical powers of its editor.

IV

Some of the implications of the Dickinson problem for editorial theory are discussed by R. W. Franklin at the end of his important book *The Editing of Emily Dickinson: A Reconsideration* (1967). Franklin correctly asserts that "from the variant fair copies of a single poem we should choose its best" (p. 133), and he objects to any nonliterary or mechanical basis of selection among alternatives in unfinished manuscripts as resulting merely in "a worksheet without all the work" (p. 134). Since an uncompleted manuscript obviously lacks finality, he concludes, "The principle of editing that a text exactly represent the author's intention is inadequate." He therefore calls for "a new editorial procedure for material unprepared by the author for publication"—a procedure which would be "a compromise between the demands of authorial intention and the demands of the poems" (pp. 142-143). One might carry the argument a step further, however, and note that since authorial intention is ultimately ascertainable only through the poems, no compromise is necessary except in the sense that two kinds of edition, rather than a single one, may be desirable: a complete transcription, faithful to the demands of the document, and a reading text (or more than one), faithful to the demands of the work of art.

Generalizing upon the specific situation, Franklin points to the "conflicting bases of criticism and editing"—conflicting because the modern critical position upholds "criticism divorced from authorial intention." Is there an inconsistency, he is asking, within the discipline of literary study, if a text, presented to the literary critic for analysis in the light of one set of principles, is prepared for him by the editor under a different set of principles? An author's final intention, he believes,

is like a Platonic archetype, unchanging, complete, and perfect in its own way, against which any one of its appearances in print can be corrected. Unfortunately, an author's intentions are not necessarily eternal and may exist as precariously as do any of their appearances: destroying a manuscript may destroy all trace of intention. Moreover, the separate appearances, even as an altered poem, have an existence as real as the archetype. (p. 142)

Readers of literature, he says, are not accustomed to dealing with multiple wordings in a final text nor with composite authorship. Yet one Dickinson "poem," "Those fair—fictitious People," has twenty-six variants that fit eleven places, amounting to 7680 possible poems; and other poems, as traditionally printed and studied, would have to be called "Dickinson-Todd-Higginson's," since editors were responsible for some of the words. In the end, Franklin observes, "the fact that we are not organized to talk about an altered poem as a poem shows how little the subject of our pursuit is poetry" (p. 141).

Two issues are involved in these considerations, and they are basic to all kinds of editing, whether the copy-text is an uncompleted manuscript or a printed edition: (1) What does "intention" signify, and when is it final? (2) Does it matter whether the *author's* wording is recovered, particularly when emendations by others are improvements? These questions ask for definitions of the three words "final authorial intention" and for justification of them as an expression of the goal of editing. I hope that what I have said up to now has provided some answers to them and will serve as background for the following brief replies, specifically directed at Franklin's conclusions.

The second of the questions is easier to answer than the first. No one presumably would deny that any alteration in a literary work could be regarded as producing a different work and that the new work could be made the subject of critical analysis. Neither would anyone deny that nonauthorial revisions could produce a work superior to the original and more rewarding for study.[67] Nevertheless, if an editor sets out to edit the works of a particular writer, he has under-

67. James Thorpe, however, does not seem to me to give adequate recognition to this possibility in the opening chapter ("The Aesthetics of Textual Criticism," originally published in *PMLA*, 80 [1965], 465-482) of his *Principles of Textual Criticism* (1972). He grants that "status as a work of art is not affected by whether [the work's] intentions all belong to the titular author"; but he immediately adds that "the integrity of the work of art depends very much on the work being limited to those intentions which are the author's," and he then insists that it is this "final integrity which should be the object of the critic's chief attention" (p. 31). Of course, his book is concerned with editing which seeks to establish what the author wrote; but the nature of that activity might have been more helpfully defined in relation to other possi-

ble editorial goals. Instead, there is the implication (which contradicts the first statement quoted above) that the work of art can only be preserved through the efforts of editors who purge it of the nonauthorial features that it continually attracts. We are told that "forces are always at work thwarting or modifying the author's intentions" and that the work "is thus always tending toward a collaborative status" (p. 48); therefore, "aesthetic objects . . . must be protected in order to preserve the work from becoming a collaborative enterprise" (p. 49). The scholarly editor is not so much "protecting" the work as restoring a particular form of it which has historical (and perhaps also aesthetic) interest; purely as an aesthetic object the work might well be better off without protection.

taken a task of historical research, and his goal must necessarily be the recovery of the words which the author actually wrote. That the bulk of scholarly editorial work has been of this sort does not imply that all critics will find this kind of edition appropriate for their purposes or that no other approach to editing is legitimate. A critic may choose to discuss a series of poems on death, say, rather than a series of poems by Milton, Shelley, Tennyson, and Dickinson; so long as he operates outside of a historical framework and makes no references to the authors or their times, he need not be concerned with whether he has the precise words of a particular author but only with whether he has the "best" version of each poem from an aesthetic point of view. Similarly, an editor could edit a collection of poems on death, letting his own aesthetic judgments guide him in improving upon any previously known version of each poem; the editor would become a self-invited collaborator of the original author, and the editorial process would be creatively, rather than historically, oriented. This kind of editing occurs regularly in publishing houses, and many books normally attributed to a single author are already the work of more than one person by the time of their first publication (one thinks immediately of the editorial labors of Maxwell Perkins at Scribner's).[68] The crucial point

68. See A. Walton Litz, "Maxwell Perkins: The Editor as Critic," in *Editor, Author, and Publisher*, ed. William J. Howard (1969), pp. 96-112. The author's attitude toward such changes is of course a separate matter, taken up in section II above. Morse Peckham has questioned whether it is meaningful to think of the "author" as distinguishable from others who work on the same text, and thus whether the recovery of authorial intention is a possible goal, in "Reflections on the Foundations of Modern Textual Editing" (see note 14 above). Whenever an author revises his work, Peckham argues, he is looking at something already created and is no longer in the position of the creator (or the "initiator" of the "discourse"); he may be the first to revise the work, but his activity is no different from that of publishers' readers or editors who come along later. Peckham's point is similar to the one I am making here, because it recognizes that the activity of "editing" need not have any connection with a concept of "author." I would go on, however, as Peckham does not, and claim that the initiator of a dis-course can be identified as a historical figure (whether or not his name is known —cf. note 5 above), distinct from others because he is the initiator; that an interest may attach to this initiator; and that the task of attempting to segregate his contributions to the discourse from those of others is therefore one legitimate scholarly pursuit. I have commented in somewhat more detail on this argument of Peckham's in *SB*, 28 (1975), 215-219. Cf. also the remark by Anthony Savile (see note 7 above): "If art conveys value through intentional means it is entirely natural that we should single out for attention the agent whose intentions these are" (p. 106). Zeller's position (see notes 26, 42, and 52 above) is similar to Peckham's in stressing "the difficulty, indeed the impossibility, of obtaining a text attributable exclusively to the author" (p. 249). But, unlike Peckham, he does not reach the point of questioning the individuality of the "author"; indeed, he distinguishes between the attitude of the author toward his text and the attitude of "the reader, the exegete or the editor" (p. 258). Baender (see note 42 above) also

is that once a critic refers to two poems *because they are by the same author*, he has introduced a consideration extrinsic to the poems, and he must thereafter be concerned with the words which the author wrote. Studying poems by particular authors or representative of particular historical periods, therefore, requires a knowledge of what the authors themselves wrote; studying poems by theme or type, without regard for biographical and historical contexts, requires only poems, and the number of hands through which a poem has passed to reach its present state of excellence is irrelevant. Academic departments are usually organized to study the historical development of literature, and it is not surprising that scholars in those departments produce editions which attempt to recover authorial wording. That they do so, however, is not indicative of a split between editorial and critical theory.

The other question—the meaning of "intention"—is too complicated a philosophical issue to be settled here; but we can at least agree that authorial intention in literature cannot simply be equated with an explicit statement by the author explaining his motives, purposes, aims, wishes, or meaning, for intention must surely exist even if no such statements were made or are extant, and any available statements may be inadequate or misleading. The only direct evidence one has for what was in the author's mind is not what he says was there but what one finds in his work. An editor, only through his analysis and understanding of the meaning of the work in the light of his knowledge of the author and the times, will be in a position to use authorial active intention as a basis for editorial choice. That is to say, of the meanings which the editor sees in the work, he will determine, through a weighing of all the information at his command, the one which he regards as most likely to have been the author's; and that determination will influence his decisions regarding variant readings. Recognizing "finality" of intention, in turn, depends on his ability to distinguish revisions which develop an intention in the same direction from those which push it in another direction: the former represent final intentions, the latter new intentions. Whether the editor rejects such "new" intentions or edits a separate text embodying them will vary with the particular situation. But so long as he is producing an edition of an author's writings, he must choose among the author's uncanceled

---

agrees with some parts of Peckham's discussion; but he is opposing Peckham when he affirms his belief "that human beings are discrete, that an individal has the power and privilege of self-expression and of changing his mind, and that other individuals do not have the privilege of altering that self-expression or of forcing that change of mind" (p. 141).

variants or published revisions in the light of his total understanding of the work and its author.

If it is objected that this conception of the editorial process gives an editor excessive freedom and substitutes subjectivism for rigorous discipline, two answers may be made. In the first place, a scholarly editor (as opposed to a creative one) is still pledged to print only the author's words. He may select readings on the basis of his own literary judgment only when the alternatives are authorial variants; when he chooses an authorial reading previous to the author's last one (or what he judges to be the last one), his justification is that the reading is "final" in terms of his view of the work as an organic whole and that the later reading either creates a new work or is an isolated alteration at odds with the spirit of the work. Beyond that, one may observe that critical perception is necessarily crucial to any act of historical reconstruction, any evaluation of evidence, and thus any edition labeled "critical"; therefore, as Greg says, "it would be disastrous to curb the liberty of competent editors in the hope of preventing fools from behaving after their kind." Perhaps the principal source of difficulty lies in thinking of the editorial and the critical functions as essentially distinct. When one recognizes that justice can be done to an author only by doing justice to his text, one also understands that the editor and the critic must be inseparable.

External Fact as an Editorial Problem

WHEN KEATS IN HIS SONNET ON CHAPMAN'S HOMER WROTE of "stout Cortez," rather than Balboa, staring at the Pacific with eagle eyes, he created what has become the classic instance of a factual error in a work of imaginative literature. Yet few readers have been bothered by the error or felt that it detracts from the power of the sonnet, and editors have not regarded it as a crux calling for emendation. Amy Lowell, after mentioning the possibility that Keats was thinking of Titian's painting of Cortez, dismisses the matter: "at any rate he put Cortez, probably by accident. It is no matter."[1] Classroom editions of Keats have often included some similar comment, such as Clarence DeWitt Thorpe's note that begins, "Historically, 'Cortez' should be read 'Balboa,'" and ends, "Poetically, it does not matter; the poem is true and magnificent."[2] Scarcely anyone would dispute Thorpe's conclusion that the poem is "true and magnificent," as it stands, or would advocate the substitution of "Balboa" in it. But the consensus of opinion on the question does not mean that no significant issues are raised by it. The view that an historical error does not detract from the greatness of a poem is of course grounded on the argument that an imaginative work creates its own internal world for the communication of truth: the work can express a "truth" relevant to the outside world without being faithful to that world in the details out of which the work is constructed. No one is surprised by the expression of this principle, which is, after all, central to an understanding of literature as metaphorical statement. What is less often considered, however, is the complexity of its editorial implications.

Certainly a critical editor cannot take as a general rule Thorpe's comment that "Poetically, it does not matter." Whether or not a particular error matters depends on more than whether or not it occurs in a poem or a "creative" work: sometimes a factual error in a poem may indeed call for correction, while at other times it may not, and the editor

1. *John Keats* (1925), p. 181.
2. In the Odyssey Press edition of the *Complete Poems and Selected Letters* (1935), p. 45.

must decide which is the case in any given instance, and why. If "Cortez" need not be or should not be corrected, the reason is not simply that factual inaccuracies are necessarily irrelevant to the artistic success of poems; the reason must instead focus on why it is either impractical or unwise to make a change in this particular case. Is "Cortez" so much a part of the pattern of versification as to rule out an alteration to a word of so different a sound as "Balboa"? Does "Cortez," calling up in the reader's mind the early days of the Spanish in Central America, manage to convey the meaning that was intended—or, at least, is it not too far off the mark to prevent the reader from grasping that meaning? (If the word, through some error of transmission, had been misspelled in such a way as not to be recognizable as "Cortez"—resulting perhaps in a name with no allusive significance or one with an inappropriate association—what would the editor do?) Or, on another level, does the long familiarity of the "Cortez" reading have any bearing on the editor's feeling that a change cannot now be contemplated? If so, does it make a difference whether the traditional, if unfactual, reading is one (like "Cortez") known to have been written down by the author or whether it is one whose origins are less certain? However simple or obvious it may seem at first to say that the "Cortez" reading should not be disturbed, questions of this kind are inevitably involved.

The editor of a critical text sets out to eliminate from a particular copy-text what can be regarded as errors in it; defining what constitutes an "error" is therefore basic to the editorial procedure. Any concept of error involves the recognition of a standard: an editor can label certain readings of a text erroneous only by finding that they fail to conform to a certain standard. Determining appropriate standards for editorial judgment must take into account the nature of the piece of writing as a whole and the nature of each individual passage in it as well as the nature of the edition that is to result, and it must recognize that errors may fall into discrete classes, each demanding different treatment. One may feel that errors of historical fact, for instance, should be corrected in some kinds of works (or passages) and not in other kinds, but that decision involves some consideration of authorial intention and will thus be affected by the attitude that the edition is to take toward questions of intention. If the goal of an edition—as with most scholarly critical editions —is to attempt to establish the text intended by the author at a particular time, one's decisions about what constitutes errors will be affected accordingly. Intention and error are inseparable concepts, because errors are by definition unintended deviations (unintended on a conscious level, that is, whatever unconscious motivation for them there may be). If a writer intentionally distorts historical fact for the purposes of a work, that distortion is not an error in terms of the work, nor is it a textual error from the editor's point of view.

An editor must distinguish, however, between accepting factual errors because they are intended features of a literary work and accepting them because they reveal the mental processes of the author. The latter interest is a legitimate and important one, but it may conflict with the aim of establishing the intended text of a work. Both interests can be accommodated through the use of textual notes, but one of those interests must be chosen as the rationale for the editor's treatment of the text itself. If one's aim is to reproduce the text of a particular document, then obviously one reproduces it errors and all, for the errors may be revealing characteristics of the author's direction of thought and in any case are part of the historical record to be preserved. But if one's aim is to offer a critical edition of that text as a finished literary work, one can no more follow a policy of retaining all factual errors than pursue a course of correcting all such errors. In a critical edition the treatment of factual errors can be no mechanical matter, covered by a blanket rule; instead, the editor must give serious thought to the circumstances surrounding each one, thought that will involve settling basic questions about the nature of the editing being undertaken.

Errors of external fact are of course only one category of the larger class of discrepancies in general. Many discrepancies in texts are internal: that is, certain readings are identifiable as errors not because they fail to agree with recognized facts but because they are inconsistent with points established elsewhere within the text. When, for example, Minnie Mavering is referred to as "Molly" in Howells's *April Hopes* or Tashtego is called "Daggoo" in *Moby-Dick*,[3] the discrepancies are matters of internal, rather than external, fact. The authors in these cases cannot have intended to refer to their characters by the wrong names, and the editor of a critical text will rectify such errors. Not all internal errors can be corrected by the simple substitution of a name, however. As alert readers have long noticed, the *Pequod* is described early in *Moby-Dick* (Chapter 16) as having a tiller ("Scorning a turnstile wheel at her reverend helm") but later in the book is given a wheel helm with spokes (Chapters 61, 118—in which the helmsman is said to "handle the spokes" and "ostentatiously handle his spokes"). Similarly, Pip is referred to as an "Alabama boy" (Chapter 27) and is told that a whale would sell for thirty times what he would in Alabama (Chapter 93); but there is also a reference to his "native Tolland County in Connecticut" (Chapter 93) and his father "in old Tolland county" (Chapter 99). Melville evidently did not intend

3. See the Indiana edition of *April Hopes*, ed. Don L. Cook *et al.* (1974), pp. 221–222; and *Moby-Dick*, Chapter 61.

these discrepancies, but a scholarly editor who attempts to eliminate them faces the difficult problem of guessing how Melville would have rewritten the passages. In some instances of this kind the editor's educated guess may be the best solution, but often the wiser course is to let the discrepancies stand.

It should be clear, however, that the editor who allows such errors to remain does so only in the belief that nothing better can be done and not because they are regarded as part of the author's intended text. Internal errors resemble external errors in the sense that they are recognizable by reference to something outside the immediate context: a reading in one sentence (or phrase) is erroneous or discrepant because it fails to match what is said in another sentence (or phrase) elsewhere in the work. But the "external" facts in such instances are still within the limits of the piece of writing, and the author's intention with respect to the internal consistency of the work is made clear to the reader in the work itself. The editor is normally in a position to know, in other words, whether the world of the work is a realistic one, in which a person named Minnie cannot suddenly become Molly and a wheel cannot change into a tiller, or a surrealistic one, in which such "facts" are not stable. In the case of allusions that extend outside the limits of the work, however, the editor is in a more difficult position. Because the reference is to something with an independent existence, one is faced with the question whether the author is attempting to be accurate in citing an external fact or is adapting it so as to give it a new existence within the work. Errors of external fact, therefore, pose quite a different problem from internal discrepancies. They are worth investigating in their own right and because they lead one to consider the fundamental assumptions of editing.

I

One of the most common situations involving external allusion occurs when a writer quotes from an earlier piece of writing. Insofar as the emphasis of the reference is on a verifiable independent source, the quotation should be exact. But insofar as the writer's intention is to adapt the quotation, it becomes a created element in the new work and cannot then be deemed incorrect merely because it fails to correspond with an external source. In many cases the motivation is mixed: the writer wishes to call on the authority of a previous author (expecting readers to recognize the author or the work cited) but at the same time wishes to alter the quotation to serve a particular purpose in the new context. Of course, a writer sometimes simply misquotes without intending to, and if no consequences follow from the misquotation, it is merely an error and nothing more; but if the misquotation becomes the basis for discussion or implication, then it has become an integral part of the new work, whether the misquotation was consciously intended or not.[4]

Many of the possible editorial problems involving quotations can be illustrated by a single famous instance, the section of "Extracts" prefixed to *Moby-Dick*. In this section Melville draws together eighty quotations, ranging from the Bible to mid-nineteenth-century fiction, constituting a massive epigraph to the book. One might at first feel that epigraphs are not part of the text they introduce and that there would thus be no legitimate reason for their not being accurate; but a moment's reflection reminds one that an author selects an epigraph in order to set up a relationship between its implications and those of the text to follow and that one should not be surprised, therefore, if the epigraph were intentionally slanted to make the relationship clearer. Epigraphs are as much a part of a text as the quotations embedded in it. In the case of Melville's "Extracts," the creative nature of epigraphs is evident: the sweep of the assembled material is intended to suggest the greatness and universality of the subject of whales and whaling.[5] Melville furthermore places his quotations in a dramatic framework: they are said to be "Supplied by a Sub-Sub-Librarian," who has "gone through the long Vaticans and street-stalls of the earth" in search of them. The fact that supposedly they have been prepared by a created character does not, of course, mean that any errors in them must necessarily be accepted as contributing to the characterization, but it does strengthen the point that misquotations may at times be functional, and intentionally so. Whether misquotations are in fact intended as part of a characterization can only be determined by the context, and in this instance there is nothing to indicate that Melville wished the reader to regard any errors as lapses on the Sub-Sub-Librarian's part; on the other hand, he may well have wished to alter certain quotations to make them more appropriate as epigraphs to the work that follows, and misquotations in the "Extracts" must be judged critically with this possibility in mind.[6] A survey of some of the editorial

4. This point is taken up in more detail below, in Part II.

5. The two-paragraph prefatory note to the "Extracts" warns the reader not to take the "whale statements, however authentic, in these extracts, for veritable gospel cetology" and claims for them only that they provide "a glancing bird's eye view of what has been promiscuously said, thought, fancied, and sung of Leviathan, by many nations and generations, including our own."

6. Some critics, such as Viola Sachs in *La Contre-Bible de Melville* (1975), assume that all readings of the American first edition were intended by Melville, and they erect their interpretations on that assumption. This approach is uncritical and unrealistic in that it does not admit the possibility that the American text might contain transmissional errors or other unintended readings. But it does draw attention to the fact that the critical editor, in deciding what constitutes an error in the text, may be called upon to assess the soundness of various critics' commentaries.

questions raised by the "Extracts" can provide a convenient introduction to the issues involved in dealing with external references in general.

Perhaps the most straightforward situations are those in which misquotations result from obviously intended alterations by Melville. In the second extract, for example, from Job 41:32, the wording of the printed text[7] (the manuscript does not survive) exactly matches that of the King James Bible except that "Leviathan" is substituted for "He" in "Leviathan maketh a path to shine after him." Clearly no one, in the process of transmission from manuscript to print, could have misread Melville's "He" as "Leviathan"; furthermore, the indefinite reference of "He" calls for some explanation when the passage is quoted out of context. It seems certain that Melville wrote "Leviathan," intentionally altering the wording of his source. Similarly, the extract from Montaigne contains the clause "the sea-gudgeon retires into it in great security," whereas the passage in Hazlitt's Montaigne (Melville's source) reads "this little fish" instead of "the sea-gudgeon." Again, the change cannot have resulted from a misreading of handwriting. Although it is perhaps conceivable that Melville wrote "sea-gudgeon" as a result of losing his place momentarily—since "sea-gudgeon" occurs in an earlier (unquoted) part of Montaigne's sentence—it is much more likely that he wished not to lose this term and substituted it in what is otherwise essentially an accurate quotation. Even undistinctive words can sometimes be recognized as Melville's alterations: the extract from Waller consists of two couplets, separated by a row of asterisks indicating ellipsis; in the second couplet "his" (twice) and "he" appear, rather than Waller's "her" and "she"— substitutions obviously made so that the gender of the pronouns would match that in the first couplet, now that the two couplets are juxtaposed (in the original, forty lines separate them).[8] In instances of this kind the

7. References such as this to the text of *Moby-Dick* are to the text of the original American edition (Harper & Brothers, 1851), which was set from the manuscript furnished by Melville and which must serve (in the absence of that manuscript) as the copy-text for a scholarly critical edition. The attention only to wording—and generally not to punctuation and spelling—is commented on below. In the examples to follow, I draw on information turned up by various members of the editorial staff of the Northwestern-Newberry Edition of Melville. The problems in the "Extracts" will be more fully and systematically dealt with in the forthcoming *Moby-Dick* volume in that edition. For valuable comments on an earlier version of this essay—both the part on Melville and the more general part—I am indebted to Fredson Bowers, Harrison Hayford, and Richard Colles Johnson.

8. In the passage from William Tooke's edition of Lucian (1820), Melville's alterations seem clearly to result from his wishing to change the diction: "sea" replaces "deep" and "monstrous" replaces "enormous" (though this second change could involve a misreading of handwriting). In the extract from William Scoresby, the distance at which one can hear the shaking of the whale's tail is said to be "three or four miles" rather than the "two or three miles" of the original, an obvious change for exaggeration. And in the quotation from Thomas Beale "Sperm Whale" is substituted for "sea beast," a change making more explicit the reference to whales.

editor of a critical edition will retain what are in fact misquotations, recognizing that the aim is to reproduce Melville's intended form of the quotations. (The accompanying apparatus should of course inform the reader in each case of the relation between the source passage and the passage of text being edited, for the retention, as well as the alteration, of an "error" in a quotation constitutes an editorial decision that must be put on record.)

Thinking about these examples leads one to see some of the conditions under which emendations in the "Extracts" would have to be made. Unintended slips—authorial, scribal, compositorial—can be present in the text of the "Extracts" just as in the body of the book, and a critical approach to the text demands that all "misquotations" be evaluated and not automatically accepted as intended alterations. When, in the quotation from Blackstone, "caught near the coast" appears instead of "caught near the coasts," and, in the extract from Frederick Debell Bennett, "these weapons" replaces "those weapons"—or when the passage from Uno von Troil contains "lime-stone" instead of "brim-stone"—the substituted word in each case could easily have resulted from a simple transmissional error (such as a memorial lapse or a misreading of handwriting), and in none of these cases does there seem to be any reason for an authorial change. A number of such examples occur in poetic quotations from prominent sources: in the second extract from *Paradise Lost*, Leviathan is said to be stretched like a promontory "in," rather than "on," the deep and to spout out a sea "at his breath," rather than "at his trunk"; and in the extract from Cowper we read that "rockets blew [rather than 'flew'] self driven, / To hang their momentary fire [not 'fires'] / Around [not 'Amid'] the vault of heaven." All these misquotations are conceivable misreadings of handwriting or slips in copying, and it is difficult to see why Melville (or anyone else) would wish to make them intentionally ("fire" for "fires" is a clear instance of error, because the word is supposed to rhyme with "spires" two lines earlier). Slips of this kind, which probably occurred in the process of transmission from authorial manuscript to printed book, call for emendation by the critical editor.

Of course, some of these erroneous readings may have been present in Melville's manuscript, but as long as they can be argued to be unintentional slips the case for emendation is not altered.[9] When the printed

9. Some evidence suggesting that Melville intended to quote accurately in certain instances is available at those points where the original English edition (set from Melville's revised proofs of the American edition) corrects the American, since no one other than Melville would have been likely to bother making such changes. One example is the correction in the English edition of the reading "stuffed with hoops" to "stiff with hoops" in a line from *The Rape of the Lock*; for other examples, see note 10 and the discussion of the

text reads "Hosmannus" at a point where the name in Browne's *Pseudo-doxia Epidemica* is "Hofmannus," the error may well have been Melville's own: since he was probably using his copy of the 1686 edition and was accustomed to transcribing long *s* as "s," he may have mistaken the "f" in this proper name for a long *s*. Some instances are less clear-cut but still make the same point. A line from Elizabeth Oakes Smith is printed in the "Extracts" as "A mariner sat in the shrouds one night," although the original reads "on the shrouds." The reading "in" could simply be a scribal or compositorial misreading of Melville's "on"; but it is also possible that Melville wrote "in," not because he wished to alter the wording but because he was not copying carefully, the "in" perhaps coming naturally to him as the more idiomatic wording. Unless there is reason to believe that Melville intended to revise the quotation—which seems unlikely here—the possible presence of the "in" in his manuscript should not deter the editor from emending to "on."[10] In other words, whenever the possibility of a misreading of handwriting or of an authorial slip outweighs the possibility that the misquotation is an intended one, the editor seeking to establish what the author wished will emend to correct the quotation. Whatever interest there may be in Melville's writing "Hosmannus" and "in the shrouds"—if indeed he did so—belongs to a different level of concern; such evidence will be preserved in the notes but does not belong in a text aimed to satisfy another concern.

An additional example or two may serve further to clarify the role of arguments based on possible slips or misreadings of handwriting. In the Smith quotation, four lines after "in the shrouds," there is the clause "it floundered in the sea," where "it" refers to "whale"; in the original the subject is "he," not "it," but here the conservative editor is likely to feel that the possibility of an intentional change is enough stronger to war-

---

Bunyan citation below. (Of course, some literate person in the English printing- or publishing-house could conceivably have been responsible for certain corrections of this kind; but the pattern of the corrections and the nature of some of the sources involved suggest a greater likelihood that the corrections are Melville's.)

10. Another example possibly involving an idiom could result in a different decision, because of differing circumstances. The quotation from Charles Wilkes's *Narrative of the United States Exploring Expedition* (1844) contains the phrase "with look-outs at the mast-heads," although Wilkes uses the singular "mast-head." To employ the plural when more look-outs than one are involved is an idiom Melville uses repeatedly (as in "the business of standing mast-heads," "the earliest standers of mast-heads," and "modern standers-of-mast-heads" in Chapter 35); furthermore, he apparently gave close attention to this extract in preparing the proofs to send to England, because the reading "her near appearance" in the American edition is altered to the correct one, "her mere appearance," in the English, and it is unlikely that anyone other than Melville would have made such a correction from this kind of source. Under these circumstances, then, there seems stronger reason to leave "mast-heads" than to change it, even though the possibility always remains that it results from a slip or a misreading of handwriting.

rant the retention of the "it." This misquotation could of course have been a mere slip, but at least a misreading of handwriting does not seem to be involved in this case, and that in itself lends some weight to the argument against emendation—though it cannot be the decisive factor. The opening line of the extract from Waller reads "Like Spenser's Talus with his modern flail," but the adjective in Waller is actually "iron," not "modern." There would seem little possibility that "modern" could result from a misreading of handwriting (or from a slip of the pen, for that matter); but "modern" makes no sense, and the editor may well take the position that the word cannot have been intended (even if its presence as an error cannot be explained) and that an emendation is in order. The argument is somewhat strengthened by the fact that Melville a few years later, in "The Bell-Tower," referred to Talus as an "iron slave." But this information is fortuitous: the point is that the editor's critical judgment carries more weight than inconclusive speculation about the transmissional process. That "modern" cannot be explained as arising from a particular kind of error of transmission does not mean that it must therefore be retained by a conservative editor, if that editor considers the change unlikely to have been intended by the author. The critical editing of a text must extend to the quotations that are a part of the text. Because quotations have external sources, the editor has access to one more stage of antecedent document at these points than elsewhere in the text and thus is in a more informed position for detecting erroneous readings.

The process of locating those external sources, however, raises some important questions of editorial procedure. First is the problem of deciding what particular edition of a source text is the proper one to use for comparison. If the text of a quotation in the "Extracts" matches the text of the corresponding passage in the first edition of the work quoted from, the problem does not exist, for it does not matter whether Melville used the first edition or some other edition, as long as the resulting quotation is accurate.[11] But when the text in the "Extracts" does not correspond with that of the first edition, one cannot assume that the difference necessarily results from a transmissional error in the process of writing and printing *Moby-Dick* or from a deliberate change on Melville's part; it may be that Melville copied accurately, but from a different edition. If

11. The possibility that Melville used either a revised or a corrupt text and misquoted from it in such a way as to produce the reading of the first edition is hardly worth the editor's while to think about in most instances. It is conceivable, however, that such a situation could occasionally be of some importance, if an author were attempting to reproduce a passage from a revised edition of a work and through an unlucky slip managed to recreate the reading of the unrevised text; but this occurrence would of course depend on an extreme coincidence.

so, the editor's thinking about the passage will be affected, and it is there-fore important to know, if possible, the immediate source of each quota-tion. Yet in the case of many classics that have gone through numerous editions and have been excerpted and quoted even more often the editor cannot be expected to have searched through all possible sources. It is conceivable, for example, that Melville happened to take the Waller passage from a secondary source that misquoted "iron" as "modern"; but an editor cannot begin to find all the places where Waller's lines may have been quoted and has no choice but to proceed on the basis of the available knowledge. Frequently, however, an editor will know some of the favorite sources that an author is likely to use and may even have some information about the particular copies read. That Melville's ninth extract—identified only as *"Other or Octher's verbal narrative taken down from his mouth by King Alfred. A.D. 890"*—comes from Robert Henry's *The History of Great Britain* (1771) is not difficult to learn when one knows that J. Ross Browne's *Etchings from a Whaling Cruise* (1846), one of Melville's principal sources, also quotes this passage; furthermore, it is clear that Melville took the passage directly from Browne, and did not go back to Henry, because his extract agrees with Browne in reading "this country" at a point where the first edition of 1771 reads "these parts." A similar instance is the extract from Bunyan, which does not re-produce the relevant passage from the 1682 edition of *The Holy War* but instead follows the wording (except for a sixteen-word ellipsis) of a paraphrase of this passage in Henry T. Cheever's *The Whale and His Captors* (1849).[12]

The question that all this leads to is how the editor should handle errors or alterations that were already present in the immediate source of the quotations. If Melville quotes a corrupt text under the impression that he is providing the reader with another author's words, is it part of an editor's duty to replace that corrupt text with an accurate text? An-swering this question goes to the heart of the concept of scholarly critical editing. Expecting editors to make such "corrections" of quotations is in effect asking them to establish the text of each quoted passage so as to fulfill its author's intentions. Such a procedure would mean treating each quotation as if it were an individual item in an anthology, not a part of a context created by another writer. The reader comes to Mel-ville's "Extracts" not to seek established texts of Waller and Bunyan but

12. In some cases another extract may provide a clue to the source. The quotation from John Hunter is a paraphrase of the original wording in the *Philosophical Transactions* of the Royal Society for 1787; but it matches exactly (except for the omission of "an") the wording quoted by William Paley in his *Natural Theology* (1802)—which is the work Mel-ville cites for the immediately following extract.

to see what Melville does with those authors; the editor's job is to establish Melville's versions of Waller and Bunyan, which may turn out to
be considerably different from the texts that would appear in scholarly
editions of them. If a corrupt text of a quotation is the one that Melville
knew, responded to, and wished to set before his readers, then that text
is the intended one under these circumstances. Emendation may be necessary if it is clear that the copy-text version of a quotation contains readings unintended by Melville, but the test for emendation is not whether
the readings were unintended by the original writer. In order to be in a
position to make intelligent decisions on this question, an editor is obviously required to perform some textual research among editions of
the quoted work: if the copy-text version of a quotation does not match
the text of the first edition of the quoted work, the editor must attempt
to locate another edition that does match, for otherwise there is no basis
for judging whether the variants were present in Melville's immediate
source or originated at a later point (either in his own copying—intentionally or inadvertently—or in the succeeding steps of transmission).
The scholarly editor must be able to draw the line between restoring an
author's intended wording of a quotation and collaborating with the
author by pushing the process of "correcting" the quotation to a point
never contemplated by the author. To claim that Melville intended to
quote accurately is not to the purpose: aside from the historical question
of the degree of accuracy implied at a given time in the past by the act of
"quoting" (discussed below), this claim mixes up different kinds of intention. That Melville may have "intended" in advance to quote accurately the sentiments of various writers does not alter the fact that the
scholarly editor's concern is with Melville's active intention as he wrote,
reflected in the quotations themselves.[13] The immediate sources he accepted and used become the authoritative sources for the quotations in
this context.

   Thus the extract from Thomas Fuller's *The Holy State, and the Pro-
fane State* reads "mighty whales which swim" at a point where the first
edition of 1642 and the "second edition enlarged" of 1648 read "mighty
whales who swim"; but because "which" is the reading of the London
1841 edition—the edition borrowed by Melville, according to Merton
M. Sealts's *Melville's Reading* (1966)—there would seem to be no reason

   13. These different kinds of intention are discussed in more detail in G. T. Tanselle,
"The Editorial Problem of Final Authorial Intention," *Studies in Bibliography*, 29 (1976),
167–211 (which includes references to many other treatments of the subject). An important
and still more recent discussion, containing some useful criticism of that essay, is Steven
Mailloux's "Authorial Intention and Conventional Reader Response," Chapter 7 (pp. 171–
206) of his University of Southern California dissertation, "Interpretive Conventions and
Recent Anglo-American Literary Theory" (1977).

to emend. The editor is not called upon to investigate whether any authority could attach to "which" as a reading in Fuller's text, for Melville evidently copied accurately the wording of the passage that struck him in the 1841 edition; whether or not that wording corresponds exactly to Fuller's intention is irrelevant, because it is the wording that Melville encountered and used. In the case of the Waller extract, if an edition or secondary source available to Melville could indeed be found containing the phrase "modern flail," no emendation would be required, however peculiar the reading seems, because the passage with that reading in it would be the one that Melville reacted to and found appropriate for inclusion in the "Extracts." Until such a source is found, however, the inherent unlikelihood of the reading will weigh more heavily with an editor than the theoretical possibility that Melville came upon the reading somewhere; the editor is acting responsibly if, after a reasonable search in Waller editions and books known to have been used by Melville, the reading is regarded as an error to be emended. Some textual research is nevertheless clearly necessary. An editor who looked only at the original 1645 edition of Waller's *Poems* would find that the line reads "Like fairy Talus with his iron flail" and might conclude that "Spenser's Talus," as well as "modern flail," is an erroneous reading (though possibly one intended by Melville to identify the allusion). But a little further research would reveal that "fairy" was changed to "Spenser's" in the 1664 edition and would thus place "Spenser's" in a different class of readings from "modern." Without such textual investigation, editors are not in a position to make informed judgments; but pursuing that research by no means implies that they are shifting their focus from the intentions of the quoter to those of the quoted.[14]

14. Melvyn New has encountered a situation in which he believes that an editor should employ as the copy-text for a long quotation the first edition of the work quoted from. In *Tristram Shandy* Sterne quotes the entire "Memoire" from Heinrich van Deventer's *Observations importantes sur le Manuel des accouchemens* (1734); New argues that "Much of the wit of the 'Memoire's' inclusion in *Tristram* lies in the fact that Sterne could use it verbatim," that "it is not a fiction but an historical record of an actual deliberation." One can guess, New says, that "had Sterne had photoreproductive processes available to him, he would have used them for providing a printer's copy of the 'Memoire'" and that one "comes closest to Sterne's intention" by using the 1734 Deventer text. New recognizes, however, that this text would have to be emended with what seem to be Sterne's intended alterations and that punctuation "remains a difficult problem, whichever text is used as copy text"—thus in fact reopening the question of how much is gained by adopting the earlier copy-text. Whether or not one is persuaded by New that presumptive authority here should be given to the 1734 text, one can agree that the problem is to separate Sterne's "function as copyist" from his "function as artist" (due allowance, of course, being made for contemporary conventions of "copying") and that "in the text underlying any borrowed material there is the possibility of a wealth of bibliographical and critical information." See "*Tristram Shandy* and Heinrich van Deventer's *Observations*," *PBSA*, 69 (1975), 84–90; and "The Sterne Edi-

A related element in considering a writer's intentions in making a quotation is an understanding of the contemporary conventions of quoting. Generally before the twentieth century (and in some cases even into the century) quotations were not thought of as "inaccurate" or "incorrect" if they occasionally departed from the wording—to say nothing of the punctuation and spelling—of the source, as long as they did not distort the gist of its meaning. It was not considered wrong, even in expository writing (that is to say, writing not usually classed as "imaginative" or belletristic), to place between quotation marks what we would now think of as a paraphrase or an adaptation. For an editor to make such "quotations" conform to modern standards of accuracy, therefore, would be to modernize (that is, to employ a modern approach—for the corrected quotation would often be less "modern" in form); and the scholarly editor will not wish to engage in modernizing here any more than with the punctuation and spelling of the rest of the text. In checking Melville's extracts against their sources, then, an editor need not be concerned with spelling, punctuation, capitalization, or other formal matters except to the extent that discrepancies markedly affect meaning (or obviously result from slips or nonauthorial styling) or that agreements point to Melville's immediate sources. It clearly never occurred to Melville to be troubled about taking a twenty-word middle section out of a long sentence of Davenant's and beginning it with a capital letter; or juxtaposing, without ellipsis marks (and actually in reverse order), two sentences from Bacon's *History Naturall and Experimentall of Life and Death* (1638) that are in fact separated by six of Bacon's "Items"; or running together two lines of verse without indicating the line break, as in the extracts from Bacon's version of Psalm 104 and from *1 Henry IV*. When Melville inserts "Fife" in parentheses after "this coast" in his quotation from Robert Sibbald and "whales" in parentheses after "these monsters" in his extract from Darwin, he is using parentheses to mark explanatory insertions in the way that we would now use square brackets.[15] An editor who injects ellipsis dots, virgules, and brackets into these quotations is modernizing, by requiring Melville's quotations—and each of the extracts is in fact printed in quotation marks—to conform to present-day standards. The place for showing these relationships between the

---

tion: The Text of *Tristram Shandy*," in *Editing Eighteenth Century Novels*, ed. G. E. Bentley, Jr. (1975), pp. 86–87.

15. The extract from Darwin in fact illustrates two practices: the insertion of "(whales)" occurs within the quotation, whereas the quotation is interrupted—by the use of closing and then opening quotation marks—for the insertion of "(Terra Del Fuego)" after "the shore."

quotations and their sources is the textual apparatus or other editorial end-matter; in the text itself the scholarly editor will wish to respect nineteenth-century customs in the use of quotation marks (and what they imply about the enclosed material) just as much as nineteenth-century practices in placing apostrophes, commas, and other punctuation.

This custom of allusive quotation is represented among Melville's extracts by a wide diversity of situations, which thus help further to define the nature of the accuracy that is attempted. In addition to substitutions, which often could be the result of a slip of the pen or a misreading of handwriting, there are instances of insertion, omission, and paraphrase that cannot reasonably be considered inadvertent. For example, the extract from the account of Schouten's sixth circumnavigation in John Harris's *Navigantium atque Itinerantium Bibliotheca* (1705) begins, "Here they saw such huge shoals of whales," whereas the passage in Harris reads "saw an incredible number of Penguins, and such huge shoals of whales." Obviously Melville wished to omit the six words after "saw" as irrelevant to his purpose; deleting the reference to penguins focuses more attention on the whales, but Melville saw no reason to note his ellipsis.[16] Similarly, in the quotation from Jefferson there is an unmarked omission of fifty-one words between the subject and the verb; the sentence from Daniel Tyerman and George Bennet's *Journal* (1831) silently omits eleven words; and five are left out of the sentence from James Colnett's *Voyage* (1798).[17] Sometimes omissions and substitutions occur together, as when four words are omitted and four other alterations are made in the sentence from Richard Stafford, causing it to refer only to one man and one whale instead of to a group of each. The motivation for some of these changes is not always as obvious as in the omission of the reference to penguins or the insertion of "Whale-" in "The Whaleship Globe" (the extract from William Lay and Cyrus Hussey), but there can be no doubt that such alterations are intentional and that they did not, in Melville's view, prevent the results from being regarded as "extracts" from the works named. Indeed, passages placed in quotation marks could depart even further from the originals and consist entirely of paraphrase: the sentences from Stowe, Boswell, and James Cook are far enough from the original wording that they have to be considered paraphrases made by Melville (unless he was following secondary sources

16. The same situation occurs in the quotation from Margaret Fuller's translation of Eckermann's *Conversations with Goethe*, where Melville has silently omitted "and sea-monsters" following "whales."

17. Transitional words in source passages form another obviously intended class of omissions. The omission of "other" from "what other thing" in the extract from Philemon Holland's edition of Plutarch and of "on the other hand" from a quotation from Frederick Debell Bennett are necessary adjustments when the passages are taken out of context.

that have not yet been located). And the first sentence of the extract from Uno von Troil was apparently constructed by Melville's rearranging parts of the original sentence. It is impossible to analyze precisely the various reasons underlying these changes; but it is clear that the desire to alter passages so as to emphasize their connection with whaling is not the sole explanation. The pattern of the extracts as a whole shows that the concept of what constitutes "quotation" here is a much looser one than present-day writers are accustomed to. As in any other piece of writing, intention is ultimately defined by the work itself, and the extracts, as a group, establish their own standards. When Melville's departures from his sources result simply from his practice of approximate quotation, they cannot be thought of as "unintended." Errors, to be emended editorially, can certainly be located in the extracts, but the process of identifying them must be founded on an understanding of the level of accuracy attempted in the first place. (And in a scholarly edition the information used by the editor for determining this level will be available to the reader in the notes that record or explain the differences between the extracts and their sources.)

Melville's twisting of quotations for his own purposes—beyond any customary casualness in quoting—does, however, play a significant role in producing the wording found in the "Extracts." When Melville paraphrases a passage, places the result in quotation marks, and labels the source, he is engaging in allusive quotation but is approaching the border line—even by nineteenth-century standards—between quotation and fresh composition. He apparently crosses that line in the passage that purports to be from Antonio de Ulloa, describing the breath of the whale "attended with such an insupportable smell, as to bring on a disorder of the brain"; these words seem in fact to be Melville's own elaboration of the three-word phrase "an insupportable smell," which refers in Ulloa to a fish called "cope." The next step is to create an entirely new passage and provide it with a fictitious source: the extract following the one from John Ramsay McCulloch is labeled *From 'Something' unpublished* and is presumably Melville's own extension of a point raised by the McCulloch quotation, for it is clearly designed to follow McCulloch's statement but does not occur there in the original. Melville does not engage in this practice often, but the presence of one or two examples further strengthens the view of the "Extracts" section as a creative work and not a mere anthology.

Suggesting that something created on the spot has an independent existence outside the work tends to break down any rigid boundary between what is external and what is internal, and references to "real" sources can sometimes partake more of the internal world of the work than of external reality. One extract, which describes some white crew members returning from the pursuit of a whale to find "their ship in bloody possession of the savages enrolled among the crew," is credited to a *"Newspaper Account of the Taking and Retaking of the Whale-ship Hobomack."* In fact, however, no such mutiny took place on board the Falmouth ship *Hobomok.* Melville's recollection of stories he must have heard probably resulted in the mixing together of details of two differ- ent events: the 1835 fight between some Namorik Islanders and the crew of the Falmouth ship *Awashonks,* and the 1842 mutiny by some Kings- mill Islanders on board the Fairhaven ship *Sharon.* The details of the *Sharon* mutiny fit more closely with those described in the extract; but one of the officers of the *Awashonks* in 1835 was captain of the *Hobomok* in 1841, when Melville's ship encountered it, and Melville may therefore have been thinking partly of his account. After investigating this tangle, Wilson Heflin decided that this extract must be "a piece of Melville's invention."[18] If so, no substantive emendation would be appropriate. To replace *"Hobomack"* with *"Awashonks"* or *"Sharon"* (which one?) would probably not restore what Melville intended to write; and, while either one would fit the facts somewhat better, there is no reason why Melville should be required to follow facts here. Whether or not the spelling of the ship should be corrected to *"Hobomok"* is a separate ques- tion. Because Melville did know of the actual *Hobomok* and because "o" and "a" are sometimes difficult to distinguish in his handwriting, it may be that he wrote "Hobomock" rather than "Hobomack," and one could defend an emendation to *"Hobomock"* (as a permissible variant of the correct spelling) or possibly to *"Hobomok."* Recognizing that what the extract describes never took place aboard the real *Hobomok* does not prevent one from correcting the spelling of the ship's name on the assumption that the actual ship *Hobomok* is being referred to in the citation—for the likelihood is that Melville was thinking of the real ship but confusing what happened on it.[19] The supposed quotation is thus

18. "Herman Melville's Whaling Years" (Vanderbilt diss., 1952), p. 224.

19. Knowledge of the range of variant spellings recorded in the *DAE* for the Indian evil deity—including "Hobomoko," "Abamacho," and "Hobbamock"—might cause one to argue that "Hobomack" falls within the range of permissible deviation, but presumably such a range did not exist for the ship's name. A different kind of argument against emend- ing the spelling would be to say that the correction does not make the citation fit the extract better than it did before and that under the circumstances the *Hobomack* becomes in effect a fictitious ship of Melville's invention. The great similarity between "Hobomack" and "Hobomok," however, makes it difficult to believe that Melville did not have the real ship in mind. And an editor's intervention to correct Melville's intended reference in the citation carries no implication that the extract and the citation are being brought into closer agree- ment: there is no reason why Melville cannot be allowed to place on board a real ship events that never occurred there, and no reason why an editor cannot make a local correction of a spelling error without being obligated to produce factual accuracy in the larger context.

inspired by real events and refers to a real ship; but the *"Newspaper Account,"* and the *Hobomok* mutiny it reports, exist only within Melville's "Extracts."

Discussion of *"Hobomack,"* which occurs in a citation rather than an extract, calls attention to the fact that problems of external reference are just as likely to occur in the citations. Some of the questions they raise are the same as those connected with quotations in general. Thus the citations of Darwin's *"Voyage of a Naturalist"* and Lay and Hussey's *"Narrative of the Globe Mutiny"* should not be considered errors simply because these are not the actual titles of the two books; the works alluded to are easily identifiable from such references, which are examples of the widespread nineteenth-century custom of allusive citation.[20] And when Robert P. Gillies's *Tales of a Voyager to the Arctic Ocean* (1826) is reported as *"Tales of a Whale Voyager to the Arctic Ocean,"* one knows that the inaccurate citation, with *"Whale"* inserted, is intended by Melville. Or when *"Most Extraordinary and Distressing"* is omitted and *"Spermaceti-Whale"* becomes *"Sperm Whale"* in the long title of Owen Chase's *Narrative* (1821), one can allow the altered wording to stand on the grounds that it seems more likely to have resulted from intentional alteration than inadvertent slip. But another long title, for Henry T. Cheever's *The Whale and His Captors* (1849), is transcribed so precisely as to suggest that exact quotation is intended, and the one slight omission —an "as" introducing the last phrase—should therefore probably be rectified.

Citation of an altogether wrong title raises a more interesting issue. The extract from James Montgomery is credited to *"World before the Flood"* but actually comes from his "The Pelican Island"; the error is one that Melville takes from a secondary source, because Cheever's book quotes the same lines from Montgomery and provides the same citation. The question, raised earlier, whether an editor is called upon to correct the errors of a secondary source, requires further thought in a case of this kind. Misquotations in the text derived from a secondary source— and there are two in the Montgomery passage deriving from Cheever— generally do not require emendation because they constitute part of the passages as the quoter knew them.[21] But allowing an erroneous citation of this sort to stand is a different matter. It is true that Melville was equal-

20. A related kind of approximate citation occurs in the reference to *"Opening sentence of Hobbes's Leviathan."* The sentence quoted is actually the fifth, but *"Opening"* should not therefore be called an error: *"Opening sentence"* is apparently what Melville wrote, meaning "a sentence that is part of the opening," "an early sentence."

21. A third error in the Montgomery extract, "instincts" for "instinct," should be corrected because the word is correct in Cheever and because the misreading could easily have resulted from a slip.

ly trusting of Cheever here and accepted the title as *"World before the Flood"*; but surely his intention in writing it down, judging from his practice in the "Extracts" as a whole, was simply to provide a factual reference. Of course, one can also argue, as with the misquotations in the text, that he may have responded to the wording of the title he found in his source and that the title should similarly not be corrected. Another extract (although the situation is not quite parallel) may provide some relevant evidence: *"Pilgrim's Progress"* is corrected in the first English edition to *"Holy War,"* a correction that was evidently among those made by Melville on the proofs sent abroad and one that reflects a concern for correct citations. In any case, the decision on the Montgomery citation is a difficult one. Editors could argue either way; but there would seem to be enough difference in function and effect between a citation of source and a quotation to justify differing treatments, and a case can be made for correcting the Montgomery reference. (Even if no emendation is made, a note should of course call attention to the correct title and explain Melville's source of the incorrect one.) Other corrections of factual errors in citations are less debatable: the man who wrote on the Bermudas in the *Philosophical Transactions* of the Royal Society in 1668 was named Stafford, not "Strafford," and the date of Jefferson's *"Whale Memorial to the French minister"* was 1788, not "1778."[22] There is no pattern in the "Extracts" suggesting the deliberate alteration of facts of this kind: although the "Extracts" section can be called an imaginative work, it maintains a firm link with external reality.

Another, much shorter, preliminary section precedes the "Extracts" at the front of *Moby-Dick*, and it raises similar problems because it, too, is made up of material having an existence outside the work and is assigned a fictional compiler, a "Late Consumptive Usher to a Grammar School." Called "Etymology," this section consists of three quotations, followed by a list of the words for "whale" in thirteen languages. Such a list would appear to be purely a factual matter, but the critical editor, interested in Melville's intention, will find that it raises some intricate questions. One of them can serve as a kind of conspectus of the considerations involved in dealing with external fact in a literary work. Just before the English word "WHALE" in the list appears the entry for the Icelandic, and the word given in the original edition is "WHALE," identical with the English. Because this is not the Icelandic for "whale"

22. On another occasion, a date in a citation identifies the actual edition used. The citation *"Captain Cowley's Voyage around the Globe. A.D. 1729"* is not an error, even though Cowley's voyage took place in 1683–86 and an account of it appeared in William Hacke's *A Collection of Voyages* in 1699, because another edition of Hacke appeared in 1729. Melville's date, therefore, refers to his source and not to the actual voyage.

and because it seems unlikely that Melville would have wished to have two identical words in his short list (one of the purposes of which appears to be to display a variety of words)[23] it would at first seem reasonable to regard the Icelandic "WHALE" as a scribal or compositorial error (influenced by the word in the next line), or as an authorial slip. But the situation is not that simple: Melville himself may very well have intended to write the word "whale," because in Uno von Troil's *Letters on Iceland* (1780), in the paragraph just preceding the one from which Melville took one of his extracts, there occurs the expression "*illwhale* (bad whales)," in which the first word is offered as the Icelandic and the parenthesis as the English translation. From this Melville may have concluded that if he dropped the "ill" from "illwhale" he would be left with the Icelandic for "whale." If so, he was doubly wrong: in the first place, "illwhale" is not an Icelandic word, and the second edition of Troil (1780) corrects it to "*Illhwele*"; in the second place, removing the "Ill," even from this corrected form, does not produce the word for "whale." What is the editor to do? If Melville is misled by an error in a source and bases a discussion on the error, nothing can be done; but here there is no discussion, only a simple listing in which Melville apparently intended to give the correct word. But if one applies to Troil's corrected text the operation Melville seemingly performed on the first text, one still has an incorrect word; the editor would be in the position of making an emendation no more correct than the original reading. If one decides to correct the text, then, one must bypass Melville's presumed source entirely and insert the modern Icelandic word "hvalur."[24] One could reasonably defend this action by arguing—as with certain facts in the citations of sources for the extracts—that Melville's intention, evident in the text, to provide correct facts justifies the editor's going beyond Melville's knowledge to make the correction, so long as the error does not achieve a possible significance of its own within the text. On the other hand, one could argue against the emendation by saying that, if Melville did indeed, on the basis of consulting an outside source, regard "whale" as the correct Icelandic word, "whale" is thus his intended form and should

23. The last two words in the list differ by one letter: "pekee-nuee-nuee" for Fegee, and "pehee-nuee-nuee" for Erromangoan. Whereas "pehee" is an acceptable rendering of the word for "fish" usually transcribed as "pihi," "pekee" is not; yet an editor must be cautious about emending it, for Melville's desire to show different words may have taken precedence here over any desire to offer precisely accurate information. (Using this argument here would not prevent an editor from correcting a factual error elsewhere in the list where the circumstances were different.)

24. Assuming that Melville would not have intended to give the Old Icelandic "hvalr." (If "whalr" were a variant of "hvalr," it might be a tempting possibility, differing from "whale" by only one letter; but it is a highly improbable form.) The Northwestern-Newberry editors are grateful to Richard N. Ringler for help with this problem.

remain. But Melville's use of Troil's erroneous *"illwhale,"* while highly likely, is after all conjectural and should not be elevated to the status of fact. One cannot dismiss entirely the possibility that first suggested itself: "whale" as a scribal or compositorial error for the correct word (presumably "hvalur") in Melville's manuscript, or even Melville's own lapse (with "hvalur" as what he meant to write). Even if one finally emends on this basis, the speculation about Melville's possible use of Troil is not wasted effort, for in suggesting one explanation for the appearance of "WHALE" in the text it focuses attention on a crucial issue: the degree to which Melville wished to respect external fact in this instance. Besides, the critical editor cannot be in a position to make informed judgments at such points without investigating all available leads to external sources. This illustration draws together a remarkable number of basic editorial questions and shows how references to external fact can provide peculiarly effective test cases for revealing how thoroughly an editorial approach has been thought through.

II

If the "Extracts" and the "Etymology" in *Moby-Dick* are unusual in providing such a concentrated array of editorial questions, the questions themselves are not at all extraordinary but are in fact the characteristic ones that arise whenever external references are involved. Sampling the thinking that goes into answering those questions in this particular instance should serve as preparation for considering the general problem in a larger framework. To begin with, determining what is "external" to a piece of writing—and what in it should therefore be expected to correspond with a standard outside itself—is a difficult task of definition. As soon as one starts to check quotations, titles of books, dates, and names of persons and places against external sources, one begins to ask how these elements differ from the spellings of all the ordinary words of the text and whether there is actually anything in the text that does not have to be measured against an external standard. On one level, of course, any communication has to be regarded as made up largely of external elements: a writer or speaker would not be able to communicate without utilizing a set of conventional symbols that are interpreted in the same way by other persons. The words and grammar of a language are external in this sense, for writers must in some degree conform to linguistic conventions that are a social product and are not their own personal inventions. Editors are concerned with such matters, and in attempting to establish unmodernized texts they take pains to see that the spelling and punctuation, for instance, conform to the standards of the writer's time or fall within the range of possibilities conventionally tolerated at that time. But editors will feel that they are not quite doing the same thing when they "correct" a date or a quotation or the spelling of an historical figure's name; they will feel, in other words, that specific historical facts constitute a different category from the medium—words and grammar—employed for communication and are external to the communication in a different sense.

In thinking about these matters, Ferdinand de Saussure's seminal distinction between *langue* and *parole* is basic, for it separates language, with its infinite possibilities for expression, from each particular act of speaking—it separates "what is social from what is individual." *Langue* is "a product that is passively assimilated by the individual," whereas *parole*, the individual act of execution, is "wilful and intellectual" and is "never carried out by the collectivity."[25] This distinction can, by extension, help to explain the editor's role. Editors, of course, deal with individual acts of expression, and their task, in reconstructing an author's intention, is to determine just what in the expression, as it has come down to them, is "wilful"; they constantly examine the characteristics of the preserved *parole* in the light of the *langue*, as it were. When a word is not spelled conventionally or a singular verb follows a plural subject, are these "wilful" deviations by the author or are they simply errors of transmission (including authorial slips) at points where the author was passively following (or intending to follow) the conventions of the language? An author may, for the purposes of the immediate act of expression, decide to violate the rules of the language, and that violation can become an effective part of the communication; but if such violation proceeds too far it can prevent communication and turn the utterance into a purely private one.[26] The act of critical editing is a constant weighing of the extent to which a work can be autonomous. At each point of possible deviation from the norm, the editor is called upon to adjudicate the claims of idiosyncrasy against those of convention. In most instances, all there is to go on is the intention manifested in the work itself; the editor's decisions are based on an understanding of the internal workings of a particular act of expression.[27] For this reason one can think of these

25. *Course in General Linguistics*, ed. Charles Bally, Albert Sechehaye, and Albert Reidlinger, and trans. Wade Baskin (1959), pp. 13–14.

26. No distinct line separates the two. What may seem nonsense in one context may become concrete poetry in another.

27. Archibald A. Hill, in "The Locus of the Literary Work," *English Studies Today*, 3rd ser. (1964), pp. 41–50, after discussing the bearing of Saussure's distinction on literary study, defines "intention" as a "structural hypothesis derived from analysis of the text" (p. 50). A fuller discussion of this point occurs in G. T. Tanselle's "The Editorial Problem of Final Authorial Intention" (see note 13 above).

matters as internal, even though in handling them one must naturally refer to the external conventions of the medium.

The difference at points where quotations, dates, and the like occur is that in these instances there is something external to be taken into account in addition to the potentialities of the language itself. These parts of the expression make external reference in a way that the rest of the words do not; they are second-hand elements, so to speak, because they are taken over from a previous *parole*, a previous specific use. The situation is most obvious in the case of quotations: words quoted (or even paraphrased) from a particular passage by another writer have lying behind them, when placed in a new context, an external standard of reference besides that of the words and grammar involved—namely, the specific configuration of words and syntax that constituted the other writer's communication. This additional standard poses for editors an additional problem: at such points they have to consider not only words, punctuation, and grammar—as they would anywhere—but also what relation the passage is meant to bear to the original (or some other earlier) occurrence of the same passage. Determining what makes it in fact the "same" passage (when the two are not identical) is analogous to deciding when authors' revisions of their own works produce new works and when they do not. Indeed, authors returning to work they have previously written stand in much the same relationship to it as they would to the work of other authors. The central question faced by editors whenever they are confronted with a piece of writing that contains within it fragments from earlier pieces of writing is the one formulated by E. D. Hirsch, Jr., in his summary of Saussure: "should we assume that sentences from varied provenances retain their original meanings or that these heterogeneous elements have become integral components of a new total meaning?" Put another way, "should we consider the text to represent a compilation of divers *paroles* or a new unitary *parole* 'respoken' by the new author or editor?" Hirsch replies that "there can be no definitive answer to the question, except in relation to a specific scholarly or aesthetic purpose."[28]

28. *Validity in Interpretation* (1967), p. 233. The role of literary sensitivity in determining the function of misquotation in an author's writing is well illustrated by Christopher Ricks in "Pater, Arnold and Misquotation," *Times Literary Supplement*, 25 Nov. 1977, pp. 1383–85. Ricks concludes that Pater reads "what he wishes to have been said": he creates a " 'world within' . . . only by a violation of a world without, another man's 'world within' as it had become embodied . . . in the inter-subjective world which is the words of a poem." Whereas "Pater's misquotations are the rewriting of his authors so that they say special Paterian things," Arnold's "are the rewriting of his authors so that they say unspecial things," reducing "something individual to something commonplace." Another discussion of the creative use of quotations, pointing a parallel with the developing text of a ballad through oral tradition, is M. J. C. Hodgart's "Misquotation as Re-creation," *Essays in Criticism*, 3 (1953), 28–38. Misquotations that become integral parts of the works in which

In scholarly editing, the editor aims to conform to the desires of the author and must therefore attempt to understand the author's aesthetic purpose in quoting. There may be times when an author intends to be factually accurate in making a quotation and other times (even within the same work) when the author is less concerned with the quotation as a quotation than with making it a supporting element in the new context. The editor of a critical text cannot escape the responsibility of judging which is the case at any given point.

If quotations are perhaps the most immediately obvious examples of second-hand, or repeated, *paroles*, they are by no means the only elements of a discourse that can be so classified. References to actual geographical locations, specific historical figures, dates of real events, and so on are also instances where words are taken over from a prior use. Ordinary concrete nouns, like "chair" and "table," refer to any member of a given class and not to individual objects until employed by a writer or speaker to do so; spelling or pronouncing "chair" correctly is a function of the conventions of the language, not of the particular use in referring to one specific actual or imagined chair. The same can frequently be said of words like "Jefferson" and "1788": a writer can create an Oliver Jefferson, spell his name "Jeffarson," and have him participate in a fictitious battle at a fictitious location in 1788. To do this is to pin "Jefferson" (as well as "1788") down to one among the infinite possibilities of denotation it contains. But if the context shows that the reference is to Thomas Jefferson's whale memorial of 1788, the writer is using a "Jefferson" and a "1788" for which precise denotations have already been established. If indeed the reference is to the real Thomas Jefferson and to the whale memorial actually issued in 1788—and that is a crucial editorial question—the writer is not assigning the denotations to the words but is in effect quoting an earlier specific assignment, one that many readers may already be familiar with and will recognize without explanation. Although it is not customary in written material to place quotation marks around a proper name whenever a previous use of the name is meant, the similarity between such references and quoted passages of writing is obvious. In either case the writer is employing words over which there is an external control beyond the ordinary conventions of the language. These words, then, are the ones that can be said to involve "external fact" and to add thereby an additional dimension to the editorial problem.

That dimension can be illustrated by the treatment of the spelling of proper names as well as by the handling of quotations. When the edi-

---

they occur are to be distinguished, of course, from incidental slips, even when those slips may have some kind of psychological significance (this point is discussed further below).

tors of the Centenary Edition of Hawthorne emend a governor's name from "Burnett" to "Burnet" and another one from "Phipps" to "Phips" in "The Prophetic Pictures," "Smollet" to "Smollett" in "Old News," and "Glumdalea" to "Glumdalca" in *Fanshawe*,[29] they are acting in each case on the judgment that the reference is to a figure (whether real or fictitious) with an existence independent of Hawthorne's work and that the name therefore has an externally verifiable spelling. Whereas the "correct" spelling of ordinary words is determined by the usage of the people who employ those words and continually evolves along with the language, the spelling of an individual's name, it would seem, is fixed:[30] departures from that spelling, no matter how common, are errors. The matter cannot simply be left there, however. To do so would be analogous to saying that quoted passages must conform to the original and that all misquotations are errors requiring emendation. Two factors complicate decisions about emending personal names. One is the attitude toward spelling during the lifetimes of the individuals concerned and their own attitudes toward the spellings of their names; many Elizabethans, for instance, spelled their own names in different ways—in keeping with the approach to spelling in general at the time—and as a result more than one "correct" spelling can exist, just as more than one authorized form of a quotation may be possible, at points where its author has revised it. Even in periods when spellings in general are less flexible, it is not unknown for certain people to spell their names differently at different times in their lives, and various traditions of using one or another of such "correct" forms to refer to these people may grow up, just as one of the authorized versions of a passage may be more widely cited than the others at certain periods. There may be some range of possibilities, in other words, all of which are "correct." A second factor influencing editorial decisions is the possibility of legitimate motives for utilizing "unauthorized" spellings. A spelling that is in fact incorrect may become part of an established literary tradition, and writers using such a spelling are merely drawing on that tradition; or, alternatively, writers may alter a spelling on their own for its effect in the context where they are using it. The former possibility is not the same as saying—as one can with ordinary words—that the correct spelling changes with time, for the ways in which people spell their own names are historical facts that cannot be altered, even though a writer may choose to make refer-

29. *Twice-Told Tales*, ed. J. Donald Crowley, Fredson Bowers, *et al.* (1974), pp. 169–170; *The Snow-Image and Uncollected Tales* (1974), p. 142; *The Blithedale Romance and Fanshawe*, ed. Fredson Bowers *et al.* (1964), p. 408.

30. Within a given language, that is, for the spelling is sometimes altered for representation in other languages.

ence to a tradition of spelling certain names differently. The editor who allows such spellings to stand has gone through a process of finding defensible support for historical errors—a process unnecessary in the case of ordinary words whose conventional spellings at the time a writer used them were no longer what they had been at an earlier time.

When Melville refers in the "Etymology" section to "Hackluyt,"[31] one can argue that the spelling is not simply an error for "Hakluyt," both on the grounds that greater latitude was permitted in spellings in Hakluyt's time and on the grounds that Melville was drawing on (or assumed he was drawing on) an established tradition represented by the occurrence of "Hackluyt" in Charles Richardson's *Dictionary*, his source at this point. But when George Bennet's name appears as "Bennett" at the end of the sixty-fifth extract, the likelihood that the spelling is a mere slip outweighs other possibilities, for the man is a nineteenth-century figure, there is no established tradition of referring to him as "Bennett," and there seems no plausible reason for Melville to have introduced such a change intentionally; the spelling should therefore be corrected. And Melville's repeated spelling of Owen Chase's name as "Chace" (in the "Extracts," in Chapter 45, and in other places outside of *Moby-Dick*) is also an error, no matter how consistently Melville used it, for he had Chase's 1821 book in front of him, he was clearly referring to that particular writer, and there is no other acceptable spelling for that writer's name. The same line of reasoning applies to geographical names as well as personal names, although the continuing existence of places means that traditions of "unofficial" spellings of place names may be stronger than in the case of personal names. When "Nuremburgh" turns up in Hawthorne's "Ethan Brand," the Centenary editors correct it, as an outright error, to "Nuremberg."[32] But when "Heidelburgh" appears consistently in *Moby-Dick* (Chapter 77), one can argue that what is actually an incorrect spelling conveys for Melville a certain flavor and that in any case the presence of this spelling in one of Melville's important source books (John Harris's *Navigantium atque Itinerantium Bibliotheca*) suggests that Melville was aligning himself with whatever tradition that book represents in this matter. "Heidelburgh" remains an erroneous spelling, but the editor may decide, with good reason, that it is not an erroneous reading in this particular text. These arguments, of course, are based on the prior assumption that the references are to the "real" Hakluyt, Bennet, Chase, Nuremberg, and Heidelberg and not to invented people and places with similar names. But the question must al-

31. This spelling also occurs in Chapter 75.
32. *The Snow-Image and Uncollected Tales* (1974), p. 96.

ways be considered, for a change of spelling in a proper name can be said to produce a new name, not just a different form of the old one,[33] in the same way that an altered quotation can be regarded as a different piece of writing. Therefore, in dealing with proper names that are identical with, or closely resemble, those of real people and places, editors must first determine from the context whether the reference is indeed to those people and places and then decide, again from the context, the extent to which a departure from the external facts can be justified as a part of the writer's active intention—an intention either to draw on a tradition or to introduce something new. The issues raised by the spelling of the names of real people and places do resemble in some respects those associated with any questions of spelling. But the crucial difference is the additional level of external reference involved in employing words whose individualized denotations have been established outside the context in which those words are now placed. It is true that only through the context can one finally decide which words these are; but once they are located, they fall into a different class from the other words by virtue of their reference to external facts. In thinking about them, editors need to go beyond the preparation they bring to other words, for they need to be acquainted with the forms these words have taken in their historical association with particular people and places. Like quotations, proper names force editors to ask themselves what status a "fact" has when it is moved from one context to another.

The issues involved show themselves clearly when a fact is moved into a work of fiction. Within a fictional world, facts can be altered in any way the author sees fit; yet to the extent that the author wishes a fact to be recognized it retains some connection with the outside world. These proportions—and their implications, both in the immediate passage and in the novel or story as a whole—are what the editor has to think about in order to decide whether or not to correct an error of external fact. One of the most pervasive questions has to do with setting. If a novelist places the action in real locations at a particular time, how much accuracy is intended in the details referring to that setting? Or, put another way, if certain datable events are employed, do all the other details have to be consistent with the date thus suggested? In Howells's *A Hazard of New Fortunes* an adverbial variant in one sentence alters the time-setting of the entire novel. The *Harper's Weekly* text reads, in a reference to Washington Square, "The *primo tenore* statue of Garibaldi had not yet taken possession of the place"; in the other texts "not yet" is replaced with "already," shifting the action to some time between the erection of

33. For some additional comment on this point, see G. T. Tanselle, "Textual Study and Literary Judgment," *PBSA*, 65 (1971), 120–121.

that statue in 1888 and the completion of the novel in 1889. The editors of the Indiana Howells, recognizing that this variant involves "a question of the historical perspective of the novel," argue for the "already" reading on the grounds that Howells finished the novel in 1889 and that his "choice of detail" suggests a fictional setting at the same time.[34] There is at least one detail, however, pointing to an earlier date: Lindau refers to his wife's death "Right after I got home from the war—twenty years ago," placing the action in the middle 1880s.[35] If one adopts the "already" reading as Howells's final intention, the question is whether this discrepancy makes any difference. It is not, after all, an internal discrepancy, for neither the date of the end of the Civil War nor that of the erection of the Garibaldi statue is given in the novel, and there is no reason why, for fictional purposes, the two sentences need to be regarded as inconsistent. On the other hand, these references are in fact externally verifiable, and Howells's intentions as to factual accuracy can only be gauged by his methods as revealed in the text itself. Since this novel is essentially "realistic," one could argue that inconsistencies involving external fact do matter and that the two sentences should be brought into alignment. Whether the authority attaching to the "already" reading carries enough weight to require the editor to add a word altering Lindau's statement or whether the earlier "not yet" reading (presumably authorial at least, even if superseded) is preferable so as to obviate further editorial intrusion is a delicate editorial question. Even if one believes that the "already" must be adopted as Howells's intention and that consistency in external fact is also intended, one may feel that the addition of even a single word to the other sentence goes beyond an editor's prerogative and that the inconsistency must stand, even though contrary to the spirit of the work. Certainly a great amount of rewriting cannot be undertaken, but deciding whether the insertion of a single word (what word? "over" or "about" before "twenty"?)[36] is excessive constitutes another question of

34. This is what I take to be the meaning of the sentence reading "Howells' choice of detail seems to place the fiction at roughly the same time as the historical events upon which it draws." See *A Hazard of New Fortunes*, ed. David J. Nordloh *et al.* (1976), pp. 55, 537–538.

35. As Harold H. Kolb, Jr., points out in his review of this volume of the Howells edition in *American Literary Realism 1870–1910*, 10 (1977), 314–317. Another possible detail suggesting a pre-1888 date for the early part of the novel is the streetcar strike described late in the book, if it is to be identified with the New York strike of early 1889 (certainly it was inspired by that strike.

36. Of course, if "twenty years ago" can be taken to mean "roughly twenty years ago," there would be no inconsistency with either version of the other sentence. But the theoretical question remains, even if the present illustration, in that case, were not particularly apt; and there would still be the problem, in this illustration, of choosing between "not yet" and "already," even though one difficulty in making the choice would have been removed. (Determining how exact the reference to twenty years was intended to be involves some consideration of linguistic customs and traditions: the vagueness about round numbers prevalent

editorial judgment. The crucial issue for present purposes is not how the inconsistency is rectified but the considerations involved in deciding whether it can be and needs to be rectified—whether, first of all, the editor can reasonably do anything about it and then, if so, whether it is actually an inconsistency in the fictional world.[37]

More often a factual problem in a novel involves only a local context and does not affect the entire time-scheme or setting of the work. But even so, sensitivity to the nature of the whole, as well as to the local context, is necessary for deciding when factual accuracy is in order. Frequently an historical figure becomes a character in a novel and engages at times in events that actually took place and at other times in events that are fictitious; in assessing any particular "factual" error, therefore, the editor must consider both the historicity of the immediate context and the methods of weaving together fact and fiction used throughout the book. Even in a *roman à clef*, where the historical figures are given new names, the relation of the depicted characteristics and events to actual ones (or traditional ideas of the "actual" ones) cannot be ignored, for an editor may be able to decide among variants or detect corrupt readings by knowing those external facts. The elusive nature of fact in fiction[38] is a fascinating subject for speculation and has been much written about,

in Elizabethan times, for instance, seems to be of a different order from the attitude toward such figures in Howells's time.)

37. A similar instance, involving the dating of the narration of a novel, occurs in *Moby-Dick*. A speculative passage in Chapter 85 refers to "this blessed minute" and then defines it (in the first American edition) as "fifteen and a quarter minutes past one o'clock P.M. of this sixteenth day of December, A.D. 1851." Because the book was published in London in October 1851 and in New York in November 1851, the year in this passage is probably a compositorial error for "1850" (the reading in the first English edition, set from proofs of the first American). As far as internal consistency is concerned, of course, "1851" would cause a problem only if there is another historical reference in the book with which it would come in conflict. But it seems most likely that Melville's intention at this point was to make the internal world of the book and the external world of reality coincide and to refer to a date that was realistically conceivable as the actual date of composition of this passage (if not in fact the actual date). John Harmon McElroy, in "The Dating of the Action in *Moby Dick*," *Papers on Language & Literature*, 13 (1977), 420–423, comments on the 1850 date of narration and on other historical references that date the *Pequod*'s voyage in 1840–41.

38. I am not suggesting that fact is ever anything but elusive, even outside of fiction; but this is not the place to raise the philosophical question of what is real. By "fact" here, as I have tried to define it earlier, I mean specific people, places, things, and events with an existence independent of the work under consideration. Saul Bellow has interestingly discussed the role of facts in fiction in "Facts That Put Fancy to Flight," New York *Times Book Review*, 11 Feb. 1962, pp. 1, 28. Many readers, he says, are concerned with the accuracy of the realistic surface, and publishers' editors will therefore wish to check on such questions as "How many stories does the Ansonia Hotel really have; and can one see its television antennae from the corner of West End Avenue and Seventy-second Street?" He proceeds to contrast writers who are "satisfied with an art of externals" (and who produce "a journalistic sort of novel") with those "masters of realism" in whose work "the realistic externals were intended to lead inward."

particularly by literary critics and biographers seeking correlations between authors' lives and their works; the subject also turns up in the popular press, discussions in recent years having been stimulated by Truman Capote's concept of the "nonfiction novel" and by television dramatizations based loosely on real events. These commentaries—some of which are concerned with the ethics of placing real people in compromising situations they are not known to have found themselves in[39]— generally deal with different questions from those the editor must think about. The editor's interest is not basically in whether a real person has been slandered by a fictional representation or whether a real event has been misrepresented but whether the details present in the text are those that the writer intended to be there. In order to be in a position to make an informed judgment on that matter, however, the editor has to learn, as far as possible, what the external facts are and to analyze—like the critic and biographer that the editor must in part be—the nature of the transmutation of those facts into fiction.

The border lines between external fact and fictional fact are constantly shifting, as Melville demonstrates when in Chapter 72 of *Moby-Dick*, after describing the "monkey-rope" tying together the harpooneer (on the whale's slippery back) and the bowsman (on deck), he appends a footnote beginning, "The monkey-rope is found in all whalers; but it was only in the Pequod that the monkey and his holder were ever tied together. This improvement upon the original usage was introduced by no less a man than Stubb." A fictional fact—a usage invented by a fictional character on a fictional ship—is here thrust out into the real world as the *Pequod* is compared with all other ships; or, rather, the real world is pulled into the novel, for the external truthfulness of the statement about all ships is irrelevant to the fictional world, in which it becomes a fact that the *Pequod* differs from all other ships in its use of the monkey-rope. Yet external facts may have to be called on when there is an internal discrepancy. In the American first edition of *Moby-Dick*, a passage discussing some famous whales (Chapter 45) refers to "Timor Tom" and "New Zealand Jack," but the next paragraph cites "New Zealand Tom"; in the English edition the discrepancy was evidently noted, for "Tom" in the third instance is changed to "Jack," thus producing consistency. It is clear that the American text must be emended, but the change selected in the English edition is not the only one that would make the names consistent, and the editor must decide which way to do it. Knowing that Melville's source, Thomas Beale's *The Natural History*

39. See, for instance, the comments on "Washington: Behind Closed Doors" in *Time*, 19 Sept. 1977, pp. 92–93, and in Michael J. Arlen's "The Air" department in *The New Yorker*, 3 Oct. 1977, pp. 115–124.

of the Sperm Whale, gives the names as "Timor Jack" and "New Zealand Tom" should settle the matter. Melville was of course free to alter these names if he wished; but since the editor has to make some emendation and since there is no evidence in this passage to suggest that Melville wanted to change the names, the obvious course is to emend them in conformity with the external source. At another point (Chapter 99) Flask figures that a doubloon worth sixteen dollars will buy him 960 two-cent cigars. At first this discrepancy seems purely an internal one, a matter of incorrect arithmetic. But of course the idea that it is a discrepancy rests on the assumption that American dollars of one hundred cents are meant or that no bulk rate was customary for two-cent cigars. If one argued that the "dollars" were Spanish-American dollars, freely circulating among American seamen as the equivalent of a British crown or $1.20, the discrepancy would vanish, as it would if one were to establish that two-cent cigars sold for 20¢ a dozen. External facts are relevant, in other words, to determining whether or not Melville could have intended the figures in the printed text.

Many references to external facts in novels do not involve such internal discrepancies (or seeming ones) that call attention to themselves but rather are discrepant only when compared with an outside source. *Moby-Dick*, again, can conveniently illustrate how the treatment of these "errors" must vary with the immediate context. At one point (Chapter 101) the narrator presents some statistics about the stocks of food on a whaling ship, statistics said to be taken from a book called "Dan Coopman." A check of Melville's source for this passage, William Scoresby's *An Account of the Arctic Regions* (1820), shows that a double "error" is present: the book, according to Scoresby, is "Den Koopman," and he actually cites the statistics from a different work. But the playful nature of Melville's passage makes any "correction" out of the question. First of all, he takes "Dan Coopman" to be "the invaluable memoirs of some Amsterdam cooper in the fishery, as every whale ship must carry its cooper." This use of the name would in itself prevent an editor from altering the spelling or substituting another name. In addition, the spirit of the passage is suggested by the reference to "Dr. Snodhead, a very learned man, professor of Low Dutch and High German in the college of Santa Claus and St. Pott's, to whom I handed the work for translation." Within such a context the misattribution of the statistics is of no moment, for Melville is not expecting the reader to think of "Dan Coopman" as any more or less real than "Dr. Snodhead." An earlier passage, near the reference to "New Zealand Tom" (Chapter 45), offers a contrast. There the captains who insistently search for particular celebrated whales are said to have "heaved up their anchors with that express object as much

in view, as in setting out through the Narragansett Woods, Captain Butler of old had it in his mind to capture that notorious murderous savage
Annawon, the headmost warrior of the Indian King Philip." In fact it
was Captain Benjamin Church who pursued Annawon in Rhode Island
in 1676; Colonel William Butler's expedition was against the Indian
leader Brant in upstate New York in 1778. The sentence could be made
factually correct by substituting "Church" for "Butler," and an editor
could persuasively argue in favor of this emendation: the reference seems
to be a simple factual allusion, in a context stressing facts, and there
seems to be no literary reason for Melville's wishing to alter the name.
"Butler" is probably a mere slip (since Melville knew the story of Brant
also) for the intended word "Church"; and because no further discussion
in the text depends on the word "Butler" (that is, the error is confined to
this one clause), it is feasible for an editor to make the change. *Moby-
Dick* may be more extreme than many works of fiction in its oscillation
between the imaginative and the factual, but it illustrates a point applicable to all fiction: that a fictional framework does not preclude the existence within it of passages (of whatever length, whether a chapter or
only part of a sentence) that aim to be factually accurate. An editor,
therefore, can justifiably make factual corrections in a work of fiction;
deciding when they are justified entails literary sensitivity and is one of
the responsibilities of the critical editor.

The editing of another of Melville's works has occasioned some debate over this principle, and the argument put forth can be instructive.
Harrison Hayford and Merton M. Sealts, Jr., in preparing their reading
text (1962) of *Billy Budd, Sailor,* follow the reasoning just outlined and
correct errors of fact when in their judgment the context shows that Melville was trying to be factually accurate.[40] Thus when Melville refers to
the execution of "a midshipman and two petty officers" aboard the actual ship *Somers,* Hayford and Sealts alter "petty officers" to "sailors,"
since only one was in fact a petty officer. Peter Shaw has attacked this decision and, with a notable lack of restraint, calls it "Possibly the most
stunning liberty with an author's text in the twentieth century."[41] Shaw's
objection is based on the argument that errors are revealing. "Freud's
doctrine in *The Psychopathology of Everyday Life,*" he says, "offers the
definitive argument against unconsidered editorial corrections." Naturally editorial emendations should never be "unconsidered," but he
seems to be saying that corrections of factual error should probably never
be undertaken in the first place: "Freud's book made it a matter of com-

40. They discuss this category of emendations on pp. 215–216.
41. "The American Heritage and Its Guardians," *American Scholar,* 45 (1975–76), 733–
751 [i.e., 37–55]; quotation from p. 742.

mon sense that an error usually reveals more than does a controlled statement of intention." Shaw unnecessarily confuses the issue here, for statements of intention are beside the point: obviously a statement of intention does not necessarily match the actual realized intention, and editors
are not concerned with statements of intention but authors' intentions as
manifested in their works. At any rate Shaw is correct to observe that
errors can be revealing, and his application of the point here is to say
that, because Melville's cousin had been a first lieutenant on the *Somers*,
"Any unconscious exaggeration by Melville of the rank of those executed has possible significance for the astute reader." The question he
does not go on to address, however, is why this kind of significance is
appropriate to be preserved in the *critical text* of a literary work like
Billy Budd (that the original reading should be preserved in the notes
goes without saying).

What Shaw fails to take into account in his discussion is the difference
between working papers or private documents and finished literary prod
ucts intended for an audience. When editors prepare private papers for
publication, there is no doubt that they should not smooth out the text
by eliminating factual errors, misspellings, deleted phrases, and the like.[42]
All these features are part of the essential nature of such documents, and
their psychological significance is one of the reasons for the importance
of the documents. When Sir Walter Scott in his journal refers to an
acquaintance whose real name was Durham Calderwood as "Calderwood
Durham" or speaks of a marriage that actually took place in 1825 as oc-
curring "in the beginning of 1826," these slips are integral parts of the
text of the document, and one would be losing part of what the document has to offer if they were corrected; W. E. K. Anderson is right to
leave them in the text in his Clarendon edition and merely to point out
the errors in footnotes.[43] There is no question, in other words, that
Shaw's point is correct in regard to the texts of private documents. Literary works and other works intended for publication, however, open up
additional possibilities. They, too, can be treated as documents, and editors can prepare *literatim* transcriptions of any extant manuscripts, or
facsimiles of particular copies of printed editions. Such work is valuable
in making important evidence more widely available. But works intended for publication also demand to be edited in another way, which
results in texts incorporating their authors' final intentions about what
was to be placed before the public. Such works—by virtue of the fact they

42. The rationale for this position is set forth by G. T. Tanselle in "The Editing of
Historical Documents," *SB*, 31 (1978), 1–56.
43. *The Journal of Sir Walter Scott* (1972), pp. 425, 412.

are intended for publication—have a public as well as a private aspect. When one is concerned to retain in the edited text all the readings of a particular document, one is focusing on a single stage in the growth of the work. The document is of historical significance because it preserves that stage; but usually no single extant document preserves a text that is free of error, in the sense that it contains all the readings finally intended by the author.[44] Therefore it is important, in approaching these intellectual products as *works* and not simply as specific *documents*, that editors use their informed judgment to produce eclectic texts, drawing critically on the available evidence and on their own sense of what constitutes an error in a given text. The evidence present in the extant documents can (and should) be recorded as notes to the critical text, but the text itself does not attempt to reproduce exactly any particular document.

In the case of *Billy Budd*, the preserved papers are clearly a private document, a working draft; but they contain a work of fiction, a work of the kind normally intended for a public audience, and not a diary or notebook entries. Recognizing this dual interest in the papers, Hayford and Sealts have prepared two edited texts. One of them, a "genetic" text, attempts to provide an accurate transcription of the textual features of the document, showing in the process the order of Melville's deletions, insertions, and alterations; the other, a "reading" text, attempts to offer a critical text representing Melville's intentions for the work as discernible from the document. The former aims to do justice to the manuscript as a document of Melville's biography and of American literary history; the latter aims to do justice to its text as a work of fiction. In the former, Melville's phrase "a midshipman and two petty officers" naturally appears, for there is no question here of emending what Melville actually put on paper, even if it was not what he intended to write. But in the latter, critical judgment must be employed to decide whether that factual error is one that Melville intended to make for the purposes of his fiction; Hayford and Sealts conclude that it is not, and they correct it. To believe that in doing so they have exercised an unwarranted liberty is to fail to understand the nature and the value of critical editing. Obviously another critic may disagree with them and argue that there are reasons for thinking that Melville particularly wished to say "petty officers" here; the issue involves literary judgment, and differences of opinion about it are bound to exist. But criticizing Hayford and Sealts's decision

44. This is not to suggest that a critical text cannot be undertaken to represent any particular stage in the history of a work, for the same point can be made about the relation of the surviving documents to the author's final intention at any specific time. Producing a critical text of some version of a work that was later revised further by the author is not the same thing as editing a transcription of one document.

on this basis is not to object to the *process* of emending a text in conformity with the editor's view of the author's intention.

Shaw's criticism, on the other hand, in effect questions the validity of critical editing: Shaw disapproves of the Hayford-Sealts emendation because the original reading may provide psychological insight into Melville's motivation, and he is thus objecting to a critical text for not being a transcription. The confusion in his thinking is suggested by the two possible interpretations that he offers of "Any unconscious exaggeration by Melville of the rank of those executed": Melville may have exaggerated "to increase the importance of the parallel with the *Somers*" or "out of a vaguely shared guilt over his cousin's complicity in the matter." The first, which would not have been unconscious, has to do with the literary effect of the comparison and could presumably be a reason for retaining the original reading in a critical text; the second, insofar as it is conceivable, is a reason for being interested in the error but not a reason for leaving it in the critical text of a literary work.[45] When Shaw concludes that the Hayford-Sealts emendation is "as significant as a nineteenth-century editor's excision of an entire paragraph of sexually explicit or politically dangerous material," he reveals his failure to understand that editorial alteration of a text can ever be anything other than a kind of censorship, something standing in the way of the author's expression rather than promoting it. This episode illustrates in dramatic fashion how the discussion of a factual error in a work of fiction demands a clear understanding of the different editorial approaches that can productively be employed. The essential prerequisite to clear thinking on the matter is recognizing the difference between a transcription, in which the editor must faithfully reproduce the errors of a particular document, and a critical text, in which the editor is not bound to retain a factual error simply because it is present in an authoritative document. A critical editor may finally decide to retain such an error on critical grounds but not because the error is a revealing Freudian slip, suggestive of the author's state of mind at the time of the preparation of a given document. The two approaches are distinct, and neither can be carried out competently if considerations applicable to one are allowed to intrude into the other. Errors of external fact often seem to provide the test cases for determining how well an editor has learned that lesson.[46]

45. In a footnote, Shaw gives another, and more far-fetched, example of a slip "useful to the critic": the appearance of F. R. Leavis's name as "F. L. Leavis" in an essay of Fredson Bowers. Shaw believes that "Leavis evidently has been confused with the older English critic F. L. Lucas" and that this slip reveals a "slightly old-fashioned" cast of mind. Surely such tenuous speculation offers no real grounds for preserving what is clearly an unintended reading, very likely a compositor's error.

46. Another Hayford-Sealts emendation in *Billy Budd* has been questioned by another

If factual errors in fiction need not always be corrected in a critical text, one might at first assume that the situation would be different with "nonfiction" writing—any writing that is expository in nature, attempting to deal with the real world directly, not through the creation of an imagined world. Surely, one might think, factual errors and misquotations cannot be a legitimate part of the intended texts of such works. Everyone senses the distinction that René Wellek speaks of when he says, "There is a central and important difference between a statement, even in a historical novel or a novel by Balzac which seems to convey 'information' about actual happenings, and the same information appearing in a book of history or sociology."[47] The difference is undeniable, and yet there seem to be intermediate shadings. One reads a "book of history" like Gibbon or Macaulay as a work of literary creativity, and not merely because it is from the past and limited in its information by what was known at the time. Or one reads an essay of sociological or philosophical analysis for its mastery of exposition, recognizing that some of its points may be half-truths or distortions employed to advance a particular argument. Of course, the truth or falsity of the information conveyed does not alter the fact that in such works the author is speaking directly to the reader, not through a fictional persona or a created world. Any author, whether producing novels and poems or writing essays, may undertake to alter facts for the purposes of the work, and what we think of as "creative literature" does not exclude so-called "nonfiction."[48] Many attempts have been made to distinguish writing that is "literature" from writing that is not,[49] but no satisfactory dividing line has ever been established. The implication of all this for the editor of a critical text is to suggest that a blanket rule regarding the correction of factual errors in nonfiction would be just as shortsighted as such a rule for more obviously "literary" works. Since deciding whether a given work can be regarded as "literature" is itself an act of critical judgment, no such classification

---

critic in a different way. In his Bobbs-Merrill edition (1975), Milton Stern differs from Hayford and Sealts on the necessity of correcting Nelson's rank, from "Vice Admiral" (as it appears on leaf 70 of the manuscript) to "Rear Admiral" (as Hayford and Sealts correct it). Stern does not rule out all corrections of fact and believes in making critical distinctions between one situation and another. His argument in this case is that Melville "makes a point of Nelson's rank more than once"; therefore "he might have attached significance to the ranks he assigned" (p. 165). This argument, however, is not critical: the fact that the error appears more than once is no guarantee that it was intended; the crucial question, not taken up, is whether there is reason to believe that Melville did attach significance to "Vice Admiral."

47. *Theory of Literature* (1949), p. 15.

48. See, for instance, Stanley Edgar Hyman's *The Tangled Bank: Darwin, Marx, Frazer and Freud as Imaginative Writers* (1962).

49. A number of them are listed by G. T. Tanselle in *SB*, 29 (1976), 176, footnote 19.

can serve to delimit for the editor certain writing to be treated in a different way from other writing. Instead, the critical editor must approach so-called "nonfiction" in the same way as fiction: the author is just as capable of altering facts intentionally, just as likely to develop a point based on an error, and just as much bound by the customs of the time; and the editor therefore has the same responsibility to assess each factual error in the light of the evidence offered by its context.

Perhaps even more than with fiction, a common situation in nonfiction is the occurrence of quotations from other works. Several philosophers have now been accorded careful critical editions, and the problem of quotations has been confronted in them. In the first volume (1969) of Jo Ann Boydston's edition of *The Early Works* of John Dewey, Fredson Bowers contributes a statement of textual policy that records a central point: "In Dewey's texts," he says, "all quotations have been retained just as he wrote them even though not always strictly accurate, since that was the form on which he was founding his ideas" (p. xvii). A basic reason for allowing inaccurate quotations to stand, in fiction as well as nonfiction, is that the quotations in that form may have ramifications that are unemendable—they may be the subject of a discussion in the text or may have influenced the author's thinking. Retaining Dewey's quotations "just as he wrote them," however, raises another problem, for it is conceivable that what he wrote at times contained mere slips and did not always reflect what he intended to write (whether or not what he intended to write was accurate), and it is also possible that some errors in quotations in printed texts or in nonauthorial manuscripts or typescripts are slips by people other than Dewey. Bowers does not go into this question because no emendations in quotations are in fact made in this volume; but the relevance of the issue is clearly recognized by Jo Ann Boydston, who, in her introduction to the appendix that prints the correct wording of the inaccurate quotations,[50] says, "It should be noted that specific changes, both in substantives and in accidentals, may have been instituted in the transmission rather than by Dewey himself. The variable form of quoting does suggest that Dewey, like many scholars of the period, was not overly concerned about precision in accidentals, but many of the changes in cited materials may well have arisen in the printing process" (p. lxxxix). Recognition of that fact underscores the necessity for a critical approach to each quotation, an attempt to judge on the

50. Bowers suggests that one of the uses of this appendix is to help the reader decide "whether Dewey had the source open before him or was relying on his memory" (p. xvii)—a problem the editor will already have thought about in determining whether any emendations are justifiable, for certain kinds of slips are more common when one is copying (intending to copy accurately) than when one is remembering (intending perhaps only to paraphrase).

basis of the available evidence—including the editor's understanding of the author's methods in general and aims in the particular passage—just which inaccuracies of quotation were probably slips. It is also worth observing that Boydston's statement calls attention to the importance of knowing contemporary standards: in an unmodernized edition it would clearly be wrong to hold Dewey to stricter standards of accuracy in quotation than were customary among his colleagues.

In later volumes of the Dewey edition some emendations in quotations are made, and the critical approach implicit in Boydston's comments in the first volume is more explicitly remarked upon. Bowers adds to his essay the point that sometimes "special circumstances in a specific text require the correction of quotations within the text itself" (IV, xlix; V, cxxviii); and Boydston notes that some house-styling of Dewey's periodical pieces encompassed the quotations as well, giving the editor a reason for restoring certain punctuation to those quotations (V, clxxvi). Sometimes an internal contradiction calls attention to what was intended in the quotation: Dewey quotes a sentence from Paul Bourget, but the text omits a clause on Stendhal, leaving four writers mentioned; because Dewey refers to the "five" writers in the quotation, it is clear that he intended for that clause to be present, and it is of course restored (III, 37). In other cases, the internal contradiction may be less mechanical but no less forceful: when a quotation from Alexander Bain reads, "a mental association is rapidly formed between his [the child's] obedience and apprehended pain," it is clear that Dewey could not have intended to substitute "obedience" for the "disobedience" of the original and could not have believed that the original read that way, and an emendation is rightly made (IV, 330). Generally, however, misquotations pose more debatable questions for an editor. The Dewey edition does not emend a misquotation from F. H. Bradley that reads "it is here the intellect alone which is [instead of "has"] to be satisfied" (*Middle Works*, IV [1977], 58) or one from F. J. E. Woodbridge that reads "by insisting that by [instead of "from"] the nature of mind" (p. 224). It is unlikely that Dewey made these changes intentionally, but one could argue that they are so insignificant as to be allowable in the tradition of approximate quotation;[51] on the other hand one could argue that the "is" and "by" are slips induced in each case by the presence of the same word earlier in the line and that they are simply mistakes that ought to be corrected. Even though approximate quotation is justifiable as a contemporary convention, any

51. Boydston points out in the first volume of *The Early Works* that "Dewey used source material in the whole range of possible ways, from paraphrase recall to verbatim copying out. . . . quotation marks do not necessarily signal a direct, precise quotation" (p. lxxxix).

misquotation can be expected to alter the meaning slightly, and one must therefore give thought to whether or not the change was intentional. If it appears not to be, then at least where substantives are involved the arguments for retention of the error as an example of the tolerated imprecision of the time would seem in many instances to carry less force than the arguments for emendation.[52] In the Dewey edition a phrase from William James appears as "any one part of experience" (p. 99), whereas the original contains "our" before "experience." How does one draw the line here between allowable imprecision of quotation and a slip that violates the author's intention? Considering the shade of difference in emphasis produced by the omission, one might feel that Dewey could not have regarded the shorter version as an acceptable paraphrase or approximation of the longer and that—unless the shift in nuance can itself be seen as intentional—the omitted word should be restored. These are difficult critical questions, and it should be clear that they are no less difficult because the piece of writing happens to be "nonfiction."[53]

Since decisions on such matters must grow out of the immediate context of the passage and the larger context of the author's times and general practice, they will vary from situation to situation; they will also

52. The same cannot necessarily be said about accidentals: because it is more difficult to reason about which discrepancies in accidentals are intentional and which inadvertent, the decision whether or not to correct the accidentals of a quotation falls back more heavily on a consideration of contemporary attitudes toward accuracy in quotations. (For works in which some looseness of quotation is tolerated, there is the companion question of the extent to which readers need to be informed about the accidentals of the original; whereas discrepancies in substantives between copy-text and source should always be reported in the apparatus, one can argue that the desirability of reporting such discrepancies in accidentals varies with the situation—perhaps, for instance, being more important for some expository works or passages than for some "creative" ones.)

53. Some debate over editing quotations in such works has recently occurred in connection with the omission of a "not" in a quotation from Joseph Spence as it appears in the first edition of Johnson's *Life of Pope* (1781). Colin J. Horne's proposal that the word be restored ("An Emendation to Johnson's *Life of Pope*," *Library*, 5th ser., 28 [1973], 156–157) has been objected to by J. P. Hardy, who argues that "surely the modern editor's prime duty is to reproduce the most authoritative text that can, on all available evidence, be attributed to Johnson" (29 [1974], 226). Horne's reply (30 [1975], 249–250) tries to clarify the nature of critical editing, especially in regard to quotations: such an editor, Horne recognizes, does not simply reproduce an authoritative text but corrects it so that it can be printed "as the author *intended* it to be and not as what, by some oversight, he actually wrote in error"; and this principle, he makes clear, must apply to the entire text, quotations and all (he underscores the illogic of holding "that one principle should apply to quotations and quite another to the main body of the text"). That certain misquotations in "nonfiction" or expository works must, however, be allowed to stand is effectively stated by Horne: "No editor, I think, would correct the habitual misquotations in Hazlitt's writings because, it may fairly be claimed, they are, in that form, what Hazlitt intended. They are authentic as being precisely how he remembered them and as such they are evidence of his adaptive memory of his extensive reading and his partly deliberate adaptation of the quotation to what he was himself writing."

inevitably vary, as with any question involving judgment, according to the person making the decision. Thus Fredson Bowers, editing another late nineteenth-century American philosopher, William James, reverses in his statement of procedure the relative emphasis on retention and correction of misquotation announced in the Dewey edition. In the James edition, he says, "an attempt has been made to identify the exact edition used by James for his quotations from other authors and ordinarily to emend his carelessness of transcription so that the quotation will reproduce exactly what the author wrote." But at some points, he adds, "James altered quotations for his own purposes in such a manner that his version should be respected" (*Pragmatism* [1975], p. 182). Correction of misquotation is here the general rule, and retention the exception; and many emendations in quotations, often to correct punctuation or small differences of substantives, are in fact made.[54] There is no question that the approach is critical, and some misquotations are not emended; but there is a bias toward the correction of misquotations, just as there is one toward the retention of them in the Dewey. This difference in emphasis ought to spring from a difference in the evaluation of these authors' intentions in quoting, seen against a background of the conventions of quoting in their time. If in practice it also springs to some extent from the fact that two different editors are performing the work, there can be no objection, so long as all the factors have been taken into account and the evidence is recorded. Critical editing depends on individual judgments, made by people intimately acquainted with the authors and their methods of working; the treatment of quotations can never rest on a mechanical rule, for it must always involve an understanding of the authors' intended use of the quotations as well as of the conventions for quoting within which they are operating.[55]

If those conventions even in scholarly writing in the late nineteenth and early twentieth centuries allowed more flexibility than we are now accustomed to, it hardly needs to be stated that the situation was still freer in earlier periods. The point has been well put in the Yale edition

54. The list of emendations in this edition is designed as the place to record all differences in the texts of quotations, even those that are not emended. The principle of providing readers with this information (handled in the Dewey by the section called "Correction of Quotations") is important, for without it readers are not in a position adequately to evaluate the editors' treatment of quotations; readers need to know where misquotations have been allowed to stand as well as where they have been emended.

55. James's preface to *The Meaning of Truth* illustrates the delicacy of judgment involved, because James there quotes from his own earlier *Pragmatism*. The editor is faced not only with the usual questions that quotations raise but with the additional consideration that James may be taking this occasion to revise what he had previously written. Bowers's text (1975) allows James to make unmarked omissions but generally restores the punctuation and italicization of the original.

of Jonathan Edwards, where in the second volume (*Religious Affections*, 1959), John E. Smith explains how the difficulty in the eighteenth century of conveniently consulting all the books one might need made it "necessary to rely upon memory and extracts copied somewhat hastily and stored up for use at a later time" (p. 81). He goes on to describe the kinds of misquotations that occur, in a passage that could apply equally well to many earlier and later writers:

> Very few of the direct quotations in the *Affections* are to be found in exactly the same form in the original editions, even though most changes are minor and do not materially affect the meaning involved. Edwards often paraphrased his source, and some of this paraphrased material appears within inverted commas along with direct quotation; the result is that the line between the two is difficult to draw. Edwards also made minor modifications, such as the changing of tenses or the dropping of an article or pronoun, and he often strung together passages from different parts of a book, omitting material in between without use of ellipsis dots. What appears in some cases to be a sentence or paragraph from one page of a work is actually a construction from several pages, and it is identified by him in the citation only by the first page (or the last) from which the quotation is taken.

The sentence that follows, however, concludes the paragraph on a questionable note: "The quotations in this edition are left as they appeared in the first edition, so that the interested student might be enabled to examine Edwards' own practice." This approach is an uncritical one, taking for granted that the first edition accurately represents "Edwards' own practice" and not inquiring into the possibility that some readings of the first edition might be errors introduced in the printing process. The editor is right not to make all quotations conform to their sources, but he should not therefore go to the opposite extreme and assume that the quotations as they appear in print are necessarily what the writer intended. The earlier volume of the Edwards edition, Paul Ramsey's text of *Freedom of the Will* (1957), exhibits the same problem, though the policy is defended somewhat differently. After pointing out the varieties of "quotation" that Edwards engaged in, Ramsey says that in no instance is Edwards "unfaithful to the original author's meaning, or, between the quotation marks, unfair to him" (p. 122). He then adds, rather irrelevantly, "To correct his quotations so as to make them formally quite exact would mutilate the text with bracketed insertions, and to repeat the quotation accurately in a footnote would needlessly burden the page." The basic argument here is that editorial emendation of the quotations is unnecessary because they accurately reflect the gist of the original authors' statements. Such a position does not question whether Edwards intended to represent those statements in exactly the way they appear in the first edition. The Yale Edwards edition, in other words, admirably describes the nature of Edwards's quoting but does not take a critical approach to the treatment of his quotations as they are found in the printed texts.[56]

If quotations in nonfiction works should be treated in a critical spirit, it is equally true that bibliographical citations and other references to external facts in them must also be so treated. In Bowers's edition of James's *Essays in Radical Empiricism* (1976), James's citation of A. S. Pringle-Pattison's book as *"Man and the Cosmos"* instead of *Man's Place in the Cosmos* (p. 53) is not emended (though of course the correct title is recorded in the notes), for there is no question about what James wrote, which is a characteristic example of nineteenth-century allusive citation. On the other hand, when Washington Irving, in *Mahomet and His Successors*, begins a sentence with "The Arabs, says Lane," and ends the paragraph with a correct reference to *"Sale's Koran,"* it is clear that "Lane" is merely a slip for "Sale," and Henry A. Pochmann and E. N. Feltskog make the emendation (p. 374) in their Wisconsin edition (1970). Joseph J. Moldenhauer and Edwin Moser, in their volume of *Early Essays and Miscellanies* (1975) in the Princeton edition of Thoreau, attempt to distinguish between erroneous information and typographical errors in Thoreau's sources: when Thoreau gives James Hogg's birthdate as 1772 instead of 1770, they do not correct it, because his source also gives 1772 as the year; but when he follows that source in citing "Madoc of the Moor," they emend "Madoc" to "Mador" on the grounds that the source reading was merely a typographical error. Other editors might disagree with this distinction and argue the case differently; but one cannot quarrel with the Thoreau editors' recognition of the necessity for applying critical judgment to each factual error and not handling all errors by a ready-made rule. In some cases, as the Thoreau edition illustrates, the basis for correcting a factual error in a copy-text may be provided by an author's earlier draft. In Thoreau's fair-copy manuscript of his early essay on "Sir Walter Raleigh," the year 1592 is said to be eight years before Raleigh's imprisonment, but the correct year, 1595, is present in two previous drafts (p. 188); and in *The Maine Woods* (ed. Moldenhauer, 1972) the copy-text statement that "our party of three paid two dollars" (p. 160) can be corrected by reference to the first draft, where the fare is recorded as three dollars per person (Thoreau's "2" and "9" resemble one another). Factual errors can of course be corrected without such documents, but their existence helps to confirm the author's inten-

56. And this edition, it should be added, is not one that excludes all editorial emendation; in fact, it is a modernized edition. (Ramsey's point that the text is not "put forth in completely modern form" refers only to the fact that idioms and other matters of wording are not modernized.) But the inappropriateness of modernization for a scholarly edition of this kind is an entirely different point from the one I am concerned with here.

tion. And that intention is what is crucial: the fact that a piece of writing is "nonfiction" cannot relieve the scholarly editor of the obligation to investigate the author's intention (as perhaps influenced by the customs of the time) before deciding to "correct" what is technically a factual error.

These considerations call attention to the fine line that an editor must draw between correcting in the sense of emending a text in the light of the author's intention and correcting in the sense of revising. Henry Pochmann, in the *Mahomet* edition, is well aware of the problem when he notes that he cannot correct Irving's grammar or syntax "short of making the transition from editing to revising Irving's text" (p. 602). After he describes Irving's methods of constructing approximate quotations, he adds, "Because the primary concern is to reproduce what Irving wrote, or intended to write, the editor has concentrated on what Irving's text shows and has noted or corrected Irving's alterations [of quotations] only when it can be shown that his modifications are erroneous or unintentional, or both." Although the inclusion of the word "erroneous" makes the sentence less clear (since from the editor's point of view the only things that can be erroneous within the text are those that are unintended), this statement is useful both because it sets forth a sensible point of view for handling quotations (and, by extension, other matters involving external fact) and because its seeming ambiguity forces one to focus on the vexing problems of intention. To say that an editor reproduces what an author "wrote, or intended to write" is obviously meant to allow the editor to correct the author's slips of the pen. It is not meant to imply that all factual errors are necessarily slips and are to be corrected by the editor; but the difficulty of constructing a sentence making that distinction explicit suggests the difficulties of the distinction itself. A factual error is not a slip, of course, if an author intentionally alters the facts; but neither is it a slip if the author has copied accurately from an inaccurate source. That the author in the latter case intended to get the facts right does not give the editor license to correct them if there is a reasonable possibility that the erroneous facts have had some influence on the author's thinking and thus have ramifications elsewhere in the text. One is dealing, in other words, with the author's immediate intention in the act of writing; basing editorial decisions on some more programmatic intention to be "accurate" would frequently mean becoming a collaborator of the author and undertaking a new stage of revision which that author never got around to.

The editing of Thoreau's college papers, though rather a special case, illustrates the point. Thoreau made some revisions in his papers before submitting them to Edward T. Channing; when Channing marked those papers he was carrying the process of revision—or indicating how to carry it—one stage further. Moldenhauer and Moser, in their *Early Essays* volume, accept into the text Thoreau's revisions before he submitted the papers but not those made as a result of Channing's directives—"unless," they add, "the original reading is an error that the editors would have emended had Thoreau himself not corrected it" (p. 311). Thus one can correct slips of Thoreau's pen, for to do so is to act in accordance with his intention at the moment of writing; but to adopt revisions prompted by a schoolmaster's markings is to accept an altered intention imposed from outside. The reader is interested in what Thoreau wanted to write, not in what someone else wished him to do. In the same way, any editor who corrects factual errors in texts merely because they are factual errors, without carefully considering the relation of those errors to the author's active intention, is playing the role of the schoolmaster, concerned more with maintaining an *a priori* standard than with understanding the internal demands of a particular situation. The critical editor is pledged to use judgment: deciding in advance to reproduce the copy-text exactly is not appropriate, for the goal is not a facsimile or diplomatic text; but neither can the critical editor decide in advance to correct all errors of external fact, for the goal is not to carry forward the authorial process of revision. Editorial emendations in a critical text that aims to respect the author's intention must be made in the light of the intention manifested in the version of the work being edited. Whether the work is "fiction" or "nonfiction," the editor must strive to make emendations that are faithful to the spirit of the historical document under consideration and that do not move on into the area of prescriptive correcting.

This point of view, particularly when applied to "nonfiction," is bound to raise a question in many readers' minds. Surely, they would say, writers of "nonfiction" set out to be informative, and if one does not correct all their errors one is caring more about the writers as individuals of interest in their own right than about the subjects they are discussing. Where, in other words, do we draw the line between an interest in a piece of writing for the information it conveys and an interest in it as the expression of a particular individual at a specific time? Irving's historical works were intended to be informative, but today we turn to them more to experience Irving's prose and to observe his handling of the material; if we wish to learn the "facts" about the historical events he dealt with, we feel that more recent accounts, based on further research, have superseded his treatments. Similarly, we are not indignant over James's and Dewey's misquotations, because we are interested in the versions that influenced their thought; but if we read current scholarly treatments of the same subjects we regard misquotations and factual errors as faults. The reason is not merely that conventional standards may have become more rigorous; it is that in the former case our interest is historical and in the latter it is not. But what is read today for its "truth" is read tomorrow for its "historical interest"; the same pieces of "nonfiction" move from one status to the other, and the editor is not faced with two discrete bodies of material, but only one, which in fact comprises all writing. The distinction to be made is between kinds of editing, not kinds of writing. What is called editing in a magazine- or book-publisher's office is not historically oriented, and publishers' editors hope to find and eliminate factual errors—that is, what can be regarded as errors in the light of current knowledge—in the manuscripts they prepare for publication. When a scholarly editor undertakes to edit a text, however, the task is retrospective and the interest historical, no matter how recent the piece of writing happens to be.

If a publisher's editor had informed F. O. Matthiessen that he was quoting a corrupt text of *White-Jacket* with the reading "soiled fish" for "coiled fish," he would have revised his discussion accordingly, for it was not his aim to analyze a phrase Melville never wrote. But if a scholarly editor were to prepare an edition of Matthiessen's book, nothing could be done about rectifying the erroneous "soiled," which forms the basis for an analysis of "the unexpected linking of the medium of cleanliness with filth."[57] Even if Matthiessen had not made a point of the word "soiled," the scholarly editor would have to think very carefully before correcting it in the quotation, for Matthiessen quoted accurately the Constable text, assuming it to be correct, and that text is the one lying behind his commentary. The critical activity of the scholarly editor is directed toward recovering what an author intended at a particular time, whether that time was yesterday, four decades ago, or four centuries ago.[58] This principle applies to matters of external fact just as much as to any other feature of the work, although editors sometimes seem more tempted to abandon their historical orientation when dealing with those matters.

Reference to Matthiessen's discussion of "soiled" is a reminder that on many occasions an author's elaboration of an erroneous point makes any emendation out of the question: it is fruitless to consider—except as an exercise—whether or not one would emend "soiled" if Matthiessen

57. *American Renaissance* (1941), p. 392. The error was originally pointed out by John W. Nichol in "Melville's '"Soiled" Fish of the Sea,'" *American Literature*, 21 (1949–50), 338–339.

58. The result may be a "new" version in the sense that the text never existed physically in this form before, but the aim is still historical reconstruction, not the application of critical ability to the further "revision" or "improvement" of the work beyond the point where the author left it.

had not discussed the word, because in fact he did discuss it, and one cannot rewrite the passage for him. Quite apart from questions of intention, then, there is always the practical question of whether or not any alteration is feasible. Presumably Yeats did not intend to misquote two lines from Burns so that they contain the phrase "white moon" rather than "wan moon," but his penetrating analysis of the use of "white" in the passage eliminates any possibility of editorial correction.[59] Situations involving internal contradiction as well as external fact may be such that an editor has no alternative but to leave them alone. When Ahab appears in "his slouched hat" (Chapter 132) just two chapters after a hawk has flown off with it (and we are told that it "was never restored"), an editor is powerless to make a change that will produce consistency. Similarly, when Melville describes the baleen of the right whale (Chapter 75), he has a sentence pointing out that "One voyager in Purchas" calls these bones one thing, "another" calls them something else, and "a third old gentleman in Hackluyt" speaks of them in a still different way. The fact is that the third quotation is a paraphrase of Purchas, not Hakluyt; but if "Purchas" were to be substituted for "Hackluyt," Purchas would be named twice, and the rhetorical effect of the sentence would be changed. What is a factual error must be allowed to stand (whether or not Melville meant to be accurate here) because the error plays a role in the rhetoric of the passage as he wrote it, and correcting the error would amount to stylistic revision.[60]

There are thus two considerations that need to be kept in mind in dealing with factual errors. First one must consider whether a correction can realistically be undertaken. If a correction involves only a simple substitution, then it can be seriously considered; but if the erroneous information has been referred to repeatedly or been made the basis of further comment, there is no way to make the correction, short of more extensive rewriting and alteration than a scholarly editor can contemplate. This consideration is purely a practical one and has nothing to do with authorial intention: some errors can be considered for correction, others cannot. In the latter case, there is no point debating what the author intended, for no alteration can be attempted; besides, the use to which the error has been put makes it in effect an intended part of the

59. This example, and other similar ones, are discussed in Hodgart's "Misquotation as Re-creation" (see note 28 above), pp. 36–37. The creative nature of Yeats's misquotations is also taken up in Jon Lanham's "Some Further Textual Problems in Yeats: *Ideas of Good and Evil*," *PBSA*, 71 (1977), esp. 455–457, 467.

60. The situation is somewhat more complicated, since the first reference has not been found in Purchas, and it may be erroneous also. But neither has it been located in Hakluyt, so there is no basis for switching the two names. These difficulties may support the view that Melville was more concerned here with rhetorical effect than with factual accuracy.

text, even if it originated as a slip. But in the case of errors that can feasibly be corrected, the editor must take up the second, and more diffi-cult, kind of consideration, to determine whether or not they *ought* to be corrected. It is here that the editor's critical assessment of all relevant factors is crucial—an assessment of the nature of the sentence and passage where the error occurs, the observed habits of the author, the conven-tions of the time. Decisions to emend must rest on informed critical judg-ment, and no less so where questions of external fact are concerned. Clear thinking about emendations of factual errors requires that these two levels of consideration be thoroughly understood: the recognition, first of all, that some errors by their nature are unemendable; and, second, the awareness that any mechanical rule of thumb for handling the emendable errors involves an abandonment of the editor's critical func-tion.

The reasons for leaving Keats's "Cortez" alone are therefore some-what more complicated than those Amy Lowell seems to imply when she says that Keats used the name "probably by accident" but that "It is no matter." To say that what an author puts into a text "by accident" is "no matter" suggests an uncritical approach to the text; it implies an accep-tance of whatever is present in a particular text, as if one were approach-ing the text of a working document, where one is interested in preserving false starts and errors for their psychological significance. But the sonnet is a finished work of art, not merely a literary document, and it demands to be edited critically, with attention to possible emendations to restore the author's intention. Whether Keats intended to disregard historical fact or confused the historical Balboa with Cortez, however, need not be pondered, for there is no question that "Cortez" is the word he put into the poem at this point, and the role which that word plays in the patterns of sound and rhythm in the poem makes it an integral element of the work. Furthermore, the connotations of "Cortez" are such that it is able to serve as a vehicle to carry the intended tenor of the figure. This is one of those situations where an "error" is unemendable because the use made of it within the work rules out any editorial attempt to rectify it. "Cortez" must remain, not because author's accidents do not matter, but because it—accident or not in origin—became, as Keats wrote, an inex-tricable part of the work. Probably Amy Lowell had such points in mind, but her elliptical statement does not make them clear and even seems to encourage the view that the accuracy of external references in literary works need not be seriously investigated.

References to external fact, as in this instance, raise textual questions because they call attention to a second "text" (the historical fact) with which the text under consideration can be compared. Editorial attention is necessarily drawn to variants between two or more texts of a work; but a critical editor's duty is also to try to identify any errors in a text at points where variants do not exist or in cases where there is only one text. If quotations or other references to external fact or uses of external documents are involved, the editor has assistance in this task that is not otherwise available, for a point of comparison outside the immediate text can be established. At many other places in a text one has no basis for speculating about whether a reading is erroneous, but when words are quoted from another writer or a date is cited, for example, one can compare the text with the outside source or fact. Even in cases of paraphrase (or translation), where a passage is loosely based on an external source, knowledge of the wording of that source is relevant. Differences found in the text are not necessarily to be regarded as errors, but in many cases familiarity with the external facts enables one to recognize a slip of the pen or a misreading of handwriting that could not have been detected any other way. And in instances where only printed texts or late manuscripts are available, such knowledge allows one to speculate about certain readings in now lost anterior documents, for one can know the sources that underlie parts of those documents. Recognizing that writers need not be held to strict accuracy in their historical allusions does not eliminate the critical editor's responsibility for checking each allusion and making a textual decision about it. The presence in a text of quotations, paraphrases, or references to historical fact undoubtedly raises some perplexing editorial questions; but it also provides editors with a splendid opportunity of demonstrating what critical editing at its most effective can accomplish.

Some Principles for Editorial Apparatus

NYONE WHO UNDERTAKES TO EDIT A TEXT MUST NECESSARILY make some basic decisions about the kind of editorial apparatus that is to accompany that text. Sometimes these decisions are so thoughtless that they are hardly recognized as decisions at all — as when a publisher's editor selects a particular early edition to be photographically reproduced, without commentary of any kind, in a cheap paperback series. At other times they are the result of careful deliberation — as when a scholarly editor who has constructed a critical text sets forth in several lists the data he had at his disposal in examining variants and making emendations. In between, the spectrum includes a wide variety of kinds of apparatus: one edition may be entirely unannotated except for a prefatory note explaining the source of the text and perhaps generalizing about certain changes made in it; another may record variant readings (or the more important of them) in brackets within the text or at the foot of the page; another may limit its annotation, at the foot of the page or at the end of the volume, to definition of obscure words and identification of historical allusions; and still another may be principally concerned with citing previous critics' remarks about individual passages. But whatever form the apparatus takes — from the rudimentary to the elaborate — it represents some sort of thought about the extent to which the editor should make himself visible to the audience at which he is aiming.

Some kinds of apparatus, of course, are in part determined by the purposes of the edition: thus a variorum edition must by definition include apparatus which records variant readings. But an editor's basic job is to produce a text, and normally neither the exact form nor the extent of the apparatus is automatically determined by that job. A careful and reliable text obviously could be published without any accompanying apparatus, while an irresponsible text could be offered with extensive notes and tables. Such is not usually the case; but the fact remains that the precise nature of the apparatus is determined by a different set of decisions from that which lies behind the establishment of the text. It is true that most of the recent editions based on Greg's rationale for choosing a copy-text[1] have similar categories of lists in the apparatus. But there is nothing in his theory itself which requires such lists; rather, it could be said that these lists provide the most important kinds of information which ought to be supplied in any scholarly edition, regardless of the principles followed in constructing the text. Decisions affecting the text involve questions of authorial intent; decisions affecting the apparatus involve questions of editorial responsibility. When an editor prepares a text for a scholarly audience, it is his responsibility to furnish all the information required for evaluating and rethinking his textual decisions; in a popular edition, on the other hand, he may feel with some justification that his primary responsibility is to provide explanatory annotation rather than textual evidence — but of course the care with which the text itself is prepared would not be less merely because the apparatus is simpler.[2] It should be clear, therefore, that a general rationale for editorial apparatus can be discussed independently of any rationale for editing. And equally obvious is the basic principle to be borne in mind in making decisions about apparatus: that the kind of apparatus presented is an indication less of the nature of the text than of the type of audience for which the edition is intended.

Just what apparatus is appropriate for a particular audience is a matter about which opinion naturally changes over the course of time, as scholarly techniques develop and bibliographical knowledge accumulates. In the nineteenth century, conventional practice for scholarly editions was to list variant readings (usually a selection of those considered most significant) in footnotes, with more discursive notes placed either at the end (as in William Aldis Wright's Cambridge Shakespeare, which began in 1863) or in a second set of footnotes, below the first (as in Horace Howard Furness's Variorum Shakespeare, which began in 1874). A new standard was set in 1904, when the first volume of R. B. McKerrow's edition of Nashe appeared; though in arrangement it was similar to earlier editions (variants in footnotes, with discursive notes in a supplementary volume), it marked a turning point

1. "The Rationale of Copy-Text," *SB*, 3 (1950-51), 19-36; reprinted in Greg's *Collected Papers*, ed. J. C. Maxwell (1966), pp. 374-91.

2. The ground rules might be different— if this were what Fredson Bowers calls a "practical edition"—so that less research would be expected. But the *care* devoted to establishing the text on the basis of the available evidence would be no less, for this is the editor's essential task.

in its discussions of the bibliographical history of each work, leading to a careful choice of "copy-text" (the term was first used here) — which in turn lent an added sense of objectivity and control to the record of variant readings, for it was defined to include *all* departures (with a few minor exceptions) from that copy-text, as well as other significant variants. McKerrow went on, in his *Prolegomena for the Oxford Shakespeare* (1939), not only to refine and elaborate his editorial procedure but also to discuss in detail the form which he believed editorial apparatus should take; although in general arrangement he advocated the old system of two sets of footnotes (one of variant readings, one of historical and linguistic information), his discussion of the symbols and form to be employed in each entry for a variant reading (pp. 73-98) was by far the most extensive that had ever appeared, and its influence is still present today.

But the event which has been most important in influencing the form of the apparatus in many of the more recent scholarly editions was the publication in 1953 of the first volume of Fredson Bowers's Cambridge edition of Dekker. What Bowers did to make the apparatus more conveniently usable was to break down the listing of variants into several parts: only the substantive departures from the copy-text were recorded in footnotes; the departures in accidentals were then gathered into a separate list at the end of the text; and two more lists at the end dealt with press-variant formes and with substantive variants in other pre-1700 editions ("historical collation"). Since that time many editions have employed some variety of Bowers's plan, most notably the series of editions now in progress under the auspices of the MLA Center for Editions of American Authors. These editions maintain Bowers's distinction between lists of emendations and historical collation; but since they are "clear-text" editions, no apparatus appears on the pages of text, and all the emendations of the copy-text — both substantives and accidentals — are usually joined in one list. The adoption of this approach to editorial apparatus by the CEAA editions of Clemens, Stephen Crane, John Dewey, Hawthorne, Howells, Irving, Melville, and Simms[3] suggests that a new pattern for the treatment of

3. Informal citations of these editions throughout this essay refer to the following: *The Mark Twain Papers*, ed. Frederick Anderson *et al.* (Berkeley: University of California Press, 1966-   ), esp. *Hannibal, Huck & Tom*, ed. Walter Blair (1969), and *Mysterious Stranger Manuscripts*, ed. William M. Gibson (1969); *The University of Virginia Edition of the Works of Stephen Crane*, ed. Fredson Bowers (Charlottesville: University Press of Virginia, 1969-   ); *The Early Works of John Dewey, 1882-1898*, ed. Jo Ann Boydston, in consultation with Fredson Bowers (Carbondale: Southern Illinois University Press, 1969-   ); *The Centenary Edition of the Works of Nathaniel Hawthorne*, text ed. Fredson Bowers, with Matthew J. Bruccoli (Colum-

apparatus in scholarly editions seems to be emerging—at least for works of the sixteenth century and later. The elements in this pattern are basically four: a set of discursive textual notes, a list of emendations in the copy-text, a record of line-end hyphenation, and a historical collation. Other lists are sometimes added to cover special problems, but these four, along with an essay setting forth the textual situation which accounts for the particular choice of copy-text, have come in recent years to represent one established kind of scholarly apparatus.[4]

Although the form of the apparatus in a large number of scholarly editions from the last twenty years is therefore similar, it is by no means identical, even in those which follow the same basic plan. There is no reason, of course, to insist on such identity in outward appearance, so long as the approach to the material is sound, since different circumstances naturally entail somewhat different treatments. Never-

---

bus: Ohio State University Press, 1962-); *A Selected Edition of W. D. Howells*, ed. Edwin H. Cady, Don Cook, Ronald Gottesman, David J. Nordloh *et al.* (Bloomington: Indiana University Press, 1968-); *The Complete Works of Washington Irving*, ed. Henry A. Pochmann *et al.* (Madison: University of Wisconsin Press, 1969-), esp. *Mahomet and His Successors* (1970); *The Writings of Herman Melville: The Northwestern-Newberry Edition*, ed. Harrison Hayford, Hershel Parker, and G. Thomas Tanselle, with Richard Colles Johnson (Evanston and Chicago: Northwestern University Press and The Newberry Library, 1968-); *The Writings of William Gilmore Simms: Centennial Edition*, ed. John Caldwell Guilds and James B. Meriwether (Columbia: University of South Carolina Press, 1969-). In addition, the following are referred to allusively throughout: *The Dramatic Works in the Beaumont and Fletcher Canon*, ed. Fredson Bowers *et al.* (Cambridge: Cambridge University Press, 1966-); *The Dramatic Works of Thomas Dekker*, ed. Fredson Bowers (Cambridge: Cambridge University Press, 1953-61); *The Journals and Miscellaneous Notebooks of Ralph Waldo Emerson*, ed. William H. Gilman *et al.* (Cambridge: Belknap Press of Harvard University Press, 1960-); *The Wesleyan Edition of the Works of Henry Fielding*, ed. W. B. Coley, Fredson Bowers, *et al.* (Mid-

letown, Conn.: Wesleyan University Press, 1967-), esp. *Joseph Andrews*, ed. Martin C. Battestin (1967)

4. Standard brief descriptions of this kind of apparatus appear in two essays by Fredson Bowers: "Textual Criticism," in *The Aims and Methods of Scholarship in Modern Languages and Literatures*, ed. James Thorpe (1963; rev. ed., 1970), esp. pp. 53-54; and "Some Principles for Scholarly Editions of Nineteenth-Century American Authors," *SB*, 17 (1964), esp. pp. 227-28. See also *Statement of Editorial Principles: A Working Manual for Editing Nineteenth Century American Texts* (CEAA, 1967), pp. 9-10. During the same years there have, of course, been proponents of other approaches to editing and to apparatus. Among the best known are Edmund Wilson (represented by his essays in the *New York Review of Books* on 26 Sept. and 10 Oct. 1968, reprinted the same year in pamphlet form as *The Fruits of the MLA*) and F. W. Bateson (represented by his editorial plan for "Longman's Annotated English Poets" and reflected in his letter in the *TLS* on 1 Jan. 1971, pp. 14-15). Some discussion of Wilson's views can be found in *Professional Stndards and American Editions: A Response to Edmund Wilson* (MLA, 1969) and of Bateson's in Thomas Clayton's letter in the *TLS* on 18 Dec. 1970, p. 1493.

theless, if a standard form exists and if there is no special reason to depart from it, following that form can be a positive advantage: it makes the apparatus easier to use, since readers acquainted with other editions will already know the system and will not be distracted from the content by trying to keep in mind a new plan or new symbols. Because one possible standard of this kind has been developing in recent years, it seems worthwhile to give further thought to the rationale of apparatus and to the implications of certain differences in form. The comments which I offer in the following pages are not intended as an attempt to establish "rules" but simply as a discussion of some of the considerations involved in thinking through the details of an editorial apparatus. Although I shall be mainly concerned with scholarly editions, many of the principles apply equally to more popular editions. Some remarks on the general arrangement of the apparatus and on the symbols to be employed will be followed by discussions of the four main divisions of modern apparatus enumerated above: textual notes, emendations, line-end hyphenation, and historical collation.

i. Arrangement

The first decision to be made about the arrangement of apparatus is its location. Are variant readings or editorial symbols to appear within the text itself? Or is the annotation to be provided at the foot of each page? Or at the end of the text? Or in some combination of these places? The tendency in recent years has been toward "clear text" — that is, no editorial intrusions of any kind on the pages of the text itself — and there are at least two important reasons for encouraging this practice. In the first place, an editor's primary responsibility is to establish a text; whether his goal is to reconstruct that form of the text which represents the author's final intention or some other form of the text, his essential task is to produce a reliable text according to some set of principles. Relegating all editorial matter to an appendix and allowing the text to stand by itself serves to emphasize the primacy of the text and permits the reader to confront the literary work without the distraction of editorial comment and to read the work with ease. A second advantage of a clear text is that it is easier to quote from or to reprint. Although no device can insure accuracy of quotation, the insertion of symbols (or even footnote numbers) into a text places additional difficulties in the way of the quoter. Furthermore, most quotations appear in contexts where symbols are inappropriate; thus when it is necessary to quote from a text which has not been kept clear of apparatus, the burden of producing a clear text of the passage is placed on the quoter. Even footnotes at the bottom of the text pages are open to the same objection, when the question of a photographic reprint arises. Once a scholarly text of a work has been established, every effort should be made to encourage publishers who plan to issue classroom or other practical[5] editions of the work to lease that text and reproduce it photographically, thus assuring wider circulation of a reliable text.[6] But in such cases it is the text which is leased, not the apparatus; and while the apparatus, like any other published research, is available for all to draw upon, it would not necessarily be appropriate for inclusion in such leased editions, which might more usefully carry an apparatus emphasizing explanatory rather than textual annotation. The presence of any apparatus on the pages of the text, therefore, may prove in the long run a hindrance to the dissemination of a responsible text.

Arguments can of course be advanced for inserting editorial apparatus into a text, and it is true that on certain occasions this arrangement is desirable. For instance, the nature of such materials as letters, notebooks, and journals — works never intended for publication — may not always be accurately reflected in clear text, which requires a choice among alternative readings that is often alien to the spirit of a private document. In these cases a text which includes editorial insertions and symbols recognizes that canceled readings and uncanceled variants are in fact integral parts of such works and comes as close as possible (short of a facsimile) to reproducing their essential character.[7] In

5. The term "practical edition" is used here in the sense established by Fredson Bowers in "Practical Texts and Definitive Editions," in *Two Lectures on Editing* (1969), pp. 21-70. Further comment on the relation between definitive editions and widely disseminated reading editions appears in his "The New Look in Editing," *South Atlantic Bulletin*, 35 (1970), 3-10.

6. Encouraging such reproduction does not imply that only one reliable text of a work can exist. Obviously more than one text can be prepared following sound scholarly procedures, for there may legitimately be differences of opinion about certain emendations which rest on critical evaluation. (For discussion of this point, see G. T. Tanselle, "Textual Study and Literary Judgment," *PBSA*, 2nd Quarter 1971.) The point is that a practical edition should

embody *some* reliable text, and, if such a text exists, the publisher of a practical edition should be encouraged to lease it rather than reprint, with no rationale, whatever previous text comes most readily to hand.

7. Some works of this kind may be of such importance that they will be frequently quoted; in these cases it may be more convenient to have a clear text (with variant readings recorded at the end), even at the sacrifice of the basic texture of the original. This sort of decision, involving a weighing of what is gained against what is lost, has to be made separately for each individual case. For further comment on this problem, see G. T. Tanselle, "The Editorial Problem of Final Authorial Intention," forthcoming in *Bibliographia*.

addition, manuscripts of works which conform to genres ordinarily intended for publication — whether or not they were so prepared — may be of interest in their own right as revealing steps in the author's creative process. Such manuscripts may appropriately be edited in the form of a "genetic text," which through symbols (often, necessarily, elaborate ones) makes clear the various stages of alteration and revision. The document being edited is still a private one (like letters and journals), even though it happens to embody a text intended for eventual publication. An outstanding example of a genetic text is the one prepared by Harrison Hayford and Merton M. Sealts, Jr., from Melville's *Billy Budd* manuscript (1962); because a genetic text is not easily readable, however, and because *Billy Budd* is a work of fiction rather than a private journal, the editors have also established a "reading text," free of all apparatus on the pages of the text. (Another method of dealing with this sort of manuscript — footnotes describing the revisions — is discussed below.) Thus it can be said that clear text may often be inappropriate when the material to be edited is a working document of a private nature; but when a work of the kind normally intended for publication is being edited as a finished piece of writing[8] rather than as a semifinal document, any intrusion into the text works against the editor's ultimate goal of presenting a text as the author intended (or would have intended) it to be presented.[9]

Notes at the foot of pages of text also can be defended at times. There is no denying the argument that the location is more convenient for reference than the end of the text, and editors may wish to place the most important apparatus there, even when they reserve the bulk of it for the end. Fredson Bowers, in his move to make apparatus less cumbersome, took the view that scholarly editions "should be made more attractive to the general user, first by removing all but the most immediately pertinent of the apparatus to appendices in the rear, thus freeing the text page from all information that is only of reference value and so of no immediate concern to the reader."[10] In his edition

8. I use the term "finished piece of writing" rather than "literary work" in order to include historical, technical, and scientific writings or any other work completed for publication or of a type usually intended for publication.

9. Another use of symbols in the text, convenient in certain situations in practical editions, is to draw the student's attention to important revised passages. In the Signet *Typee* (ed. Harrison Hayford, 1964), passages which Melville deleted in the revised American edition of 1846 are enclosed in square brackets, and those which he revised are both bracketed and numbered, with the revised wording given at the end of the volume according to the reference numbers.

10. "Old-Spelling Editions of Dramatic Texts," in *Studies in Honor of T. W. Baldwin*, ed. D. C. Allen (1958), p. 14.

of Dekker, only substantive emendations are given at the foot of the page, and other editions have followed a similar plan — the California *Works of John Dryden* (first volume, 1956), for example, which records only the emendations (substantive and accidental) in footnotes. Once the decision has been made, however, not to clutter the text pages with the entire apparatus, it is a difficult question to decide just how much of the apparatus is of such immediate importance that it should be retained on those pages, separated from the rest of the apparatus. What the issue comes to in the end is whether the advantages of having some data available without turning any pages outweigh the decided disadvantages of having the text pages encumbered with visible signs of the editorial process. And the advantages of the former are less strong when related information must be turned to at the back anyway, while the disadvantages of the latter are strong enough to have dictated this shift of at least some of the material in the first place.[11] Of course, footnote apparatus is not objectionable in editions of manuscript drafts or journals, for the same reason that genetic texts are appropriate there. Sometimes footnotes, rather than symbols in the text, are used in such editions to record manuscript alterations: a good example is Bowers's parallel-text edition[12] of *Whitman's Manuscripts* (1955), in which footnotes to the manuscript texts describe in words rather than symbols the exact nature of the manuscript alterations (footnotes, that is, without reference symbols in the text, so that the text remains clear). At other times footnotes are used in addition to symbols in the text, as

11. The question takes a slightly different form for practical editions, since it may be felt that a classroom edition with little apparatus except explanatory notes should offer those notes as easily accessible footnotes. It is perhaps true that more students will read them as footnotes, but the price paid for this attention is a high one: not simply the distraction from the text (which is after all more important for the students to read), but the cumulative psychological effect of always (or nearly always) encountering classic works encased in an obtrusive editorial framework which sets them apart from other books read outside of class.

Sometimes it is objected that references to line numbers are awkward and inconvenient when side-numbers counting the lines do not appear on the text pages. Side-numbers have been so widely used in connection with poetry that they probably constitute little distraction there (and thus do not prevent a poetic text from being "clear"); but their presence on a page of prose remains an intrusion and lends the page a "textbook" air. The psychological advantages of clear text, therefore, can be said to compensate for the minor inconvenience of having to count lines.

12. The use of parallel texts is often a more sensible way of exhibiting complicated revisions than to present one established text with the revisions recorded in apparatus; besides, some complex revisions result in what amounts to a different work, so that both forms of the work deserve to be presented as texts in their own right. Placing two texts in parallel columns or on facing pages is in itself a kind of apparatus; but, except for that, the comments made here about the texts of other editions would also apply to the individual texts of a parallel-text edition.

in the Harvard edition of Emerson's journals, where the footnotes (keyed to numbers in the text) provide both textual and historical information in discursive form. In neither case are the footnotes intrusions as they would be on the pages of the finished text of a novel or poem. But whenever footnotes do appear on any kind of text pages, the proximity of note to text should not lead an editor into thinking that his decisions about the readings of the text itself are less important. H. H. Furness, in the first volume of his Variorum Shakespeare, declared that, "in such an edition as the present, it makes very little difference what text is printed *in extenso*, since every other text is also printed with it on the same page" (p. viii). To take such a point of view is practically to abandon editing a text in favor of constructing an apparatus, for the text then exists largely as a frame of reference for the apparatus. A record of variants presented as a work of scholarship in its own right can be useful,[13] but there should be no illusion about its being an edition.[14] In the end, a decision to use or not to use footnotes reflects an editor's critical judgment about the nature of the text he is editing combined with his evaluation of the relative importance, in terms of psychological effect on the reader, of clear text as opposed to text with simultaneously visible apparatus.[15]

If an editor decides to place his apparatus at the end rather than on the text pages, several questions of arrangement still remain. One of the first is whether, if a volume contains more than one work, the apparatus pertaining to a given work should come immediately after the text of that work or whether the entire apparatus should be gathered at the end of the volume. Practice has varied in the CEAA editions: the Ohio State Hawthorne and some volumes of the Virginia Crane have apparatus following each work, whereas the Southern Illinois Dewey has apparatus at the back of each volume. Of course,

13. Indeed, sometimes the apparatus appended to a text is more important to scholars than the text itself, since, if it is well done, it provides the evidence on which other editions can be constructed by editors who do not agree with the interpretation of the evidence represented in that particular edition. A good example of an apparatus presented as a piece of research in its own right is Matthew J. Bruccoli's "Material for a Centenary Edi-.tion of *Tender is the Night*," *SB*, 17 (1964), 177-93.

14. Even a facsimile or a diplomatic edition of one particular impression of a work or one particular copy of an impression is based on a decision to present a given text and cannot be approached with the attitude that "it makes very little difference what text is printed *in extenso*."

15. Since the basic goal of an edition is to establish a text rather than to present an apparatus, the effect which the text makes would apparently—if it comes to a choice—be given somewhat more weight than the convenience with which the apparatus can be located.

the number of separate works involved has some bearing on the decision: the first volume of the Dewey edition contains many individual
essays never before collected, whereas the first volume of the Crane
edition and the third of the Hawthorne each contain the texts of only
two separately published books. In the case of the Dewey, therefore,
apparatus after each work would have produced a cumbersome volume
in which editorial material continually alternated with the text and
in which reference to the apparatus was inconvenient since the reader
would never know just which pages contained the apparatus to any
given work; in the case of volumes made up of only two or three works,
on the other hand, it could be argued that the proximity of the apparatus following each work is an advantage and further that this arrangement emphasizes the discreteness of the texts which happen to be
published in the same volume. Nevertheless, even when the number
of separate works is small, the act of consulting the apparatus seems
more difficult when the apparatus is placed at the ends of the works
rather than all together at the end of the volume;[16] in addition, the
occurrence of apparatus at scattered points throughout a volume,
though it does not violate the idea of clear text, is undeniably a greater
editorial intrusion than would exist if all the editor's data were collected at one location. Essentially the difficulty arises out of the fact
that, from the textual point of view, one is concerned with two or more
"books," while from the point of view of design one is dealing with a
single physical volume. Since the placement of apparatus does not
affect an editor's principles for establishing a text but does affect the
design of the finished volume, and since the volume, as the smallest
separate physical unit in an edition — and not the literary work or
"book" — is the unit which the reader must manipulate, it seems
reasonable to suggest that the apparatus (once the decision has been
reached to place it at the "end" rather than on text pages) should
probably in most circumstances be gathered in one section at the end
of each physical volume.[17]

16. Both because one knows less readily
where to turn to find the apparatus and
because comparative study involving several works requires more extensive page-
turning. In addition, the editor may have
practical reasons for preferring a single
block of apparatus at the end, since it
enables him to key all his apparatus to
page proof at one time. If sections of
apparatus are scattered through a volume,
the process is inevitably less efficient; for if

the editor gets galleys first, he must wait to
key the apparatus for his second text until
the apparatus for his first has been made
into pages, so that the pagination of the
second text is known, and so on through
the volume; and if the editor receives
pages directly, then the apparatus must
be set up with blank references ("oo.oo")
and all the figures later altered.

17. Considerations of the ease with which

A related question is the precise arrangement of the material at the end of the volume. Just as it seems easier to turn to the apparatus if it is all at one location, so is it simpler to refer to the information about a particular work if it is presented at one spot within that section of apparatus. Normally when a reader consults the apparatus he is studying a single work, and he finds the apparatus more convenient if all the lists pertaining to that work occur together, so that he does not have to turn back and forth from the relevant part of a long list of emendations for the whole volume to the relevant part of a full historical collation, and so on. One might argue, of course, that to have only one list of each type for the whole volume — as in the Dewey edition — consolidates the information more economically and is in conformity with the view of the volume as a single physical entity. The difficulty, however, is that the volume is still composed of individual works, each with its own textual history and each requiring separate editorial consideration; any apparatus which does not segregate the material relating to each work is likely to obscure the variations in copy-texts and in numbers of authoritative editions involved and to suggest a greater uniformity than in fact exists. Obviously this is not to say that the true situation cannot be perceived by a careful reader — after all, neither system, in the hands of responsible editors, conceals relevant information. The whole point is whether one system is clearer and easier to use than the other, and the advantage in this regard would seem to lie with the system which presents separate blocks of data for each individual work. The greater ease with which, under this system, one can move from one category of data to another and gain an overview of the kinds of editorial decisions involved (even without remembering which pages the work covers) surely outweighs the slightly greater expenditure of space entailed.[18]

---

individual texts and apparatus can be reproduced photographically have little relevance here, for even when the apparatus immediately follows the work the pagination would be appropriate for separate issue only for the first work in the volume; and when pagination must be altered in any case, there would be no additional problem in taking the apparatus from the end of the volume and altering its page numbers also. A real problem might arise, of course, if the apparatus for a given work were not presented as a unit and if apparatus pertaining to other works appeared on some of the same pages; but

there is no reason why apparatus at the end of a volume cannot be so arranged as to avoid this problem. (See the following paragraph and footnote 18.)

18. Some extra space is required, of course, for the additional headings which would be needed. Further space would generally be used if one always began the section for a given work on a new page, in an attempt to facilitate photoreproduction of an individual text with its apparatus (see footnote 17). But if only a few long texts were involved, little space would be wasted in this way, while for shorter texts,

Whether or not a volume contains more than one work or has apparatus arranged by work, another question which an editor must decide is the order in which the various parts of the apparatus are to be presented. Although the record of emendations in the copy-text generally precedes the historical collation, there is otherwise little consensus on this matter. Some editions place the discursive textual notes after the list of emendations, while others give them first; some put the list of line-end hyphenation last, while others insert it immediately after the record of emendations. The issue is not one of major importance: what is important is that these kinds of information be present, not that they be present in a particular order. Still, they have to appear in some order; and the editor, if he does not settle the question by flipping a coin, must have some rationale for selecting one order over another. If an advantage, however slight, does exist favoring one arrangement, that arrangement is preferable to a purely random order hit upon by an individual editor — preferable not only because there is some reason for it but also because its adoption would result in greater uniformity among editions. At any rate, the editor should be aware of the various considerations involved in the ordering of the lists.

One common arrangement is to place the list of emendations first (if it does not appear as footnotes), since it could be considered of most immediate importance, recording as it does the editorial alterations in the copy-text. Generally this list is followed (as in the Ohio State *Scarlet Letter*, the California Mark Twain, and the Dewey edition) by the discursive textual notes; because a common practice now (following Bowers's Dekker) is to mark with an asterisk those emendations which are discussed in the notes, the section of notes can in a sense be regarded as an appendage to the list of emendations. On the other hand, most editors find it necessary occasionally to comment on readings they have not emended, giving their reasons for not altering what might at first seem to be incorrect. Notes of this kind obviously do not relate to the list of emendations, since no emendations are recorded at these points. One way of solving this awkwardness is to insert asterisked entries in the list of emendations calling attention to

such as essays, stories, and poems (where more space might be wasted, since more of these works could be included in a volume), there would be less reason to accommodate photoreproduction, because less demand exists for separate reprints of individual short works. There would be little reason, in other words, for beginning the apparatus to each work on a new page except when a volume contains only two or three long works.

these notes, simply by citing the reading involved and adding *"stet"* to show that the reading was the same in the copy-text.[19] The result is that every discursive note can be located by means of the asterisks in the list of emendations; but the price paid for this convenience is that the list of emendations is no longer, strictly speaking, a list of emendations, because it also contains certain instances where emendations have not been made. This list is then less easy to use for surveying the emendations as a whole or compiling statistics about them, since one would have to be alert for those items which are not emendations at all. The function of such a list would be less clear-cut and less easy for the reader to comprehend; and the convenience of having asterisk references to all the notes (if, indeed, it really is a convenience) is probably not worth so high a price. An alternative, and more satisfactory, solution is simply to reverse the order of the two sections, placing the textual notes before the list of emendations. One effect of this change is to remove any implication that the notes are tied to the list of emendations; asterisks can still be used in the list of emendations to call attention to notes, but no awkwardness results from the fact that some of the notes take up readings not entered in the list. This arrangement emphasizes the real function of the notes: to comment on any readings — whether emendations or not — which raise some problem from a textual point of view and which thus require some explanation. Many readers not interested in rejected variants will be reading carefully enough to wonder about certain peculiar expressions and will turn directly to the textual notes to see what explanation is offered for the adoption (whether through emendation or retention) of these expressions. Placing these notes nearest the text is both suggestive and convenient: suggestive of the fact that the notes make direct comments on readings in the established text, and convenient because it allows all the sections of the apparatus in tabular, rather than discursive, form to fall together.[20] In recent years this position for the textual notes has

19. Bowers's Dekker employs this system, though the situation is somewhat different since the record of substantive emendations appears as footnotes. It is also used by Matthew J. Bruccoli in "Material for a Centenary Edition of *Tender is the Night*," *SB*, 17 (1964), 177-93, but again there are special circumstances since here the apparatus is presented independently of the text. And the Virginia Crane edition uses the *"stet"* system even though the list of emendations follows the textual notes.

20. Still another arrangement is employed in the first volume of the Simms edition, where the list of emendations and the textual notes are merged: that is, whenever a reading requires comment, the comment is inserted at the appropriate point in the list of emendations. The advantage, of course, is a reduction in the number of separate sections of apparatus, so that the reader is involved in less cross reference between sections. But, as usually happens when notes are tied to a list of emenda-

been gaining favor and has been employed in the Crane, Howells, Irving, and Melville editions and in the Hawthorne edition beginning with the second volume.[21]

Once it is decided to make the textual notes the first of the four main divisions of the apparatus,[22] it is not difficult to settle on the list of emendations as the second. Of the standard lists, it is the one most directly connected with the edited text, since it records the editorial changes which that text embodies and enables the reader to reconstruct the basic document, the copy-text. The question that remains, then, is the order of the other two basic lists — the historical collation and the record of line-end hyphenation. The hyphenation list is often put in last position (as in the Dewey, Howells, and Irving editions, in certain volumes of *The Mark Twain Papers*, and in the first volume of the Hawthorne edition); apparently the reason is that hyphenation seems in some intangible sense less "significant" than the instances of substantive variation in the authorized editions. Yet if one of the reasons for giving precedence, among the lists, to the record of emendations is that it is concerned with editorial decisions, consistency would suggest that the hyphenation list should follow immediately, since it too records editorial decisions — that is, one half of it does, the half that lists line-end hyphens in the copy-text. And the other half — noting the established forms of compounds divided at line-ends in the edited text — is of direct use to any reader who wishes to make a quotation from the text. The historical collation, on the other hand, is simply a factual register of the variations (usually only the substantive ones) present in a given group of editions; although it is valuable in setting forth much of the textual evidence at the editor's disposal, its purpose is not pri-

---

tions, some entries for unemended readings have to be included in the list. Furthermore, there is the danger that the insertion of blocks of discursive material into the list will make the list less easy to follow; in the case of the first Simms volume, the number of notes is small enough that this difficulty does not arise to any significant extent, but it remains a possibility when there is a considerable number of notes— and when the number is small, the notes may actually prove less readily accessible if imbedded in a list. Finally, difficulties of design in joining paragraphs and lists (as when lengthy notes must be accommodated to a double-column page designed

primarily for listed items) provide an additional argument against using this system under ordinary circumstances.

21. The Cambridge Dekker and Beaumont-Fletcher editions also place the textual notes immediately after the text, but in effect these notes follow the substantive emendations, since the substantive emendations are recorded in footnotes on text pages.

22. The positions of various other special lists which may be required are commented on below, at the points where these lists are discussed.

marily to list editorial decisions,[23] and it is thus set apart from the other main sections of the apparatus in this regard. If the principle of arrangement is to be — as seems sensible — a movement from what is most directly associated with the final edited text to what is least directly connected with it, there is little doubt that the hyphenation list should precede the historical collation (as it does in the Crane, Fielding, and Melville editions and in the Hawthorne beginning with the second volume).

A suggested standard order, therefore, for the four basic parts of the apparatus is as follows: (1) textual notes; (2) emendations; (3) line-end hyphenation; and (4) historical collation. Another essential part of the editorial matter is an essay describing the editorial principles followed in the edition, the textual history of the individual work, and any special problems emerging from the application of those principles to that particular historical situation. This kind of essay is frequently labeled as an "introduction" and placed at the beginning of the volume, preceding the text. Although such a location does not contradict the notion of clear text (since it obviously does not affect what appears on the text pages), it does result in the editor intruding himself at a very prominent place in the volume; what is probably more in keeping with the spirit of the clear-text principle and with the decision to place apparatus at the end is to think of the textual essay not as an introduction to the entire volume but only as an introduction to the apparatus — and thus to be placed at the end, though preceding the other parts of the editorial matter dealing with textual concerns (a plan followed by a number of editions, such as the Howells, Irving, Melville, and Simms).[24] In cases where related documents of textual interest exist (a manuscript fragment from an early draft, a published preface differing from the one in the copy-text edition, a map or other nontextual appurtenance of the copy-text edition, and the like), they can properly be printed or discussed as another section of the editorial apparatus — a section which should probably come last, since such material often is not keyed directly to the established text and in any case is only peripherally related to it. Finally, the editorial apparatus

23. Though incidentally it does list the substantive ones, since each entry has to be keyed to the reading which appears in the edited text.

24. In the Dewey edition, both a textual introduction and a historical introduction precede the text; but the pages on which they appear are numbered with small roman numerals, and this sequence of pagination is resumed at the back of the volume for the remainder of the apparatus. This arrangement thus makes it simple, in other printings or photographically reproduced sub-editions, to bring all the editorial matter together.

in some instances may include explanatory, as opposed to textual, annotation: many editions provide a historical essay on the background, composition, publication, and reception of the work, and some —especially those of nonfiction — also offer notes identifying allusions and an index. The historical essay is sometimes placed at the beginning of the volume, even when the textual essay follows the text (as in the Howells and Simms editions), and at other times it is put in the end matter, preceding the textual essay (as in the Irving and Melville editions); the argument for the latter position is the same as in the case of the textual essay — to allow the edited work to have the opening place in the volume. The explanatory notes — if they are not treated as footnotes[25] — might reasonably be the first section to follow the text, preceding any of the textual apparatus (as in the Howells edition), though they might logically follow the historical essay, if that essay were in the end matter; and an index, whether or not it covers the editorial contributions, should retain its conventional position at the very end of the physical volume (as in the Dewey edition). Since the nontextual annotation is discursive in form or is set up in forms (such as indexes) about which much has already been written, and since the related documents by their nature usually present special situations which must be treated on an individual basis, the remarks on form in the pages which follow will be limited to the strictly textual apparatus.

ii. Symbols

Practically every edition makes some use of symbols or abbreviations; indeed, they are almost unavoidable unless one is dealing with a text so uncomplicated that scarcely any apparatus results. The primary motive behind most (but not all) symbols and abbreviations is economy, for if an editor is going to refer dozens (or even hundreds) of times to a particular impression, published at a given time by a given publisher and identifiable perhaps only by certain typographical peculiarities, it is merely common sense that he devise some concise way of making the reference. But he must also realize that, beyond a point, the interests of economy work in the opposite direction from those of clarity. In 1863 William Aldis Wright recognized (as every editor must) this dilemma: "We will now proceed," he said in the introduction to the Cambridge Shakespeare, "to explain the notation employed in the foot-notes, which, in some cases, the necessity of com-

---

25. In the Wesleyan Fielding, though the textual apparatus is at the end of the volume, the explanatory notes are placed at the bottom of the text pages (keyed to footnote numbers in the text).

pressing may have rendered obscure" (p. xxii). When symbols are multiplied to the point where it is difficult for the reader to keep them in mind, so that he must constantly consult a key to decipher what is being said, the time has come to rethink the whole system. In some fields, such as mathematics or chemistry, symbolic statements, however complex, are admirably suited to the purposes they are intended to serve; but the apparatus to a literary text is generally directed toward the readers and students of that text, for whom a knowledge of special symbols is not necessary in their principal work of understanding the text. It is not reasonable, therefore, to ask the users of a textual apparatus to become acquainted with an elaborate symbolic structure, since that apparatus is only a reference tool, rather than the central focus of their attention. Nineteenth-century editors tended to make excessive demands along these lines; and even McKerrow's *Prolegomena*, though its thoughtful treatment of symbols is important and though the symbols it advocates are individually sensible, sets up too many of them, with the result that in combination they can be bewildering. Fortunately, the recent trend, since Bowers's Dekker, has been toward the simplification of symbols. In thinking about editorial symbols, the essential principle to be kept in mind is that for this purpose the value of a symbol ought to be judged on the basis of convenience rather than economy (though economy is often a prime element in convenience): if a symbol, both in itself and in combination with others, makes the apparatus easier to refer to and understand, it is a good one; if it does not, it should be abandoned.

Perhaps a distinction should be made between symbols which stand for particular editions or impressions and those which stand for concepts. One cannot object to a multiplicity of symbols representing editions, if there happens to be a large number of editions involved, for the symbols are still easier to manipulate than cumbersome identifications of the editions in words; but further symbols to be used in conjunction with the edition-symbols for making comments about particular situations may easily proliferate to the point where they are less easy to follow than the same concepts expressed in words. Thus when McKerrow uses parentheses to indicate "a reading which is not *identical* with the one given but which is *substantially* the same in meaning or intention so far as the purpose of the note is concerned" (p. 82) and then inserts two parallel vertical lines within the parentheses "as a warning that, although the editions thus indicated support the reading in question, the *context* in which their reading occurs is not identical with that of the other texts" (p. 85), one may begin to feel that the goal of the apparatus has become compression rather than ease of comprehension.[26] Yet no one would be likely to have strong objection to the many abbreviations and symbols — such as "Theo.," "Johns.," "Cap.," "Camb.," "Fl," "Q1"—which McKerrow employs as shorthand designations for individuals editions. Indeed, these abbreviations, though numerous, are largely self-evident and rarely would need to be looked up more than once; even aside from their economy and ease of transcription, therefore, they have the positive advantage of being recognizable at a glance (whereas a fuller identification in words normally would take somewhat longer to read).

If it can be agreed, then, that the use of symbols is desirable for reference to editions and impressions, the practical question which arises is what system to use in establishing the symbols. There are two basic approaches: one is to arrange the editions in chronological order and then to assign them arbitrary sequential designations, such as the letters of the alphabet or numbers; the other is to construct each symbol so that it contains enough rational content connecting it with its referent to serve as a mnemonic. The choice of system depends on what kind of information is deemed most useful in connection with a given text, since each system, in order to make certain facts obvious, sacrifices other facts. In the first system, one can tell immediately that a particular reading is, for example, from the third edition (by means of a "C" or "3") but cannot tell (and may not be able to remember without checking) the year of that edition and whether it was English or American. The second system, conversely, might provide in the symbol the information that the edition was an 1856 American one (through some such symbol as "A1856" or "A56") but would not at the same time reveal its position in the sequence of editions. A variety of the first system has conventionally been used for pre-nineteenth-century books: a letter designating format (such as "F" for folio and "Q" for quarto), followed by numbers indicating the succession of editions within each format. Thus "Q4" would identify the fourth quarto but would not indicate the year of publication nor whether the edition came before or after the second folio. Attempts to combine the two approaches have not been successful because forcing too much significance into a symbol renders the symbol more cumbersome and to some extent defeats the purpose of establishing symbols as simple and easily recognizable designations. An edition reference like "3A56" is,

---

26. McKerrow was clearly aware of this feeling and admits that compression was his principal consideration: "I may say here that the conventions, which at first sight may appear somewhat complicated and even perverse, have only been adopted after careful thought and experiment, and actually do—at least in my deliberate opinion—make it possible to give all necessary facts in the minimum of space" (p. 77).

on the fact of it, not simple, particularly when it occurs in a table full of similar references; furthermore, it contains a possible ambiguity (whether the 1856 American edition is the third edition or the third American edition) which may cause its meaning to be less easy to remember and may keep one turning to the key for reassurance. If it is also necessary to take impressions into account, the symbol becomes even more unwieldly, whether it is "3A2 (56)," "3Ab56," "AIIIii56," or whatever. It is clearly a mistake to try to construct symbols which reveal edition, impression, year, and country of publication at the same time; if a symbol is to serve efficiently its basic function of providing a convenient and unambiguous reference, it cannot bear the weight of so much information, and the editor must decide which pieces of information will produce the most useful symbols in a given situation.

For earlier periods (before the beginnings of machine-printed books), the bibliographical and textual information conveyed by reference to format makes such symbols as F_1, F_2, Q_1, etc., more revealing than reference to years of publication would be — and simpler as well, since the common situation in which more than one quarto appeared in a single year would have to be reflected in letters or other marks appended to the year designations. This system is one of the few well-established conventions in reference notation, and, with usefulness and simplicity on its side, there is little reason to oppose its popularity. For later books, however, format cannot always be determined and in any case is a less useful fact for incorporation in the symbol, since the variants to be reported are likely to be between impressions as well as editions. The most obvious adjustment would be merely to eliminate the format designation and use consecutive numbers (or letters) to refer to successive editions, with attached letters (or numbers) to indicate impressions within any edition. The Hawthorne edition assigns capital roman numerals to editions, with superscript lower-case letters for impressions (e.g., "III^c"), while the Howells edition employs capital letters for editions, with arabic numerals for impressions (e.g., "B2").[27] Such a system is simple and neat; but, if a large number of editions and impressions are involved, it is difficult, even

27. In both cases, however, some of the symbols do not follow the same system. In *The Scarlet Letter*, the first two editions are designated not by roman numerals but by "1850^1" and "1850^2"; and in *Their Wedding Journey* the serial publications are referred to as "S1" and "S2" (chronologically S1 would precede A, and S2 would follow C). Both editions use the mnemonic symbol "MS" for manuscript texts, and the Hawthorne uses "E" to distinguish English editions. In the Wesleyan *Joseph Andrews*, the five editions published during Fielding's lifetime are designated by simple arabic numerals, 1 through 5.

with repeated use, to remember with certainty what many of the symbols stand for, and continual reference to the key is unavoidable. A mnemonic system, on the other hand, may generally be somewhat less simple; but, so long as it is not a great deal more cumbersome, the fact that the user can remember numerous symbols without difficulty may be regarded as an offsetting advantage. (Besides being easier to use, brief symbols may be preferable for practical reasons of economy, especially if the apparatus is set in double column, where longer symbols might produce additional run-over lines.) Probably the most workable and adaptable mnemonic system is to identify editions by letters and to attach years for particular impressions. Thus if only one English and one American edition are involved, the letters "E" and "A" are sufficient, with a given impression referred to as "E1855" or "E55." When more editions are involved, letters representing the name of the publisher or the city of publication could be used; and when more than one impression occurs in a particular year, appended lower-case letters could indicate the sequence within the year. References to manuscript, typescript, and proof could employ the usual symbols "MS," "TS," and "P," as in the Howells edition. Obviously other adjustments would be required in certain situations. If, for example, there is more than one edition from the same publisher, a prefixed number could indicate the fact (as "2H," where "H" stands for the publisher's name), unless year-designations are going to appear so often as to make the symbol cumbersome. In that case the technique of consecutive lettering could be applied, though with some lessening of the mnemonic value of the system, which would then be evident principally in designations of later impressions ("C75" would be the 1875 impression of the third edition).

Regardless of the variations in the basic system, an extremely useful convention which emerges is that a letter by itself stands for all impressions of an edition and a year is attached only when a particular impression is meant. But even this convention is best modified in certain situations: in the case of Irving's *Mahomet* there is only one English impression but nine American printings, all from the same publisher; the sensible way in which the Wisconsin edition assigns symbols here is to use "E" for the English impression and simple year designations without attached letters ("50" for "1850") for the Putnam impressions.[28] This arrangement is perfectly clear and is

28. The system referred to in *Mahomet*, p. 584, note 17, as the standard system for the Irving edition uses such symbols as "1A1," "1A2," etc. It is difficult to decide whether the mnemonic value of these symbols is greater than that of symbols

simpler than if a superfluous "A" or "P" were prefixed to the numbers. In another kind of situation, a letter may even be made to stand for more than one edition. Some volumes of the Crane edition, for example, involve syndicated newspaper pieces, for which the text in one newspaper is no closer to the syndicate's master proof and no more authoritative than the text in many other newspapers. In these instances of "radiating texts," Fredson Bowers introduces (in the fifth volume of the Crane) the symbol "N" to stand for all the located newspaper texts, attaching superscript figures when necessary to identify specific newspapers. The generic letter suggests the essential equality of the various newspaper editions, and the superscript figures distinguish themselves from the regular figures used in other symbols to indicate chronological sequence. The basic principle in each situation is to make the symbols as simple as the textual situation will allow, so long as they retain enough substance to be easily remembered. (Certain symbols which are sometimes used to stand for groups of edition-symbols are commented on below in the discussion of the historical collation.)

In regard to symbols which stand for abstract concepts or relationships rather than concrete documents or impressions, the most prudent course of action is to keep their number as small as possible. Only two such symbols (both suggested in McKerrow's *Prolegomena*) have gained any currency in recent editions, and the reasons for their importance will suggest the kinds of circumstances in which symbols are desirable. Both symbols are used in reporting variants in punctuation: one, the centered tilde or wavy dash ($\sim$), stands for the word previously cited, when the variant is not in the word but in the punctuation associated with it; the other, the caret ($_\wedge$), calls attention to the absence of punctuation at a given point. The justification for the first is not simply that it saves the effort of repeating the identical word, for the small amount of effort saved would be no justification at all if the repetition of the word would be clearer; the fact is, however, that the information is conveyed more clearly with the symbol than without it:

> 218.4 indefatigable,] A; $\sim$;
> 218.4 indefatigable,] A; indefatigable;

In the second example, the reader may see the difference in punctua-

---

incorporating references to years; but under most circumstances of any complexity, symbols which employ the last two digits of the year (instead of the second figure here) and initials of publishers (when more than one publisher in a given country is involved) are probably easier to remember.

tion immediately, but he cannot be sure that no other difference is involved until he examines the two words closely to see that they are identical;[29] in the first, the curved dash tells him instantly that the only variant reported here is that of punctuation. Furthermore, using the curved dash eliminates the possibility of introducing a typographical error into the word the second time it is set; hopefully such an error would be caught in proofreading, but there is no point in needlessly setting up situations in which errors of this kind can enter. The caret is similarly useful in providing a clearer statement than is possible without it:

188.23 approaching,] 57; $\sim_\wedge$
188.23 approaching,] 57; approaching
188.23 approaching,] 57; $\sim$

The difficulty with the last two examples is that in them empty space is made to carry the burden of significance for the entry. It is true, of course, that no foolproof way exists to guarantee the accuracy of what appears in print, and it may be that in proofreading the danger of overlooking an unintentional omission of punctuation is no greater than that of failing to notice an incorrect mark of punctuation. Nevertheless, it is reassuring to the reader to find a caret calling attention to an intended lack of punctuation. In any case, the whole point of the entry is to inform the reader that punctuation is absent at a given spot in a particular text, and it is more straightforward to make this point positively by actually noting the lack than to imply it by simply printing nothing. As these two symbols illustrate, therefore, conceptual symbols are justified when they reduce the chances of error in proofreading, when they are clearer in the context than their referents would be, or when they eliminate the necessity of regarding the absence of something as significant. The wavy dash and the caret may take a few seconds to learn, but the importance of what they contribute easily outweighs whatever unfamiliarity they may at first present to some readers. When a symbol fails to meet these tests — that is, when it is merely a shorthand device and makes no positive contribution to clarity — it is better not adopted, for only a slight proliferation of such symbols can render an apparatus needlessly forbidding. Except in certain editions of manuscripts,[30] there is rarely any need to have more

29. Of course, if a variant in punctuation were not involved, the punctuation would not be included in the reading at all; but the fact that it is included does not rule out the possibility that a spelling variant also exists at this point.

30. As stated above, editions of manuscript material which attempt to show stages of composition may require more

symbols than the curved dash and the caret, along with the symbols for individual documents.

iii. Textual Notes

The section of discursive notes on textual matters is generally entitled "Textual Notes" but sometimes (as in the Irving and Melville editions) is called "Discussions of Adopted Readings." Both titles suggest an important point about the content of these notes: they are comments on individual problematical readings in the text which has been established, and any reading which appears there is the "adopted reading," whether it results from emendation or retention of the copy-text reading. The notes, in other words, discuss not simply emendations but also places where emendations might have been expected and yet, after careful consideration, have not been made. (The principal reason for putting the textual notes before the list of emendations, of course, is to emphasize the fact that they refer to the text itself and not to the emendations.) Since these notes deal with individual readings, it is important to keep general matters out of them and to limit them to cases which raise special problems. Any textual problem which recurs a number of times ought to be taken up in the textual essay, since it then constitutes a general textual problem and since a repetition of the same explanation several times in the notes or extensive cross-references between the notes would be more awkward and, indeed, less clear than one coherent discussion in which all the evidence is brought together.

The most convenient form which the textual notes can take is a citation of page and line number (or act, scene, and line),[31] then the reading under discussion (shortened by an indication of ellipsis if

---

elaborate sets of symbols (including perhaps angle brackets for canceled matter and vertical arrows for insertions, both of which have been fairly widely used); but the general principles for evaluating symbols outlined here would still apply. (Useful examples of symbols for editing manuscripts are found in the Hayford and Sealts *Billy Budd* and in the Emerson and the Irving journals.) It should be noted that complicated alterations in a manuscript can also be set forth in verbal descriptions, without any symbols at all, as in the Ohio State *House of the Seven Gables* and in the California *Hannibal, Huck & Tom* and *Mysterious Stranger Manuscripts*. Fredson Bowers, in his review of the New York

Public Library edition of *Walt Whitman's Blue Book* (ed. Arthur Golden), makes some comments on the relative merits of the two approaches and finds Golden's method an uneconomical mixture of the two—see *JEGP*, 68 (1969), 316-20.

31. A sensible convention which has become well established is to use periods to separate the elements of these reference numbers (e.g., "240.17" or "III.ii.75"). All references in the apparatus should obviously be to the edited text (though in the textual essay a discussion of type damage or defective inking in an early edition might well involve page-line references to that edition).

necessary) , followed in turn by the discussion itself. Generally a square bracket, the conventional sign to distinguish a lemma, separates the reading from the discussion but is of course not essential.[32] The note itself need not say what has been substituted or retained, because the reading of the edited text is the one fact which the reader inevitably knows at the time he consults the note, and if, in addition, it is cited at the head of the note, he has that reading before him on the same page. It is superfluous and uneconomical, therefore, to begin a note by saying, "We retain x at this point because . . ." or "This text adopts the reading y here owing to the fact that . . . ." Instead, all that is required is a direct statement, as simple as possible, of the facts which led to the decision which is already obvious. Thus a note might begin, "X, though unidiomatic, appears in a similar context at 384.27 . . ."; or, "No evidence has been discovered which would support z, the copy-text reading, as standard usage at the time, and the phraseology at 412.16 suggests that z is probably a compositorial error for y . . . ." The notes should be kept as few as possible: there is no point explaining matters easily checked in standard dictionaries or encyclopedias, nor is there any reason to refer to those general problems more cogently handled in the textual essay. Annotation which is unnecessary for either of these reasons only wastes the reader's time[33] and reveals the editor's failure to give sufficient thought to the rationale for textual discussions.

iv.   List of Emendations

The purpose of the list of emendations is to provide a convenient record of all the changes of textual interest[34] — both substantive and

32. A space, for example, would suffice; or, as in the Howells edition, the reading itself need not be cited, since the discussion can be constructed so as to make clear what word or words in the cited line are in question.

33. It might not literally waste a particular reader's time if a given fact, though easily ascertainable in the dictionary, were not already known to him. But an editor cannot pitch his annotation at his text's least informed reader, even if he could discover who that is; some minimum level must be recognized, and it seems reasonable to say that spellings or usages readily discoverable in standard dictionaries fall below that level. (Explanatory, as opposed to textual, annotation is of course a different matter; in an explanatory note it may well be useful to have a brief identification of a historical figure, even though he is listed in the basic biographical reference works. The essential difference is that historical allusions, however numerous, are manageable in number and affect one's understanding of the meaning of the text, whereas the kind of textual notes ruled out here might logically involve half or more of the individual words of a text and by definition would not raise such special problems as interpretation or meaning.)

34. As opposed to those which may be classed, for one reason or another, as nontextual—about which more is said below.

accidental — made in the copy-text by the editor(s) of a given edition. The essential parts of each entry are simply the page and line citation, the reading of the edited text, the symbol representing the source of that reading, and the rejected copy-text reading. The general form which these items usually take includes a square bracket to signify the lemma and a semicolon to separate the source of that reading from the copy-text reading which follows:[35]

10.31   whom] W; who

Another possibility, employed in the Melville edition, eliminates the bracket and the semicolon and places the two readings in separate columns. It could perhaps be argued that this scheme makes the list slightly easier to use for purposes of surveying the nature of the emendations as a whole or constructing various kinds of statistics about them, since the source symbols would more readily show up along the right side of the first column and the copy-text readings would have a common margin in the second column. In any case, if the list is limited strictly to those readings of the copy-text which do not appear in the edited text, no symbol is required after the second reading, since in each case it is by definition the copy-text reading. (In those unusual instances in which a deficient copy-text is rectified by intercalations from another text, so that the copy-text is in effect composite, symbols following the second reading are helpful, even though a separate list of the intercalations would presumably be available.) It is important, however, to understand the reason for setting up a list restricted in this way. So long as a historical collation is to be included in the apparatus, the readings of the copy-text could be ascertained from it and would not necessarily have to be presented in a separate list. But this arrangement would be awkward and inconvenient in two ways: first, since the historical collation is normally limited to substantive variants and since the reader may legitimately wish to know all emendations, including accidentals, the absence of a separate list of emendations would cause the historical collation to become an uneven mixture, combining a complete record of substantive variants with an incomplete record of variants in accidentals; second, discovering what emendations had been made would be somewhat less easy if notation of them were imbedded in the larger historical collation. There is no question about the necessity of having at hand a record of all editorial

---

35. Often each of these entries is placed on a separate line, but sometimes, to save space, they are run on in paragraph form (a form which makes individual entries somewhat less easy to locate).

alterations in the basic authoritative document chosen to provide copy-text; and the greater convenience of having that record as a discrete unit, along with the resulting greater consistency of the historical collation, provides compelling reason for what might otherwise seem a superfluous or repetitive list. The situation is a good illustration of the principle that some sacrifice of economy is more than justified if the result is truly greater clarity and usefulness.

In the light of this summary of the general rationale behind the idea of a separate list of emendations, two common variations in the basic form outlined above are worth examining. One is the segregation of substantives and accidentals into two different lists. This system is used in Bowers's Dekker and the Cambridge Beaumont and Fletcher (where emendations in substantives are listed at the foot of the page and emendations in accidentals at the end of the text), as well as in the Virginia edition of Crane's *Maggie* and the Wesleyan edition of Fielding's *Joseph Andrews* (where both lists come at the end of the text). Since the purpose of a list of emendations is to make the whole range of emendations easier to examine and analyze, it follows that under certain circumstances — particularly when there is an especially large number of emendations in accidentals — the separation of substantives and accidentals will make such examination easier still. In other words, if the total number of emendations is small or even moderate, little is gained by exchanging the simplicity of one list for the complication of two; but when there are a great many emendations, with the possible result that the emendations in substantives would be obscured by being included in the same list as a large number of emendations in accidentals, the data may be much easier to use if the two categories are listed separately. To do so is only to extend the principle of convenience and clarity on which the whole list is founded in the first place. And, by a further extension, certain large categories of automatic alterations within the list of accidentals itself may be separated so as not to overwhelm the other individual alterations of probably greater significance. For example, in the Northwestern-Newberry *Typee* 224 words ending in "-our" in the British copy-text are changed to the American "-or"; once the policy of making this category of changes is adopted, the changes themselves are automatic, and to list all 224 instances in a list of emendations would place an unnecessary impediment in the way of using the list to trace the more important alterations. Yet it is unwise to make any textual changes silently;[36] so these

36. Nontextual changes—those affecting the design of the document embodying the copy-text but not the text itself—may of course be made silently. But to make tex-

224 alterations of spelling are recorded in a footnote to the textual essay. In the Dewey edition many emendations are made in the capitalization of words standing for concepts, and these emendations are gathered into a separate list of "concept capitalization."[37] Whenever there is a large separable category of emendations, this practice is a useful way to avoid, on the one hand, overburdening the main list and, on the other, risking the dangers of silent emendation.

A second variation from the most basic form of an emendations list is the inclusion of at least some of the further history of the rejected copy-text readings. That is, instead of providing simply the copy-text reading at those points where the copy-text has been emended, the entry includes the sigla for certain other editions which agree with the copy-text and sometimes includes the full history of the reading in the collated editions. One often-used plan,[38] following Bowers's Dekker, is to trace, at each point of emendation, the readings of all collated editions (that is, all which might contain textual authority) down to the earliest which can serve as the source of the emendation. Thus in the entry

IV.iii.19   we] Q3; me Q1-2

the earliest edition to contain the adopted emendation is Q3, and the history of the reading down to that point is given (Q1 and Q2) , rather than just the copy-text (Q1) reading; what the history of the reading in any collated editions after Q3 may have been is not revealed here

tual changes silently, even though the categories of such changes are announced and discussed in the textual essay, is to deny the principle that it is risky to allow the absence of a positive designation to be significant (cf. the comments on the caret above). Thus, in the Melville example, merely informing the reader that "-our" spellings are changed to "-or" does not allow him to reconstruct the copy-text with the certainty he would have if he could follow an actual list of changes; for he could not be sure that every "-or" word in the edited text was originally "-our," whereas with a list he would know explicitly just where the changes were made. Furthermore, the specific instances of any type of textual alteration, however trivial they may seem, may be of particular concern to some linguistic, literary, or historical scholar, and the burden of locating these instances should not be placed on the user of the text but is rather the editor's responsibility.

37. The same principle is followed in the Ohio State *Fanshawe* and the California *Mysterious Stranger Manuscripts*, where a number of groupings of identical changes in accidentals are made; here, however, the references are cited in paragraph form in the list of emendations at the point of first occurrence of each type. To some extent this arrangement disrupts the smooth sequential flow of the list of emendations and makes it somewhat less easy to follow; but there is no doubt that it is an advantage to the reader to have these groups of identical emendations brought together somewhere.

38. It is used, for example, in the Fielding, Hawthorne, and Crane editions.

but can be ascertained from the historical collation. In other editions (such as the Howells and the Irving), the complete history (in the collated editions) of the readings at certain points of emendation is given, either explicitly or through a specified system of implication; when this plan is followed, none of these entries reappears in the historical collation, which is then limited to rejected substantives. In both of these arrangements, the distinction between the historical collation and the list of emendations has been blurred to some extent; as a result, the functions of these lists are less clear-cut, and therefore more cumbersome for the editor to explain and less easy for the reader to comprehend. Including in the emendations list the history of the readings down to the point of emendation means that the emendations list becomes partly historical in function and repeats part of the material from the historical collation; but the presence of some historical information in the emendations list does not obviate the need for turning to the historical collation, since anyone wishing to examine the evidence available to the editor at a given point of substantive emendation must look at the historical collation in any case to see if there were variants in editions later than the one from which the emendation is drawn.[39] In the other system, the emendations list takes over even more of the function of the historical collation — indeed, it becomes the historical collation for certain emended readings.[40] And though none of this material is repeated in the other historical list (now containing only rejected substantives), there is no one place where the reader can go to survey all the evidence at the editor's disposal relating to substantive variants. So long as it is agreed in the first place that there is value in having a separate list of emendations, the simplest way of dividing the data is to make one list strictly a record of emendations and the other strictly a historical record. The functions of the two lists are then easier to understand, and the lists are correspondingly easier to refer to and work with.

The question of distinguishing between substantives and accidentals is often not an easy one, because some alterations of punctuation, for instance, do have an effect on meaning; but unless the substantives and accidentals are to be placed in separate lists, the question does not arise in constructing the record of emendations. Two other basic

39. Only if the source of the emendation were the editor himself or the last of the collated editions could the reader know that no additional information would be found in the historical collation.

40. In the Howells edition, when editions later than the one from which an emendation is taken agree with that edition, the complete history is implied in the entry. But when a later edition reverts to the reading of the copy-text, that further history is not offered in the emendations list. See footnote 66.

problems of definition always have to be faced, however: since the list aims to enumerate emendations in the copy-text, the editor must have precise definitions of what constitutes an "emendation" and what is meant by "copy-text" if he is to have a firm basis for deciding what to include in the list and what to leave out. In practice, defining the two concepts becomes a single problem, for however one is defined affects the definition of the other. Editors of critical editions[41] generally agree that there is no point listing as emendations such changes as those in the display capitals at the opening of chapters, in the typographical layout of chapter headings, in the length of lines, or in the wording of running titles. Whether an editor defines "emendation" so as to exclude changes concerned with styling or design, or whether he defines "copy-text" to exclude purely typographical features of the text, the result comes to the same thing in the end. Technically, of course, an "emendation" is simply a correction or alteration, and it is the qualifying phrase "in the copy-text" which through precise definition serves to delimit the kinds of alterations to be listed. There should be no difficulty in defining "copy-text," if the distinction between "text" and "edition" is observed: "text" is an abstract term, referring to a particular combination of words, spelled and punctuated a particular way; "edition" is a concrete term referring to all copies of a given printed form of a text. Thus a "copy-text" is that authoritative text chosen as the basic text to be followed by an editor in preparing his own text, and it does not include the formal or typographical design of the document which embodies that text.[42] The type-face, the width and height of the type-page, the arrangement of headings and ornaments, and the like, are all parts of the design of an edition but are not elements of the text which is contained in that edition; similarly, the formation of letters, the spacing between words, the color of the ink, and the like, are not parts of the text embodied in a manuscript. It does no harm for an editor to enumerate certain features of design which he regards as nontextual, but it is not actually necessary for him to do so if he has defined "copy-text" carefully, for his definition will have excluded such details as external to the text.[43] Omission of any

41. Of course, editors of facsimile or diplomatic editions are necessarily concerned with formal and typographical matters and must take them into account.

42. See G. T. Tanselle, "The Meaning of Copy-Text: A Further Note," SB, 23 (1970), 191-96.

43. Nontextual details often play a great role in the bibliographical analysis which leads to the establishment of the text (as when wrong-font types allow a bibliographer to learn something about the timing of the distribution of type from preceding formes or about the order of formes through the press), but they are nevertheless not a part of the text.

notice of alterations in design does not constitute a category of silent emendations in the copy-text, since the design is not a part of that text at all.

One problem in the specification of copy-text is raised by the existence of variations within an impression. Such variations may be caused by stop-press corrections or by type which slipped or shifted during the course of printing. The precise definition of copy-text in terms of particular states of the variations obviously determines which of these readings qualify for inclusion in the list of emendations: thus if uncorrected formes are taken as copy-text, the only press-variants which would turn up in the emendations would be those adopted from corrected formes; and if the correct spacings at points where letters shift around are regarded as characteristics of the copy-text, the only variants of this kind which would be reported in the emendations list would be those for which no copy with correct spacings had been found. The decision as to whether correct or incorrect states are taken as copy-text may vary in individual circumstances, but the point is that the copy-text must be defined in terms of the specific variants within the impression which embodies it; for this abstract "text" must have one and only one reading at any given point,[44] and to define a copy-text merely in terms of an impression is not sufficiently rigorous, since more than one reading may exist at many points within various copies of that impression.[45] Because sheets embodying corrected states of some formes (or correct spacings of letters) will be bound with sheets embodying uncorrected states of other formes (or incorrect spacings of other letters), it is unlikely — when more than a few press-variants occur — that any single physical copy can be found which contains the entire copy-text.[46] Emendations in the copy-text, therefore, are not simply emendations in the text of a particular copy; and the copy-text remains an authoritative documentary form of the text, even though no one existing physical entity (or even no one physical entity that ever existed)

44. With the exception that, when all variants are manifestly incorrect and their order is indeterminate (as in the example cited in footnote 48), designating only one of them as the copy-text reading becomes a pointless exercise. (In the case of a manuscript copy-text, of course, alternative uncanceled readings may well exist at individual points.)

45. Thus Bowers, in the general textual introduction to the Cambridge Beaumont and Fletcher, defines the copy-texts as embodying the readings of corrected formes: "The normal assumption is that the present edited text reproduces the corrected readings when press-variation is present if no contrary record is made" (I,xix).

46. Since a photographic reproduction of a single copy is often used as printer's copy for a critical edition, it follows that not every textual alteration marked on that copy is an emendation in the copy-text, for some may bring the printer's copy into conformity with the copy-text.

happens to preserve it. The exigencies of producing a book — the fact that the forme is the unit in printing and the sheet the unit in gathering a copy of a book together for binding[47] — makes it natural that the finished product may contain a mixture of states. One may have to examine a large number of copies of a given impression to discover the press-variants in it, and one can never be sure that any copies left unexamined do not contain additional variants. In the Ohio State *Scarlet Letter*, for instance, collation of eight copies of the first impression produced five variants, all examples of loosened type which either shifted position or failed to print. At four of the points of variance, some copies carried the correct reading; but in the remaining case one copy read "t obelieve," and the others read "tobelieve." Since the correct spacing in this one instance did not occur in any of the examined copies, it had to be listed as an emendation, whereas the other four variants do not enter the emendations list at all, since the correct form of each did appear in at least one copy.[48] If, however, another copy were to be collated in which "to believe" appeared correctly, that form would no longer be an emendation and should not appear on the emendations list. As with any other research, the conclusions must be based on the evidence at hand; and that evidence, in any inductive investigation, is probably incomplete. If the number of surviving copies is small, one can examine all the available evidence and still be far from the truth; if the number is large, one may reasonably wish to set some practical limits on the extent of the investigation. But in either case the results are liable to modification by the next copy which turns up. The danger is unavoidable; but at least one can operate with precision and rigor within the limits of the located evidence. Part of what that entails is defining the copy-text in terms of press-variants (saying, for example, "the text in a copy of the 1850 impression with x at 172.15, y at 234.21, and z 278.11"), for only in this way can one know what constitutes an emendation and belongs in the list.

There are some variations among copies of a given impression which are nontextual and need not be reported, any more than differences in design between the copy-text print and the critical edition

---

47. Some further discussion of this point appears in G. T. Tanselle, "The Use of Type Damage as Evidence in Bibliographical Description," *Library*, 5th ser., 23 (1968), esp. 347-48.

48. When neither form is correct, as in "t obelieve"/"tobelieve," it makes little difference which is considered the copy-text form, since an emendation is required in either case; in such instances, especially when the order of the variants is not clear, there is no point in choosing among incorrect forms, and both readings might as well be listed as the rejected copy-text readings.

need be specified. Usually it is not difficult to distinguish between these nontextual press-variants and the press-variants of textual significance just discussed. They are frequently due to differences in inking or in the amount of damage which a particular piece of type (or letter in a plate) has suffered. Variations in inking need not be reported if all the letters are visible, but if the inking is so poor that some letters do not show up at all in any copy examined, the variation is in effect a textual one of the kind described above. Battered letters or marks of punctuation — whether or not the batter varies from copy to copy — can be silently corrected without involving textual emendation, so long as there is no question what letters or marks are intended. But if the damage is great enough to raise possible doubt about their identity, any attempt at correction becomes a textual emendation and must be listed. Thus if a dot appears in the middle of a sentence at a place where it could be the upper half of either a colon or a semicolon, and if no examined copy shows enough of the lower half for identification, a textual decision is required to correct the punctuation; or if a small mark appears between two words where it could perhaps be a hyphen, and if no examined copy clears up the matter, the editor's decision to consider it a hyphen rather than, say, a part of the damaged preceding letter is a textual one; or if a letter which ought to be "e" appears to be a "c" in every examined copy, the correction is a textual emendation. The importance of having access to a large number of copies for this kind of checking is obvious. Most editors rightly feel that it is unfortunate if their lists of emendations have to be overburdened with entries which are probably not really emendations at all and which might be eliminated if more copies were available for examination. But without those copies, there is no alternative to recording them as emendations, since there is no documentary proof that the copy-text contained the correct readings.

Finally, a few minor points about form should be noted. (1) First, the list will be clearer in the end if each lemma consists simply of the word or words which constitute the emendation, without any of the surrounding words.[49] Occasionally an editor will feel that it would be helpful to the reader to have an additional word or two of the context, to enable him to see more clearly the nature of the alteration involved, while he is looking at the list. It is difficult to say, however, what would be sufficient context for this purpose, but generally a few words would not be enough; and as the cited readings become longer, the actual

49. Similarly, punctuation following (or preceding) a word need not be cited when only the word, and not the punctuation, is at issue.

emendations become less easy to pick out, with the result that this approach makes the list more difficult to use (as well as less consistent, since there would be no way of defining objectively how much should be cited). The only times when a word in addition to the actual emendation should be reported are when the same word as the emendation appears elsewhere in the same line (so that one of the two words adjacent to the emendation is required to identify it), when a mark of punctuation is emended (so that the word preceding the punctuation— or after it, in the case of opening quotation marks — is convenient, and sometimes essential, for locating the emendation), and when something is deleted from the copy-text (so that the point of deletion can be located). (Even the first of these can be eliminated if one adopts Greg's device of using prefixed superscript numbers to indicate which of two or more identical words is at issue, but this system is perhaps somewhat less easy for the reader to follow.) (2) A second formal matter which might cause difficulty is the notation of a missing letter (or letters). When loosened type causes letters to shift, without any letters failing to print, there is of course no problem because the usual between-word spacing can be used (as in "t obelieve"); but when loosened type or a damaged plate results in the complete disappearance of letters, it is important to show that space for these letters exists. It clearly makes a difference whether a reading is reported as "race" or as "[ ]race," for the second shows that a letter has dropped out and that the original word was "brace," "grace," or "trace." These empty spaces can be noted in various ways. The Hawthorne edition simply uses a blank space, which works well enough between words but is less clear if the missing letter is at the beginning or end of a word; Kable's edition of *The Power of Sympathy*[50] employs a caret to mark the space, creating an ambiguity since the caret is also used to signify the absence of punctuation; and the Melville edition uses square brackets, which may be somewhat cumbersome but are fairly suggestive and do not conflict with another symbol. (3) Another question of notation concerns those emendations which are in fact additions to the copy-text — that is, words or passages for which there is no counterpart in the copy-text. One common editorial device is to use the abbreviation "*Om.*" or "*om.*" to signify the lack of corresponding text at a given point in the copy-text. If the abbreviation is specifically defined in this way, it is clear enough; but if it is not explicitly defined and is allowed to suggest "omitted," it can be misleading, since the omission of anything implies

50. William Hill Brown, *The Power of Sympathy*, ed. William S. Kable (Columbus: Ohio State University Press, 1969).

that something was available to be omitted, whereas the additions to a copy-text are often passages not yet written at the time the copy-text was completed. A phrase like "[*not present*]," which suggests no direction of change, would avoid the problem and would require no explanation.[51] (4) There remains the question of adjusting the symbols for editions and impressions to take variant states into account. If one of the uncorrected formes of a particular sheet is taken as copy-text but requires emendation at several points from the corresponding corrected forme, the symbol indicating the source of the emendations must note the state involved. For hand-printed books the conventional method is to attach a "u" or "c" in parentheses to the symbol for the edition — "$Q1$ (u)," "$F2$ (c)" — though of course superscript letters could also be employed. For later books, if the symbol for a given impression ends with figures, states can be represented by suffixed letters ("$A55a$," "$A55b$") or — regardless of the makeup of the symbol — by superscript letters ("$A55^a$"); these letters signify the sequence of presently known states of individual readings within an impression (not necessarily "uncorrected" and "corrected" states of formes).[52] Because no single copy of a book may contain all the uncorrected or corrected formes, or all the earliest or latest states of variants, these attached letters — for books of any period — must be understood to refer, not to physical "books" (that is, not to entire copies of a given impression), but to readings that may or may not be present in any individual copy of the proper impression. A copy containing one $Q1$ (u) reading may contain other $Q1$ (c) readings, or a copy containing some $A55^a$ readings may have other $A55^b$ readings. For this reason the superscript letter may have an advantage over the suffixed one in emphasizing the fact that it is essentially a different kind of symbol — referring to a stage of variation at a particular point within an impression, not to the whole impression (or edition), as does the basic symbol to which it is attached. Many formal matters such as these may seem of minor consequence in themselves, but, taken together, the decisions regarding them may make the diffrence between a list of emendations

51. Editorial comments of this kind should of course be enclosed in square brackets to show that they are not actual readings; italicizing them is usually not sufficient, since italic words could appear in the text.

52. In other words, the letters do not stand for general stages of revision or alter- ation but refer only to the sequence at a given point. Thus there is no reason to suppose that one reading labeled "$A55b$" occurred at the same time or in the same process of revision as another with the same label; all that the symbol implies is that these are the second readings at each of these points.

which is cumbersome and perhaps misleading and one which is convenient, logical, and easily understood.

v.   List of Ambiguous Line-End Hyphenation

Until Fredson Bowers called attention to the matter in 1962,[53] no
consideration (to my knowledge) had been given to the editorial problems raised by possible compound words hyphenated at the ends of
lines. Such hyphenation clearly presents problems in two ways: first,
when a possible compound is hyphenated at the end of a line in the
copy-text, the editor must decide whether to print the word in his
edition as a hyphenated word or as a single unhyphenated word; second, when a possible compound is hyphenated at the end of a line in
a scholarly critical edition, the editor must have some means for
informing his readers whether this word should be reproduced, in any
quotation from the text, as a hyphenated word or as a single unhyphenated word. As a result, the necessity of including two hyphenation
lists in the apparatus of critical editions cannot be denied. The first
of these lists, recording line-end hyphenation in the copy-text, is essential to complete the record of editorial decisions. The editor's decision
whether or not to retain a line-end hyphen in a given word can be
more difficult than some of his decisions reported in the list of emendations. Yet it does not really produce an emendation, for if he prints
the hyphen he is only retaining what, after all, is already present in the
copy-text; and if he eliminates the hyphen he is only treating it as the
printer's convention for marking a run-over word. Obviously some line-
end hyphens present no problems: those simply breaking a word
which cannot possibly be a compound (as "criti-|cism"), where the
hyphen is only a typographical convention, not to be retained when
the word will fit within a line; and those dividing compounds in which
the second element is capitalized (as "Do-|Nothing"), where the
hyphen is to be retained whenever the word is printed. But in between
is a large area of possible compounds where no automatic answers can
be given; the treatment of these hyphens depends on various factors
(the author's characteristic usage, the conventions of the time, and the
like), and the editor is not providing readers with a full record of his
textual decisions unless he specifies these cases. The second list, recording line-end hyphenation in the editor's own text, is necessary if the
editor is to complete his task of establishing a text — for if there are
places in a text where a reader does not know precisely what reading

53. In the Ohio State edition of *The
Scarlet Letter* and in his paper before the
South Atlantic Modern Language Asocia-
tion (cited in its 1964 published form in
footnote 4 above).

the editor has adopted, the text cannot be considered established. An editor has failed in part of his responsibility if he produces a text in which the reader, quoting a particular passage, has to make decisions on his own about the hyphenation of certain possible compounds.[54] Both these hyphenation lists, then, are indispensable parts of an editorial apparatus. (For convenience, I shall refer to the first kind of list described here as the "copy-text list" and the second as the "critical-text list.")

Because the Center for Editions of American Authors has required editions prepared under its auspices to include the two hyphenation lists (as specified in its 1967 *Statement of Editorial Principles*), the value and importance of these lists are becoming more widely recognized. Among the CEAA editions themselves, however, there are some variations in form, arrangement, and approach; and a glance at the principal variations will suggest some of the factors which need to be considered in setting up these lists. Probably the most noticeable difference among editions is in the order of the two lists. One may feel that it makes little difference about the order, so long as the two lists are there; but if an editor is trying to follow some consistent rationale in the overall arrangement of the entire apparatus, then surely one arrangement of the hyphenation lists fits that scheme better than another. Several editions (the Crane, Fielding, Hawthorne, and Simms and *The Mark Twain Papers*) place the critical-text list before the copy-text list, while several others (the Dewey, Howells, Irving, and Melville) reverse this order. The general rationale outlined above suggests placing nearest the text those parts of the apparatus taking up decisions affecting the edited text. Following this plan, the copy-text list should precede the critical-text list, for the copy-text list does record editorial decisions and in this sense is an appendage to the list of emendations (the immediately preceding section, according to this arrangement); the critical-text list, on the other hand, does not involve editorial decisions in establishing the text[55] but only printer's decisions

54. And obviously, if the reader is accurately to reconstruct the copy-text from the critical text, he must have this information for interpreting the critical text.

55. If a possible compound coincidentally hyphenated at the end of a line in both the copy-text and the critical text is not recorded in a separate list, then it would appear in both these lists, and to that extent words involving editorial decisions might appear in the critical-text list. But their presence there has nothing to do with the fact that their established forms result from editorial decisions; they are there only because they are hyphenated at the ends of lines in the critical text. The fact that editorial decisions are involved can be learned only by noting the reappearance of the same words in the copy-text list.

in setting the text (decisions necessitated by the exigencies of right-margin justification).

Indeed, the functions of the two lists are so different that it is somewhat artificial to place them side by side; only the superficial fact that both deal with hyphenation has caused them to be grouped together. The copy-text list fits logically into the textual apparatus because it is historically oriented: that is, it records certain words in a historical document about which the editor of a critical text has to make decisions. But the critical-text list is merely a guide to the proper interpretation of certain fortuitous typographical features (hyphens) of a given edition of that critical text; its usefulness is not in studying textual problems but simply in *reading* the edited text. In other words, the edited text is not really complete without the critical-text list, for without it certain hyphens in that text would be ambiguous. The other parts of the apparatus are important to certain audiences, but the edited text could of course be printed without them; the critical-text list, on the other hand, is essential to all audiences, and the edited text should never be printed without it. If, for example, a publisher leases a CEAA text and reproduces it photographically, he should include the critical-text list, whether or not he is including any other apparatus; if, instead, he sets the CEAA text in type anew, he should prepare a new critical-text list which applies to his own edition. It is extremely unfortunate that the copy-editors' convention for indicating to the printer which hyphens are to be retained (one hyphen above another, resembling an equals sign) has never become a generally accepted convention for use on the printed page; if an editor could utilize such a double system of line-end hyphens, the printed form of his edited text would be self-contained, without any typographical ambiguity requiring a separate list to elucidate.[56] As matters stand, however, to do so would violate the notion of clear text, since the double hyphen would strike the reader as an unfamiliar symbol. It will not be possible, therefore, in the foreseeable future to eliminate the critical-text list, and yet it presents something of an anomaly in the textual apparatus. Logically it should be separated from the rest of the apparatus and placed as an independent entity immediately following the text. Yet it is unrealistic to think that the easy grouping together of all matters connected with hyphens will be readily superseded; and

56. Of course, an editor could insist that the lines of the text be reset until no hyphen which should be retained in quotation fell at the end of a line; in practice, this approach is often prohibitively expensive and, in some cases, virtually impossible of achievement.

one can only hope that this arrangement does not obscure the widely different purposes of the two lists nor cause reprint publishers to over-look the relevance of the critical-text list to their concerns.

Some editions contain more than two lists in the section on line-end hyphenation. For instance, a third list that sometimes appears (as in the Crane, Dewey, Fielding, Hawthorne, and Simms editions) is a short one recording those instances in which a line-end hyphen occurs in a possible compound in the critical text at the very point where a line-end hyphen also falls in the copy-text. The function of a separate list of these words is to show that the established forms in these cases result from editorial decisions. Nevertheless, these words do not logi-cally constitute a third category; they merely belong to both the preced-ing categories. A simpler arrangement, therefore, would be to have only the two lists — the copy-text list and the critical-text list — with certain words appearing in both. The introductory note to the critical-text list could not then say — as these notes do in some editions — that the words occurred with hyphens (or without hyphens) in the middle of lines in the copy-text; it would have to say that for each word the "established copy-text form" is listed. If the reader wishes to know which forms were established through editorial decision, he can quickly check the appropriate spot in the copy-text list to see if the word also turns up there.[57] Still another hyphenation list which has been employed (as in *The House of the Seven Gables* and *The Marble Faun*) records line-end hyphens in the critical text which are true emendations (that is, hyphens at points where none are present in the copy-text). Again, such words do not form a separate category but, rather, readings that belong in two categories — in this case the critical-text hyphenation list and the list of emendations. The simplicity of an arrangement which keeps the number of word-division lists down to the basic two is not merely an advantage to the bewildered reader who may never have encountered any hyphenation lists before; it also dramatizes the logical division between the two functions which hyphenation lists serve.[58] Furthermore, it sets as few obstacles as

---

57. And if the editor feels that it is of some help to the reader to have such words noted, a symbol can be placed beside those words which appear in both lists. (The Melville edition uses a dagger for this purpose.)

58. And emphasizing this division helps to make clear—as removing the critical-text list to another location would make still clearer—why some words turn up in two lists: since the critical-text list has nothing to do with editorial decisions, any word in it which in fact results from an editorial decision must naturally be found also in one of the two lists which record editorial decisions—the list of emendations or the copy-text hyphenation list.

possible in the way of the quoter or reprint publisher by presenting one, and only one, consolidated list of ambiguous hyphens in the critical edition.

The matter of deciding just which line-end hyphens are to appear in these lists can be approached in two ways. One method is to list all compound words and all words which might be regarded as compound, if they are hyphenated at a line-end, recording the forms they should take when they fall within the line; such a list would contain both hyphenated and unhyphenated words. Another method is to list only those words whose line-end hyphens are to be retained when the words come within a line and to say that all other line-end hyphens can be ignored as compositorial word-division; such a list would contain only hyphenated words.[59] Each method has its advantages and disadvantages. The first system has the advantage of being explicit (listing all words about which a question might arise), whereas the second proceeds by implication (making the absence of a word assume positive significance); on the other hand, the second system has the advantage of covering in condensed fashion — through its combination of direct statement and implication — every instance of line-end hyphenation in an entire work, whereas the first may result in an extremely long list and still omit words that some readers would consider "possible compounds." Presumably one could infer, even in the first type of list, that omitted instances of line-end hyphens are not significant (that is, that those hyphens should not be retained in transcription), but the fact remains that the actual content of the list is not precisely defined, since the question of what constitutes a "possible compound" is a subjective one. It might never occur to one person to think that the line-end hyphens in "cup-|board" or "inter-|view," for example, should be retained, while another person might expect to find them in the list for explicit guidance. The first kind of list, in other words, is somewhat inefficient, because for all its length it may always fail to note words considered "possible compounds" by some people; the second type of list, in contrast, can in shorter space be positively complete, because

59. It should be clear that the opposite possibility (employed in the first volume of the Simms edition)—that is, recording only those instances of possible compounds hyphenated at line-ends in the critical text which should be transcribed as single unhyphenated words—leaves ambiguities unresolved, for the reader still has to distinguish between purely compositorial hyphens, dividing unhyphenated words at line-ends, and the hyphens which should in fact be retained. (Of course, listing *every* line-end hyphen which should be eliminated in transcription—the only way to make this approach unambiguous—would be foolishly inefficient, since the majority of line-end hyphens in any printed work normally fall into this category, and the list would be extended inordinately.)

the criterion for inclusion does not involve any attempt to define "possible compounds."

This second type of approach, then, might seem preferable for the hyphenation lists in a scholarly edition, were it not for two further considerations. In the first place, this approach, for full effectiveness, requires that one have at hand the edition referred to. That is, if an editor says that all line-end hyphens, other than those listed, are merely compositorial, the reader who wishes to look over those allegedly compositorial hyphens must consult the edition under discussion and run his eye down the right margin of the pages. Furthermore, if the policy of an apparatus is to record all the editor's textual decisions, those instances in which a line-end hyphen in a possible compound has been dropped are just as significant for inclusion as those instances in which it has been retained; to define the first category by a process of elimination (as what remains after the second category is specified)[60] is as unfair to the reader as to make silent emendations, for it requires him to search through a text himself to locate the individual instances. It becomes obvious, therefore, that one of these methods is more appropriate for one of the hyphenation lists, and the other method is more appropriate for the other list. The copy-text list should follow the method of noting all possible line-end compounds and showing the editorially established form of each, with or without hyphens — for this list refers to a document outside the volume which the reader has in his hands at the moment, and it records editorial decisions necessary for the reader to know about in evaluating the editorial process or in reconstructing the copy-text. The critical-text list, on the other hand, more appropriately follows the system which notes only those line-end hyphens to be retained in transcription — for this list refers to the printed form of the text in the volume already in the reader's hands, and it has nothing to do with editorial decisions. In other words, the more explicit system is necessary for a full recording of editorial decisions, whereas the more concise system is preferable for elucidating purely typographical ambiguities of the new edition. Once again, the differences in the purposes of the two lists are reflected in differences in method. If the hyphenation lists are set up in this way, and if their introductory comment[61] and their form[62] are kept as simple as possible,

60. Of course, what remains is actually made up of two categories: possible compounds which, by editorial decision, should not contain hyphens, and words which are not possible compounds and which naturally do not contain hyphens.

61. Because the functions of these lists are not always grasped at first by the general reader, it is important that the headnote to each list not make the lists sound more complicated than they are. For the copy-text list, nothing more is needed

the reader should have no difficulty following them or understanding why, in their different ways, they are important.

vi. Historical Collation

The remaining principal division of the apparatus is the one which records the variant readings that have occurred in significant editions of the text. Its emphasis is historical, as distinguished from the list of emendations, where the emphasis is on the changes made by the present editor in the basic text he is following. Some of those changes were probably adopted from (or noted in) other editions, but the primary function of the entries in the list of emendations is not to provide the history of the variant readings at those points;[63] such history, as well as the history of other variants (where no emendation of the copy-text occurred), is reserved for this "historical collation," as it is often called. Two limitations are normally imposed on the historical collation. In the first place, it does not usually survey (at least in the case of nineteenth- and twentieth-century works) every edition of the text which has ever appeared, but only those of possible textual significance; thus all authorized editions which were published during the author's lifetime are included (since any changes present in them could have resulted from his revision), as well as any posthumous editions which purport to utilize newly available authoritative documents or which could conceivably have utilized such evidence.[64]

---

than a statement of this kind: "The following are the editorially established forms of possible compounds which were hyphenated at the ends of lines in the copy-text." And for the critical-text list: "In quotations from the present edition, no line-end hyphens are to be retained except the following."

62. The simplest form is merely to list, following the appropriate page-line number, the word in its established form. Since the place where line-end division occurred is obvious in most cases, there is usually no need to mark it with a vertical line. Of course, when the point of division is not obvious—as in a compound with three elements and two hyphens—a vertical line can be used; but even then the vertical line is useful only in the copy-text list, not in the critical-text list. (The Dewey edition, in the critical-text list, gives the word first as a lemma, showing the line-ending with a vertical stroke, and then the established hyphenated form; such repetition does not make the function of the list clearer and indeed would seem to add a needless complication.) Furthermore, in the critical-text list, where every page-line citation would technically contain two line numbers (since each cited word runs over a line-end in the critical text, to which all citations are keyed), the awkwardness of the double-line reference serves no real purpose, and each page-line citation might as well refer simply to the line on which the word begins.

63. Sometimes certain of these entries do in fact provide histories of the readings involved, but that is not their primary function.

64. Certain other editions which, because of their wide popularity or impressive

Second, the historical collation is generally limited to substantive variants, on the grounds that variants in accidentals from edition to edition
are of so little significance (particularly in light of Greg's rationale for
selecting a copy-text) as not to justify the great amount of space and
labor which a record of them would entail.[65] This limitation obviously
necessitates distinguishing substantives from accidentals, not always an
easy task; but if the distinction is to be meaningful, one should guard
against admitting variants in punctuation into the historical collation
as "semisubstantives" unless they clearly involve substantial alterations
of meaning.

Some editions (such as the Howells and the Irving) limit the historical collation in one further way: by entitling it "Rejected Substantives" and listing in it only those substantive variants which are not
adopted as emendations in the copy-text. Under the basic form of this
system, each entry in the list of emendations must provide the full
history of the readings at that spot, because none of these entries will
reappear later in the historical collation. In effect, the historical collation is split into two lists, one containing entries involving emendation
of the copy-text and another covering the remaining substantive variants, where no emendation is involved. (In another version of this
system, any agreements with the rejected copy-text reading in editions
later than the one from which the emendation is drawn — or any
additional post-copy-text readings — would appear in the list of rejected
substantives, and thus in these cases the list of emendations would not
provide the entire history of the variants.) [66] The obvious motive for
this arrangement is economy, and there is no doubt that in many
cases the apparatus can be considerably shortened by the procedure;
how much it is shortened depends on the number of substantive emendations (exclusive of those initiated by the editor at points where no

---

scholarship, have been influential in the
history and study of the text may also be
included in the historical collation, even
though the variant readings present in
them can carry no authorial sanction; indeed, editions of Elizabethan works often
include practically every previous edition
in their historical collations and thus provide the complete history of the treatment
of the text with regard to substantives.

65. In the Melville edition the historical
collation is entitled "List of Substantive
Variants."

66. This plan is followed in the Howells
edition (note the entries in *Their Wedding
Journey* for 102.28 or in *Literary Friends
and Acquaintance* for 223.23). As a result of
the overlapping function of the two lists
under this plan, the reader cannot know,
when looking at the list of emendations,
whether or not any given substantive entry
contains the complete history of the variants at that point and must turn to the
list of rejected substantives to see if any
additional history is recorded there.

other variants exist), since under this system none of them would have to be repeated in the historical collation. If a particular text requires an extremely large number of substantive emendations, it is possible that so much space might be saved as to justify this method on grounds of economy alone; but in most situations it is perhaps questionable whether the saving of a few pages is the most important consideration. The price paid for the economy, after all, is some loss of clarity and convenience. For one thing, the functions of the two lists become less clear-cut and distinct and therefore less easy to explain to the reader and less easy for him to comprehend: one list serves both as a record of editorial emendations (substantives and accidentals) in the copy-text and as a partial historical collation, and the other completes the historical collation (for substantive variants only). In addition, the reader making a serious study of the variants may be somewhat inconvenienced by not having the full range of historical evidence regarding substantive variants brought together in a single list or at a single place,[67] necessitating a search through the emendations list. Of course, if the emendations are divided into two lists, one for substantives and one for accidentals (as they probably should be whenever a list of "rejected substantives" replaces a full historical collation), this objection carries less force. But the fact remains that an emendations list is predicated on the idea that it is important to have a concise and readily accessible record of all textual changes made in the copy-text; if that list is made to carry part of the burden of the historical collation as well, then it becomes in effect a segment of the historical collation, and the logic of having two lists becomes less clear. In most cases, it would seem that the slightly greater space required for a full historical collation (that is, one which includes adopted as well as rejected substantive variants) is offset by the advantages of keeping the historical evidence intact — and separate from the record of the editor's conclusions based on that evidence.

The form of the entry in a historical collation is essentially the same as in a list of emendations, except that the sources of the rejected readings must be specified (whereas in a list of emendations the rejected readings are by definition from the copy-text and thus do not have to be individually identified as such). In addition, since the reading from the edited text provides the lemma in each case, there is strictly speaking no necessity to identify its source, since if it is not from the copy-text its source is recorded in the list of emendations.

67. There might be more than one list with historical emphasis, as discussed below.

Even in a simple entry, therefore, these differences reflect the differing functions of the two lists:

> 10.31   whom] W; who   [*list of emendations*]
> 10.31   whom] who 50-60,E [*historical collation*]

Although it is not necessary in the historical collation to specify the source(s) of the lemmata, it does no harm, particularly in the cases of those which are emendations. Furthermore, the list of emendations names only the immediate source of an emendation, and if the historical collation does not specify later editions in which this reading occurs, the history of the variant is provided only by implication:

> 127.4   moan] moon 37-42; mean 60-70
> 127.4   moan] 45-57; moon 37-42; mean 60-70

Both these entries convey the same information, but in the first the reader has to be told that any of the collated editions not specified agree with the lemma, while in the second the history of the lemma is provided explicitly. It is a common practice to say that editions not listed agree with the reading to the left of the bracket; when a great many editions and variants are involved, the economy of this system no doubt makes it a sensible one, but it does require that the reader be familiar enough with the editions collated to remember which ones are not specified (or else he has to turn to the list of collated editions to see which ones they are). Although the entries can be run on in paragraph form, they are generally presented on separate lines, and specifying the history of the lemma does not usually cause an entry to spill over into a second line; under these circumstances, there seems little reason not to aid the reader by naming explicitly (or in inclusive form, as "45-57") all the editions covered.[68] One of McKerrow's symbols, the plus sign, has frequently been used to signify all collated editions later than the one indicated; using the plus sign is preferable to allowing this information to be implied by the absence of certain

68. However, impressions of an edition need not be specified when there are no variants in them. Thus if "A" stands for the only American edition, that symbol alone could signify all the collated impressions of the American edition. But if a variant first shows up in, say, "A1847" (or "A47"), its history will be represented more clearly by "A47-76" than by defining "A47" to include all subsequent collated impressions. The use of inclusive notation, of course, does not result in the appearance of every siglum in each entry, but, when the symbols include mnemonic allusions to years or sequences, the grouping which would include any given siglum is obvious. For convenient reference, a list of all collated editions (or impressions) with their sigla should be included in the headnote to the historical collation (as well as in the headnote to any other sections in which the sigla are used).

sigla, but unless the number of editions is very large it would be still better to specify them individually.[69] When they are so specified, the reader can study the variants of any given edition by running his eye down the page and noting the appearances of the proper siglum (or the groupings which include it), without having to remember or figure out where that siglum would fall in entries which do not list it (or clearly refer to it). Finally, the form of the entire list may be further modified by leaving out the brackets and semicolons and arranging the readings in columns. The advantages are the same as when the column form is used in the emendations list, but the limitation of this arrangement is that it is awkward if more than two or three variants are involved in individual entries. When, for example, there is only one American and one English edition — as in the case of Melville — a two-column historical collation is feasible;[70] but when a work went through more than two editions, with the resulting possibility of more variant readings (but not the same number in each instance), the conventional form, with brackets following lemmata and semicolons following sigla, is to be preferred.[71]

69. A related symbol of McKerrow's, the plus-and-minus sign (±), is put to good use in Bowers's Dekker to stand for a general but not exact agreement among several editions, where the minor variations are irrelevant to the main fact which the entry is recording The same method could be applied to the specification of individual editions by enclosing in parentheses those sigla which refer to editions containing the slightly variant readings. (Such a practice would conform to McKerrow's use of parentheses, referred to above, to indicate "a reading which is not *identical* with one which is given but which is *substantially* the same in meaning or intention so far as the purpose of the note is concerned" [p. 82].) Sometimes earlier editions went too far in multiplying symbols of this sort: in the opening volume of the Variorum Shakespeare (1874), for example, Furness employs "&c," "*et cet.*," and "*the rest*" to stand for different groups of editions.

Another symbol relevant to the matter of inclusive notation is the dollar sign, which has been borrowed from descriptive bibliography and introduced into textual apparatus by Bowers in the fifth volume of the Crane edition; it is used there to mean "all" or "every" when attached to symbols which subsume a number of documents (such as "N," the syndicated newspaper texts of a given work). The symbol is useful in "$N" to emphasize the fact that all the examined N texts agree and "$N (—N4)" to reinforce the statement that all but one agree; but since "N" is already a generic symbol, defined as all the examined newspaper texts, the dollar sign is essentially a device for adding emphasis rather than for condensing the statement.

70. Even in such a case, a variant at a point of emendation is somewhat awkward, since the reading in the edited text must be cited as the key for the entry, and it is different in these instances from the first-column (copy-text) reading.

71. It would be highly undesirable to have a situation in which a reading from a third edition had to be placed in a third column, even though it agreed with the reading in one of the other two editions; such an arrangement would make it more difficult for the reader to note agreements among editions and would open up more possibilities for typographical errors in the list.

Variants within impressions raise special problems for the historical collation, just as they do for the list of emendations. Since a knowledge of such variants in the copy-text edition is necessary for the precise specification of copy-text, they should certainly be recorded (at least those which involve more than variations in inking or slight type damage) ; but since these variations are likely to be in accidentals as well as substantives, not all of them would be appropriate for recording in the historical collation (if, as usual, that collation is limited to substantives). It seems sensible, therefore, to set up a special list to record such variants[72] (examples are the lists of press-variants in the Dekker and Beaumont-Fletcher editions and the lists of variants within the first and within the second editions in the Ohio State *Scarlet Letter*); alternatively — or additionally — these variants can be discussed in the textual essay as part of the definition of copy-text or of the bibliographical comment on other editions (as in the Melville edition). If any of the variants do turn out to be substantives, they should also be reported in the regular historical collation, since they form a part of the full history of the readings at these points. But determining which ones are substantives sometimes turns — as information about variants within impressions necessarily turns — on the particular group of copies collated or examined. In Chapter 70 of Melville's *White-Jacket,* for instance, the American edition (copy-text) reads "President" at a point where many copies of the English edition read "[ ]resident"; the space suggests that a "P" failed to print, but what did print — "resident" — is a different word, and, if no copies of the English edition could be found with the "P," the word would technically be a substantive variant. Copies reading "President" were eventually located, however, and this variant — though it deserves mention in the textual essay (or in a special list) — need not be entered in the historical collation. Once again, the intimate connection between descriptive bibliography and editing is evident: the greater the number of copies which are examined, the more reliable the evidence on which the edition is based.

The idea of separating certain categories of historical information for presentation in special lists can be applied to other situations as well. Two kinds of special lists may result. One kind merely repeats data present in the full historical collation — data which the reader may find useful to have brought together in one spot. In the Hawthorne edition, for example, there are sometimes (as in *The*

---

72. Sigla in these lists would refer to particular copies of books, not just to particular impressions.

Blithedale Romance and *The Marble Faun*) lists of rejected first-edition substantive variants (rejected in favor of manuscript readings). The entries in these lists are included in the full historical collation, but because of their importance for critical study they are made more easily accessible by this additional listing as a separate group.[73] This type of list is purely for the reader's convenience and can be a great help when there is an important category of variants difficult to survey as a whole in the regular historical collation. The other kind of special list (like the list of variants within an impression) records information which should be made available to the reader but which, though historical in nature, does not readily fit into the historical collation. This situation often arises in treating pre-copy-text variants (such as alterations in a manuscript), especially if variants in accidentals as well as substantives are to be reported. Of course, if only substantive pre-copy-text variants are recorded, and if they are not of such quantity as to overwhelm all the later substantive variants, they can simply be included in the regular historical collation (as in the Wisconsin *Mahomet*), and no separate list is required. But when either of these conditions does not apply, a special list is advisable. In the Hawthorne edition, both accidental and substantive alterations in the manuscripts of *The Blithedale Romance* and *The Marble Faun* are listed, and the number of substantive alterations alone is far greater than the total number of substantive variants in the later editions; under these circumstances, the wisest course, adopted by the Ohio State edition, is to provide separate lists entitled "Alterations in the Manuscript."[74] These special historical lists including both substantives and accidentals are also appropriate on occasion for post-copy-text variants, as when a particular later edition is of enough importance in the history of the text to warrant recording all its textual variants. An example, in the Ohio State *Scarlet Letter*, is the list of variants between the first and second editions; any substantive variants in this list naturally occur in the regular historical collation as well, but they are repeated here along with the variants in accidentals to facilitate study of the precise relationship between the two texts. The basic historical collation, there-

73. These lists do not record the complete history of the variants listed, for their function is only to note that the variants were present in a particular edition and are not adopted in the critical text. (Strictly speaking, therefore, no sigla at all would be required in such lists.)

74. When only a brief manuscript fragment survives, it can be treated either in a separate list (as "The Ohio State University Leaf" in *The Blithedale Romance*) or in a complete transcription with accompanying apparatus (as in the Northwestern-Newberry *Typee, Mardi,* and *White-Jacket*).

fore, will often be buttressed by additional lists, sometimes regrouping information for the reader's convenience and sometimes reporting supplementary information.[75]

Any consideration of editorial apparatus is misguided if it loses sight of the convenience of the reader. For some audiences, the apparatus may be irrelevant and need not accompany the edited text; but for most scholarly audiences an edition without apparatus resembles any other work that lacks documentation — it may be brilliantly done, but it provides no aids for facilitating the scholar's independent investigation of the evidence. The apparatus (as the word itself suggests) is a tool for expediting further study, and a tool, to be effective, must be as simple and as easy to use as the circumstances allow. Fredson Bowers — through his connections with editions of Dekker, Beaumont and Fletcher, Fielding, Hawthorne, Crane, and Dewey — has done more than anyone else to set the course of modern apparatus along these lines. As a result of his efforts, there is now not only a widespread acceptance of an efficient basic approach to apparatus but also an increased awareness of the significance of apparatus. Though just a tool appended to a text, the apparatus may well be the only part of an edition that can meaningfully be called "definitive": there may legitimately be differences of opinion about certain emendations which an editor makes, but a responsible apparatus is a definitive statement of the textual situation (within the limits of the copies examined). What constitutes an apparatus responsible in both form and content is therefore a matter worth serious consideration. Only by being fully cognizant of the issues and problems involved in setting up an apparatus can an editor make those decisions which will establish his apparatus as a lasting contribution to literary study.

75. Placing all such lists immediately after the basic historical collation helps to make clear that they are parts of the historical record, appendixes in a sense to the historical collation. (The attempt to make the list of emendations serve as a partial historical collation is not an extension of the principle that certain categories within the historical collation can be conveniently separated, for it mixes the functions of the lists; all these special supplementary lists are purely historical in function.) Some-times certain of these lists—especially those dealing with variants within an impression —are placed first in the apparatus, since they often deal with material which chronologically precedes that taken up in other lists; but chronology is not the general basis for the organization of the apparatus as a whole, and readers can probably find their way around in an extensive apparatus more easily if the arrangement is based on the distinct functions of the several lists.

APPENDIX: EDITORIAL APPARATUS
FOR RADIATING TEXTS

IN HIS ESSAY "MULTIPLE AUTHORITY: NEW PROBLEMS AND CONCEPTS OF COPY-Text" (*Library*, 5th ser., 27 [1972], 81–115), Fredson Bowers makes an important contribution to editorial theory by analyzing the editorial principles involved in handling "radiating texts," that is, the situation in which "two or more substantive texts radiate from a lost original." Greg's rationale for choosing a copy-text[1] assumes that one is dealing with texts which have a linear relationship, since in his theory the authority for accidentals and for the majority of the words normally resides in that text which is genetically closest to the lost manuscript. When, however, two or more surviving texts each represent a separate line of descent from a single lost document, no one of them, when they are equidistant in descent from the lost document, is qualified to serve as a copy-text in Greg's sense. By drawing examples from Stephen Crane's syndicated newspaper pieces (in which each newspaper text derives from a common typesetting—the proofs distributed by the syndicate), Bowers shows that an analysis of all the variants in a group of radiating texts enables one to approach (with greater or lesser confidence, depending on the number of texts extant) the goal of reconstructing that lost text which was the common ancestor of the surviving texts. In such a situation the text which an editor establishes is based on a statistical and critical analysis of all the variants, accidentals as well as substantives; no one surviving text, as Bowers says, carries any "greater presumptive authority" than any other. Therefore the established text does not result from a process of emending a copy-text but instead from a process of combining certain features present in various surviving texts.

Since the two processes are radically different, it would seem likely that

1. "The Rationale of Copy-Text," *SB*, 3 (1950–51), 19–36; reprinted in Greg's *Collected Papers*, ed. J. C. Maxwell (1966), pp. 374–391.

somewhat different kinds of apparatus would be appropriate to each. The standard apparatus attached to a text established according to Greg's rationale includes a list of emendations made in the copy-text and a historical collation recording the substantive variants in the authorized texts; but in the case of a text reconstructed from radiating texts, there is no copy-text, and it would seem that the apparatus would have to be adjusted accordingly. When I surveyed "Some Principles for Editorial Apparatus," I was concerned only with texts amenable to Greg's rationale;[2] it seems in order now to say a few words, as an appendage to Bowers's discussion, about the apparatus appropriate to radiating texts. Bowers clearly states the problem:

> The choice [of copy-text], therefore, is theoretically indifferent because the only function of the copy-text in such a situation is to serve as the physical basis not for a purified reprint in the shape of a modern edition but instead for a reconstruction of the immediate lost printer's-copy, in which process all the preserved documents will participate. Although it is perhaps hypothetically true that a modern text edited by such a method might be said to accept as its copy-text this reconstructed proof, nevertheless the problem of what form an apparatus would take for such a non-extant copy-text is acute, and it is a matter of economy to select some one of the documents that as a whole conforms most closely to the reconstructed proof in respect to its accidentals and to use it as the copy-text or basis for the emendation that will embody the reconstruction. Since, in fact, an editor in this situation selects his copy-text only after he has reconstructed the lost, common printer's-copy, it is largely a question of convenience which document he uses. That one requiring the least amount of apparatus to record the necessary alterations (it is hard to call them emendations) is the most economical in printing costs and certainly the most convenient for a reader's use of the apparatus. (pp. 101–102)

What Bowers recognizes here, but does not say, is that to think in terms of the usual copy-text apparatus is a hindrance in this situation. If one assumes that an apparatus must contain a list of emendations made in a copy-text, then of course one could not have "a non-extant copy-text." But, as Bowers points out, editorial alterations (based on variant readings) made in whichever one of the radiating texts is chosen as "copy-text" are not really "emendations." In fact, to speak of a "copy-text" at all in such a case is to alter the meaning of the word; to choose one of the radiating texts as a "copy-text" means simply to use it as the basis for printer's copy.[3] And if for economy

---

2. This article, *SB*, 25 (1972), 41–88, provides a detailed explanation of what in the present note are referred to casually as the "usual" list of emendations, historical collation, and record of line-end hyphenation.

3. In his ensuing discussion Bowers suggests that even with radiating texts a "copy-text" with some degree of "presumptive authority" can sometimes be found: "It must be admitted that as the number of witnesses decreases the importance of selecting a copy-text on qualitative grounds may well increase. . . . It may well be in such a situation that the

one chooses that text quantitatively closest to the editorially reconstructed text and then feels that only the alterations in that text need be recorded in a "list of emendations," one is depriving the reader of information which would have been made available if a different text had been selected. In a footnote to the paragraph quoted above, Bowers acknowledges this point: "Paradoxically, the copy-text most faithful to the reconstructed printer's-copy conceals more information in its list of emendations by recording fewer of the multiple variants than would be the case for a copy-text less faithful." It seems clear that trying to fit a radiating-text apparatus into the form appropriate for the usual copy-text apparatus creates difficulties in getting on record the facts which a reader of a critical text deserves to have at his disposal.

Furthermore, preserving the distinction between substantives and accidentals, central to copy-text theory, seems unnecessary here, since no one text has presumptive authority for the accidentals, as a true copy-text does. The historical collation for a "copy-text edition" normally lists only substantive variants, since no question of emending the copy-text with accidentals variants from later editions usually exists. But in a "radiating-text edition," the variants (within the radiating texts) in accidentals, just as much as those in substantives, are part of the relevant evidence bearing on the editor's final decisions; and if a "list of emendations" based on that radiating text closest to the final reconstruction conceals some of this evidence, then it should be revealed in the "historical collation." In the footnote previously quoted, Bowers goes on to say, "How far this concealment of the evidence

over-all opinion he [an editor] has formed the general fidelity of the accidentals of his copy-text can materially influence his judgement in cases of honest doubt. Yet an editor should to the best of his ability exhaust his qualitative evidence (in combination with the quantitative) before throwing back on the copy-text the responsibility for the authority of a reading" (p. 102). But how, even in cases of "honest doubt," can an editor legitimately make a decision by falling back on a particular text out of the group of radiating texts? One text, of course, may happen to contain more of the readings which an editor decides—on qualitative and quantitative evidence—to adopt; but when he decides to adopt still another reading from that text because that text seems more generally faithful, what he is doing is making another qualitative decision—and not simply reverting to a text with presumptive authority. Each decision in this situation is an active one; none can be settled passively by falling back on a "copy-text," for no copy-text in the usual sense can exist. Bowers makes a similar point later, in his discussion of a case in which there are only two radiating texts: "Because both documents are of equal authority I suggest that it would be a clear case of abnegation of editorial responsibility and of tyranny of the copy-text if an editor treated the document he chose as copy-text in the conventional manner as if it had more inherent authority than the other. Multiple authority inevitably creates an eclectic text and the copy-text cannot be treated with the respect accorded a primary, single document heading a linear series of derivations" (p. 105).

on which the work was edited can be rectified by including among the substantive variants of the Historical Collation the accidentals variants rejected from the other witnesses is a procedure sometimes practicable on a limited basis." One may wonder, however, whether it is proper to allow the listing of variants in accidentals to be less than complete, when the status of those variants in radiating texts is no different from that of substantive variants.[4] In a "copy-text edition" the editor is expected to list all the substantive variants in authorized texts, no matter how certain he feels that some of them have no connection with the author; in a "radiating-text edition," therefore, it would seem reasonable to expect him to list *all* variants in the radiating texts (accidentals as well as substantives), since the authority of all is at issue.

What this line of reasoning leads to is obvious. Since the historical collation would consist of all variants except those in the list of emendations, and since the text on which the list of emendations is based would represent an arbitrary choice from a theoretical point of view, there would seem to be no reason to construct two separate lists. A single list which records all readings in the radiating texts that differ from those adopted in the editor's critical text would provide the reader with all the evidence necessary to examine the editor's decisions; it would be easier to use than two lists by giving all the information at one place; and it would carry no implication, as a division into two lists would seem to, that certain of the variants have a different status theoretically from the others.

The way in which this kind of listing would work out in practice can be illustrated by taking some of the variants in one of the stories Bowers discusses, Crane's "A Grey Sleeve." In *Tales of War* (1970), volume 6 of The University of Virginia Edition of the Works of Stephen Crane, the first few entries in the list of emendations are as follows:

67.0   I] PM, FLW; PART I $N; *omit* EIM
67.5   him,] $N(–N^1), PM; ~$_\wedge$ N^1, FLW, EIM
67.12 far-away] N^5, FLW, EIM; faraway N$^{1-4}$, PM; ~ -|~ N^6
67.15 but,] N$^{3-6}$+; ~$_\wedge$ N$^{1-2}$
67.21 column$_\wedge$] $N(–N^1)+; ~, N^1

---

4. Indeed, one could even argue that a full listing of accidentals is the more crucial, because, particularly when the number of radiating texts is small, the editor may have greater difficulty (and less confidence) in judging the accidentals variants than the substantive ones. See Bowers, pp. 104–105.

And the entries in the historical collation covering the same passage:

67.0   I] PART I $N; *omit* EIM
67.3   ¶So] *no* ¶ N^5
67.6   at us] us N^6
67.10   an] *omit* N^5
67.11   the eternal] he eternal FLW
67.17   him] *omit* N^2
67.18   the] an N^6
67.19   the brigade] a brigade EIM
67.22   the colors] colors EIM

This volume of the Crane edition (along with volume 5, *Tales of Adventure*, published the same year) represents a pioneer effort to deal with radiating printed texts, and in it Bowers adopts the convenient symbol "N" to stand for all the radiating newspaper texts. (He also adds to that symbol the "$" from descriptive bibliography, meaning "all" or "every"; see his discussion in volume 5, p. 211, and volume 6, pp. 335–336.) Individual N texts can then be specified with superscript figures, and lack of agreement can be indicated by a minus sign. In the case of "A Grey Sleeve" there are six radiating newspaper texts, plus three magazine texts (designated PM, FLW, and EIM) which also radiate from the same syndicate master-proof. Of these nine radiating texts, the one chosen as "copy-text"—that is, the one which serves as the basis for the list of emendations, of which an excerpt is quoted above—is N^1.

The solution to the complicated textual problem here is brilliant, but one may question whether the traditional apparatus is equipped to reflect the subtlety of the textual situation. By combining the information in the list of emendations with that in the historical collation, one can reconstruct all the radiating texts in terms of substantives. But, as for the accidentals, why is it more important for the reader to be able to reconstruct the accidentals of N^1 than of the other eight texts? Even in connection with the substantives, one could say that it is somewhat misleading to have certain substantive variants relegated to a second list, since the only reason they are there—instead of in the first list—is that the text in which they appear was not chosen on practical grounds as the basis for that first list. (Of course, the second list, the historical collation, does bring together all the rejected substantive readings, regardless of their source; but the fact remains that those from N^1 are also recorded in the emendations list, whereas those from one

or more of the other radiating texts and not from N^1 are recorded only in
the historical collation.) The very fact that the two-part arrangement—
a list of emendations followed by a historical collation of substantives—has
become established means that a number of readers will have become con-
ditioned to interpreting the lists in a certain way; thus they may have some
initial difficulty in recognizing that, in a radiating-text situation, entries in
the historical collation are not necessarily post-copy-text variants for the
most part but consist of many readings from texts contemporaneous with and
of equal authority with the so-called "copy-text." Using the two-part division
for both kinds of textual situations, in other words, runs the risk of blurring
the important distinction between them, particularly since that arrangement
does not efficiently reflect the nature of the textual problem in cases of radiating texts.

Let us see, therefore, how the two excerpts quoted above would look
when combined into a single list:

67.0	I] PART I $N; *omit* EIM
67.3	¶So] *no* ¶ N^5
67.5	him,] $\sim_\wedge$ N^1, FLW, EIM
67.6	at us] us N^6
67.10	an] *omit* N^5
67.11	the eternal] he eternal FLW
67.12	far-away] faraway $N^{1\text{-}4}$, PM; $\sim$ -|$\sim$ N^6
67.15	but,] $\sim_\wedge$ $N^{1\text{-}2}$
67.17	him] *omit* N^2
67.18	the] an N^6
67.19	the brigade] a brigade EIM
67.21	column$_\wedge$] $\sim$, N^1
67.22	the colors] colors EIM

Of course, this list is not quite what would appear in an actual edition following this plan, for presumably there are additional variants in accidentals (not
recorded in the presently published historical collation) which would have
to be included. Even so, it suggests some of the merits of the single-list form.
There is the greater simplicity of the entries which were formerly in the
list of emendations,[5] plus the simplicity of having everything in one list.

5. Of course, this is not a necessary consequence of combining the two lists, because
an editor might choose instead to expand the entries from the historical collation: that is,
every entry could include, immediately after the bracket, the source(s) of the reading to the

And there is the implied recognition, through the inclusion of such entries as 67.5 and 67.6 in the same list, that (1) both substantive and accidentals variants are equally deserving of attention, and (2) readings in the critical text which vary from N^6 (or any other of the radiating texts) are just as important to report as those which vary from N^1. The list would simply be a record of all the variants in the radiating texts (keyed to the critical text), and from it the reader would be able to reconstruct all the relevant features (whether accidentals or substantives) of each text examined as part of the basis for editorial decisions.

If this approach to a radiating-text apparatus seems reasonable, there remain several specific problems which must be dealt with. First of all, the entries in the example above do not involve any instance of emendation in which the editor supplies a reading that does not occur in any of the radiating texts; but there is no reason why such an entry could not be incorporated into the same list. As the following hypothetical example shows, one could either insert a symbol (here V, for Virginia Edition) to stand for the present edition, or merely allow the fact that all the collated texts are accounted for to indicate that the reading to the left of the bracket occurs in none of them and is provided by the editor:[6]

$$67.3 \quad \text{does,"}] \text{ V; } \sim,_\wedge \$N+$$
$$67.3 \quad \text{does,"}] \sim,_\wedge \$N+$$

The first emphasizes the fact that the reading has been editorially supplied, while the second is consistent with the form of the other entries in identifying the source of the adopted reading as any text(s) not otherwise mentioned (out of a specified group of texts). Entries of this kind are undeniably different from those which involve a choice among variant readings in the radiating texts, and for that reason one might feel that they should be segregated into a separate list. But to do so would probably be more confusing than helpful for at least two reasons: (1) the consolidated list of variants in the radiating texts, while it is serving as a "historical collation" of those texts, is also providing the record of editorial decisions, and to place certain other editorial decisions in a separate table would in most cases constitute an unnecessary

---

left of the bracket. One could argue that such a system would be clearer in some cases, because it would be more explicit; but the point is that a combined list would have the simplicity of presenting all entries in the same form—and that form need not involve sigla following the bracket, as lists of emendations ordinarily do.

6. Instances in which a substantive emendation comes from a later authorized edition rather than from the editor himself are touched on in the footnote to the next paragraph.

proliferation of lists; (2) whenever the editorially supplied reading is at a point where variation among the radiating texts already occurs, the entry would have to go into the list of variant readings in any case, keyed of course to the new reading in the critical text, and any separate listing of such occurrences would be simply a duplication. It is probably better, therefore, to include all editorial decisions in one list, but, as a way of making it easier to locate those readings supplied by the editor, the insertion of the siglum for the critical edition (the "V" in the example above) is probably a good idea.

So far no mention has been made of authorized texts which come later than the series of radiating texts. Clearly such texts are comparable to the post-copy-text editions in the usual situations in which there is a single copy-text. The radiating texts are like the copy-text in that it is important to be able to reconstruct them in terms of both accidentals and substantives; but for the later editions, in either situation, the variants in accidentals are of less concern and normally need not be recorded. The question, then, is whether to include references to such later collated editions in the kind of variants list for radiating texts proposed above or whether to set up a separate list for them. The answer, I suppose, would vary with particular situations, but as a general rule it would seem preferable to incorporate those references into the same list. If they were put into a separate list, which would be a "historical collation" in the usual sense, a great deal of duplication would result. Besides, the list of variants in the radiating texts is already serving a "historical" function, and it would seem sensible to place the rest of the historical evidence at the same location. After all, any substantive variant in those later editions could conceivably supersede the reading(s) of the radiating texts (whereas the accidentals variants in them—in the terms of Greg's rationale of copy-text—could not normally provide emendations for the radiating texts). Incorporating all this information in the same list, therefore, provides a single historical record of relevant textual evidence— variants in substantives and accidentals for the radiating texts and variants in substantives alone for the later authorized texts. Of course, in using the list one would have to keep in mind that the group of texts being reported on in the entries for accidentals is not as large as the group being reported on in the entries for substantives, but doing so seems to offer little practical difficulty,[7] certainly less than working with two lists whose functions overlap.

7. If one looks back at the consolidated list presented earlier and imagines that several later texts—say X, Y, and Z—are also being reported on there, it is a simple matter to know that in such entries as 67.6 or 67.10 X, Y, and Z agree with the bracketed reading,

Finally, there is the question of how the record of line-end hyphens is affected by a radiating-text situation. Obviously the list dealing with line-end hyphens in the critical text is not affected at all, but the other list, recording editorial decisions about possible compounds hyphenated at line-ends in the copy-text, does require modification. As the entry for 67.12 in "A Grey Sleeve" shows, the Crane edition records in its lists of emendations certain line-end hyphens in radiating texts rather than including them in the regular section of "Word-Division":

67.12   far-away] N^5, FLW, EIM; faraway N^{1-4}, PM; $\sim$ -|$\sim$ N^6

It is clear why this practice must be followed. The editor's decision is based on the evidence of all the radiating texts (along with his knowledge of the author's practice), and, if one of those texts is ambiguous, that fact is relevant. In this example, to join N^6 either with N^5 or with N^{1-4} would be misleading, for it would conceal a prior editorial decision, and it would be equally misleading simply to enter "far-away" in the regular word-division list, for to do so would conceal the fact that variation in hyphenation exists among the radiating texts. Only when all radiating texts concur in a particular line-end hyphen does the situation resemble that in which there is a single copy-text; in such cases it is adequate to list the editorially established form of the compound in the usual way in the word-division list. But whenever a possible compound hyphenated at the end of a line in one or more radiating texts is not broken by a line-end (or is not hyphenated) in one or more others, that variation must be included in the list which records the other variations among the radiating texts. Thus in radiating-text editions, the record of line-

---

whereas in such entries as 67.12 and 67.15 nothing at all is being implied about X, Y, and Z. Similarly, if the editor were to adopt a substantive variant from one of these later texts, that fact would be clear because the symbol for that text would be excluded from the group named (e.g., "$N, X, Y" or "$N, X, Z"). Nevertheless, there is a certain awkwardness in this arrangement, for occasionally there may be some question as to whether a given entry is a substantive or an accidental, and the reader is then placed in the position of having to judge which way the editor regarded it. In order to be explicit and to make his entries unambiguous, the editor employing this kind of list probably should adopt a symbol to distinguish the entries for accidentals, the entries, that is, which record only the readings of the radiating texts and do not go on to record (directly or through implication) the readings of later editions. One convenient symbol for this purpose which has been suggested by Bowers (in a letter to me) is a vertical line at the end of the entry. Thus if the entry given above for 67.15 were written "but,] $\sim_\wedge$ N^{1-2} |", the reader would be told unequivocally that editions later than N, the group of radiating texts, are not involved in this entry.

end hyphenation may still include the usual two lists, but the list devoted to copy-text hyphens will contain only those instances in which the radiating texts are in agreement.[8]

Some of the details in the kind of apparatus I have outlined here are obviously open to debate. But the important point is to recognize that it is misleading and unproductive to set forth the evidence about radiating texts in the terms we have grown accustomed to using for a different situation. Fredson Bowers has performed a great service in offering a rationale for cases not encompassed by Greg's rationale. As we make practical use of these rationales, we should not be surprised to find that different theoretical positions result in different forms of apparatus.

8. If there are only a few of these instances (so that it seems awkward to make a separate list of them), even they could be included in the consolidated list of variants—e.g., "tonight] ~-|~ $N". But they do form a separate class of entry; and if, as in a composite volume, like *Tales of War*, containing some pieces with single copy-texts, there is to be an inclusive copy-text hyphenation list anyway (as opposed to separate apparatus for each individual work), these entries are best recorded there.

II

Problems and Accomplishments
in the Editing of the Novel

I
T HAS BEEN A QUARTER OF A CENTURY SINCE GORDON RAY COMPLAINED THAT "Readers generally remain remarkably uninformed regarding the extent to which nineteenth-century books were revised by their authors." After naming a number of books, mostly novels, as examples, he added, "Our state of contented ignorance has generated a culpable carelessness about the versions of nineteenth-century books that we read. We do not even demand that publishers of reprints state the sources of their texts."[1] Soon after, Kathleen Tillotson said, "We have virtually no edited texts of Victorian novelists, and no means, short of doing the work ourselves, of discovering how (and why) the original edition differed from the text we read."[2] And several years later Bruce Harkness published his now well-known article on "Bibliography and the Novelistic Fallacy,"[3] in which he pointed out that "everyone ignores the bibliographical study of the novel. People who would consider it terribly bad form to slight the textual study of a play or poem— or even doggerel—commit bibliographical nonsense when handed a novel" (p. 24). His survey of examples of textual corruption in novels demonstrated the fallacy of regarding novels as textually "a different order of thing from poetry." At roughly the same time John Butt observed, "The energy ex-

---

1. "The Importance of Original Editions," in *Nineteenth-Century English Books: Some Problems in Bibliography* (1952), pp. 3–24 (see p. 9).

2. *Novels of the Eighteen-Forties* (1954), p. vii. A similar comment occurs in the preface to her and John Butt's *Dickens at Work* (1957): "Dickens studies have hardly passed beyond the early nineteenth-century phase of Shakespeare studies; while the study of his text seems arrested in the early eighteenth century" (p. 10).

3. *Studies in Bibliography*, 12 (1959), 59–73; reprinted in *Bibliography and Textual Criticism*, ed. O M Brack, Jr., and Warner Barnes (1969), pp. 23–40. The later printing is cited in the text because it is said to contain "slight changes."

pended during the last forty years in supplying reliable editions of our major writers has not yet been directed towards our great novelists."[4]

The situation today is much less dismal, for comments such as these both reflected and stimulated a growing awareness of textual problems in fiction. In this climate it was possible for a Center for Editions of American Authors to be established as a committee of the Modern Language Association of America. Given the nature of nineteenth-century American literature, it was inevitable that a considerable part of the Center's efforts would be concerned with works of fiction, and the CEAA editions which have appeared over the last decade constitute a landmark in the development of novel-editing. Although there has not been universal approval of the CEAA's editorial principles, the debate about them has itself served to call attention to the size and significance of the undertaking. As a result, the editing of novels has received more serious discussion and more widespread interest in recent years than ever before.

In some ways, however, the situation has not much improved, for teachers still seem willing to adopt irresponsible editions for classroom use—or, at least, seem reluctant to investigate the trustworthiness of available editions. No one expects classroom editions (or "practical editions," as they are now often called)[5] to be the equal of full-scale scholarly editions, either in the research they entail or in the amount of textual data they present; but one is justified in expecting them to reflect the results of previous research and to specify just what text is being offered. That so many of them do not is a gauge of the general state of textual awareness: many scholars and teachers still do not demand better editions, and an unreliable text does not necessarily lose sales in competition with a reliable one. The questions Harkness asked in 1959 are still the key questions: "Can not we have sound texts reproduced and publisher's history stated by the editor? Can not we know *what it is* we have in our hands?" (p. 40). These questions are essentially the ones being asked in an extremely helpful series of analyses of practical editions appearing in *Proof*. As Joseph Katz formulates them in examining classroom editions of *The Red Badge of Courage*,[6] one should ask of any edition whether it reprints an authoritative source, states that source, reproduces the source accurately, and records any alterations made. After checking fifteen editions, he

4. "Editing a Nineteenth-Century Novelist (Proposals for an Edition of Dickens)," in *English Studies Today, Second Series*, ed. G. A. Bonnard (1961), pp. 187–195 (see p. 187).

5. See Fredson Bowers, "Practical Texts and Definitive Editions," in Charlton Hinman and Fredson Bowers, *Two Lectures on Editing* (1969), pp. 21–70.

6. "Practical Editions: Stephen Crane's *The Red Badge of Courage*," *Proof*, 2 (1972), 301–318.

concludes, "Nearly every one is unsatisfactory; most are disgraceful" (p. 301). Similarly, John C. Gerber finds that the available texts of *Tom Sawyer* and *Huckleberry Finn* are "unsatisfactory, in some instances dramatically so. At best, our students are reading approximations of what Mark Twain wanted them to read." Don Cook discovers that the texts of the five largest-selling paperback editions of *The Rise of Silas Lapham* differ substantively in about forty places from the CEAA text, and Hershel Parker reports that only one out of twenty-six editions of *Moby-Dick* can be regarded as satisfactory.[7]

Novels are not alone in being offered in unreliable practical editions. But it is undeniably true that they are repeatedly so offered, and the nature of the novel itself may in part be responsible. The current scholarly interest in the editing of novels makes this an appropriate time to survey the field. Recognizing what kinds of problems are encountered in editing novels and what achievements have so far been attained may help lead toward further development and more widespread understanding.

I

The problems of editing novels are essentially, of course, the same as those of editing poems, plays, stories, and essays. All are verbal constructions, and all can have corrupt readings which an editor tries to rectify by determining what the author intended. If the novel can be thought of as having any special problems, they are all attributable to one characteristic of novels: length.[8] For one thing, it simply takes more time to compare the texts of a novel than of a shorter work; the whole process of recording and studying variants is more tedious and more costly. In addition, the argument is often made that this effort is less worthwhile for novels precisely because of their length: individual variants, it is said, cannot have as much significance in a novel as in a lyric poem. Most people agree that large passages deleted from or added to a novel are important, but many feel that lesser alterations do not materially affect one's experience of a long work. Furthermore, the question of how to display the variant readings is complicated by length. An extensive listing, whether at the foot of the page or at the end of the volume, is costly to set and may greatly increase the bulk (and price) of the book; and the idea of employing parallel texts, which might be more effective in cases of extensive revision, is generally impractical for a long work because of the expense

---

7. John C. Gerber, *Proof*, 2 (1972), 285–292 (see p. 292); Don Cook, *Proof*, 2 (1972), 293–300; Hershel Parker, *Proof*, 3 (1973), 371–378.

8. Some poems are as long as novels, but the vast majority are much shorter; many works of nonfiction are long, and they, like novels, have been much less frequently edited than poetry and drama.

involved and the difficulty (without further apparatus) of locating all the variants of a given class for study. Even the survival of documents is affected by length. While fragmentary manuscripts of lyric poems certainly exist, there is a much greater likelihood that manuscripts of novels, when they survive at all, will be incomplete. The hundreds of pages of large manuscripts, if they are not discarded for lack of space, tend to become separated over the years (or deliberately dispersed, as when manuscript leaves are bound into large-paper or limited issues of published books). As a result, the editor of a novel may find that his choice of copy-text is made more difficult by the fact that the document which he would normally choose exists in fragmentary form.

The quantitative problem which novel-editing offers can be illustrated by the works of Samuel Richardson: his novels are long, they went through a number of editions which show extensive changes, and the changes deserve the closest scrutiny because, for many of the editions, Richardson was his own printer. In recent years there has been a series of excellent articles surveying Richardson's revisions and suggesting the magnitude of the task facing an editor. From them one learns, for example, that the number of alterations in both the second and the fifth editions of *Pamela* approaches a thousand and that over 8,400 changes appear in the first two volumes of the last revision (published posthumously). Three of the four revised editions of *Sir Charles Grandison* contain nearly a thousand changes each, and the other one about half that many. *Clarissa*, which was considerably revised before its initial publication in seven volumes, was altered in its second edition at about 4,000 points in the first four volumes, and the third edition was a whole volume longer than the first.[9] Examining and categorizing such a large number of variants is naturally difficult, but, as Shirley Van Marter recognizes in her work on *Clarissa*, one must look at them all and not begin with the assumption that small changes, given the mass of the whole, are unimportant. "Only the full scope of the evidence," she says, "can help scholars determine whether it is true that the substantial difference between the editions lies not in 'small and subtle variations' but primarily in the large blocks of material inserted into the third version" (1973, p. 109). Her examination of the revisions in the

9. See T. C. Duncan Eaves and Ben D. Kimpel, "Richardson's Revisions of *Pamela*," *SB*, 20 (1967), 61–88; Robert Craig Pierson, "The Revisions of Richardson's *Sir Charles Grandison*," *SB*, 21 (1968), 163–189; Eaves and Kimpel, "The Composition of *Clarissa* and Its Revision before Publication," *PMLA*, 83 (1968), 416–428; Shirley Van Marter, "Richardson's Revisions of *Clarissa* in the Second Edition," *SB*, 26 (1973), 107–132; Van Marter, "Richardson's Revisions of *Clarissa* in the Third and Fourth Editions," *SB*, 28 (1975), 119–152.

second edition demonstrates that the size of a revision has no necessary relation to its effect or significance, and she makes a useful statement of the position: "Quantitatively Richardson's revisions form a continuum from the
very tiny to the very large, and certain patterns of qualitative strengths and
weaknesses, certain stylistic features peculiar to him, certain goals that he set
himself, turn up at many different points throughout this continuum" (1973,
p. 131).

Two related questions are being faced in discussions of this kind. One
is how to decide what text is to be presented to the reader; the other is how
(or whether) to record all the variant readings. In response to the first, it can
be argued that the nature of Richardson's revisions for certain editions
actually creates different works and that the editor cannot produce a single
critical edition representing the author's "final intention"; since more than
one "final intention" exists, there is more than one work to be edited. Thus
Eaves and Kimpel have suggested that the first and last revisions of *Pamela*
be offered simultaneously in a parallel-text edition; and M. Kinkead-Weekes
has argued that the revisions for the third edition of *Clarissa* represent "the
earliest example of the effect upon a novel of audience reactions" and that
the resulting work, aimed at a differently conceived audience, does not supersede the work as completed and presented to the public in the first edition.[10]
But even after arriving at an answer to the difficult question of whether there
is more than one "work" here and, if so, which one is to be edited, there is still
the question of the presentation of the evidence. If one is editing either the
first or the third edition of *Clarissa*, does the reader of a scholarly edition require the full record of variants? An affirmative answer is implied by the view
that an individual small alteration can have great significance: if every alteration, even in a long novel, is of potential significance, the reader is not in
a position to understand the history of the work or the editor's reasoning
about it if he does not have all the evidence. Shirley Van Marter makes the
point emphatically:

scholars should never be satisfied with anything less than a complete record of Richardson's art. His efforts to revise *Clarissa* are so varied and voluminous, so reflective
of his inventive strengths and weaknesses, so much a part of his own peculiar genius
for delving into the heart's recesses in homage to moral norms, they deserve detailed
attention. Any critical edition which excluded all this testimony from an apparatus
would deprive scholars of one of the richest sources of evidence that can stimulate
a more exact understanding of this novel, of Richardson's creative talent, and of his
role in the development of the novel form. (1975, p. 152)

10. "*Clarissa* Restored?", *Review of English Studies*, n.s. 10 (1959), 156–171.

It is not only in connection with long novels that editors confront questions of authorial intention and the possibility of revisions creating new works, but dealing with those questions is complicated by the practical problems imposed by a long work. When Van Marter summarizes that "the evidence presented by Richardson's revisions is voluminous and exceedingly complex" (1973, p. 109), we understand that part of the complexity is a result of the sheer quantity.

Another scholar who has struggled with similar problems is Bernard Weinberg, though in his thinking about editing Balzac he does not always come to similar conclusions.[11] Balzac was an endless reviser who engaged in substantial rewriting on two or three successive sets of galley proof, sometimes doubling the length of his work in the process; then, after serial publication, he made extensive revisions for the first book edition, again for various later editions, and yet again when fitting the work into the *Comédie humaine.* As Weinberg says, "The problem of editing Balzac is a problem in infinite variation" (p. 65). Yet in all this mass of material, an individual minute change, Weinberg finds, does have significance: "a single phrase or sentence or passage may reveal the whole of the form," he says; "a new conception of the form may penetrate down to a substitution for a single word" (p. 76). Nevertheless, he does not recommend that all variants be recorded. The reason there has been so little critical editing of Balzac, he believes, is not merely the great complexity of the surviving material but also the nature of what is customarily expected in a critical edition. He cites William Leeper Crain's edition of *Le Secret des Ruggieri,* prepared as a dissertation at Chicago in 1937, and calls it "unpublished because unpublishable" (p. 66)—unpublishable because of the voluminous apparatus which records as notes to one text all the prepublication variants and as notes to a parallel text all the postpublication variants. It is his contention that such editions are "philological" —an inheritance from the scholarly work on earlier literature, intended to provide data for the historical study of language. Balzac's intended text, he thinks, can be defined simply as "the last text published during Balzac's lifetime" (p. 67), and a record of the variants would provide no information about nineteenth-century language "that could not more easily be learned from more accessible documents" (p. 70). What the editor should do, in his opinion, is to offer a critical analysis of each version, showing the artistic differences among them and recording variants selectively as support for these analyses.

11. "Editing Balzac: A Problem in Infinite Variation," in *Editing Nineteenth Century Texts,* ed. John M. Robson (1967), pp. 60–76.

It is difficult to reconcile Weinberg's recommended procedure with his belief in the importance of individual variants. An editor's critical abilities are naturally crucial to the success of a critical edition, but the editor is not providing his readers with adequate documentation for examining his position or his textual decisions if he records only those variants which seem to him to support his views. Even if one leaves aside Weinberg's overconfident assumption that the author's last approved text is "definitive" (p. 67), it is hard to conceive how he can regard any evidence about a major writer's revisions as historically or philologically unimportant. The answer, of course, is that he is speaking from a practical, not a theoretical, point of view. Obviously he understands the historical value of such information, but he is saying, in effect, that it is worth sacrificing some of this detail if as a consequence dependable editions will be published. The quantity of the data is clearly the stumbling block: when he speaks of the materials being "so recent and so abundant" (p. 67), the key word is "abundant." It seems doubtful that he would have raised these points if he had been dealing with a sonnet or an ode (however many stages of revision were involved) rather than with the immense structure of the *Comédie humaine*. One can sympathize with the desire to compromise in order to get results, and it is possible to say that it is better to have editions being produced with abbreviated apparatuses than to have no editions being produced at all. Yet this is a shortsighted position, for scholarship requires documentation. If the job is well done, the effort will be no less merely because less information is to appear in print, but the publication of more information not only gives the reader a greater basis for judging the quality of the work but also contributes to the available store of facts on which others can draw. No one would suggest that all classroom editions need contain a comprehensive apparatus, but a climate of opinion conducive to the widespread production of reliable classroom editions is best encouraged by the publication of the results of intensive textual investigations.

This matter becomes an issue principally in connection with fiction, because of the large amounts of data involved and the cost of putting them in print. But it is significant that both Van Marter and Weinberg assert the importance of small revisions; neither believes that the mass of a novel necessarily renders the effect of such alterations nugatory. This view must lie at the heart of any serious approach to the editing of novels. Many people, of course, can agree that theoretically the change of a single word produces a different work of art, but they have often found the consequences of this position more disturbing and awkward when applied to novels than when applied to poems.

An editorial rationale which has been gaining prominence in Germany and which has been summarized by Hans Zeller[12] carries the position to its logical conclusion. A text, Zeller explains, "does not in fact consist of elements but of the relationships between them"; thus "variation at one point has an effect on invariant sections of the text" (p. 241). If this is so, it follows, according to Zeller, that each "version" of a text which an author approves (even if it contains only one variation from another version) is an entity that must be respected by the editor. It is not possible, in this view, to construct through emendation any one text which reflects the author's "final intention";[13] instead, there are various texts—each a finished work—which represent the author's intention at different times. Zeller does not regard this approach as precluding critical decisions on the part of an editor, for the editor would still be expected to recognize and correct errors and to determine which of several texts is most appropriate to reproduce; but to prohibit an editor from incorporating into one text particular variants from another certainly restricts the area in which the editor's judgment can operate. In many respects Zeller's position coincides with Weinberg's, for Weinberg states that the "aggregate of all the changes introduced into one stage of the composition makes of it an independent work different from its predecessor" (p. 74), and he concludes that "the editor's reference would be to the total form at any given stage in the development of the work" (p. 76).

Many editors of novels, when confronted with this theory, are likely to feel uneasy. They would recognize that the length of novels makes it unrealistic to envisage the full publication of multiple texts of most novels; yet the more realistic alternative—selecting one text for full publication, accompanied by an apparatus recording the variants in the others—tends to violate the integrity of all the texts but one, making them recoverable only through the apparatus and thus implying that they are in some way subordinate. Al-

12. "A New Approach to the Critical Constitution of Literary Texts," *SB*, 28 (1975), 231–264.

13. Zeller does not believe that an author's "final intention" in an artistic sense can be separated from the other forces which affect his decisions. In Zeller's words, "It is not possible (or only rarely, in exceptional cases), when a work is revised, to give a detailed account of the extent to which the reception of the first version, a change in society, a change in the author himself and in his relationship to his environment, a different incentive or purpose in publication, may be involved in the revision, and this holds all the more true since right from the beginning, before he even thought of writing, the author was exposed to this play of forces from all sides" (p. 244). Or, as he puts it more succinctly, "the magnetic needle of the author's wishes is quivering in the field of non-aesthetic forces" (p. 245). However, one could argue that, since authors do sometimes make revisions which they would prefer not to make because they are under pressure to do so, an editor's task properly entails the analysis of an author's motives in revision.

though this reaction is a practical one, stemming from the economic realities of publishing long works, it points to a theoretical difficulty as well. But first one must recognize that Zeller's argument begins from an unexceptionable position: it is scarcely debatable that literary works are entities defined by the relationships of their parts and that an editor (or critic) can comment perceptively on a particular part only if he understands its relation to the whole. He is also right to assert that eclectic editing—the emending of one text with variants from another—presupposes the author's "intention" in both texts to be the same. The next step logically would be to examine the problem of determining authorial intention and of distinguishing among different intentions as manifested in different texts. Zeller, however, retreats from this problem, saying in effect that the task of identifying intention is an impossible one and that there is no alternative to regarding each authorized text as reflecting a different intention. The theoretical difficulty with his position, therefore, is that it neither refutes the commonsense belief that some revisions differ in kind from others nor accepts that belief by attempting to distinguish among them.

Whenever one speaks of revisions producing a new work, one really means "a new work in some sense," because the two "works" will remain more closely related to each other than they are to a "totally different work." Zeller, implicitly recognizing this distinction, uses the word "versions" to designate texts "with authorial variation" (p. 236). If "versions" are not to be exactly equated with "works," there is no theoretical necessity for always treating "versions" like "works"; instead, the nature of "versions" ought to be examined, to see if there are times when they should indeed be regarded as analogous to separate works and other times when they should not. Henry James's revisions of his early works for the New York Edition of 1907–09 constitute a classic instance of creating versions so different in effect that they deserve to be regarded as new works; those revisions are surely of a different order from the ones made, for example, by Melville for the English edition of *Moby-Dick*—local alterations which affect individual passages but not the total impact of the book. Yet the difficulty of defining this difference in borderline cases has been perhaps the single most troublesome point in recent editorial theory, particularly acute in relation to fiction. Clearly the distinction is not quantitative, though sometimes editors act on the assumption that it is; but the number of revisions in the third edition of *Clarissa* is less crucial than their nature. No precise rule can be formulated for making the distinction, since it must depend on critical insight. But one can follow a general observation: that "horizontal revisions"—revisions within the plane of the work as presently constituted—do not reflect an altered intention and do not produce a new "work"; but that "vertical revisions"—revisions which move the work to a different level—do represent a changed intention and thus do result in an essentially different "work."[14]

Two elements in Zeller's position make it impossible for him to give the editor the liberty to make such a decision. For one thing, he believes that a writer's artistic motivation cannot be separated from other kinds of motivation affecting the text which the writer finally approves; because "influences on the author" and "influences on the text" are inseparable, "uninfluenced artistic intentions" are "something which exists only in terms of aesthetic abstraction" (p. 248). Second, he maintains that errors ("violations of a principle") can be identified only in "utilitarian texts," which are rhetorically "predictable," because "it is an idiosyncrasy of artistic structures that they themselves transgress the rules or codes which they have set up in the text, in favour of new codes" (p. 259). If the editor is permitted to decide that certain texts do not constitute separate works, he is then faced with the question of whether to emend one text with particular variants from another; and in determining what emendations to make, he is inevitably attempting to distinguish variants which reflect the author's artistic intention from those which either are errors or are revisions forced on the author or prompted by nonartistic considerations. These distinctions cannot be easy or certain, but to eliminate them is essentially to deny the value of a critical approach. The editing of individual texts of a work or the preparation of a record of the variants in them is a valuable accomplishment. To go a step further and to apply critical intelligence to the evaluation of those variants is, of course, to take the risk of making mistakes; but that risk is the price that must be paid for the possibility of obtaining a single text which represents, as closely as available evidence will allow, what the author wished his text to be. One could perhaps argue—though I think not very convincingly—that for short works the first stage is sufficient, since readers will be in a position to judge the different versions for themselves. But certainly for novels and other long works, readers deserve to have the benefit of the editor's critical decisions; it is unrealistic to expect multiple texts of a novel to be published or to expect readers (whether comparing multiple texts or examining an apparatus) to hold in mind the different categories of variants in order to make informed judgments. I am not saying that the theoretical position is affected by the length of the work, for I believe that any text can benefit from the critical

14. For a fuller discussion of this whole issue, see G. T. Tanselle, "The Editorial Problem of Final Authorial Intention," *SB*, 29 (1976), 167–211.

attention of one who has become a specialist in that text and its background; I am only pointing out that there are practical problems, not met with in short works, which further complicate the editing of long works.

Because of those problems, textual investigation into novels often results in articles rather than editions. There has been an increase in the number of such articles since the time, twenty years ago, when Harkness complained of their scarcity; by now a considerable number of studies treating the texts of novels are available. Many of them are excellent, like those on Richardson mentioned earlier. And many of them convey more clearly than a list of variants could the nature of the alterations in heavily revised texts. An attempt to record all the variants between the early and late texts of certain of James's novels, for instance, would produce an unwieldy list, but an essay, through selection and subordination, can conveniently outline the kinds of revision undertaken and suggest the relative importance of each. Lists of variants present the raw material; textual essays offer interpretations of that material. The strength of essays thus also points to their weakness, for the reader of an essay is dependent on the evidence selected for inclusion and is not in a position to adduce further evidence in evaluating the conclusions of the essay. Textual essays are not substitutes for lists of variants, however useful and convenient they may be, particularly for novels. Recognizing the necessity for lists as well as analysis and commentary, several scholars in recent years have proposed that textual apparatuses for individual work be published as articles in journals. In 1964 Matthew J. Bruccoli published in *Studies in Bibliography* a complete apparatus—including, that is, a list of proposed emendations as well as a list of variants—for *Tender Is the Night*;[15] and in 1969 James B. Meriwether provided the fullest description of the rationale for this procedure in his proposal that Faulkner be edited in this way.[16] The idea of publishing all the editorial matter for an edition separately from the actual text offers the only way of proceeding in many instances, when a work is still in copyright and the copyright-holder does not wish to go to the expense of altering the present text. But, as Meriwether points out, this plan is also appropriate for "many out-of-copyright literary works which are badly in need of a better text, but which are unlikely to receive the financial sup-

15. "Material for a Centenary Edition of *Tender Is the Night*," SB, 17 (1964), 177–193.
16. In a paper delivered at the Toronto Editorial Conference in that year and published as "A Proposal for a CEAA Edition of William Faulkner," in *Editing Twentieth Century Texts*, ed. Francess G. Halpenny (1972), pp. 12–27. See also Bruccoli, "The SCADE Series: Apparatus for Definitive Editions," *Papers of the Bibliographical Society of America*, 67 (1973), 431–435, and the first volume in the series of South Carolina Apparatus for Definitive Editions, Bruccoli's *Apparatus for F. Scott Fitzgerald's* THE GREAT GATSBY (1974).

port that would make possible a new letterpress edition" (p. 26). This situation, of course, is directly attributable to the cost of printing and publishing works of novel-length. It is understandable, therefore, that textual research on novels may be published in the form of an essay or a separate apparatus. The increasing use of both forms is certainly to be welcomed and encouraged, and yet the fact remains that they are not *texts*. The existence of the material to accompany a reliably edited text is a very different thing from the existence of the edited text itself. How many readers can be expected to enter the necessary corrections into their copy of a novel or to hold a list of emendations in one hand and a novel in the other? Bruce Harkness ended his discussion of the "novelistic fallacy" by asking, "Can not we somehow insist that editing actually be done . . . ?" It is perhaps less difficult today than it was then to find people who will undertake the editing of novels, despite the problems which length entails; but length remains the crucial factor which complicates the process of getting the edited text published, disseminated, and accepted.

II

Editors of novels face other problems, of course, some of them related to the matter of length and some common to all editing. A convenient way to survey a number of these problems is to look at the editions which have been produced under the auspices of the Center for Editions of American Authors (CEAA). Of the authors so far accorded CEAA editions, six have written novels—Crane, Hawthorne, Howells, Melville, Simms, and Mark Twain.[17] More than twenty-five novels by these writers have been edited, and collectively these editions represent the outstanding achievement thus far in the editing of the novel.[18] The editorial theory behind them is Greg's rationale

17. The editions are as follows: *The University of Virginia Edition of the Works of Stephen Crane*, ed. Fredson Bowers (1969–); *The Centenary Edition of the Works of Nathaniel Hawthorne*, text ed. Fredson Bowers (1962–); *A Selected Edition of W. D. Howells*, ed. Edwin H. Cady, Don L. Cook, Ronald Gottesman, David J. Nordloh, *et al.* (1968–); *The Writings of Herman Melville: The Northwestern-Newberry Edition*, ed. Harrison Hayford, Hershel Parker, and G. Thomas Tanselle (1968–); *The Writings of William Gilmore Simms: Centennial Edition*, ed. John Caldwell Guilds and James B. Meriwether (1969–); and *The Mark Twain Papers*, ed. Frederick Anderson *et al.* (1966–). The dates of individual volumes are cited in the text, along with the names of the editors when they differ from those listed here.

18. Another edition of an American novel which should be mentioned here is William S. Kable's edition of William Hill Brown's *The Power of Sympathy* (1969); though it is not officially one of the CEAA editions, it fulfills the CEAA requirements, both in editorial approach and in presentation of material. See my review in *Early American Literature*, 6 (1971–72), 274–283.

of copy-text:[19] as a rule, therefore, the text chosen as the basis for the newly edited text is the fair-copy manuscript or, if it does not survive, the earliest printed edition based on that manuscript. If there is convincing evidence that an author gave careful attention to all details of a later edition, that edition would be the copy-text; but normally authors, even when they make changes in words (substantives) in later editions, do not reexamine all the punctuation, capitalization, and spelling (accidentals), with the result that later editions generally exhibit a progressive deterioration of accidentals. An editor who accepts the accidentals of the manuscript or earliest edition and emends that text with authoritative revisions from later editions is recognizing this divided authority. CEAA editors follow this procedure and thus produce *critical* texts—texts which are not simply reproductions of particular documentary forms of a text but which result from the application of critical judgment to the problem of correcting and emending a text so that it will more nearly reflect the author's intention than any of the surviving documentary forms. Greg's rationale has proved to be a satisfying and effective approach to critical editing because it does not attempt to substitute an arbitrary rule for editorial judgment, but it does offer the editor a way of thinking which enables him to maximize the chances of incorporating the author's wishes in instances where he otherwise has no basis for reaching a decision.[20]

The textual apparatus in the CEAA editions is more detailed than had previously been accorded to novels. Although the precise form of the entries and the physical arrangement of the different parts of the apparatus vary from edition to edition, all the CEAA editions include the same categories of information.[21] In addition to an essay setting forth the textual history of each novel, there are basically four sections in the apparatus, all of which are

19. "The Rationale of Copy-Text," *SB*, 3 (1950–51), 19–36; reprinted in Greg's *Collected Papers*, ed. J. C. Maxwell (1966), pp. 374–391. See also Fredson Bowers, "Some Principles for Scholarly Editions of Nineteenth-Century American Authors," *SB*, 17 (1964), 223–228, and "Textual Criticism," in *The Aims and Methods of Scholarship in Modern Languages and Literatures*, ed. James Thorpe, 2nd ed. (1970), pp. 29–54; and Center for Editions of American Authors, *Statement of Editorial Principles and Procedures*, rev. ed. (1972).

20. There have been a number of objections raised to Greg's approach, but most of them have arisen from a misunderstanding of what Greg actually said or a misconception of the CEAA's use of Greg. For an analysis of Greg's essay and a critical survey of the discussion it has provoked, see G. T. Tanselle, "Greg's Theory of Copy-Text and the Editing of American Literature," *SB*, 28 (1975), 167–229.

21. For a more detailed examination of CEAA apparatus, see G. T. Tanselle, "Some Principles for Editorial Apparatus," *SB*, 25 (1972), 41–88.

placed at the end of the volume. The decision to keep the text pages completely free of editorial matter is sensible, for it allows one to read the text
without the distraction of notes and makes the text pages more appropriate
for photo-offset reprinting in classroom editions. One section of the apparatus
consists of discursive notes explaining problematical readings or emendations.
(Some of these readings may have been used as illustrations in the textual
essay, but it is convenient in any case to have discussions of specific cruxes
gathered in one place for reference.) The other three parts of the apparatus
are lists: a list of the emendations (both substantives and accidentals) which
the editor has made in his copy-text; a list of the line-end hyphens in compound words in the copy-text and in the newly edited text; and a list of the
variant readings in authorized editions during the author's lifetime. With the
first of these lists the reader can reconstruct the copy-text and can examine
for himself each of the editor's decisions to emend it. The hypenation list is a
logical necessity because of the fact that it is not conventional in printed
books to distinguish line-end hyphens which merely mark a break at the end
of a line from those which would appear in a word regardless of its position
in the line. If the editor is to present a complete record of his decisions, he
must indicate how he has interpreted the ambiguous line-end hyphens of his
copy-text; similarly, if the reader is to know whether or not to retain certain
line-end hyphens in quoting from the newly edited critical text, the editor
must provide a list of those to be retained. Before the CEAA *Scarlet Letter*—
the first of the CEAA volumes—no edition had included information about
line-end hyphens; now, after the example of the CEAA volumes, no scholarly
edition can responsibly ignore it. And the remaining list gives the history
of the readings at each point of variation; if there are pre-copy-text materials
extant, a separate list may also record the variants in them—as when the
Hawthorne edition lists the alterations in the manuscript of *The House of
the Seven Gables* or the Crane edition lists those in *The Red Badge of Courage*. It is only in this historical listing that the characteristic CEAA apparatus
can be criticized for lack of thoroughness. Whereas the list of emendations
includes accidentals as well as substantives, the record of variants in authorized editions is normally limited to substantives, because the number of
variants in accidentals is often so enormous that to list them would be very
expensive and would greatly expand the apparatus. It is true that variants in
accidentals in later editions are less likely to be authorial than variants in
substantives, but without a record of them the reader is deprived of some of
the textual evidence on which editorial decisions were based. And when the
copy-text is a manuscript, this lack is more serious, for the variants in punc-

tuation between the manuscript and first edition (which would not be recorded) are of particular interest, especially if the intervening proofs have not survived; it may be that few, if any, of the differences are attributable to the author's alterations in proof, but the question cannot be reexamined by the reader without the evidence. That one has only this deficiency to complain about, however, is a mark of the thoroughness of the CEAA apparatuses. They have set a new standard not only because they do in fact include a great amount of data but also because they define with precision what is not included, so that the reader knows exactly where he stands in utilizing them.

The textual situations represented in CEAA editions of novels can be divided broadly into two classes: those in which the author's fair-copy manuscript or typescript is extant and those in which it is not. Of the former, the least complex situation is that in which the manuscript is the only source for the text, either because the text has never been published or because the only published versions are unauthorized or clearly corrupt. Mark Twain's *The Mysterious Stranger* (1916) was published posthumously in a version put together and altered by Albert Bigelow Paine, Twain's literary executor, and Frederick A. Duneka, an editor for Harpers. This distorted text obviously has no authority; and the California edition (ed. William M. Gibson, 1969)—which calls the earlier edition "an editorial fraud"—takes as its copy-texts the three manuscript versions of the work, emending them with Twain's own corrections on the surviving typescripts. In his admirable statement of editorial policy, Gibson points out that Twain was "a good speller" and was "meticulous about his punctuation" and that accidentals in his manuscripts have been altered "only when what he has written is obviously in error or inconsistent with his general and clear preference for one usage over another" (p. 494). Some emendations for consistency are made on the grounds that Twain "expected a publisher to impose a consistent texture on his accidentals," but whenever he appears to be "indifferent about usage" alternative spellings are "allowed to stand unchanged since they present no problem for an understanding of the text."

A less straightforward case, but one that again illustrates the importance of returning to a manuscript for copy-text, is Howells's *The Son of Royal Langbrith* (ed. David Burrows, Ronald Gottesman, and David J. Nordloh, 1969). Leaves from the author's manuscript and typescript survive for about half the text, and these are taken as copy-text for that portion of the novel in preference to the serial text in the *North American Review* or the first book edition (1904); for the rest of the book the copy-text is printer's typescript or, where it does not survive, the serial text. Since it appears unlikely that Howells read serial proofs against copy, some of the variants between the published serial text and the printer's typescript may be alterations occasioned solely by the errors in that typescript—alterations which Howells might not have made if his original text had been correctly reproduced. This consideration at least raises doubts about the serial variants at such points, and the chances of incorporating what Howells intended are greater by taking the manuscript-typescript readings. But, of course, where no prepublication material survives, there is no choice but to use the serial text. In following this procedure, the editors are employing a copy-text which represents more than one stage of the text; but that should be no argument against the procedure, for the chance of preserving more of the author's intended readings outweighs whatever desirability there might be in preserving the texture of a single document. Indeed, whenever consistency becomes an issue, it is the practice of the manuscript rather than the serial which carries more weight: for example, Howells's manuscript-typescript and the printer's typescript invariably spell the contraction "wont" without an apostrophe, and the Indiana editors therefore remove the apostrophe from the word in those parts of the novel for which the serial serves as copy-text.

Complete manuscripts survive for some of Hawthorne's and Crane's novels. As the Ohio State editions of *The Blithedale Romance* (1964), *The House of the Seven Gables* (1965), and *The Marble Faun* (1968) show, the extant fair-copy manuscripts of these works were used as printer's copy for the original editions. The characteristics of the accidentals in these three manuscripts are similar, and in each case there are thousands of differences in the accidentals of the printed texts, making a strong demonstration, even without the proofs, that the printed accidentals reflect house styling more than they do Hawthorne's preferences. It is possible, of course, that Hawthorne was responsible for some of the alterations, but it is generally not possible to determine just which ones. As Bowers points out in *The Blithedale Romance*,

> With comparatively few exceptions, therefore, a definitive edition must follow the forms of the manuscript, and not of the print. In doing so, the editor will perhaps lose some few Hawthorne alterations in the accidentals; but in these unknown and undeterminable cases he will at least preserve an authorial reading even though not a final one, and he will protect himself from accepting hundreds of printer's house-style variants as if they were the author's. (p. xl)

The same point is made in the other two volumes, and the three present an effective exposition of the basic argument for preferring the manuscript to the first edition. It is difficult to deny that accidentals are part of an author's expression and that normally, therefore, the author's accidentals are to be preferred to those supplied by the publisher (even when accepted by the author). The fact that manuscripts do not survive for some of Hawthorne's novels and that those novels must be edited from a printed copy-text does not affect the argument any more than the existence of only a partial manuscript does for *The Son of Royal Langbrith*; the texture of accidentals will not be the same throughout Hawthorne's works, but it will be based on the most authoritative documents available in each case. For Stephen Crane's novels, the available manuscripts are not the original printer's copy; as the Virginia editions of *The O'Ruddy* (1971) and *The Red Badge of Courage* (1975) show, a now missing typescript stood between the surviving manuscript and the first printed text of each of these books.[22] The latter case well illustrates some of the characteristic problems faced by editors of late nineteenth-century novels, involving as it does carbon typescripts and serialization: the missing typescript and a carbon copy of it were apparently revised by Crane independently to serve as printer's copy for the Bacheller syndicate master proof and for the first book edition. Determining the authority of substantive variants in such situations is naturally made more difficult by the absence of the printer's copy, but the choice of the manuscripts as copy-texts is not altered by the fact that in these instances the manuscripts were not printer's copy. In Bowers's words, most of the accidentals of Crane's *Red Badge* manuscript represent "what he intended to write according to his idiosyncratic system that is worth preserving for its own interest and for the importance that it may have for indicating the rhythms and pauses that he heard in his own ear as he wrote" (p. 222).

The fact that a holograph manuscript is generally the proper choice for copy-text over the first printed text, however, does not mean that it is always the preferable choice. This point is well illustrated in the Indiana edition of Howells's *Their Wedding Journey* (ed. John K. Reeves, with textual commentary by Ronald Gottesman, 1968), where the *Atlantic Monthly* serial text rather than the preserved holograph manuscript is used as copy-text. The principal reason for rejecting the manuscript is that it is only a provisional, and not a final or fair-copy, draft. When Howells made substantive alterations in this manuscript, he did not always make the necessary accompanying alterations in accidentals; his usual practice in finished manuscripts was to employ conventional punctuation, and the uncharacteristic incorrectness and inconsistency of the accidentals of this manuscript suggest that he had not given much attention to them. Therefore, as the editors rightly point

22. For Robert Barr's part of *The O'Ruddy*—chapters 26–33—the earliest surviving text is page proof.

out, "it makes no sense to preserve the great proportion of these readings, even on the argument that one can at least be sure that they represent
Howells' intentions, final or not" (p. 209). A second reason for preferring the
Atlantic text to the manuscript is that Howells was the editor of the *Atlantic*
at the time; he was extremely thorough in his revision and proofreading of
all contributions, and it seems likely that he would have been at least as
careful in going over his own contribution. In other words, the manuscript
here is a preliminary one, and the earliest printed text is one which the author
could oversee and control to a degree rarely possible; the printed text is
clearly the sensible choice for copy-text. In view of some of the misunderstanding that has arisen, it is worth pointing out that there is nothing in Greg's
theory or in the CEAA regulations which requires an editor to choose the
manuscript when compelling reason exists to do otherwise. What constitutes
compelling reason is of course a matter of judgment, but the CEAA editors
have effectively demonstrated that the mere fact of an author's having seen
the proofs for a given edition does not in itself constitute compelling reason
for choosing that edition as copy-text.

For about two-thirds of the novels so far published in CEAA editions,
however, no finished manuscript survives, and the copy-text has to be one
of the printed texts. In many cases the choice is straightforward and the
textual situation relatively uncomplicated. The American first edition becomes the copy-text in the Ohio State edition of Hawthorne's *The Scarlet Letter* (1962) and *Fanshawe* (1964), in the Virginia edition of Crane's *George's
Mother* (1969), and in the Northwestern-Newberry edition of Melville's *Pierre*
(1971) simply because no other text of these works carries any authority. The
choice of copy-text is no more difficult for most of Melville's other books, as
the new editions of *Omoo* (1968), *Mardi* (1970), *Redburn* (1969), and *White-
Jacket* (1970) show. Yet these works of Melville can illustrate a common
problem faced by editors of novels in the English language: that of determining the authority and chronology of variant readings in transatlantic editions.
An English edition of each of these titles was set from proofs of the American
(and published before the American, to secure English copyright); when a
conceivably authorial variant reading occurs, the English reading could be
the later one, if it were a revision which Melville entered on the proofs for
England, but the American could also be the later one, if it were an alteration
which Melville made after the proofs had already been sent to England.
There are not in fact many differences between the American and English
texts of *Omoo*, *Mardi*, and *Redburn*, but the two texts of *White-Jacket* vary
at a considerable number of points. Since Melville took the proofs of that

book to England himself, he had time on shipboard and several weeks after he arrived in London to make revisions, but he also returned to the United States in time that he could have made further revisions on the proofs for the American edition. The Northwestern-Newberry editors conclude that the nature of the variants themselves does not suggest that the American readings are later. But, in the absence of physical evidence, such a determination can rest only on critical judgment.[23] When a manuscript survives, of course, one has further evidence with which to make a judgment, as when certain readings in the English edition of *The Blithedale Romance* agree with the manuscript against the American edition, suggesting that the American readings at these points are later alterations in proof.

One way in which the textual history of novels is affected by their length is the possibility that they may be first published serially in periodicals or in separate parts. Several of the CEAA editions are of novels originally serialized, although serialization does not necessarily complicate the editorial process. In fact, two volumes in the South Carolina Simms edition, *Voltmeier* (1969) and *Paddy McGann* (1972), had not previously been published in book form, so the serial texts were the only available texts. But the serial is generally chosen as copy-text even when book editions exist, for the serial in most cases is the text set from the author's manuscript and is thus one step closer to that now missing manuscript. Scott Bennett, in the Indiana edition of Howells's *The Altrurian Romances* (1968), shows that Howells, though he revised the *Cosmopolitan* texts of *A Traveller from Altruria* and *Through the Eye of the Needle* for book publication, did not concern himself with the accidentals of the book texts; these novels therefore offer, as he says, "a textual problem of classic simplicity" (p. 465), the only problem being to determine which substantive variants in the book texts are authorial and are to be incorporated into the serial copy-texts. The situation is essentially the same for Howells's *A Chance Acquaintance* (ed. Ronald Gottesman, David J. Nordloh, and Jonathan Thomas, 1971), where the *Atlantic Monthly* serialization is copy-text. Several other volumes of the Howells edition utilize serial copy-texts but involve more complicated textual histories which can raise more interesting questions about the authority of substantive variants. The basic pattern is illustrated by *The Shadow of a Dream* (ed. Martha Banta, Gottesman, and Nordloh, 1970), where the *Harper's Monthly* proof was the copy for David Douglas's Edinburgh edition (to secure English copyright)

23. In addition to the discussions in the volumes of the Northwestern-Newberry Edition, comment on these situations is made in G. T. Tanselle, "Bibliographical Problems in Melville," *Studies in American Fiction*, 2 (1974), 57–74.

and where the American book publication consisted of impressions from the Douglas plates, with some revisions by Howells being made at each stage. In *Indian Summer* (ed. Scott Bennett and Nordloh, 1971) and *April Hopes* (ed. Don L. Cook, James P. Elliott, and Nordloh, 1974), there is evidence to suggest that Howells probably made further substantive revisions on the magazine proofs after sending one set to Douglas, thus providing an additional reason for editorial reliance on the serial text. David J. Nordloh gives the fullest discussion of this situation, and of some further related complications, in the Indiana edition of *The Rise of Silas Lapham* (ed. Nordloh and Walter J. Meserve, 1971). In the first eighteen chapters of that book, Howells was able to make additional revisions on Douglas's copyright proof after final revision had been completed for the serial (indeed, after the *Century* installment had been published); but the timing of Douglas's publication of his book edition (June 1885) meant that it was almost certainly impossible for Howells to have had the opportunity to see the copyright proofs of the last nine chapters. As a result, the status of a substantive variant differs according to where it occurs: in the first eighteen chapters, the Douglas edition is likely to contain a number of late revisions, whereas in the last nine chapters the serial text is likely to have the latest readings. The editors' policy, therefore, in cases where the copyright proofs agree either with the Douglas edition against the magazine or with the magazine against the Douglas edition, is to accept the unique substantive reading in each case. There is no problem, in others words, about the choice of the *Century* serialization as copy-text; the complications arise only in determining what emendations to make in that text, and Nordloh has set forth very clearly and concisely the guidelines for emendation which the facts in this case impose on an editor.

One issue which emerges briefly in the editing of *Lapham* is the extent to which Howells made alterations because of outside pressures. Two alterations in particular are at issue: the deletion of a discussion of the Jews and of a reference to dynamite. Since Howells apparently made the former deletion before he received criticism of the passage, the editors accept the deletion as reflecting Howells's own intention; but because Howells eliminated the reference to dynamite only after the editor and publisher of the *Century* expressed their concern, the editors have restored it. It is difficult, certainly, to reconstruct an author's motives, and one might argue the first case the other way. But one cannot avoid, in a critical text, making judgments about the extent to which an author's revision reflects his real intention as opposed to his acquiescence to outside pressures. This issue is more central to the editing of *Typee*, for Melville prepared a revised edition of that work, upon

the request of his publisher, softening or eliminating the criticism of missionaries, and then said that the revised version was an improvement. The Northwestern-Newberry edition (1968), however, takes Melville's statement as a
rationalization of the drastic alteration in the tone of the book which he
had been forced to make, and it therefore uses the original edition as copy-
text and retains the passages later deleted.[24] Perhaps the most difficult instance
of this kind so far encountered in a CEAA novel is Crane's *Maggie*. Bowdleri-
zation of the text of the privately printed edition of 1893 was a condition of
Appleton's acceptance of the book for publication in 1896, and the Virginia
edition (1969) therefore takes the original edition as copy-text and does not
accept Crane's revisions made under external pressure to expurgate. The
difficulty comes in drawing the line between those revisions and other revisions made at the same time but for literary reasons. Which category the
elimination of the episode of the "huge fat man"—to take the most famous
example—falls into can be argued both ways. Bowers's position, set forth in
detail (pp. lxxvii–xci), is that Crane deleted the passage for artistic reasons
and that the deletion cannot be thought of as producing a separate work,
and the Virginia text therefore does not include the passage. However, a
strong case can be made that the two versions of *Maggie* represent Crane's
differing conceptions of the work and are so divergent that they can only
be edited as individual works. Both positions rest on literary arguments, and
Bowers's edition represents one of the defensible ways of handling the matter.
Those who have attacked this edition have not always recognized that to
disagree with his textual decisions (which entail literary judgment) is not to
discredit the textual theory within which he is working. A critical edition is
a piece of literary criticism, as all the CEAA editions show and as this one
demonstrates in a particularly striking way. For this reason it is only the
apparatus of a CEAA edition that can really be called "definitive"; and, so
long as one believes that an author's intended text can be more effectively
recovered through the exercise of editorial judgment than through the reproduction of a single document, there is no point in wishing for absolutely
"definitive" texts. It is true that some critical texts will incorporate judgments with which one does not agree, but that is a price worth paying for
what they accomplish as a whole.

One of the most troublesome problems in editing, whether one is dealing
with a manuscript or a printed copy-text, is the extent to which the accidentals should be made consistent. CEAA editions of novels exhibit more than

24. Cf. Hershel Parker, "Melville and the Concept of 'Author's Final Intentions,' "
Proof, 1 (1971), 156–168.

one approach to the question. In the Hawthorne and Crane editions, for instance, inconsistencies are regularized according to the author's dominant practice, whereas in the Melville edition no attempt is made to produce consistency in accidentals when the variant forms are acceptable (outright errors, of course, are corrected in all the editions). There are several reasons, it seems to me, why regularizing should not be undertaken in scholarly un-modernized editions like those of the CEAA.[25] To begin with, it is faulty logic to assume that the dominant form in a given text represents the author's preferred form. Inconsistencies abound in nineteenth-century manuscripts and printed texts, and one has no assurance in most cases that the authors regarded consistency as an ideal to be striven for. Selecting one form for consistent use, therefore, may actually eliminate what the author desired and to some extent defeat the purpose of selecting an early copy-text as authority for accidentals. The notion of consistency in accidentals is given too great a weight if it leads to the position that a consistent form in a given text is not to be altered, even though it varies from the author's known practice in sur-viving manuscripts of other works, whereas an inconsistent form does require alteration, even though it is conceivable that the form which will be elimi-nated was actually the author's preferred one or that he had no desire for consistency. The principle, followed in CEAA editions, that a critical text must be based on the surviving documentary forms of a work (even if the resulting texture of an author's works varies from one book to another) is a sound one, in my view, because an author's habits do change, and it would be fallacious to assume that the practices of one manuscript were necessarily those of another, now missing, manuscript from a different period in the author's life. If it is accepted, then, that the imposition of consistency from one book to another might result in distortion of the author's intention, it is difficult to see why the imposition of consistency within a single book may not also be a similar distortion. Underlying Greg's theory of copy-text is the belief that accidentals do constitute an important part of an author's ex-pression, and CEAA practice in selecting copy-texts places a concern for getting as close as possible to the author's accidentals above a concern for uniformity of texture (the mixture of manuscript and printed copy-text for *The Son of Royal Langbrith* effectively illustrates the point). It would seem to be more in keeping with this approach to allow inconsistent forms, except those which are unquestionably erroneous, to stand. A regularized text can

25. I have also discussed this matter in "The New Editions of Hawthorne and Crane," *Book Collector*, 23 (1974), 214–229.

no longer be thought of in most instances as an unmodernized text,[26] and in this respect some of the CEAA editions can be regarded as not fully attaining their goal. For the most part, however, the CEAA editions are enormously successful both in the quality of their texts and in the fullness of their apparatuses. Certainly they have done more to raise the standards of editing novels than anything that has gone before.[27]

III

Although there has been no counterpart to the CEAA in the editing of British novels, two projects in particular deserve to be singled out, the Wesleyan Fielding and the series of Clarendon Editions. Ian Watt was right to feel that the first volumes of the Fielding and the Clarendon Dickens "mark the auspicious beginnings of a new era,"[28] for certainly both reflect more detailed textual work than any previous edition of these novels. But the picture is not as auspicious as it might be: there are important differences between the two which indicate an unfortunate divergence between American and British practice. It is worth examining in some detail the ways in which the two approaches differ, both in editorial theory and in treatment of apparatus, for it is only through an understanding of these differences that a more consolidated effort may result in the future.

The Fielding (though distributed in England by the Clarendon Press) is an American undertaking,[29] and it follows the plan of the CEAA editions. The first volume, Martin C. Battestin's edition of *Joseph Andrews* (1967), contains a textual introduction by Fredson Bowers summarizing Greg's theory and explaining its application to the textual history of the book. That history is not complicated: there were five editions during Fielding's lifetime, each of the later ones set from a copy of the immediately preceding one. Fielding made extensive revisions in the second edition and a few revisions in the third and fourth editions; the variants in the fifth edition appear to have no authority. Although most modern editions derive from the Murphy editions of 1762, eight years after Fielding's death, it is clear, in view of Greg's rationale, that an authoritative text must take as its copy-text either

26. Cf. Hershel Parker, "Regularizing Accidentals: The Latest Form of Infidelity," *Proof*, 3 (1973), 1–20.
27. Some reviews of CEAA editions are listed in the CEAA *Statement of Editorial Principles and Procedures*, p. 23. See also "The CEAA: An Interim Assessment," by Hershel Parker with Bruce Bebb, *Papers of the Bibliographical Society of America*, 68 (1974), 129–148.
28. In his review of *Joseph Andrews* in *Philological Quarterly*, 47 (1968), 379.
29. *Wesleyan Edition of the Works of Henry Fielding*, gen. ed. W. B. Coley (1967–).

the first or the second edition (the manuscript does not survive). While there is no question that most of the substantive differences in the second edition are attributable to Fielding, there is no evidence that the alterations in accidentals are his. As Bowers says, "The odds do not favour an author of the time tinkering extensively with the accidentals of printed copy so long as his meaning had not been altered as a result of house-styling" (p. xl). The situation is thus a perfect illustration of Greg's recognition that the authority for accidentals and the authority for substantives need not lie in the same text. What Battestin does, then, is to take the first edition as copy-text, in order to preserve the formal features of the extant text closest to the missing manuscript, emending it with the authoritative substantive variants in the second edition. Because of the extent of Fielding's revision of the second edition, each substantive variant in that edition is accepted as his unless there is strong reason to think it is not; in the third and fourth editions, on the other hand, where only a few revisions appear to be authorial, each variant is rejected unless there is strong reason to believe it is Fielding's. This procedure involves the critical evaluation of each variant in the light of all that is known about the text in which it occurs; in Bowers's words, "the part is always surveyed in relation to the whole so that the circumstances surrounding the production of any given edition can be used as evidence, or at least as suggesting a 'climate of opinion,' when an individual reading is under scrutiny" (pp. xli–xlii).

If this approach seems routine to those acquainted with the CEAA editions, the accompanying apparatus would also seem familiar. Battestin, like the CEAA editors, provides a list of emendations (here subdivided into two, one for substantives and one for accidentals), a list dealing with line-end hyphenation, and a "historical collation," recording the substantive and semisubstantive variants in the first five editions. These lists, placed at the end of the text,[30] enable the reader to know (with the exception of a few categories of silent alteration) what has been done to the copy-text and to examine the substantive variants which have not been accepted. The only questionable practice—as with some of the CEAA editions—involves the failure to report two groups of accidentals. First are the categories of silent emendations. The problem here is not merely that any silent alterations, however unimportant they may seem, reduce by that much the reader's ability to know precisely what the copy-text reading is at any given point; there is the prior question of whether such alterations are necessary. Bowers

30. Explanatory notes are placed on the pages of text as footnotes.

points out that Battestin "has not tried to achieve an unnatural consistency" in accidentals (p. xliii). Nevertheless, we are told that the reader's convenience is kept in mind in making certain emendations of accidentals, where the inconsistencies of the original might prove distracting. But it is very tricky to attempt to draw a line between inconsistencies in accidentals which must be retained in an unmodernized text and those which can in effect be modernized without compromising the aim of presenting an unmodernized text. Battestin silently normalizes (and modernizes) the handling of quotations in several ways: by deleting the running quotation marks along the left margin of a quotation, by supplying missing opening or closing quotation marks, by taking the dominant system of punctuation associated with quotations as a norm to be followed in each instance, by making consistent the dominant practice of not using quotation marks in connection with the parenthetical identification of speakers, and by consistently using a lowercase letter to begin indirect quotations which are placed in quotation marks. It can hardly be argued that missing opening and closing quotation marks should not be supplied (though it can plausibly be maintained that the reader ought to be informed as to where such emendations—which are, after all, acts of judgment—have been made). But it is at least debatable whether the normalizing of punctuation in relation to quotations accomplishes anything other than to suppress the practice of the period in favor of a modern preference for consistency; and as long as this issue can be raised, it would seem desirable to have a record of where such changes have been made.[31] The other major question about the recording of accidentals has to do with the fact that only substantives and semisubstantives are included in the historical collation; yet the variants in accidentals in the second edition have an important bearing on the choice of copy-text. Since Fielding made numerous revisions in substantives in that edition, it is conceivable that he revised the accidentals as well; without a record of those variants the reader has no way of reexamining the editor's conclusion that Fielding did not in fact revise them. Despite the absence of these categories of information (which are also absent from some of the editions awarded the CEAA seal), one must recognize the great merits of this edition of *Joseph Andrews*. It makes effective applica-

31. Matters of typography and design, of course, are nontextual, and one could argue that the old method of placing running quotation marks along the left margin falls into this category and is thus not a matter of accidentals at all. However, another class of silent emendations, the elimination of the small capitals at the beginning of each paragraph, is perhaps not quite so easily justified in an unmodernized edition.

tion of Greg's theory, provides an extensive apparatus, and makes explicit just what information can and cannot be found there. In following the CEAA plan, it brings a new standard to the editing of British fiction.

The first volume of the Clarendon Dickens,[32] Kathleen Tillotson's edition of *Oliver Twist* (which appeared the year before *Joseph Andrews*), is also an important achievement in editing: Mrs. Tillotson has investigated the complicated textual history of this work more thoroughly than it has been done before and impressively works out the relationships among the texts. But in two respects her edition falls short of Battestin's *Joseph Andrews*. The first of these is the defense she presents for her choice of copy-text. She selects the 1846 edition as "the only text which was thoroughly revised and corrected by Dickens throughout its length" (p. xl), and she shows that in it Dickens concerned himself with accidentals as well as substantives, experimenting with a system of punctuation which "suggests pauses for the voice rather than conventional syntactical relationship" (p. xxxvii). Her choice may well be the proper one, but the point is that her discussion leaves some basic questions unanswered, so that the argument is not fully convincing. To begin with, the status of the revised punctuation is not made clear. It is suggested that Dickens returned to more conventional punctuation soon after 1846 (pp. xxxviii–xxxix), and the 1846 text is called "a document in the development of Dickens's style, of which the punctuation is a vital part." If so, one may wonder whether the 1846 punctuation is appropriate for a text which is to reflect the author's ultimate wishes; the later editions, in 1850 and 1867, do not appear to have received careful enough attention from Dickens to be appropriate for copy-text, but it is possible that the accidentals of an earlier edition might be a better representation of Dickens's final wishes than the idiosyncratic punctuation of 1846. The manuscript survives for twenty-two chapters, and, as a result of Mrs Tillotson's excellent analysis, it is known just what printed texts were set from manuscript: the *Bentley's Miscellany* text through October 1838, the three-volume 1838 edition for the remaining chapters (so that the book could be published before the part-issue had been concluded), and the one-volume Philadelphia edition from chapter 44 on (Mrs. Tillotson is the first to have investigated the Philadelphia editions and to have discovered the early readings which they alone preserve).[33] With these

32. *The Clarendon Dickens*, gen. eds. John Butt and Kathleen Tillotson (1966–).
33. Her admirable discussion of the Philadelphia editions is for some reason relegated to Appendix A, pp. 372–381. Although she has established their importance, she does not include them in her list of "substantive editions" (p. xxx), and she seems reluctant to cite them in her textual notes. On page 379 she lists readings of the one-volume Philadelphia edition which are "accountable only as Dickens's own revisions on a very early proof of the

materials available and their relationships now known, one could choose as copy-text the surviving parts of the manuscript, filled out by the printed text set from the manuscript; this copy-text could then be emended with later authorial variants, both substantive and accidental. Proceeding in this way would seem to offer a greater possibility of avoiding compositorial errors which Dickens overlooked; since the 1846 edition was set from a revised copy of 1841, it inevitably contains a certain amount of accumulated error. Mrs. Tillotson does make fifty-two substantive emendations of the 1846 text with readings from the manuscript or first editions, but to work in this direction gives the benefit of the doubt to the 1846 text. (And the statement that Dickens's "occasional later revisions are confined to the apparatus" [p. xl] does not explain why those readings do not supersede the 1846 readings.) In regard to accidentals, it is hard to believe that a similar situation does not exist there and that they do not also involve errors which slipped past Dickens.[34] In short, Mrs. Tillotson does not explain in detail why the usual procedure under Greg's rationale is not appropriate in this instance; I am not saying that it necessarily is appropriate but only that the reader is not provided with a thoroughly documented statement of the case.[35]

The other area in which this edition of *Oliver Twist* is somewhat less satisfactory than the Wesleyan *Joseph Andrews* is its handling of textual apparatus. A distinction should be made, of course, between matters of formal presentation and those affecting the actual content of the lists. While it seems to me a mistake to place the record of emendations and variant readings at the foot of each page with footnote numbers in the text (it is distracting to the reader and makes the text less suitable for photographic reproduction as a classroom text), this is only a question of arrangement and could be argued both ways. Of more substance is the specification of what is to be listed. The

---

October instalment of *Bentley's*"; but when these readings are recorded in the regular textual notes, their source is misleadingly reported as "*early proof of* B."

34. One curious fact about the accidentals in the Clarendon text is that the quotation marks throughout were incorrectly set, apparently through a misunderstanding at the Press, and were not altered thereafter: "Single quotation marks have been substituted for double; this was not the intention of the editors, and the usage of the original editions (known to have been Dickens's own preference) will be followed in future volumes" (p. xliv, note 2). (The fact that the editor regards this usage of Dickens as significant should be compared with her policy of disregarding the "common practice [at that time] of leaving a space in contracted forms.")

35. A more detailed examination of the choice of copy-text and the policy of emendation can be found in Fredson Bowers's review of this volume in *Nineteenth-Century Fiction*, 23 (1968–69), 226–239. One of the matters he takes up is the questionable decision to accept the passages which Dickens added to make a monthly part long enough but to reject the material he deleted in order to shorten a part (pp. xxxiv–xxxvi).

record of variants is said to include "only the more important" of the deletions in the manuscript and "Almost all" of the substantive differences between manuscript and print (presumably it does include all the substantive
differences among the printed texts, but the point is not made explicitly);
it does not record differences in accidentals or "changes of form such as
farther/further, while/whilst, sunk/sank, hanged/hung" (and, still more de-
batably, *upon/on* and *till/until*); and it omits "Obvious errors" in the manuscript and "generally" omits errors in the printed texts corrected before or in
the 1846 edition, though errors in the two later editions (1850 and 1867),
"other than literal misprints," are given, "since they have become current in
modern texts" (p. xlv). The questionable logic of the latter point is not the
main issue; the important question is whether these categories are too dependent on individual judgment. A number of emendations, too, are excluded from the record. "Misprints" in the 1846 text are "silently corrected,"
and spelling, hyphenation, and the form of contractions (the placing of the
apostrophe and the spacing of the elements) are silently made consistent.[36]
Much of this regularizing seems unnecessary, but that is a different issue.
What I am questioning is whether the classes of material left out of the
printed record are clear-cut enough so that a reader can know just what he
has available. A critical text naturally depends upon critical judgment, but
the purpose of an apparatus is to document that judgment with factual information. If in too many categories judgment is involved in determining
what is to be included in the apparatus, then the usefulness of the apparatus
is seriously diminished. In the Wesleyan *Joseph Andrews*, certain categories
are perhaps unwisely excluded, but at least the categories themselves are well
defined, and the reader knows where he stands; but he is at the mercy of the

36. The principle for making the spelling consistent is similar to that in the Centenary
Hawthorne, and the same objection to it can be raised. Mrs. Tillotson says that when a
spelling in the 1846 edition is "both consistent and acceptable in its own time," it is retained; but an inconsistent spelling is made consistent on the basis of "Dickens's own
preference as shown in the manuscript" or "the relative frequency" of the spellings in the
1846 text. One of the logical difficulties with this position, of course, is that consistency (or
the domination of a particular form) does not necessarily reflect authorial preference;
another is that it assumes, without evidence, that an author's intention is necessarily to be
consistent in choosing among acceptable variant spellings. The practical result of such a
policy may be to eliminate authorial preferences. Mrs. Tillotson does, however, allow one
category of inconsistent spellings: "An exception has to be made for the spelling used
in the speech of 'low' characters, where colloquial forms and sub-standard pronunciations
are variously represented, even within the speech of a single character. Dickens's representation of such speech is impressionistic, and even if the distinction between *an't* and *ain't*
is only a visual one it seems worth preserving" (p. xliv). This line of reasoning might
profitably have been applied to other spellings as well.

editor when categories are described with such phrases as "only the more important" or "almost all." One other shortcoming of the Dickens apparatus is its failure to include any instructions for interpreting ambiguous line-end hyphens in the Clarendon text.[37] A list of those line-end hyphens which should be retained in quotations from the text would take up very little space, but such a list is an essential part of any scholarly presentation of an established text of prose. It has nothing to do, obviously, with the record of variant readings or emendations; its function is not to record historical information but to clarify the readings of the newly edited text at points where the necessity for justifying the right-hand margin has obscured that reading. This omission from *Oliver Twist* is all the more surprising because the editor has taken pains to make the hyphenation of words in the text consistent.

These remarks can equally well be applied to the second of the Clarendon volumes, Margaret Cardwell's edition of *The Mystery of Edwin Drood* (1972), for it follows the same editorial plan. But the most interesting thing about this volume is the fact that the evidence against the chosen copy-text is increased by the set of proofs which became available while the edition itself was in proof and which is summarized at the end of the volume. Although the manuscript of *Drood* survives (lacking only one leaf), Miss Cardwell chooses the 1870 first edition as copy-text because it is "obviously" the "authoritative" text (except for the last two chapters, for which "the manuscript is the guide to Dickens's intention," because he did not live to see those chapters in proof).[38] That this is an unwise decision, however, seems clear even without the evidence of the complete set of proofs. Miss Cardwell points out that Dickens engaged in a considerable amount of stylistic revision between the manuscript and the published text; but she admits, "At the same time that he was giving great care to his choice of words, he was capable of being incredibly careless over his proof-reading" (p. xxxiii). Then, in her discussion of emendations, she points out that the author's proofs for chapters 17–21 (which were available all along) contain about one hundred "printers' errors," of which only thirty-six were corrected by Dickens to the original reading and six more were altered to a new reading (he did not read proofs against copy). Her policy for this part of the book (roughly forty pages) is to restore

37. For instance, the word "book-stall" is hyphenated at the end of a line at 57.30 and 95.29, and "work-house" at 1.20 and 33.9. It is true that "book-stall," with the hyphen, also occurs within the line (as at 58.5), as does "workhouse" without the hyphen (as at 1.7); but the reader, when he wishes to quote a passage, cannot be expected to search for such occurrences.

38. By calling the manuscript "the guide to Dickens's intention" in these chapters, she does not mean that it becomes copy-text.

the manuscript reading where Dickens made no correction ("This sometimes gives a markedly improved reading"); and where "a printer's error led to a further alteration by Dickens, the manuscript reading has been restored if it seems unlikely that Dickens would have preferred a change but for the mistake in proof" (p. xxxv). For the preceding sixteen chapters, where no such proof was available, the restoration of manuscript readings is "more cautious," but no emendation is made without manuscript authority. And for the final two chapters, which Dickens could not have seen in proof, she observes that the 1870 edition contains "more than fifty printers' errors"; yet her list of substantive emendations shows that she uses the 1870 as copy-text even here and reinstates the manuscript readings. Altogether she emends the 1870 text substantively with manuscript readings at 140 points.

The pattern that emerges, therefore, supports Greg's view of copy-text and suggests that more of Dickens's intended readings would have been incorporated in the text if the manuscript had been taken as copy-text and emended only at those points where the 1870 reading can convincingly be argued to be Dickens's alteration.[39] Miss Cardwell's decision to use 1870 cannot have been based on the evidence of the substantive variants and must result from her judgment in regard to accidentals. She says, "Proofs for other novels show that Dickens normally expected the printer to revise his punctuation" (p. xliv). However, his failure to alter nearly two-thirds of the substantive differences in the proof of chapters 17–21 does not lend credence to the view that his passing in proof various differences in accidentals means that he actively wished to have the accidentals in that form. This argument for the manuscript as copy-text is made even more convincing by the complete set of proofs described in Appendix H. These proofs, originally sent to Luke Fildes, the illustrator of the volume, were in the possession of Colonel Richard Gimbel at the time Miss Cardwell was editing the volume, but he was not willing to allow her to consult them. After his death, the Beinecke Library made them available, and she was able to report on them only in that appendix. Although they are less heavily corrected than the surviving part

39. The value of the manuscript readings has been attested to by Angus Wilson in his review of this volume. Although he asserts that "an author is often happier to correct a book as he reads it in proof from his own impressions gained *at that reading*, rather than to return to his original manuscript," he admits that there are "many very vital readings which Miss Cardwell has been able to restore from manuscript" and states, "There are, I should say, about seven or eight such manuscript restorations which do so vitally affect the text that even a sceptic about scholarly exactitude like myself must be won over" (*Dickensian*, 69 [1973], 48–51).

of the proof for the printers, they do enable one to determine that certain differences resulted from the compositors rather than Dickens, especially in chapters 10–16, where these proofs are first proofs. Miss Cardwell acknowledges, "Had the material been available from the outset, more MS readings would have been restored" (p. 256); and she provides lists, supplementing the regular apparatus, detailing the evidence about substantive variants which the new proofs furnish—concluding that twenty-eight more manuscript readings would have been restored, as opposed to only eight places where the 1870 readings would now be preferred to the manuscript. It is extremely unfortunate that these proofs were not made available to Miss Cardwell at an earlier stage in her work; it must be very frustrating for her, after years of research, to have to publish the edition in this awkward form—and all because of the lack of cooperation on the part of an important collector. Although the price is too high to pay for an experiment demonstrating the correctness of Greg's theory of copy-text, that in effect is what we now have in published form in this volume.

The third volume of the Clarendon Dickens, Alan Horsman's edition of *Dombey and Son* (1974), follows the policies of the series already seen in the previous two volumes. The first edition of 1848 is chosen as copy-text, even though the whole manuscript survives (along with a considerable amount of proof). Yet the editorial comments, as with *Drood*, repeatedly suggest the superiority of the manuscript. In regard to substantives we are told, for instance, that the emendations "reinstate superior MS readings which Dickens overlooked when correcting the proof and some corrections which he made in the proof but the printer apparently overlooked" (p. xxxviii); and when an error in proof caused Dickens, in correcting, to produce an "inferior" reading, the manuscript reading is restored (p. xxxix). In regard to accidentals, so much emphasis is placed on the assumption that Dickens must have approved the alterations he found in proof that the defense of the first edition as copy-text begins to sound halfhearted. Dickens's idiosyncratic system of punctuation, Horsman says, was somewhat weakened by the printers; nevertheless,

enough of the commas where grammar would reject them, semicolons where commas would do, and colons for parentheses survive to achieve the aim of making decisive all those divisions of the sentence which must be observed in reading aloud. Dickens is presumably satisfied with the result; at any rate he makes no attempt radically to alter it later. So the editor is justified in following 48 as a general rule. Occasionally, as with substantive readings, something better is available in the MS; in such cases (relatively few) it has been restored, but silently unless it decisively changes the sense. (p. xl)

Since Dickens did not alter spelling in proof, "the inference is fair that he approved of the printer's attempts to regularize" (p. xli), even though he did not always accept the changes of capitalization in proof. In summary Horsman states, "It is no doubt a loss that a number of cases of idiosyncrasy or emphasis in the MS should disappear, but the defense is that where Dickens attached importance to them he altered the proof" (p xli). What an author fails to alter in proof, of course, does not necessarily reflect his positive preference, and it is unfortunate that the defense of the choice of copy-text here cannot be put on firmer ground. One other aspect of the editorial policy in *Dombey* should perhaps be noted. Speaking of the alterations which appear in later editions, Horsman says that "even those which seem to be the author's own are made so sporadically that it is difficult to prefer the results of such a half-hearted revision to the decisions made in the original energy of composition" (p. xxxvi). The principle involved here is well recognized and defensible, though it should perhaps be stated in such a way that it does not make the timing of the changes the sole factor. But the thinking which leads to this position would logically take one back to the manuscript, not the first edition, as copy-text.

Another Clarendon edition in progress—of the Brontës' novels[40]—follows the same general plan as the Dickens, with textual notes at the foot of the page, and takes the same approach to the choice of copy-text. The fair-copy manuscript of *Jane Eyre* which was used as printer's copy is extant, but Jane Jack and Margaret Smith's edition (1969) chooses the first edition as copy-text, citing two letters from Charlotte Brontë to her publishers thanking them for bringing her punctuation into order. The punctuation of the manuscript, in the editors' words, is "much lighter and more informal" than that of the first edition; but, they say, "it is clearly the duty of an editor to preserve the system of punctuation in the first edition, so decidedly accepted by the author herself" (p. xv). The editors, nevertheless, seem to have a lingering attraction to the accidentals of the manuscript, because one of their reasons for preferring the first to a later edition is that the first "is, as one would expect, closer to the MS in accidentals than are the second and third editions" (p. xx). There is no argument about the fact that the first is closer to the manuscript, but the statement is illogical in this context.[41] If one accepts Charlotte

40. *The Clarendon Edition of the Novels of the Brontës*, gen. eds. Ian and Jane Jack (1969–   ).
41. It is similar to a statement made later by Philip Gaskell, in *A New Introduction to Bibliography* (1972); his chapter on editing (pp. 336–360) takes the position that "in most cases the editor will choose as copy-text an early printed edition, not the manuscript" (p. 340).

Brontë's remarks at face value, then the punctuation of the first edition super-
sedes that of the manuscript, and it is therefore no merit of the first edition
to be closer to the manuscript than other editions are; on the other hand, if
an argument can be made for preferring the punctuation of the manuscript
as representing the author's real intentions, despite her statement, then the
manuscript itself would become the copy-text. The argument for the manuscript has in fact been well put by one of the Clarendon editors, Margaret
Smith, in the 1973 reprinting of the Clarendon text of *Jane Eyre* in the Oxford English Novels series:

> The printed text inevitably tones down the occasionally erratic but expressive point-
> ing of the manuscript. Charlotte made abundant use of dashes and commas instead of
> heavier semicolons or even periods. The effect is often of rapid, emotional speech or
> thought. She also used a number of capitals for various personified abstractions or
> concepts such as the Past, Memory, or Passion, and frequently, though not always,
> for the word Master. The first edition retains only a few of these, but we must pre-
> sume that Charlotte accepted it as adequate. (p. xxix)

To accept something as adequate (for any number of practical reasons) is far
different from preferring it as an artistic improvement, and this statement
only serves to whet the reader's appetite for a text based on the manuscript.
A few emendations from manuscript, we are told, have been incorporated at
places where the "first edition quite seriously distorts the intended meaning";
but this, of course, is to work backward and produces very different results
from a process which takes the manuscript as the starting-point.

Two other recent volumes, not parts of any larger series, deserve to be
mentioned. Gardner Stout's edition of Sterne's *Sentimental Journey*[42] was
published the same year as Battestin's *Joseph Andrews* and, like that volume,
has a more comprehensive apparatus than the Clarendon editions. It is unfortunate that each page of text is encumbered with two sets of notes, one textual and one explanatory, but the notes themselves are generally well handled; and the apparatus is noteworthy for its inclusion (with acknowledgment
of the Hawthorne edition) of a record of line-end hyphenation. One of the
appendixes provides a list of page-line references for all emendations, so that
the entries for them can be located in the notes; this is helpful but is not as
easy to use as if all the textual notes had been brought together at the end,
with the emendations separated from the record of variants. The textual
problem is not complicated, for Sterne apparently went over the proofs of the
first edition carefully, and he died three weeks after the publication of that

42. *A Sentimental Journey through France and Italy by Mr. Yorick,* ed. Gardner D.
Stout, Jr. (1967).

edition. The first edition is the only choice for copy-text for the second volume, but for the first there is the possibility of choosing the manuscript, which survives. Stout decides in favor of the first edition, however, arguing that it follows the punctuation of the manuscript carefully and also incorporates Sterne's revisions and the routine corrections which he expected the printer to make. In cases of indifferent variants, therefore, Stout has accepted the first-edition readings, assuming that Sterne "approved these changes even if he did not make them himself" (p. 50). After describing some of the differences in accidentals between the manuscript and the first edition, Stout repeats the point:

I have been unable, in specific instances, to assign even these more significant variants [in accidentals] with any confidence to Sterne rather than to the printing-house editor or compositor. However, since Sterne evidently proofread $A1$, all the changes in accidentals between $S1$ and $A1$ may be regarded as generally authorized even if not specifically authorial. (p. 52)

The weaknesses of this familiar argument should by now be evident. As stated here, the position is in direct opposition to that advocated by Greg; yet Stout acknowledges that Sterne "was, in general, very careful about specifying accidentals" in his manuscript. Rather than assume that differences in the first edition result from his equal care in reading proofs, the more conservative approach would be to accept the text which is known to be his as the copy-text. In any event it is regrettable, given the attention which Sterne paid to accidentals, that many of the variants in accidentals between the manuscript and the first edition cannot be recovered from the notes provided.

Four years earlier Geoffrey and Kathleen Tillotson published their edition of *Vanity Fair* (1963), which also presents its textual notes as footnotes and fails to record the differences in accidentals (and some of the substantives as well) between the copy-text (1853) and the manuscript and first edition. A peculiarity of this edition is that substantive emendations proposed by the editors without the authority of the manuscript or first edition, even when they are obvious, are only mentioned in footnotes and not incorporated into the text. Thus where the text reads "lowering covering" (p. 496), the footnote says, "So in all editions, but 'lower' was presumably intended." Where the text reads, "If even Cynthia looks haggard . . . how much more can old Lady Castlemouldy keep her head up" (p. 461), the word "more" should obviously be "less"; but the editors do not alter the text because, they say, "An occasional looseness of syntax is characteristic of Thackeray, and we have not presumed to correct him" (p. xli). Yet when it comes to accidentals, they emend punctuation "where it is obviously mistaken or ambiguous" (p. xl), making a number of silent corrections. The logic of this procedure is difficult to comprehend: on the one hand, certain substantive readings which do not make sense and are plainly erroneous are corrected only in footnotes, not in the text, suggesting a policy so conservative as not to allow any editorial corrections; at the same time, the deficiencies of the copy-text in accidentals are considered serious enough that the text itself must be altered, yet most of these alterations are not recorded in notes. One admirable feature of this edition is its insistence on the importance of the illustrations; as the editors say, "the illustrations make addition to the prime meaning of the text." The point may be more obvious here, since the illustrations are Thackeray's own, than in cases where the author merely supervised the work of an illustrator. Yet the illustrations in many Victorian novels do constitute another kind of textual problem which editors of novels face, and the significance of the problem is increasingly being recognized.[43]

This edition, like the other British editions taken up here, shows a reluctance to follow Greg's theory and turn back to an early text. Many more editions than formerly do go back as far as the first edition, but there seems to be a resistance to the idea of taking the logical next step back to the manuscript (which is also resistance to the idea that the authority for accidentals and the authority for substantives can reside in different texts). I am not suggesting that the acceptance of the manuscript as copy-text should be an automatic or inflexible rule; but, as I think this survey shows, the burden of proof must be on the editor who chooses a first edition in preference to a manuscript. That choice may at times be the wiser one, but compelling evidence for the choice must be shown. In the absence of such evidence, the manuscript has the better prima facie case. What the CEAA has demonstrated, and what some editors have not recognized, is that to reject this position is inevitably to move away from the goal of a scholarly edition.

IV

All the editions so far discussed—of both English and American novels—were produced in the 1960s and 1970s. Despite the weakness which some of them have, they clearly reflect more sophisticated editorial standards than do previous editions of novels. Before the 1960s there were, of course, some

43. See, for instance, Joan Stevens, " 'Woodcuts dropped into the Text': The Illustrations in *The Old Curiosity Shop* and *Barnaby Rudge*," *SB*, 20 (1967), 113–134; and Peter L. Shillingsburg, "Thackeray's *Pendennis*: A Rejected Page of Manuscript," *Huntington Library Quarterly*, 38 (1974–75), 189–195 (and the other articles listed on pp. 191–192).

serious attempts—a very few—to deal with the texts of novels.[44] One of the most notable was R. W. Chapman's five-volume edition of Jane Austen (1923). Although he chose revised editions, when they exist, as copy-texts, he recognized the importance of retaining the accidentals of his copy-texts and of recording variants ("If the present editor's judgement is anywhere at fault, the means of its correction are supplied in the textual notes" [I, ii]). Other landmarks from the 1920s have been revised in recent years, with varying results. When A. C. Guthkelch and D. Nichol Smith's edition of *A Tale of a Tub to Which Is Added The Battle of the Books* (1920) was revised in 1958, some unspecified changes were made in the text, but the text remained essentially that of the fifth edition of 1710, with some recorded and some silent alterations. On the other hand, when Roger Sharrock in 1968 revised James B. Wharey's edition of *The Pilgrim's Progress* (1928), which had been based on the third edition of 1679, he altered the copy-text to the first edition (1678), citing Greg's "Rationale" and making the point that a later edition containing authorial revisions may also contain many readings which the author did not sanction (p. cviii). Some editions now seem old-fashioned in their editorial policies: for example, the guidelines for the Centennial Lanier, under which *Tiger-Lilies*[45] was edited in 1945, define the authoritative text as "that text which last passed under Lanier's eyes and met with his approval" and permit the regularization of accidentals according to "Lanier's system when he had one and standard modern usage otherwise" (I, x–xi). The Hendricks House editions of Melville's *Pierre* (ed. Henry A. Murray, 1949), *Moby-Dick* (ed. Luther S. Mansfield and Howard P. Vincent, 1952), and *The Confidence-Man* (ed. Elizabeth S. Foster, 1954) stand up better, though they vary in the extent to which they alter accidentals for consistency and report the alterations. A few series of classroom editions contained the most responsible textual work on certain novels, a prominent instance being James A. Work's edition of *Tristram Shandy* (1940) for the Odyssey Series in Literature. Harry Hayden Clark's American Fiction Series (1937–39) also showed concern with texts, although the textual policy differed considerably from one volume to another: Ernest Marchand, in his edition of Charles Brockden Brown's *Ormond* (1937), worked backward by selecting the 1887 modernized edition as his copy-text

44. One convenient survey which includes some comments on texts is *The English Novel*, ed. A. E. Dyson (1974). Also useful, as selective and to some extent evaluative guides, are the Goldentree Bibliographies by Ian Watt, *The British Novel: Scott through Hardy* (1973), and by C. Hugh Holman, *The American Novel through Henry James* (1966).

45. *Tiger-Lilies*, ed. Garland Greever, assisted by Cecil Abernethy (1945), vol. 5 of the *Centennial Edition*, gen. ed. Charles R. Anderson.

and restoring to it some readings from 1799; but Claude M. Newlin, in his edition of Hugh Henry Brackenridge's *Modern Chivalry* (1937), sensibly chose the first edition of each part of the work as copy-text.

Classroom editions (or "practical" editions) cannot be expected to involve the same extensive collation of texts and publication of variants as are necessary for full-scale scholarly editions. But some series of practical editions have recently exhibited more attention to textual matters, and some of the volumes in them can serve to provide useful interim texts. The largest such series devoted to novels is the Oxford English Novels series, under Herbert Davis and then James Kinsley, although the amount of textual information supplied and the rationale of editorial approach vary widely among the volumes, making some of considerably more value than others. Many of the recent editions of Smollett and Defoe in this series merely state what text has been followed and add that "obvious" errors have been silently corrected. But the *Moll Flanders* volume, edited by G. A. Starr (1971), contains a six-page textual discussion (pp. xxiii–xxix), explaining why the first edition is chosen as copy-text in preference to the third, which has generally been the basis of modern editions. Although his decision appears to be based more on his analysis of substantive variants than on his concern for accidentals, he does recognize the merits of accepting the accidentals of the first edition. In contrast, Roger Lonsdale's edition of *Vathek* (1970) in this series takes the third English edition of 1816 as copy-text, without explaining sufficiently why the copy-text should not be the first edition (1786) of the English translation, which Beckford read, revised, and approved before publication (and which could then be emended with undoubted authorial revisions from 1816); no comment is made on the relationship between the accidentals of 1786 and those of 1816, although some discussion of this matter would be crucial to a defense of the 1816 as copy-text. Both the Defoe and the Beckford volumes are supplied with lists of variant substantives (condensed into paragraph form, yet easy to follow), but neither one presents a complete list or defines precisely what categories are excluded. The Defoe list is designed "to give readers a fairly good idea of the scope and nature" of the variants, and the Beckford list omits many of the French readings; both decisions can be justified in practical editions, but the resulting lists are obviously not adequate for scholarly purposes. Other classroom series, such as the Norton Critical Editions, the Penguin English Library, the Bobbs-Merrill Library of Literature, and the Houghton Mifflin Riverside Editions, have included some novels in carefully edited texts, but again there are great variations between individual volumes.[46] Some of these editions—like the Norton *Wuthering Heights* (ed. William M. Sale, Jr., 1963), *Hard Times* (ed. George Ford and Sylvère Monod, 1966), and *Moby-Dick* (ed. Harrison Hayford and Hershel Parker, 1967)—make real contributions to the textual scholarship on the works involved; others, though edited by persons who have investigated the textual history of the works and made collations, record very little of this information.[47]

It is encouraging to note that novels are increasingly being given more careful textual attention, even in classroom series. There is no doubt that the general awareness of the importance of textual problems in novels has grown considerably in the last fifteen years. Yet we have a long way to go before the situation can be regarded as satisfactory. Classroom editions with unreliable texts continue to be produced, to circulate, and to be adopted by teachers. At the other end of the financial scale, handsome limited editions of classic novels continue to be published, with painstaking attention given to all details except the wording of the text itself. And editions which purport to be scholarly but which are in fact uninformed and inaccurate still appear.[48] Bradford Booth could recently repeat the lament of earlier years: "It is one of the anomalies of literary history that the work of poets and dramatists should be subjected to meticulous textual collation and scrupulous annotation while the work of novelists is reprinted through successive editions with the grossest errors uncorrected."[49] The novel does offer special problems and difficult challenges for editors, and the old notion that textual accuracy is less important in a long work than in a short one is hard to eradicate. Because of the time it takes to edit a novel properly, the dissemination of reliable texts of large numbers of novels in practical editions cannot realistically be expected to occur until after full scholarly editions of those novels are avail-

46. For some useful reviews of practical editions, see "Editing Dickens," *Times Literary Supplement*, 6 April 1967, p. 285; Willard Thorp's review of the Norton *Moby-Dick* in *Journal of English and Germanic Philology*, 67 (1968), 539–541; and Barry Westbury's review of the Penguin *Barnaby Rudge* in *Dickensian*, 70 (1974), 133–134. Another series of practical editions which has paid some textual attention to novels is the John Harvard Library: Everett Carter's edition of *The Damnation of Theron Ware* (1960) records substantive variants in footnotes and discusses a few variants in a brief "Note on the Text" (p. xxv).

47. Several other firms (such as Garrett Press and Gregg Press) are publishing series of photographic reproductions of first editions of fiction. While these hardly advance textual knowledge, they at least provide the reader with identified (or generally identifiable) documents of historic significance.

48. An example is *The Major Fiction of Sherwood Anderson*, ed. Ray Lewis White (1968–   ), of which three volumes have appeared. See my review in *Proof*, 4 (1975), 183–209.

49. In the chapter on Trollope in Dyson (see note 44 above), p. 202.

able to be drawn upon. In the meantime, practical editions can at least be precisely labeled and described, so that a reader can know exactly what text he has before him and what the editor has done to that text. The novel has thus far benefited more than poetry from the new wave of editing, which Greg's "Rationale," Bowers's interpretations of Greg, and the CEAA have done much to stimulate; and these recent accomplishments have made the goal of establishing reliable texts of all our major novels appear less impossibly distant than it seemed only a short time ago.

The Editing of Historical Documents

I F THE THIRD QUARTER OF THE TWENTIETH CENTURY CAN BE CON-
sidered—as it often is—an age of editing, one of the principal reasons is the existence and influence of two American organizations:
the National Historical Publications Commission (NHPC), re-
named in late 1974 the National Historical Publications and Records
Commission (NHPRC); and the Center for Editions of American Authors (CEAA), succeeded in 1976 by the Center for Scholarly Editions
(CSE). The NHPC (NHPRC)[1] has since 1950 given encouragement and
assistance to a large number of multi-volume editions (more than four
dozen) of the papers of American statesmen, especially those of the late
eighteenth and nineteenth centuries; the CEAA, from 1963 through
1976, gave its official approval to volumes in fourteen editions, pre-
dominantly of the works of nineteenth-century American literary figures.[2] As a result, massive scholarly editions have been produced in an
unprecedented quantity during these years; hundreds of scholars have
been connected with these projects, and widespread discussion and
awareness of the problems and aims of editing have been engendered.
The presence of these editions has dramatically altered the scholarly
landscape in American history and literature within a generation.[3]

1. In what follows I shall use "NHPRC" when referring in general to the editions
produced with the assistance of the Commission from 1950 on; but for historical accuracy
"NHPC" will be used in those instances where the reference is clearly to events preceding
late 1974.

2. A comprehensive list of "Documentary Works Planned, in Progress, and Completed
in Association with the National Historical Publications Commission" appears in Oliver W.
Holmes, *Shall Stagecoaches Carry the Mail?* (1972), pp. 93–105; many of the editions are
also listed in the Brubaker and Monroe articles mentioned in note 10 below. Earlier lists
form the appendix to *"Let every sluice of knowledge be open'd and set a flowing": A Tribute to Philip May Hamer . . .* (1960) and Appendix B to the NHPC's 1963 *Report* (see note
8 below). Most of the CEAA editions are mentioned in the CEAA's *Statement of Editorial
Principles and Procedures* (rev. ed., 1972), pp. 22–23, and in *Studies in Bibliography,* 25
(1972), 43–44; all of them are listed in *The Center for Scholarly Editions: An Introductory
Statement* (1977), pp. 7–8.

3. Bernard Bailyn, for instance, states that the Jefferson edition "introduces a new
era in the history of American documentary publications" ("Boyd's Jefferson: Notes for a

When there is so much editorial activity directed toward material from a single country and, for the most part, a single century, one would expect a great deal of communication among the editors involved; indeed, the creation of coordinating organizations like the NHPC and the CEAA suggests a recognition of the need for such communication. However, the fact that two organizations have seemed necessary indicates that the communication has not very readily crossed the boundary lines between academic disciplines. Regrettably, but undeniably, editors of "literary" material and editors of "historical" material[4] have gone their separate ways; members of each group have discussed common problems among themselves but have remained remarkably uninformed about what was taking place in the other group. One does not have to examine many volumes to recognize a central difference between the historical and the literary editions: the historical editions in general give more attention to explanatory annotation than to the detailed recording of textual data, whereas the literary editions reverse this emphasis. It is a fact that most of the historical editions do not meet the standards for reporting textual information established by the CEAA and would therefore not qualify for the award of the CEAA emblem. Whether those particular standards are justifiable is a separate question; what is disturbing is that such different standards should prevail in the two fields. If one could argue that the material edited by historians is different in kind from that edited by literary scholars, there might be some reason to expect different approaches. Indeed, the NHPRC editors do have more occasion to deal with manuscript letters and journals than with texts which were published by their authors, and for CEAA editors the opposite situation prevails. No doubt these relationships are largely responsible for the lesser concern of historians with questions of copy-

Sketch," *New England Quarterly*, 33 [1960], 380–400 [p. 380]). He also refers to the "series of massive documentary publications launched since World War II" and calls it "a remarkable movement in modern American letters" ("Butterfield's Adams: Notes for a Sketch," *William and Mary Quarterly*, 3rd ser., 19 [1962], 238–256 [pp. 239–240]). Edmund S. Morgan proclaimed in a 1961 review of the Adams edition that "a new kind of scholarship has begun in the United States" ("John Adams and the Puritan Tradition," *New England Quarterly*, 34 [1961], 518–529 [p. 518]); and Esmond Wright, in another review of the Adams project, declared that this "age of the editor" is "transforming the methodology and character of American history" ("The Papers of Great Men," *History Today*, 12 [1962], 197, 213).

4. I shall not continue to place "literary" and "historical" in quotation marks but wish to make clear that these adjectives are used here only to refer to the fact that some persons are generally thought of as literary figures and some as historical figures; the adjectives are not meant to imply that there is any firm dividing line between material of literary interest and material of historical interest or that material cannot be of interest in both ways simultaneously. (In fact, all documents are of historical interest; and I trust that it will be clear when—as in the title—I use "historical" in this more basic sense. See also note 18 below.)

text and textual variants and for the greater concern of literary scholars with these matters. Nevertheless, literary editors frequently must edit letters and journals, and historical editors must handle statesmen's published, as well as unpublished, works. The editing of literary and of historical material should have many more points of similarity than of difference; and a greater understanding of mutual problems, between the two groups of editors, is bound to have a salutary effect on the editing produced by both groups.

There have recently been some encouraging signs to suggest that the dangers of editorial parochialism are perhaps becoming more widely recognized. Most notable is the broadening of the scope of the Modern Language Association's committee on editions: no longer limited to editions of American authors, it now provides simply a "Center for Scholarly Editions"—editions of any kind of material from any time and place—and it has shown itself to be concerned with promoting greater contact between editors in different fields. A similar development is the careful editorial attention which has lately been given to certain philosophers: Jo Ann Boydston's edition of John Dewey (1967–), Fredson Bowers's of William James (1975–), and Peter H. Nidditch's of John Locke (1975–)—the first two are CEAA editions—manifest an approach to textual matters which had previously been limited almost exclusively to more clearly bellettristic or "literary" writing.[5] In 1972 Edwin Wolf, 2nd, published a timely and well-considered appeal for historians to begin applying to historical works the techniques of analytical bibliography which have long been associated with literary studies, particularly with the editing of English Renaissance drama.[6] He calls attention to the historian's lack of sophistication in dealing with printed texts by pointing out that two of the most respected editors of historical manuscripts, Julian P. Boyd and Leonard W. Labaree, "never questioned the validity of the text of only a single copy of any printed work" (p. 29). After citing some examples of variants in American printed works of the eighteenth century, he again laments the "tradition of a wall separating bibliography as applied to literary works from bibliography as

5. Interest in editing scientific manuscripts is increasing also, as evidenced by a Conference on Science Manuscripts in Washington on 5–6 May 1960; one of the papers presented was Whitfield J. Bell, Jr., "Editing a Scientist's Papers," *Isis*, 53 (1962), 14–19, which takes Benjamin Franklin as its principal example.

6. "Historical Grist for the Bibliographical Mill," *Studies in Bibliography*, 25 (1972), 29–40. Cf. the way P. M. Zall begins his article on "The Manuscript and Early Texts of Franklin's *Autobiography*," *Huntington Library Quarterly*, 39 (1976), 375–384: "How odd it is that even in this bicentennial year we should know more about the texts of Shakespeare's plays than we do about the text of Franklin's *Autobiography*—especially since Shakespeare's manuscripts are nowhere to be found, while the original manuscript of the *Autobiography* lies open to the public in the gallery of the Huntington Library."

applied to historical or political works" (p. 37). Nicolas Barker has also found occasion recently to comment on this point: in one of his editorials for the *Book Collector* he rightly says, "Historians, even more than literary scholars, have been apt to neglect the physical form in which the evidence on which they subsist has been preserved."[7]

In many other respects, the situation in which historical editors find themselves is similar to that of literary editors. In each field there was increased recognition, in the years following World War II, of the need for new editions of basic writings. In each field there was one man whose work provided the impetus and model for further work: the first volume of Julian P. Boyd's edition of Jefferson in 1950 set the pattern for many later historical editions, and the publication of that volume was the occasion for President Truman's reactivating the NHPC (which had originally been established in 1934);[8] the first volume of Fredson Bowers's edition of Hawthorne in 1962 was influential among literary editors in showing how the editorial techniques developed for Renaissance plays were applicable to nineteenth-century literature, and soon after its publication the CEAA was formally constituted (1963).[9] In each field there is thus an agency which serves as coordinator and clearinghouse, though with some differences: the NHPRC[10] is a government

7. "Morgan & Brown," *Book Collector*, 25 (1976), 168.

8. The principal official statements of the position of the new NHPC are *A National Program for the Publication of the Papers of American Leaders: A Preliminary Report . . .* (1951); *A National Program . . . A Report . . .* (1954); and *A Report to the President . . .* (1963). See also Philip M. Hamer, *The Program of the National Historical Publications Commission* (1952). The 1954 report states that the NHPC's "primary responsibility, in addition to that of planning, is to cooperate with and assist other organizations or individuals in their work on parts of the national program" (p. 30); the brief section on "Editorial Policies" (pp. 32–33) stresses the importance of presenting uncensored texts of both sides of a correspondence.

9. The CEAA's position was officially set forth in 1967 in a *Statement of Editorial Principles*; this booklet was revised in 1972 as *Statement of Editorial Principles and Procedures*.

10. The history of the NHPRC—and of previous historical editing in America as background to it—has been expertly recounted in a number of essays (which also inevitably express opinions on what standards are desirable in editing). See, for example, Clarence E. Carter, "The United States and Documentary Historical Publication," *Mississippi Valley Historical Review*, 25 (1938–39), 3–24; L. H. Butterfield, "Archival and Editorial Enterprise in 1850 and in 1950: Some Comparisons and Contrasts," *Proceedings of the American Philosophical Society*, 98 (1954), 159–170; Waldo G. Leland, "Remarks," *Daedalus*, 86 (1955–57), 77–79; Julian P. Boyd, " 'God's Altar Needs Not Our Pollishings,' " *New York History*, 39 (1958), 3–21; Butterfield, "Historical Editing in the United States: The Recent Past," *Proceedings of the American Antiquarian Society*, 72 (1962), 283–308; Philip M. Hamer, " '. . . authentic Documents tending to elucidate our History,' " *American Archivist*, 25 (1962), 3–13; Leland, "The Prehistory and Origins of the National Historical Publications Commission," *American Archivist*, 27 (1964), 187–194 (reprinted, revised, as "J. Franklin Jameson and the Origin of the National Historical Publications Commission," in *J. Franklin Jameson: A Tribute*, ed. Ruth Anna Fisher and William Lloyd Fox [1965],

agency (part of the General Services Administration and housed in the National Archives building), which undertakes to do some research (such as locating relevant manuscripts in archives) for editors; the CEAA[11] was, and the CSE is, a committee of the Modern Language As-

pp. 27–36); Lester J. Cappon, "A Rationale for Historical Editing Past and Present," *William and Mary Quarterly*, 3rd ser., 23 (1966), 56–75; Butterfield, "Editing American Historical Documents," *Proceedings of the Massachusetts Historical Society*, 78 (1966), 81–104; Robert L. Brubaker, "The Publication of Historical Sources: Recent Projects in the United States," *Library Quarterly*, 37 (1967), 193–225; H. G. Jones, "The Publication of Documentary Sources, 1934–1968," in *The Records of a Nation: Their Management, Preservation, and Use* (1969), pp. 117–133; Haskell Monroe, "Some Thoughts for an Aspiring Historical Editor," *American Archivist*, 32 (1969), 147–159; Walter Rundell, Jr., "Documentary Editing," in *In Pursuit of American History: Research and Training in the United States* (1970), pp. 260–283; E. Berkeley Tompkins, "The NHPRC in Perspective," in the proceedings of the Iowa conference on *The Publication of American Historical Manuscripts*, ed. Leslie W. Dunlap and Fred Shelley (1976), pp. 89–96. The Brubaker and Monroe essays include detailed surveys of the critical reception of NHPRC editions. Historical accounts also appear in the NHPC's 1951, 1954, and 1963 reports (see note 8 above); more recent developments can be followed in the NHPRC's newsletter, *Annotation* (1973–).

Earlier discussions are J. Franklin Jameson, "Gaps in the Published Records of United States History," *American Historical Review*, 11 (1905–6), 817–831; and Worthington Chauncey Ford, "The Editorial Function in United States History," *ibid.*, 23 (1917–18), 273–286. Some analyses of earlier American editing are Fred Shelley, "Ebenezer Hazard: America's First Historical Editor," *William and Mary Quarterly*, 3rd ser., 12 (1955), 44–73; Lee Nathaniel Newcomer, "Manasseh Cutler's Writings: A Note on Editorial Practice," *Mississippi Valley Historical Review*, 47 (1960–61), 88–101; L. H. Butterfield, "Worthington Chauncey Ford, Editor," *Proceedings of the Massachusetts Historical Society*, 83 (1971), 46–82; and Lester J. Cappon, "American Historical Editors before Jared Sparks: 'they will plant a forest . . .,' " *William and Mary Quarterly*, 3rd ser., 30 (1973), 375–400.

A few other general comments on the NHPRC or recent documentary editing are worth mentioning: Dumas Malone, "Tapping the Wisdom of the Founding Fathers," *New York Times Magazine*, 27 May 1956, pp. 25, 32, 34, 37, 39; Whitfield J. Bell, Jr., "Editors and Great Men," *Aspects of Librarianship*, No. 23 (Winter 1960), pp. 1–8; Adrienne Koch, "Men Who Made Our Nation What It Is," *New York Times Book Review*, 21 February 1960, pp. 1, 22; David L. Norton, "The Elders of Our Tribe," *Nation*, 192 (1961), 148–150; Koch, "The Historian as Scholar," *Nation*, 195 (1962), 357–361; John Tebbel, "Safeguarding U.S. History," *Saturday Review*, 45, no. 25 (23 June 1962), 24–25, 52; Leslie H. Fishel, Jr., "The Federal Government and History," *Wisconsin Magazine of History*, 47 (1963–64), 47–49; [John F. Kennedy and Julian P. Boyd], "A White House Luncheon, June 17, 1963," *New York History*, 45 (1964), 151–160; James C. Olson, "The Scholar and Documentary Publication," *American Archivist*, 28 (1965), 187–193; Richard B. Morris, "The Current Statesmen's Papers Publication Program: An Appraisal from the Point of View of the Legal Historian," *American Journal of Legal History*, 11 (1967), 95–106.

11. For the history and background of the CEAA, see William M. Gibson and Edwin H. Cady, "Editions of American Writers, 1963: A Preliminary Survey," *PMLA*, 78 (1963), 1–8 (September supp.); Willard Thorp, "Exodus: Four Decades of American Literary Scholarship," *Modern Language Quarterly*, 26 (1965), 40–61; Gibson, "The Center for Editions of American Authors," *Scholarly Books in America*, 10 (January 1969), 7–11; John H. Fisher, "The MLA Editions of Major American Authors," in the MLA's *Professional Standards and American Editions: A Response to Edmund Wilson* (1969), pp. 20–26 (cf. "A Calendar," pp. 27–28, and a reprinting of Gibson's 1969 article, pp. 1–6); and Don L. Cook, "Afterword: The CEAA Program," in *American Literary Scholarship: An Annual*, 1972, pp. 415–417.

sociation of America, which draws some funds from the National Endowment for the Humanities[12] and which calls attention to excellence in editing by awarding an emblem to volumes that qualify (after being requested to inspect printer's copy for those volumes by their editors). In each field there has been some controversy surrounding the new editions, though for characteristically different reasons: criticism of the literary editions has been concerned principally with textual matters, whereas the main questions raised about the historical editions have had to do with the quantity of annotation, the justification for letterpress rather than microform publication, and the choice of material to be edited in the first place.[13] And in each field the editors have found that a great many of their colleagues neither understand nor respect editorial work;[14] in both fields an attempt has been made to improve graduate training in editing and to bring about a greater interest in and

12. The CEAA allocated NEH funds to the individual associated editions; the CSE draws NEH funds only for its own operation, and the award of NEH grants to particular editions is made directly by the NEH.

13. A history and analysis of the controversy over the CEAA editions is provided by G. T. Tanselle in "Greg's Theory of Copy-Text and the Editing of American Literature," *SB*, 28 (1975), 167–229; some of the criticism of the NHPRC editions is found in the articles cited in notes 81, 82, 83, and 84 below, and some commentary on that criticism in the paragraph to which those notes are attached.

14. For example, Julian P. Boyd has said, "I deplore the fact that these [editorial] enterprises, despite the labors of J. Franklin Jameson and others, arose on the edge of the profession, beyond it, or even on occasion, in spite of some obstacles thrown up from within it"; see "Some Animadversions on Being Struck by Lightning," *Daedalus*, 86 (1955–57), 49–56 (p. 50). He also has stated, "That a mastery of the techniques and uses of scholarly editing is not now regarded as part of the indispensable equipment of the academic historian and as being a recognizable aspect of his duty is beyond question," and he points out that many people regard "the editorial presentation of documents as being almost mechanical in nature"; see "Historical Editing in the United States: The Next Stage?", *Proceedings of the American Antiquarian Society*, 72 (1962), 309–328 (pp. 314–315). Lester Cappon, in "A Rationale" (see note 10 above), also speaks of "the academic historian's prejudice against editing as a second-class pursuit"—a view in which the editor "appears to be a lone wolf, a kind of 'sport' detached from the mainstream of teaching, engaged in a task that is useful but nevertheless expendable" (pp. 58–59). Walter Rundell, in *In Pursuit of American History* (see note 10 above), summarizes, "Traditionally, academic historians have not held the function of documentary editing in especially high regard" (pp. 262–263). And Paul H. Bergeron—in "True Valor Seen: Historical Editing," *American Archivist*, 34 (1971), 259–264—says, "Only occasional efforts are made to breach the wall of prejudice that separates historians and editors" (p. 259). Cf. Stanley Idzerda, "The Editor's Training and Status in the Historical Profession," in the Dunlap and Shelley volume (see note 10 above), pp. 11–29. Such comments as these could be applied to the literary field as well; on the general lack of understanding of editing, see also note 80 below. Occasionally one hears the opposite point of view: Leo Marx, in "The American Scholar Today," *Commentary*, 32 (1961), 48–53, is bothered by "a suspicion that the scholar-editor is in fact the type we encourage and reward beyond all others" (p. 49); but his misunderstanding of editing is revealed by his labeling the editor a "humanist-as-technician" (p. 50). In the historical field, it may be noted, there has been a greater tradition of the full-time editor, independent of academic responsibilities, than in the literary field.

acceptance of editorial projects for dissertations—though the historical field, with the various NHPRC conferences, institutes, and fellowships in editing, has been more active in this regard that the literary.[15]

Despite some differences, editors in the two fields are in similar enough positions and face similar enough problems that one would expect them not only to be conversant with each other's work but to approach each other's concerns in an understanding and constructive spirit. In fact, however, there is, in the extensive editorial literature in the two fields,[16] practically no discussion which takes up the NHPRC and CEAA editions together or which examines the textual policies of the NHPRC editions in the way those of the CEAA editions have often been examined. The most publicized article of this sort is unfortunately one which confuses the issues more than it clarifies them. Peter Shaw, writing for a general audience in the *American Scholar* and interested in exploring textual matters,[17] was in a position to inaugurate a period of productive interdisciplinary discussion; but the regrettable tone of some of his remarks, as well as the fact that they are sometimes uninformed and incoherent, results in an essay which cannot command respect or offer a fruitful basis for further discussion. Shaw believes that the historical editors "unquestionably have had far greater success than their literary counterparts" (p. 739) and finds the literary editors' "tragic flaw" to be "their respect for language" (p. 740). But when he then praises the historical editors' "respect for historical fact," since for them "both the text and its variants qualify as historical facts" (p. 743), one

15. Editing has also perhaps been the subject of scholarly meetings more often in the historical field. Examples are the "Symposium on the Manuscript Sources of American History: Problems of Their Control, Use, and Publication" at the American Philosophical Society in November 1953 (see its *Proceedings*, 98 [1954], 159–188, 273–278); the session on "Publishing the Papers of Great Men" at the 1954 meeting of the American Historical Association (see *Daedalus*, 86 [1955–57], 47–79); the discussion of "Historical Editing in the United States" at the 150th annual meeting of the American Antiquarian Society in October 1962 (see its *Proceedings*, 72 [1962], 283–328); the session on the "Publication of Historical Source Materials" at the AHA meeting in December 1964; the series of "Special Evening Gatherings on the Writing, Editing, and Publishing of American History" at the Massachusetts Historical Society in 1964–65; and the session on "Historical Editing" at the 1974 AHA meeting.

16. The literature of the NHPC has been recorded by Oliver W. Holmes in "Recent Writings Relevant to Documentary Publication Programs," *American Archivist*, 26 (1963), 137–142—supplemented by an October 1971 typewritten list prepared by NHPC. Relevant materials can also be located in the checklists of archival scholarship which have appeared annually in the *American Archivist* since 1943. The literature of the CEAA (and related editions) is surveyed in an essay, "Relevant Textual Scholarship," appended to the CEAA's *Statement* (see note 2 above), pp. 17–25, and in *The Center for Scholarly Editions: An Introductory Statement* (1977), pp. 5–19. A few checklists of material also appeared in the *CEAA Newsletter* (1968–75).

17. "The American Heritage and Its Guardians," *American Scholar*, 45 (1975–76), 733–751 [i.e., 37–55].

becomes lost. His point lacks any real substance because it is based on the superficial view that a modern literary editor produces an "eclectic text" and a historical editor a "faithful transcription of a single text" (p. 739)—without examining, for instance, what kinds of texts and textual histories may lead to a literary editor's decision to be "eclectic" or what kinds of textual facts are not recoverable from many historical editors' "faithful" transcriptions. It is naïve to suggest that "the historical editor requires a literary appreciation of nuance, while the literary editor needs the historian's respect for fact" (p. 740); but one can nevertheless agree with Shaw that "each set of editors might usefully have advised the other"—though not because they have "opposite kinds of problems."

What is needed is mutual discussion of common problems, and in this spirit I should like to raise a few questions about the textual policies of some of the historical editions, in the light of what has been learned about editing by the literary editors. In order fairly to assess Shaw's assertion that the historical editors have been more successful, one must examine carefully the editorial rationale and procedures followed by those editors. A survey of the differing practices of a number of editions of letters and journals—both historical and literary—will lead, I think, to a consideration of some underlying issues—issues basic not merely to the editing of the papers of American statesmen but to documentary[18] editing in general.

I

Three statements of editorial policy for historical editions appeared within the space of five years in the early 1950s; all three have been influential, and an understanding of modern American documentary editing must begin with them. The first, and the most influential, was Julian P. Boyd's account of his "Editorial Method" (pp. xxv–xxxviii) in the first volume of *The Papers of Thomas Jefferson*, published by Princeton University Press in 1950.[19] Boyd states that his general aim is "rigidly to

18. Although all written and printed artifacts are documents of historical interest (as pointed out in part III below), I am using "documentary" and "document" to refer particularly to private papers, such as letters, diaries, notebooks, rough drafts, and the like.

19. The method was also summarized by Lyman H. Butterfield in "The Papers of Thomas Jefferson: Progress and Procedures in the Enterprise at Princeton," *American Archivist*, 12 (1949), 131–145. The early planning of the edition is reflected in Boyd's *Report to the Thomas Jefferson Bicentennial Commission on the Need, Scope, Proposed Method of Preparation, Probable Cost, and Possible Means of Publishing a Comprehensive Edition of the Writings of Thomas Jefferson* (1943).

adhere to scrupulous exactness in the presentation of the texts as Jefferson wrote them" (p. xxviii), but he recognizes that "complete exactitude is impossible in transmuting handwriting into print"; he has therefore worked out a "standard methodology which, though sometimes consciously inconsistent, is nevertheless precise" (p. xxix). From this, one assumes that the only changes to be introduced are those necessitated by the typography. As soon as he starts to explain the methodology, however, one begins to wonder how it supports his aim of adhering to the text with "scrupulous exactness." He says that he is going to follow a "middle course" between "facsimile reproduction" and "complete modernization," except in the case of business papers and of certain important documents (like the Declaration of Independence), which are to be "presented literally." There are thus two categories of material, accorded different treatment: letters and ordinary documents, presented with some degree of "conventionalization";[20] and business papers and important documents, presented as literally as print allows. Only the treatment of the second category would seem to fulfill the goal of presenting with "scrupulous exactness" the texts "as Jefferson wrote them" or of providing "as accurate a text as possible" which preserves "as many of Jefferson's distinctive mannerisms of writing as can be done" (p. xxix).

In the first, and larger, category, spelling, grammar, and capitalization remain unchanged, except that each sentence is made to begin with a capital letter (in contrast to Jefferson's practice). As for punctuation, however, "for the sake of clarity this literal policy will be less rigorously applied" (p. xxx): periods are supplied, when lacking at the ends of sentences, and unnecessary dashes, such as those which follow periods, are deleted.[21] Although this alteration of punctuation is minimal, one may well ask what is gained by eliminating these dashes; they could not cause a modern reader to misinterpret the sense, and, if they are a characteristic of Jefferson's style, to delete them is at best to modernize and at worst to risk losing a nuance of meaning. More troublesome is the treatment of abbreviations and contractions. They are "normally" ex-

20. Except that the "place and date-line, the salutation, and the complimentary close in letters will also be retained in literal form," though "the date-line is uniformly placed at the head of a letter" (p. xxx). It is somewhat surprising that these features of letters are singled out to be rendered with greater fidelity than the bodies of the letters.

21. More liberties are taken with "documents not in Jefferson's handwriting" if the punctuation makes a passage "misleading or obscure"; but if more than one meaning is possible, the punctuation is not altered and the problem is discussed in a note (p. xxx). The trouble with such an approach is that if only one meaning is possible the reader does not really need the editor's intervention in the punctuation in order to find it.

panded, with the exception of those designating money or units of measure and weight, those standing for proper names, and a miscellaneous group containing such forms as "wou'd," "do." (for "ditto"), and "&c." (though "&" alone is altered to "and"). The rationale for this arbitrary list of abbreviated forms to be retained is not clear, especially since Boyd recognizes that some of them will require editorial expansion in brackets. If there is a value in preserving these contractions, why should others be expanded silently? Boyd gives an example to show Jefferson's extensive use of abbreviations in hurried jottings: "wd hve retird immedly hd h. nt bn infmd" is expanded into "would have retired immediately had he not been informed" (p. xxxi). The expanded text, Boyd argues, "represents the kind of clear and readable form that Jefferson himself would have used for a document intended for formal presentation in print. It makes for clarity and readability and yet sacrifices nothing of Jefferson's words or meaning." But the document was not in fact intended for formal presentation, and to smooth its text out silently is to conceal the essential nature of the preserved document. And if the nature of a document is misrepresented, even if the literal "meaning" is preserved, can one say absolutely that the meaning has in no way been sacrificed? It is true that a long passage full of such abbreviations would slow the reader down, but the reader's convenience is surely not the primary consideration here. The argument presented for expanding contractions like "wd" and "hd" could just as well be applied to "Wmsbgh," yet contractions of geographical names are allowed to stand. Perhaps this distinction is one of the conscious inconsistencies Boyd alludes to, but the reason for it remains unclear. It is disturbing because it would seem to reflect a wavering between two editorial approaches—an indecisiveness whether to transcribe or to normalize.

Three basic decisions about the nature of the edition are implicit in what has been said up to this point. One is that the text is to be critical, in the sense that it incorporates certain kinds of changes dictated by the editor's judgment. A second is that the original text will not be fully recoverable from the data provided; some editorial changes, in other words, will not be recorded. And the third is that the edited text will not be "clear text"—that is, it will incorporate bracketed editorial insertions. These decisions also evidently underlie the treatment of substantive matters, which Boyd turns to next. Conjectured readings are placed in roman type in square brackets and editorial comments (such as *"In the margin")* appear in italics in square brackets. Such intrusions suggest precision, and it is therefore unfortunate that a bracketed reading in roman type followed by a question mark can mean two different things: either a conjecture at a point where the manuscript is mutilated

and part of the text is missing or else an attempt to read a faded passage
or one that is "too illegible to be deciphered with certainty" (p. xxxii).[22]
Obvious errors in the original texts are corrected, again indicating that
the edited text is a critical one. In writings by Jefferson, the original
readings in these instances are provided in notes; in writintgs by others
(such as letters to Jefferson), the original readings are not reported—
"though," Boyd adds, "if an error has psychological significance it will
be allowed to stand, with a note when required." Once it is recognized,
however, that errors can have psychological significance, it becomes hard
to justify a policy that conceals any of them. And this treatment of errors
—emending the text and recording the original readings in notes—is a
further reflection of editorial indecisiveness, for it represents a third
approach in contrast to the treatment of conjectured readings and of
some contractions. In the case of errors, the text is emended but is kept
free of editorial symbols; conjectured readings are also placed in the
text but are marked there as such; and certain contractions remain unemended but are explained by an editorial insertion in the text. Finally,
if two or more copies or drafts of a document exist, variant or canceled
readings are reported in notes only when they are "significant." (The
variants in fact may not always be known, for it is stated a few pages
later that "The editorial policy does not call for full collation of every
document extant in more than one version" [p. xxxvi].)[23] Nothing is
said about the possibility that a variant reading could call attention to
an error in the copy-text, which might then be emended with that variant reading. Of course, if the editorial policy regards each edited text
as an edition of a single copy of a document, emendations from other
copies would not be allowed. But emendation to correct "obvious errors" is permitted here, and such a category is naturally a subjective one.
Can a policy be logically defended which allows the correction of errors
that a given editor discovers without recourse to another copy of the
text but does not permit the correction of errors that he locates only
through examination of another copy? Any procedure that might be
called "eclectic" is automatically rejected by some editors. But if a text
is not to be presented literally, then the editor's judgment is involved
in determining at each point what ought to be in the text;[24] and it is

22. When such passages are not conjecturable, they are indicated by spaced periods
within brackets if "one or two words or parts thereof" are missing; if a larger amount is
missing, "a note to this effect will be subjoined."

23. There may of course be some versions with no claim to authority. But a distinction
should be made between those copies which it is essential to collate—even for an "ordinary"
document—and those which can safely be dismissed. (In a later article ["Some Animadversions"—see note 14 above], Boyd says, "We insist upon collating every text available" [p. 52].)

24. Of course, judgment is involved, even in a literal presentation, in deciding what

hard to draw a line between being critical (using one's judgment) and being eclectic (considering readings which come from outside a given copy of a text, whether from the editor's head or from another copy of the text). Perhaps such a line could, with careful definition, be worked out; but Boyd's discussion does not acknowledge the existence of this problem, though it implicitly raises the issue.

All these points, one must remember, relate to the treatment of letters and "ordinary documents." The other category of texts, "documents of major importance," are handled very differently. They are presented literally, exactly as found in the document supplying the copy-text—though with bracketed editorial insertions when required for clarification. Variant readings, as before, appear in notes; but all of them, not just the "significant" ones, are recorded. Canceled passages, however, are now given in the text, in italics within angle brackets, placed before the revised wording. Aside from the fact that it is unclear why canceled matter should be reported within the text for major documents and in notes for ordinary documents, the approach employed for the major documents is far simpler and more satisfactory than that for the ordinary documents. With the major documents, no complicated rules are necessary, and yet the reader knows exactly what he is using (with one exception to be noted below); with the ordinary documents, in spite of the complex guidelines, he cannot always know the reading of the original or what evidence is available in other copies or drafts. It may be true that fewer people will be interested in textual details about the ordinary documents; but, if those documents are less important, why should considerable editorial effort be expended to make them more conveniently readable, especially when that effort serves to conceal some evidence that could conceivably be of use? The juxtaposition of the two kinds of texts is in itself somewhat awkward; and the straightforward handling of the major documents makes the compromises involved in the treatment of the ordinary documents appear all the more unsatisfactory by contrast.

There is, however, one serious weakness in the presentation of the major documents: the system used for recording canceled passages. The simple insertion of canceled matter in angle brackets cannot possibly inform the reader in many cases of the true textual situation, especially when no provision is made for labeling which words or syllables are entered above the line. For instance, in the edited text of Jefferson's first draft of the Virginia constitution of 1776, the following appears:

---

is in fact present in the original text; but that is a different application of judgment from the one which results in altering what is in the text. (This distinction is commented on further in part III below.)

"unless suspended in their operation for his <con> assent" (p. 338, lines 4–5). One would naturally assume that Jefferson had started to write "consent," changed his mind after writing the first syllable, then marked it out and wrote "assent." But a check of the manuscript (reproduced facing p. 414) shows that Jefferson actually wrote "consent" and at some time after that crossed out the first syllable and inserted "as" above it.[25] The printed transcription not only misrepresents the manuscript but fails to show that the revision may have occurred at a time later than that of the original inscription. A few lines later occurs the phrase "endeavoring to prevent the population of our country <by> & for that purpose obstructing the laws" (338.16–17); Jefferson's revision becomes clear only when one knows that "& for that purpose" was inserted above the line at the time when "by" was deleted. Beginning in the next line the edited text contains a phrase that is bound to leave readers even more puzzled: "raising the conditions of new appropriati<ng>ons <new> of lands" (338.18–19). One can of course read the final text here; but if one wishes to know how it read earlier, one cannot simply add the bracketed letters, because no indication has been given of what words or letters were added at the time when the bracketed material was canceled. The manuscript shows that Jefferson first wrote "conditions of appropriating lands." After this "of" the word "new" is careted in; "on" is written over the "ng" and followed by "s"; and after that another caret points to "new of" with the "new" marked out. Thus Jefferson first revised his wording to "conditions of appropriating new lands"; then he further altered it to "conditions of new appropriations of lands." These examples are enough to show that the system is inadequate; reporting cancellations in this way serves little purpose because it does not provide enough information to allow one to reconstruct the stages of revision.[26]

What I have been saying about the textual policy of the Jefferson edition is not meant to cast doubt on the accomplishment of this edition in other respects. It is surely a great achievement in its assemblage and arrangement of material, its exemplary historical annotation, and its generally efficient physical presentation (with each document followed by concise descriptive, explanatory, and—in some cases—textual notes). And it deserves to be praised for the role it has played in causing serious scholarly attention to be turned to the full-scale editing of important statesmen's papers—it has eloquently demonstrated why the scholarly

25. The identical situation occurs again at 338.25.
26. Some further remarks on Boyd's method in such texts are made by St. George L. Sioussat in *American Historical Review*, 56 (1950–51), 118–122—in one of the few reviews of an NHPRC edition to pay close attention to textual matters.

editor must place "the exacting claims of history" above "the amenities and a respect for the privacy and feelings of individuals" (p. xxviii). What is to be regretted is that an edition in such a strategic position of influence is so unsophisticated in its handling of the actual text. There is no single right way to edit a text, but the editorial policy of the Jefferson edition does not suggest that the alternatives have been clearly thought through. As a result, there is indecision as to whether the text is to be literal or critical, whether it is to be modernized or unmodernized, and whether it is to incorporate apparatus or have the apparatus appended. The reason given for retaining "&c." is that "it was widely used in eighteenth-century printing" (p. xxxi), but Jefferson's "&" is expanded in ordinary documents to "and," presumably because it would not have appeared in an eighteenth-century printed version. Yet, as Boyd recognizes, an editor cannot undertake to capitalize various nouns for Jefferson, even though Jefferson's "extreme economy" in the use of capitals was a matter in which he "differed from his contemporaries" (p. xxx). Is the question of how a given letter or private note would have appeared in print in the eighteenth century even a relevant one, when such documents were not intended for print? The way Jefferson wrote them, however unconventional it may have been, is what the reader is interested in. This view prevails part of the time, since the editor has thought it worthwhile to transcribe the major documents literally. But at other times there seems to be a feeling that formal matters are really not important and that a partially "conventionalized" rendering is all the reader needs. The statement of editorial method, in short, reflects no coherent textual rationale.

Two years later Clarence E. Carter published *Historical Editing* (1952), a 51-page pamphlet which in some ways is the counterpart, for the historical field, of the CEAA's *Statement of Editorial Principles and Procedures* (1967, 1972). Although it was not meant to be an official statement of the NHPC (as the CEAA's pamphlet was a committee position paper), it was published as Bulletin No. 7 of the National Archives and was written by a man with extensive editorial experience in connection with a government project, *The Territorial Papers of the United States* (1934–   ). Unlike the CEAA's pamphlet, which emphasizes printed texts and devotes most of its space to discussion of textual matters, Carter's booklet deals with manuscript texts and spends only ten pages on textual questions. Carter refers favorably to Boyd's work early in his discussion (pp. 10–11), but it is clear that Carter's position is more conservative than Boyd's and that he places a higher value on the formal aspects of a text.

Carter begins his account of "Textual Criticism" (pp. 20–25) with the problem of establishing the authenticity of a document, and then he turns to "the operation designed to clear up such corruptions as may have entered it" (p. 23). This statement suggests that the kind of edited text which Carter envisions is a critical one, not an exact transcription. The matter soon becomes less clear, however. Although he admits that originals may contain errors, he discusses emendations only in regard to copies. He implies that originals are not to be emended, because even in the copy retained by the writer "no editorial emendations are permissible": "it is an official record, and the only resort is to call attention to the presence of specific errors" (p. 24). A copy made by someone else, in contrast, may be emended—but whether silently or not is uncertain. "Conjectural emendations," he says, "are recommended only when it is clear that the errors are due to the inadvertence of the scribe." But, he goes on, "such emendations should be plainly identified as such in footnotes or by editorial brackets in the text" (p. 23). Yet on the next page he says that "slips of the pen" by the copyist can be corrected by "unidentified emendations." Apparently the second category is meant to consist of obvious errors, such as "the transposition of letters in words, or the repetition of words or lines," and the first of less obvious errors. But such a distinction is not definite enough to provide a workable basis for deciding which emendations are to be silent. There is a curious mixture here of strictness and leniency: nothing, not even errors, can be altered in a text from a document in the author's hand; but scribal copies can be emended, sometimes silently. This mixture also reflects an indecision similar to Boyd's about the nature of the editor's task— whether it is to produce an exact transcription of a surviving document or a critical text not identical with the text in any single extant document. The issue emerges squarely in Carter's paragraph on "the occasional needs to reconstruct a document when two or more textual versions are encountered, each of which possesses attributes which stamp it as authentic" (p. 24). The word "reconstruct" suggests the production of an emended text; but his "harmonizing of the various versions" amounts to "the choice of the one which seems to be the most complete one of chronological priority," with readings from the other versions placed in brackets or in footnotes.[27]

Carter says nothing further about emendation but instead turns to "Transcription" (pp. 25–30), where the emphasis is clearly on what he calls "exact copy." His comments are based on a thorough understanding of the value of retaining the original punctuation and spelling; he cites some useful examples illustrating the importance of punctuation

27. Carter had earlier made the same points in his article, "The Territorial Papers of the United States," *American Archivist*, 8 (1945), 122–135.

in official documents (p. 26) and notes that the "interest in bad spelling lies partially in that it indicates the current pronunciation" (p. 28).[28] He believes that superscript letters, ligatures, abbreviations, date-lines, addresses, signatures, and the like should all be reproduced exactly.[29] Canceled matter, he says, can be inserted into the text, appropriately marked, or reported in notes—but not simply ignored. To eliminate these passages, as he rightly points out, "omits an element that often indicates what was actually passing through the mind of the writer which he concluded not to set down, and of course it also represents carelessness in many instances—a not unimportant facet of a writer's character" (p. 29). Carter's discussion of "Transcription," taken by it-self, sets forth an intelligent and well-considered approach, which is admirably put in practice in his own work on *The Territorial Papers* (commented on further below).

Although he stresses objectivity here and throughout, he is aware that subjective judgment enters into transcription. When a mark of punctuation is not clearly identifiable, for instance, "it becomes the editor's responsibility to determine from the sense of the passage what was probably intended, and to proceed accordingly" (p. 26). This view is more realistic than the one expressed at the end of the preceding sec-tion, where he says that "the editor must eschew any and all forms of interpretation; he cannot deal with his documents in a subjective man-ner" (p. 25). What he is primarily getting at in this earlier statement is that the editor should not interpret the facts presented in his text, leaving that task for "the historian who uses the edited documents as a basis of historical composition." He is adamant on this point: "It cannot be too strongly emphasized that the editor's sole responsibility, after having established the purity of the documents, is to reproduce them with meticulous accuracy." Despite his insistence, the issue is not so easily settled, for it can be argued that the editor, having thought deeply about the text, is in the best position to suggest interpretations of it in his

28. A few years later, Carter made the case even more forcefully, in "The Territorial Papers of the United States: A Review and a Commentary," *Mississippi Valley Historical Review*, 42 (1955–56), 510–524. Every aspect of a document, he says there, is "part and parcel of the intellectual climate of an era. Editorial tampering with punctuation, spelling, paragraphing, and the like, which means the introduction of textual corruptions, is anathema" (p. 516).

29. The only departure he condones is in regard to spacing: "unusual spacing should not be reproduced" (p. 27), he says, and all paragraphs should begin with indentions and (surprisingly) all salutations run in with the first lines of texts. It would be more in keeping with Carter's respect for documentary evidence not even to allow these alterations. Spacing can of course be regarded as a nontextual matter; but Carter's desire to "avoid undue ex-panses of blank paper" seems a trivial justification for changing the way a writer sets off a salutation or complimentary close.

annotation. In any case, this question does not affect texual policy. But Carter does not perhaps sufficiently recognize the extent to which judgment inevitably enters the editorial process, especially when emendation is allowed. His discussion, like many others in the historical field, neglects printed texts and (perhaps partly for that reason) fails to confront adequately the issues involved in an editor's decision to produce a critical text; the issues are present even when the only choice for copy-text is a holograph letter, but they may call themselves more forcibly to the editor's attention when he has more occasion to deal with multiple versions of a text. Nevertheless, Carter's comments are generally sensible, as far as they go, and he at least takes notice of—if he does not fully pursue—the problems of choosing a copy-text when one is faced with several copies, none of which is in the author's hand, or with multiple possibly authoritative texts. Certainly his views on punctuation and spelling and on the necessity for recording variants deserve to be heeded more than they have been.

A third influential statement on historical editing was published two years after Carter's, in the *Harvard Guide to American History* (ed. Oscar Handlin *et al.*, 1954)—which contained a short section on "The Editing and Printing of Manuscripts" (pp. 95–104), prepared primarily by Samuel Eliot Morison. Because of the wide circulation which the *Guide* has achieved, a great many people have been exposed to this discussion, and it has often been referred to in historical literature as a standard account of editing. When the *Guide* was revised in 1974 (ed. Frank Freidel *et al.*), the editors apparently saw no need to alter this section, for it was retained in practically identical form ("Editing and Printing," pp. 27–36).[30] Yet it is a superficial treatment of editing which, like Boyd's and Carter's, oversimplifies or fails to touch basic questions which any editor must consider.

The discussion attempts "to set forth general principles of editing American documents" and begins with the usual point that "printing is unable to reproduce a longhand manuscript exactly." But from there on, difficulties arise. Three methods of preparing texts are announced—called the Literal, the Expanded, and the Modernized—and a preliminary section offers directions that apply to all three. Some of these directions are overly precise and unnecessary—such as specifying that a salutation should be printed in small capitals or that the date line, regardless

30. Citations below are to subsection and paragraph numbers of the 1954 edition; the identical passages can easily be located in the 1974 edition, where the paragraph numbers remain the same (the subsections are not numbered but readily identified). The only significant revision in 1974 is the alteration of the opening paragraph to include references to five more recent discussions of editing, including Carter's.

of where it appears in the original, should consistently be "printed either in *italics* under the heading, or at the end" (I.2). What such directions do reveal is that some silent alterations of the original are to be allowed—even in the Literal Method, since these directions apply to all the methods. Three other preliminary directions indicate further— and more objectionable—silent alterations. When a manuscript is torn or illegible, editorial comments are to be inserted in italics within brackets and conjectured readings in roman type within brackets, as Boyd recommended; but, unlike Boyd, the *Guide* claims that "if only one to four letters [of a long word] are missing, brackets are unnecessary and pedantic" (I.3)—on the grounds that the editor can be sure in those cases of what had originally been written. Yet obviously one cannot really be certain what spelling was used; not to indicate in some way what the editor has done misrepresents the surviving evidence by offering as a fact what is actually an inference.[31] Another direction calls for inserting "[*sic*]" after "a very strange spelling or mistake of the original writer" (I.5), implying that mistakes are not to be emended. Yet the same direction states, "One may correct, without notice, obvious slips of the writer's pen such as 'an an hour ago.' " As in Carter's discussion, nothing explicit is said about what distinguishes errors to be silently corrected from those to be retained. The two categories in fact represent very different approaches to editing, and their juxtaposition here requires further explanation. Still another direction, dealing with manuscript alterations, asserts that "canceled passages are omitted unless they contain something of particular interest, when they may be inserted in a footnote" (I.7). No discussion of what value canceled passages may have is given, nor of what might cause some to be of particular interest; if the point had been taken up and analyzed, the difficulty of regarding any cancellations in a letter or journal as insignificant would have become apparent.[32]

The subsection on the Literal Method begins with the statement, "Follow the manuscript absolutely in spelling, capitalization, and punctuation"—unaccompanied by an explanation of how this directive is consistent with such earlier rules, applicable to all methods, as the one permitting silent corrections of slips of the pen. And it is immediately followed by a troublesome exception: "in very illiterate manuscripts,

31. Besides, the arbitrary limit of four letters is illogical, since there could well be instances of more missing letters in which the intended word was equally obvious.

32. The final sentence of this rule makes the odd suggestion that a clerk's marginal glosses in "court and similar records" may "either be omitted, or used as subheadings to save expense." If they are so unimportant that they can be omitted entirely, it seems strange that an alternative is to give them a prominent place in the text itself—so prominent as to impose upon the text the sense of its structure envisioned by the clerk.

where little or no punctuation is used, a minimum necessary to understand the text may be supplied; and in documents where the writer
begins practically every word with a capital, the editor may use his
discretion " (II.1). Although the editor is told that he should state "the
practice followed" in a preliminary note, there is no requirement for
him to record his alterations. Obviously the point of a literal method is
to reproduce the text of a document exactly as it stands; if a manuscript
is "illiterate," the reader of a literal text of it will expect to see the characteristics that make it illiterate. There is no logic in setting up a category called "Literal Method" and then saying that an editor can, in
extreme cases, make changes for the convenience of the reader and still
produce a literal text. Even if there were really much difficulty in reading
a text in which most words are capitalized, the ease of readibility is not
a criterion for a literal text. A few changes, of purely typographic significance, can be defended in a literal text, such as the elimination of
the long "s"—a literal text, after all, is to be distinguished from a type-
facsimile. Manuscript abbreviations, however, constitute a difficult category: one would expect an abbreviation to be reproduced, not expanded,
in a literal text, and yet some abbreviations would require specially
cast types to be printed. The rule given here is to print abbreviations
and contractions "exactly as written *within the limitations of available
type*" (II.4) and otherwise to expand them without brackets (II.5). This
procedure is defensible as a practical compromise; but unfortunately
the impression is given that an editor need not explain exactly what he
has altered in this respect.

For the so-called Expanded Method, taken up next, the *Guide* recommends Boyd's practice, though it prefers more expansion of abbreviations and more standardization of designations for money, weights, and
measures. In fact, most of the discussion is concerned with the treatment
of abbreviations, the general policy being to "spell out all abbreviations
except those still used today . . . and those of months, proper names, and
titles" (III.2). No rationale is given for the aims of the Expanded Method, but since the goal is not to produce a modernized text (that is the
subject of the third method) it is not clear why the present-day currency
of an abbreviation is relevant. Nor is it clear just what changes are to be
made silently. All sentences are to begin with a capital and end with a
period, "no matter what the writer does" (III.1); these changes and most
expansions of abbreviations are apparently to be made without comment, but supplied letters which follow the last one in a superscript
abbreviation are, inexplicably, to be enclosed in brackets ("m^o" becomes
"mo[nth]"). Except for the treatment of the opening and closing of
sentences, the original capitalization and punctuation are to be retained

(III.1), and the spelling as well, even if inconsistent (III.5); the point in standardizing the money, weight, and measure designations, therefore, becomes less clear by contrast.[33] Indeed, the point of the Expanded Method as a whole is puzzling. It is not, as one might at first suppose of an emended but unmodernized text, to correct errors, nor is it to produce consistency, except in a few minor respects; it is simply, as the name indicates, to expand some of the abbreviations. But this expansion does not really constitute a separate "method"; it is more accurately regarded as a form of annotation. One could just as well have a literal text with the explanations of the abbreviations in brackets or notes; indeed, such a procedure would be preferable to the uncertainties suggested here. If the Expanded Method were truly a different method of editing, it would have to involve a basically different approach to the text—a critical approach, for instance, in which the text is emended to correct errors and resolve cruxes. Despite the confusions of the section on the Expanded Method, it ends with a salutary caution:

Some editors begin every new sentence with a capital letter, even if the writer does not. This is unobjectionable if it is clear where the writer intended a new sentence to begin; but often it is not clear. Punctuation in all manuscripts before the nineteenth century is highly irregular; and if you once start replacing dashes by commas, semicolons, or periods, as the sense may seem to warrant, you are asking for trouble. (III.6)

Ironically this closing statement, which contradicts the opening point of the section ("always capitalize the first word and put a period at the end of the sentence no matter what the writer does"), is the most sensible one in the whole discussion.[34]

The subsection on the Modernized Method requires little comment. Modernization is said to be for "the average reader who is put off by obsolete spelling and erratic punctuation." The extent to which the average reader is "put off" by such features of a text is probably not so great as many editors seem to think. In any case, the modernization

33. Incidentally, the rule on such designations (III.3) states, "Points after monetary abbreviations are superfluous." But a previous rule (III.2b) tells what to do if an abbreviation is "still obscure after superior letters are brought down and a point added," as if the addition of the point is a factor in producing clarity. Whether abbreviations are written with or without periods is a matter of convention; determining whether or not a period is "superfluous" does not normally involve considerations of meaning.

34. Another statement which offers valuable advice occurs in the preliminary subsection: "In reprinting a document it is better to prepare a fresh text from the manuscript or photostat; for if an earlier printed edition is used as the basis, one is apt to repeat some of the former editor's errors, or maybe add others of one's own" (I.9). The last seven words should of course be eliminated: an editor can naturally make mistakes of his own, but this danger is present whether he is working from the original or a printed edition.

recommended here is a confused concept. The first direction is the expected one: "Modernize the spelling, capitalization, and punctuation, but pay scrupulous respect to the language" (IV.1)—although one might not expect the additional statement, "Paragraphs and sentences that are too long may be broken up." What is confusing, however, is that the same instruction also contains this sentence: "Where the original writer has obviously omitted a word like *not*, or, for instance, has written *east* when you know he means *west*, the editor may add or correct a word; but he should place it within square brackets." The correction of errors is an entirely separate matter from modernization, and the two should not be linked together here as aspects of the same "method." One can modernize a text without correcting errors, and one can emend without modernizing. An introduction to editorial method which does not make this distinction will only encourage illogical thinking.

The confusions which underlie the *Guide*'s whole discussion are epitomized in the concluding remarks on "Choice of Method" (VI). The choice is said to depend "partly on the kind of document in question, but mainly on practical considerations, especially on the purpose of the publication." The nature of the document does determine whether expansion of abbreviations or modernization is required, once it has been decided that the edition is aimed at an audience which would require such alterations; but that decision comes first, since for some purposes only the literal approach will suffice, regardless of the complexities of the document. To say that documents of the sixteenth and seventeenth centuries "full of contractions" should be printed literally "in a publication destined for scholarly readers only" is both to underestimate the capacities of a wider audience and to ignore completely the possibility of accompanying a literal text with textual annotation. But why anyone, scholar or not, needs an unmodernized text does not seem to be fully grasped: an expanded text is said to be better for the student than a modernized one "because the wording, spelling, and punctuation of the original give it a certain flavor"—a statement suggesting only a trivial interest in these matters (and again including "wording" as one of the concerns of modernization). The assertion that "for a new edition of some classic such as the Virginia 'Lament for Mr. Nathaniel Bacon,' or the poetry of Edward Taylor, the Modernized Method is best" shows a complete failure to understand the serious reasons for being interested in spelling and punctuation and implies that those features are of less concern in "literary" than in "historical" documents. (An earlier similar comment claims that the "texts of recent editions of Shakespeare, Dryden, and the King James Bible have been established by this [modernized] method"—as if modernizing could "establish" a text, instead of being a way of altering a text, once established.)[35] The motto offered at the end of the section is in the spirit of the rest of the discussion: "Accuracy without Pedantry. / Consistency first, last, and always." The accuracy required for establishing a text may be regarded as pedantry by some, without affecting its desirability, and what excessive accuracy might be is not defined. If consistency of editorial treatment is the prime virtue, then surely a logical consistency of editorial rationale is a necessity; the *Guide* in this respect sets a poor example.[36]

These three statements of editorial method were not the only ones available to historical editors of the 1950s and 1960s. Thirty years earlier, for instance, the Anglo-American Historical Committee produced a two-part "Report"[37]—the first dealing with medieval and the second with modern documents—which was in many ways an intelligent and carefully considered statement. Unfortunately it recommended modernizing punctuation for all documents;[38] but, unlike some later treatments, it recognized the importance of recording cancellations and revisions and of providing a detailed account of the practice of the manuscript text in any respect in which the editor alters it.[39] Boyd, Carter,

35. A superficial reason is also given for not being literal in quotations cited in secondary works: in these cases "the Expanded Method is far preferable to the literal, since the latter clashes unnecessarily with a modern text and makes readers pause to puzzle over odd spellings and abbreviations." (The Expanded Method here sounds very similar to the Modernized.) For some reason bracketed explanations are disapproved of in such quotations, though appended footnotes are not.

36. Just before the end it is stated that every text "should be compared word for word with the original, or with a microfilm or photographic copy," as if comparison against a photocopy could be substituted for comparison against the original. Many later historical editors do in fact comment on having taken their texts from photostats, microfilms, and the like, seemingly unaware of the dangers involved; literary editors more frequently remark on the necessity for the collation of transcriptions against the original manuscripts. For an excellent statement explaining why photographic reproduction can be "the most dangerous thing of all" for persons who have "a touching faith in the notion that 'the camera does not lie,'" see pp. 70–72 of Arthur Brown's article cited in note 97 below.

37. "Report on Editing Historical Documents," *Bulletin of the Institute of Historical Research* [University of London], 1 (1923–24), 6–25; 3 (1925–26), 13–26.

38. "It is customary to adopt modern methods of punctuation, and cases are few in which departure from this procedure is advisable. The editor should, however, be careful not to alter the sense of a passage in altering the punctuation" (3, 22).

39. Two still earlier statements have much in common with the later ones. Charles Francis Adams, Jr., in "The Printing of Old Manuscripts," *Proceedings of the Massachusetts Historical Society*, 20 (1882–83), 175–182, complains about the practice of reproducing manuscript abbreviations in print and believes that fidelity to a manuscript text "can be carried to fanaticism" (p. 182), though he does recognize that at least "the scholarly few" may wish to preserve the "complexion, as it were, of the period to which the book belongs." In "Suggestions for the Printing of Documents Relating to American History," *Annual Report of the American Historical Association*, 1905, 1:45–48, the position is taken that a

and the *Harvard Guide,* however, are more important for anyone examining the NHPRC editions. Boyd's edition led the way for the later
editions and was taken as a model, and the other two discussions followed in quick succession at a time when some of the later editions were
being organized. The first and third especially have had a considerable
influence on a large number of American editions, which either refer
to them explicitly or are modeled on other editions that follow their
recommendations. If that were not the case, they would hardly deserve
the attention given them here; but their deficiencies have apparently
not been regarded as obvious. The discussion in the *Guide* is the least
satisfactory, as Carter's is the best, of the group; all three have serious
shortcomings, but the one with the most merit ironically has been cited
the least often. A recognition of the indecisiveness of these discussions—
particularly the two most influential ones—in regard to editorial theory
and procedure suggests what a weak foundation they provide for the
massive superstructure later erected.

II

A brief survey of some of the historical editions which followed, beginning in 1959 with the Franklin, Calhoun, and Clay editions, will
illustrate how similar their characteristic position is to that of one or
more of the three statements of the early 1950s.[40] Leonard W. Labaree,
in *The Papers of Benjamin Franklin* (Yale University Press, 1959-   ),[41]

---

manuscript should be printed "in the form which it would have borne if the author had
contemporaneously put it into print" (p. 47), with obvious mistakes corrected, abbreviations
expanded, and some punctuation clarified—though with certain cancellations recorded, as
offering "some indication of the mental process of the writer." A more recent discussion by
Edith G. Firth, "The Editing and Publishing of Documents," *Canadian Archivist Newsletter,* No. 1 (1963), 3–12, makes clearer the reasons for not modernizing and recognizes
that much modernization in any case results from "underestimating Everyman's ability"
(p. 4). A similar point of view was cogently set forth thirty years earlier by Hilary Jenkinson,
in "The Representation of Manuscripts in Print," *London Mercury,* 30 (1934), 429–438
(which also comments on the relation between historical and literary editing).

40. My brief comments on the editorial policies of these editions are not meant to be
comprehensive; many other features, both praiseworthy and regrettable, could be discussed in addition to those I select as relevant illustrations here. Most of the editions, for
instance, place in brackets editorial conjectures for illegible or missing words or letters, and
most report variants or canceled readings on a selective basis, but these practices are generally not referred to. Citation of page numbers in each case, unless otherwise specified,
refers to the first volume of an edition.

41. On the history and editing of Franklin's papers, see Francis S. Philbrick, "Notes
on Early Editions and Editors of Franklin," *Proceedings of the American Philosophical
Society,* 97 (1953), 525–564; William E. Lingelbach, "Benjamin Franklin's Papers and the
American Philosophical Society," *ibid.,* 99 (1955), 359–380; Leonard W. Labaree and Whitfield J. Bell, Jr., "The Papers of Benjamin Franklin: A Progress Report," *ibid.,* 101 (1957),

sets out to follow "a middle course between exact reproduction . . . and complete modernization" (p. xl)[42] and cites the *Harvard Guide* for "a discussion of principles which the editors have in general followed." The aim is "to preserve as faithfully as possible the form and spirit in which the authors composed their documents, and at the same time to reproduce their words in a manner intelligible to the present-day reader." Insofar as the second aim involves alteration of the original, it would seem to be incompatible with the first. Labaree distinguishes his treatment of printed copy-texts from that of manuscript copy-texts. The former, he says, are "considered as having been edited once from an original manuscript" and therefore are presented as originally printed, except for the silent alteration of certain typographic conventions (italic proper names are made roman and words in full capitals are made lower case) and the silent correction of "obvious" errors (otherwise, "no attempt will be made to reconstruct the original version"). In manuscript copy-texts, however, contractions are expanded, periods are placed at the ends of sentences, and punctuation is altered in various other ways: "A dash used in place of a period, comma, or semicolon will be replaced by the appropriate mark of punctuation . . . . Commas scattered meaninglessly through a sentence will be silently omitted" (p. xlii). These procedures leave the editor in the ironic position of treating printed texts—which are at least one step removed from the author's manuscript and may contain compositors' alterations—with greater respect than authorial manuscript texts, in which there is direct evidence of the author's practice. Furthermore, there is no recognition of the fact that printed texts may vary from copy to copy or that manuscript texts may be of a kind that were never intended for publication. The idea that a printed copy-text has already "been edited once" and thus requires less alteration implies that the scholarly editor's function, like that of the printing- or publishing-house editor, is to put a text—regardless of its nature—in "publishable" shape. But, as Labaree knows, a scholar is interested in the "form and spirit" of Franklin himself; and most of the silent changes described here can only take one farther away from him. Part of the texture of contemporary detail is sacrificed for the sake of a

---

532–534; Labaree, "The Papers of Benjamin Franklin," *Daedalus*, 86 (1955–57), 57–62, and "The Benjamin Franklin Papers," *Williams Alumni Review*, 59 (February 1967), 11. P. M. Zall's article (see note 6 above) illustrates the kind of work which remains to be done on the textual history of Franklin's *Autobiography*, even after the appearance of the Yale edition.

42. Cf. his generalization, in "Scholarly Editing in Our Times," *Ventures*, 3 (Winter 1964), 28–31, that recent editors "may make concessions . . . to modern usage in such matters as spelling, capitalization, and punctuation, but they reproduce to the utmost of their ability the phraseology of the original" (p. 29).

supposedly more readable text, though many of the deleted features would not have caused a reader any real difficulties in the first place. One must wonder why, if a partially modernized text of Franklin had to be produced, it could not have been accompanied by a record of editorial alterations.[43]

The same year, in *The Papers of John C. Calhoun* (University of South Carolina Press, 1959–   ), Robert L. Meriwether took a different position from Labaree, arguing that printed texts could be treated more freely than manuscript texts because Calhoun was not responsible for printed reports of speeches and the like; yet the freedom employed—involving the silent revision of capitalization and punctuation and the breaking up of paragraphs—seems excessive, especially in view of the fact that Calhoun probably revised the reporter's accounts in some cases (p. xxxv). In manuscript texts, the editor does not allow Calhoun to employ two marks of punctuation together (one is chosen), and dashes at the ends of sentences are silently changed to periods. The most confusing device in this edition is the use of roman type in square brackets to represent both editorial restorations and authorial cancellations. W. Edwin Hemphill, taking over with the second volume (1963), makes explicit reference to the Expanded Method of the *Harvard Guide* (p. xxvii). By contrast, *The Papers of Henry Clay* (University of Kentucky Press, 1959–   ), edited by James F. Hopkins,[44] says little about editorial method and nothing about punctuation, except that the lowering of superscript letters sometimes affects the punctuation. Presumably punctuation is otherwise unaltered, and the "original spelling and capitalization have been retained" (p. ix), so that this edition may come closer to offering a literal treatment than the others of 1959—although "typographical errors" in printed texts are silently corrected. The problem of variant texts, frequently slighted in historical editions, is at least commented on here: "When several contemporary copies, but not the original letter of delivery, have been discovered, that which most closely approximates the form identified with the sender has been used. When there are several versions of a manuscript in the inscriber's hand, that which most closely represents his final intent has been accepted." This statement shows no awareness of the intricacies of textual criticism. The first sentence does not recognize the possibility of constructing an "eclec-

---

43. Labaree follows Boyd's system of printing significant canceled passages in footnotes for ordinary documents and recording cancellations within the text for important documents. A few criticisms of the textual policy of the Franklin edition appear in J. A. Leo Lemay's review of the eighteenth volume in *American Historical Review*, 81 (1976), 1223–24.

44. See also his "Editing the Henry Clay Papers," *American Archivist*, 20 (1957), 231–238.

tic" text; it assumes that the task is to edit a single document, not the text which is found embodied in several documents. Yet when errors in a printed copy are silently corrected, the editor is concerning himself with an idealized text rather than with the reproduction of a specific embodiment of the text; the principle that is recognized in handling a printed text is not extended to situations involving scribal copies, though both may obviously contain departures from the author's manuscript. And the second sentence does not suggest the difficulties of determining "final intent" or the importance of variant readings among the holograph drafts.

In 1961 two more large editions began publication. One was *The Adams Papers* (Belknap Press of Harvard University Press)—which, like the Jefferson and Franklin editions, had been designated a priority project by the NHPC.[45] Lyman H. Butterfield, describing his editorial method in the first volume of *The Diary and Autobiography of John Adams*, praises those other two editions, and it is clear that his procedures closely resemble those of the Jefferson edition (with which he had earlier been associated).[46] He aims at a "middle ground between pedantic fidelity and readability" (p. lvi) and adds that scholars who are "concerned with the ultimate niceties of a critical passage" can "resort" to the microfilm edition of the Adams papers.[47] It is true that the availability of the papers on microfilm makes it easier for a scholar to check readings in the manuscripts, but that fact has no bearing on the editor's responsibility for producing a sound text in a letterpress edition. The reason for undertaking a letterpress edition of material available on

45. For general accounts of the papers, see L. H. Butterfield, "The Papers of the Adams Family: Some Account of Their History," *Proceedings of the Massachusetts Historical Society*, 71 (1953–57), 328–356 (abridged as "Whatever You Write Preserve" in *American Heritage*, 10 [April 1959], 26–33, 88–93); Butterfield, "The Adams Papers," *Daedalus*, 86 (1955–57), 62–71; and Wendell D. Garrett, "The Papers of the Adams Family: 'A Natural Resource of History,'" *Historical New Hampshire*, 21, no. 3 (Autumn 1966), 28–37. All three include some historical comments on the editing of the papers. See also *Butterfield in Holland: A Record of L. H. Butterfield's Pursuit of the Adamses Abroad in 1959* (1961), with comments by Julian P. Boyd and Walter Muir Whitehill; and *The Adams Papers: Remarks by Julian P. Boyd, Thomas B. Adams, L. H. Butterfield, the President of the United States* (1962).

46. There is thus the same difficulty here with interpreting canceled matter placed in angle brackets, when there is no symbol for interlineations: one cannot always tell whether the cancellation was made at the time of inscription or possibly later.

47. This edition (1954–59), in some 600 reels, has been influential in the movement to make manuscript collections available in microfilm form. For historical and evaluative comments on it, see L. H. Butterfield, "'Vita sine literis, mors est': The Microfilm Edition of the Adams Papers," *Quarterly Journal of the Library of Congress*, 18 (1960–61), 53–58; Merrill Jensen, Samuel Flagg Bemis, and David Donald, "'The Life and Soul of History,'" *New England Quarterly*, 34 (1961), 96–105; and Wendell D. Garrett, "Opportunities for Study: The Microfilm Edition of The Adams Papers," *Dartmouth College Library Bulletin*, n.s., 5 (1962), 26–33.

microfilm is not simply to offer a more readable (that is, partly modernized) text; it is to furnish readers with a text which has benefited from the editor's critical thinking about what the writer meant to have in that text.[48] Of course, a scholar under any circumstances may wish to consult the original manuscripts (just as he might wish to check on any other documentation); but to justify silent alterations in a printed text on the grounds that a scholar can always look at the manuscripts is to conceive of editing as little more than styling for present-day readability. In addition, the discussion suggests that only a few scholars will be interested in such matters as punctuation and even takes a disparaging tone toward anyone concerned with them. Rather than counting on the reader's agreement that it is "pedantic" to be interested in the "ultimate niceties" of a text, it would be more positive and productive to assume that readers will want to understand the text as fully as they can and will not wish to slight any aspect of it in the process.

As with many other historical editions, the determination here not to emend from a variant text is in odd contrast to the leniency with which the selected text is handled. Relevant texts are collated and "significant" differences are recorded; however, Butterfield says, "Whatever version is found *in the manuscripts being edited* has perforce been considered the 'basic' text in the present volume" (p. lix). Two years later, in the opening volume of *Adams Family Correspondence*, a supplementary editorial discussion marks a notable departure from this practice: the comparison of copies, it is said, can call attention to clarifications of grammar, corrections of spelling, and the like, and such changes are adopted silently (p. xlv). The fact that their immediate source is another document makes this an "eclectic" procedure, and the statement is a welcome recognition of the possibility of editing a text rather than a document. The Adams edition, unlike many of the literary editions of published works, does not fully carry this approach through; but it has gone farther than most of the historical editions in enunciating the principle on which the establishment of critical texts rests.[49]

The other edition beginning in 1961, *The Papers of Alexander Hamilton* (Columbia University Press), edited by Harold C. Syrett,[50] places even more stress on modernization: not only are punctuation and capitalization altered "where it seemed necessary to make clear the sense

48. And, on the nontextual side, to provide historical annotation.

49. Whether critical texts are more appropriate for some kinds of material than others is a separate question, as is the desirability of a record of all emendations in critical texts.

50. In an earlier article on "The Papers of Alexander Hamilton," in the *Historian*, 19 (1956–57), 168–181, Syrett and Jacob E. Cooke say that the Hamilton editors "expect to rely heavily on the precedent set by the Jefferson papers." See also Syrett, "Alexander Hamilton Collected," *Columbia University Forum*, 5, no. 2 (Spring 1962), 24–28.

(such as lowering superscript letters and replacing dashes with periods at the ends of sentences); otherwise, each document is "reproduced *exactly* as it appears in the original" (p. xvi), with any change marked by brackets (and deleted matter reported in angle brackets). It is true that the changes are made "for the sake of clarity," as in the other editions, but here the reader knows where they occur. Similarly, LeRoy P. Graf and Ralph W. Haskins, in *The Papers of Andrew Johnson* (University of Tennessee Press, 1967–),[57] make no changes of spelling or punctuation without using brackets (and apparently the only alteration of punctuation is the insertion of bracketed periods), although they add in the second volume (1970) that slips of the pen are eliminated. A third edition of these years, John Y. Simon's edition of *The Papers of Ulysses S. Grant* (Southern Illinois University Press, 1967–),[58] is particularly commendable. It can state flatly that "None of Grant's spelling, grammar, or punctuation has been altered" (p. xxxi), and it reports deletions in canceled type.

Most of the historical editions which followed in the 1970s unfortunately did not imitate these three editions but continued in the familiar pattern of partial modernization and selective recording of evidence. Robert A. Rutland's edition of *The Papers of George Mason* (University of North Carolina Press, 1970) states that it is following Boyd's *Jefferson*; while it retains inconsistent spellings, it silently regularizes the punctuation of sentence-endings, reduces Mason's capitalized pronouns to lower case, and inserts periods "in place of many a semicolon or colon that the writer obviously intended to function as a break rather than a pause" (p. xxii). Haskell M. Monroe, Jr., and James T. McIntosh, in *The Papers of Jefferson Davis* (Louisiana State University Press, 1971–) also silently emend punctuation according to modern standards, sometimes "correcting" a colon to a comma or a period; but, oddly, they do not insert what they regard as needed punctuation where no punctuation is present in the manuscript, representing the lack instead by an extended space. *The Papers of Joseph Henry* (Smithsonian Institution Press, 1972–), edited by Nathan Reingold, takes the Adams edition as its model and incorporates canceled matter in angle brackets if of "historical, psychological, or stylistic significance" (it is hard to

57. See also Graf, "Editing the Andrew Johnson Papers," *Mississippi Quarterly*, 15 (1962), 113–118.

58. For a survey of the history and reception of this edition, see Haskell Monroe, "The Grant Papers: A Review Article," *Journal of the Illinois State Historical Society*, 61 (1968), 463–472. In connection with the editorial archives amassed by the staff of the Grant edition, Simon has discussed the interesting question of the policy that should be established regarding access to such material, in "Editorial Projects as Derivative Archives," *College and Research Libraries*, 35 (1974), 291–294.

see how any canceled matter could be eliminated on these grounds). Although punctuation and spelling are said to be "usually faithfully preserved," "ubiquitous dashes are converted to modern commas and periods, and a few commas and periods are inserted silently where absolutely necessary for clear understanding" (p. xxxv).

Louis R. Harlan, in the second volume (1972) of *The Booker T. Washington Papers* (University of Illinois Press, 1972–   ),[59] describes his policy of silently correcting "typed and printed errors" and regularizing some punctuation, "except in semi-literate letters, which are reproduced exactly as written in order to avoid an inordinate amount of editorial intrusion into the document." A more valid reason for printing them as written is that the documents are more revealing unemended —an argument which could be applied to a much wider range of material. The first volume of this edition, containing Washington's published autobiographical writings, illustrates the way in which editors who primarily work with single manuscript texts sometimes fail to report adequately on multiple printed texts. Harlan's brief textual comment on *Up from Slavery*, for instance, merely says that the first book edition is used as copy-text in preference to the serialization in the *Outlook* because the magazine "did not include all that later appeared in the book version" and because "Negro" is spelled with a capital, as Washington wanted it, in the book but not in the magazine. Nothing is said to characterize the material added to the book or to explain the relation of the book text in other respects to that of the magazine, and no lising of variants is provided. The two texts do differ occasionally in punctuation and spelling ("coloured" in the book vs. "colored" in the magazine, for example), but the question of which text better reflects Washington's practice in these respects is never addressed.

In E. James Ferguson's *The Papers of Robert Morris* (University of Pittsburgh Press, 1973–   ), slips of the pen and "casual or incorrect punctuation" (p. xxxiv) are corrected: "Dashes and commas randomly distributed in the manuscripts are silently removed." Herbert A. Johnson's *The Papers of John Marshall* (University of North Carolina Press, 1974–   ) also silently emends some punctuation but interestingly confuses the author's intention with standards of correctness for a published work: sentences are supplied with opening capitals and closing periods "as necessary to preserve the original intention of the writer" (p. xxxvi). Apparently printed texts are reproduced with greater fidelity than manuscript texts, if that is what is meant by saying that dashes at the

59. See also Pete Daniel and Stuart Kaufman, "The Booker T. Washington Papers and Historical Editing at Maryland," *Maryland Historian*, 1 (1970), 23–29; and Harlan and Raymond W. Smock, "The Booker T. Washington Papers," *ibid.*, 6 (1975), 55–59.

ends of sentences are "silently omitted from documents other than those that reproduce a previous imprint." In other respects punctuation is not emended silently, for Johnson recognizes "the uncertainties involved in correcting any given writer's use of the comma." He very sensibly continues, "Should considerations of clarity dictate some explanatory insertion, the editors have added punctuation in square brackets, thereby permitting the reader to reach his own decision concerning the propriety of the editorial decision."[60] *The Papers of Daniel Webster* (University Press of New England, 1974–), edited by Charles M. Wiltse,[61] is similarly cautious about silent changes and makes none except to replace the dashes "intended" as periods; it is careful to retain misspellings and abbreviations or to alter them only in brackets. Merrill Jensen's two recent editions, however, go to the opposite extreme: both *The Documentary History of the First Federal Elections, 1788–1790* (with Robert A. Becker; University of Wisconsin Press, 1976–) and *The Documentary History of the Ratification of the Constitution* (State Historical Society of Wisconsin, 1976–)[62] remove capitals and italics "except when they are evidently used by the author for emphasis," add punctuation "if needed to clarify meaning," and modernize spelling except for personal names (p. xvi); although official documents and a few others are given in a literal text, other printed texts are emended to eliminate certain eighteenth-century practices, "except when capital letters and italics were evidently used for emphasis by the author or the printer."

Enough has been said to show the characteristic textual practices of the NHPRC editions and other editions modeled on them. But I do not wish to imply that "historical" editions are the only ones which have indulged in partial modernization and selective reporting of emendations and have in general taken a superficial view of textual matters. A number of editions of the letters of literary figures—not particularly influenced by the modern practice of historians—are equally unsatisfactory. The influence, in fact, may go the other way, because *The Yale Edition of Horace Walpole's Correspondence* (Yale University Press, 1937–), edited by Wilmarth S. Lewis,[63] was the first of the modern

60. Johnson, incidentally, exactly reverses Boyd's practice regarding "&" and "&c.": the former he retains and the latter he changes to "etc."—"to conform to modern usage and typography."

61. See also his "The Papers of Daniel Webster," *Source*, 1 (1971), 6–8.

62. Cf. Robert E. Cushman, "A Documentary History of the Ratification of the Constitution and the First Ten Amendments," *Quarterly Legal Historian*, 1 (March 1962), 3–6.

63. Lewis has commented on "Editing Familiar Letters" in the *Listener*, 49 (1953), 597–598—reprinted in *Daedalus*, 86 (1955–57), 71–77—and on "Editing Private Correspondence" in *Proceedings of the American Philosophical Society*, 107 (1963), 289–293 (where he confuses the issue by asserting that any editor who favors literal transcriptions of eighteenth-

large-scale editions of a single figure and has been cited as an influential force in some of the historical accounts of the NHPRC editions.[64] Lewis did set a good example in his thorough explanatory annotation and in his careful headnote to each letter giving details about the manuscript. His treatment of the text, however, raises some questions. Although he indicates, with brackets, emendations of words, he makes numerous silent emendations of punctuation and spelling. The policy is to retain Walpole's punctuation (but not that of his correspondents) and his spelling of proper names, but "to normalize other spellings and capitalization." One of the justifications offered is "a considerable gain in readability and appearance." The "considerable" is debatable, but readability is at any rate the standard argument for modernization—although the question remains why thorough modernization is not therefore undertaken to make the text even more readable. Another justification is more troublesome: "What is amusing and 'flavoursome' in small doses becomes wearisome in large, and it imparts an air of quaintness to a text which was not apparent to the correspondents themselves" (p. xxxvi). Surely no serious reader will regard any characteristics of a particular time in history as merely quaint; all characteristics are part of the evidence for historical understanding, and it is an insult to the reader to suggest that he can better perceive the intended tone of a letter if certain features of it have been altered for him.

Similar problems arise in many other literary editions. Theodore Besterman's edition of *Voltaire's Correspondence* (Institut et Musée Voltaire, 1953–65)[65] is famous because of its enormous size; the completion of an edition of 21,000 letters is indeed an accomplishment, to say nothing of bringing it out a second time in a revised "definitive edition" (*Correspondence and Related Documents*, 1968–76). Although Voltaire's alterations are recorded in notes, the treatment of the main text is disappointing: the first edition reports that apostrophes are inserted and "a minimum of capital letters and punctuation, where lacking" (p. xiii), and the revised edition follows the same policy (pp. xvii–xviii; Besterman says, "without attempting to modernize, I have introduced a measure of regularity"). The edition offers an example of the kind of inconsistency which partial modernization almost invariably leads to: "When Voltaire used an accent it has been reproduced even if

century documents should also "wear a wig while at work and give up cigarettes for snuff").

64. As in Butterfield's "Historical Editing . . . The Recent Past," in Rundell's "Documentary Editing" (see note 10 above), or in Labaree's "Scholarly Editing" (see note 42 above). See also Butterfield's comments in *The Letters of Benjamin Rush* (American Philosophical Society, 1951), p. lxxvii.

65. See also his "Twenty Thousand Voltaire Letters," in *Editing Eighteenth-Century Texts*, ed. D. I. B. Smith (1968), pp. 7–24.

it now looks wrong, but when he omitted one it has been supplied."[66] Gordon S. Haight, in *The George Eliot Letters* (Yale University Press, 1954–55), says that his "principal concern has been the reader's convenience" (p. xxxv); though he retains spelling, he treats punctuation "a little more freely, adding or deleting an occasional mark to save rereading." In the same year Allan Wade, in *The Letters of W. B. Yeats* (Hart-Davis, 1954), argues for "correcting" both spelling and punctuation on the grounds that Yeats was poor at both. To retain Yeats's spelling would "in the long run appear merely tediously pedantic" (p. 16); Yeats's "faults" in punctuation, he says, "I have silently corrected, and I have not hesitated to introduce commas into sentences which, without them, are either ambiguous or almost meaningless" (p. 17)—obviously running the risk of giving those sentences meanings which Yeats did not intend. E. S. de Beer does not attempt to normalize punctuation in *The Diary of John Evelyn* (Clarendon Press, 1955) but does supply "without note a certain amount of punctuation" aimed "solely at intelligibility," arguing that for "strict linguistic study" one must consult the manuscripts (p. 68). In *The Swinburne Letters* (Yale University Press, 1959–62), Cecil Y. Lang says, "I have always tried to make readability my first concern" (p. xlix), and he follows the practice of reproducing printed texts "faithfully" but making some alterations in manuscript texts.

The same approach continues to appear in literary editions of the 1960s and 1970s. Harry T. Moore, in *The Collected Letters of D. H. Lawrence* (Heinemann, 1962), comments on some of Lawrence's seeming deficiencies of punctuation and states, "rather than belabour the reader by calling attention to these peccadilloes I have quietly done what was needed" (p. xxi). Rupert Hart-Davis silently emends spelling, capitalization, punctuation, and paragraphing in *The Letters of Oscar Wilde* (Hart-Davis, 1962). Wilde's habitual dashes, he says, "make the letters difficult to read, and I have re-punctuated normally as the sense seems to demand" (p. xi). Wilde also liked to capitalize words beginning with "t" and "h," "presumably because he enjoyed making those particular capitals more than their lower-case equivalents." Hart-Davis believes that "to perpetuate this whim would only irritate the reader," and he has "followed the standard usage wherever the capital clearly has no significance." But he has just told us what significance those two capitals have. Why should a writer not be allowed to indulge his

---

66. Precisely the opposite policy (correcting any accents present according to modern practice, but not supplying accents when they are omitted) is applied to the French in the sixth volume (1967) of *The Correspondence of Edmund Burke*, ed. Thomas W. Copeland *et al.* (Cambridge University Press and University of Chicago Press, 1958–).

"whims" in a letter? It is a perfect place for him to do so, because the text will not have to go through the hands of a publisher or a printer before reaching the intended audience. *The Letters of Henry Wadsworth Longfellow* (Belknap Press of Harvard University Press, 1966–), edited by Andrew Hilen, is like some of the NHPRC editions in silently correcting "mere slips" but not altering errors or variations in proper names. "Occasionally," Hilen says, "I have silently provided punctuation, or deleted it, in order to clarify meaning" (p. 13). Leon Edel, in the *Henry James Letters* (Belknap Press of Harvard University Press, 1974–), makes silent corrections "where they were obviously called for" (p. xxxv), but in the letters of the young James he retains "relevant misspellings" because "they are a part of the flavor of the letters." Unfortunately he does not extend this argument to the later letters.

I do not wish to prolong this litany unnecessarily. I have merely tried to cite a sufficient number of examples to show that there is a considerable body of editors whose approach to the editing of letters and journals is in the spirit of the policies set forth in Boyd's *Jefferson* and the *Harvard Guide*. And it is by no means only the historians who fall into this group. While it is true that most of the NHPRC editions—with only a few exceptions—are of this type, there are certainly a great many literary editors whose practice coincides with that of the NHPRC editors.[67] Most of the editions mentioned are praiseworthy in many respects: most of them reflect thorough research and exemplary annotation. But their treatment of the actual texts is relatively casual and unsophisticated by comparison. It is clear, from this survey, that one widely followed approach to editing documents assumes that some modernization is essential and that a silently modernized or corrected text can serve most purposes of historical study. The assumption is made, however, without adequate consideration of the role which such features as spelling and punctuation play in private documents and the extent to which they constitute part of the total body of evidence that the historian needs to have at his disposal. What I have said about these editions can perhaps begin to indicate why their textual policies are bound to seem unsatisfactory to anyone who has given careful thought to textual matters and the nature of written communication.

III

At the time when Boyd's *Jefferson* was about to come out and the NHPC to be revitalized, there were some editions other than the Wal-

67. Although, it is fair to add, none of the editions with a CEAA or CSE emblem can be classed in this category.

pole which might have been turned to as models, and it is unfortunate that they did not have more influence at that strategic moment. The Walpole edition, because of the enormous size of the undertaking, may have seemed a closer parallel to the large editions which were projected to accommodate the masses of papers accumulated by statesmen; but certain smaller editions could have offered a sounder textual policy. Paget Toynbee and Leonard Whibley's three-volume edition of *Correspondence of Thomas Gray* (Clarendon Press, 1935), for instance, states, "The text is printed as Gray or his correspondents wrote it, with the spelling, punctuation, use of capitals, and abbreviations of the originals" (p. xxiii); and Ralph L. Rusk's six-volume edition of *The Letters of Ralph Waldo Emerson* (Columbia University Press, 1939) requires little space for an explanation of editorial policy, for Rusk says simply, "I have tried to print a literal text, with no interpolated corrections or apologies" (p. v). Gordon N. Ray's four-volume edition of *The Letters and Private Papers of William Makepeace Thackeray* (Harvard University Press, 1945–46) is a model edition. Ray presents "a literal text" and is not bothered, as so many editors seem to be, by sentences which end with dashes rather than periods. In an admirable statement, he sums up why it is important to preserve in print the spelling and punctuation of the manuscripts:

Thackeray, the most informal of letter writers, was a past master at shaping his sentences in the precise contour of his thoughts by oddities of punctuation and orthography and by whimsical distortions of words not unlike Swift's "little language" in the *Journal to Stella*. Not to reproduce these peculiarities faithfully would be to falsify the tone and blur the meaning of the letters. (p. lxxiii)

Although the details which lead to this conclusion might have to be altered somewhat in the case of other writers, it is difficult to see how the conclusion itself could be improved upon as a guiding statement for all editors of letters.

Another notable edition, which began to appear just after the first volume of the Jefferson but early enough that it could have been influential in the formative days of the new NHPC, is Elting E. Morison's eight-volume edition of *The Letters of Theodore Roosevelt* (Harvard University Press, 1951–54). The letters are "printed as written without further indication of Roosevelt's frequent and startling departures from the norm of accepted usage in spelling." Morison, like Ray, has given careful thought to the rationale for such a policy, and he makes an intelligent statement of the case:

No doubt this will strike the readers, as it has from time to time struck the editors, as a piece of unnecessarily solemn scholarship. But it seemed simpler, and safer on the whole, to leave Roosevelt's own text untouched rather than to interfere from time to time to correct or alter words or phrases to conform to what must be, in some cases, assumed meanings. Also these letters may serve as interesting documents on causation, since they were written by the President to whom the mission of simplified spelling commended itself. (p. xix)

Also during these years historical editors in particular should have been aware of the excellent example being set by Clarence E. Carter in his major project, *The Territorial Papers of the United States* (Government Printing Office, 1934–); it was in 1956, in the introduction to the twenty-second volume, that he made an important statement of his aim of "literal reproduction."[68] Even more persuasively than in his *Historical Editing*, he pleads the case for an unmodernized text:

in brief, the idiosyncrasies of both the writer and the age are preserved. To proceed otherwise would be to bypass certain significant facets of the cultural status of an earlier era as glimpsed in the character of the written record, which, it is submitted, equates with the bare facts of politics and wars as historical grist. (pp. viii–ix)

Modernization, he rightly concludes, "tends to obscure rather than to clarify." Some literary editors, too, were commenting in the 1950s on the importance of exact transcription of letters and journals. R. W. Chapman, reproducing the manuscripts "as closely as typography admits" in his three-volume edition of *The Letters of Samuel Johnson* (Clarendon Press, 1952), points out the value of errors:

I have preserved Johnson's occasional inadvertences, such as the omission or repetition of small words, partly because they furnish some indication of his state of health or his state of mind, partly because they show the sort of error to which he was prone and may therefore help us in judging the text of those letters of which the originals are lost. (p. viii)[69]

Kathleen Coburn, at the beginning of *The Notebooks of Samuel Taylor Coleridge* (Pantheon Books [later Princeton University Press],

68. For references to two similar statements of his, see notes 27 and 28 above. His earlier edition of *The Correspondence of General Thomas Gage* (Yale University Press, 1931–33) is characteristically careful but does not contain an analogous announcement of textual policy.

69. Johnson's spelling is of particular interest, too: "I have respected Johnson's spelling. It was worth while to show that the great systematic lexicographer did not in his own practice achieve a consistent orthography, and was conspicuously careless about proper names" (p. x). See also Chapman's "Proposals for a New Edition of Johnson's Letters," *Essays and Studies*, 12 (1926), 47–62.

1957–),[70] agrees, stating that "Slips of the pen are respected, in conformity with the argument of Dr. Chapman in editing Johnson, that such things have their own interest and significance" (p. xxx), and she adds that Coleridge himself remarked on this point.[71] Howard Horsford, editing Melville's *Journal of a Visit to Europe and the Levant* (Princeton University Press, 1955), suggests the importance of precision in his careful descriptions of cancellations and his thorough discussion of the difficulties of Melville's handwriting. Hyder Edward Rollins, in *The Letters of John Keats* (Harvard University Press, 1958), notes that "Keats penned his sentences rapidly and spontaneously, not carefully and artfully" (p. 17), and therefore his "queer punctuation" and "occasional grammatical slips" are indicative and should not be rectified. And Thomas H. Johnson's edition of *The Letters of Emily Dickinson* (Belknap Press of Harvard University Press, 1958) presents all holograph letters "in their verbatim form" (p. xxv), which involves many dashes.[72] With editions of this kind available to point the way, the NHPC editors of the late 1950s were unwise to turn in a different direction.

In 1960 four editions appeared which, in their somewhat differing ways, represent the approaches followed by the best of the literary editions of the 1960s and 1970s. All are characterized by scrupulous reporting of details of the manuscripts, but what distinguishes a number of them from most earlier careful editions of manuscripts is a system—not unlike that long in use for printed copy-texts—whereby certain categories of emendation can be allowed in the text, with the original readings preserved in notes or lists. Henry Nash Smith and William M. Gibson's edition of *Mark Twain-Howells Letters* (Belknap Press of Harvard University Press, 1960) involves no normalizing of punctuation or spelling, and it records significant cancellations. James Franklin Beard, in *The Letters and Journals of James Fenimore Cooper* (Belknap Press of Harvard University Press, 1960–68), does alter some punctua-

70. Cf. her "Editing the Coleridge Notebooks," in *Editing Texts of the Romantic Period*, ed. John D. Baird (1972), pp. 7-25.

71. It is surprising, however, given this policy, that she regularizes Coleridge's "careless apostrophes" (p. xxxii)—especially in view of the variable placement of apostrophes which occurs even in printed matter in the nineteenth century.

72. Examples of editions in these years which present manuscript texts almost, but not entirely, in "verbatim" or "literal" form are *The Letters of William Gilmore Simms*, ed. Mary C. Simms Oliphant, Alfred Taylor Odell, and T. C. Duncan Eaves (University of South Carolina Press, 1952–56); and *Collected Letters of Samuel Taylor Coleridge*, ed. Earl Leslie Griggs (Clarendon Press, 1956–71). Both these retain the original spelling and punctuation but silently eliminate such slips as repetitions. *The Collected Works of Abraham Lincoln*, ed. Roy P. Basler *et al.* (Rutgers University Press, 1953), silently corrects typographical errors in printed texts but brackets all emendations in manuscripts; Basler feels, however, that Lincoln's "habitual dash at the end of a sentence or following an abbreviation" must be altered to a period.

tion for clarity and amend some spellings, but these editorial alterations are recorded in footnotes (except for a few specific categories),[73] while "legible cancellations" are incorporated into the text within angle brackets. The text of Merrell R. Davis and William H. Gilman's edition of *The Letters of Herman Melville* (Yale University Press, 1960) also incorporates a few emendations of punctuation for clarity, but they are all listed in the meticulous textual notes at the end. These notes additionally include such details as foreshortened (hastily written) words: one can learn from them that what appears in the edited text as "thing," for example, resembles "thng" in the manuscript (merely misspelled words, of course, are not altered). Cancellations are all transcribed, either in the text (in angle brackets, along with braces for insertions) or in the textual notes. *The Journals and Miscellaneous Notebooks of Ralph Waldo Emerson* (Belknap Press of Harvard University Press, 1960–   ), edited by William H. Gilman *et al.*, goes farther in the use of symbols to record as much textual information as possible within the text. It aims to come "as close to a *literatim* transcription" as is feasible in print (p. xxxviii) and does indicate the stages of Emerson's revision with great precision; some categories of editorial alteration, here too, are not labeled in the text but are reported in textual notes at the end. The volumes of Emerson *Journals* which appeared after the CEAA emblem was instituted have received the emblem, and later CEAA editions of journals further illustrate the modern practice of the full recording of manuscript characteristics. Washington Irving's *Journals and Notebooks* (University of Wisconsin Press, 1969–   ), as edited by Henry A. Pochmann *et al.*,[74] is uncompromisingly literal (it respects Irving's lowercase sentence openings, for example) and contains one of the most thorough discussions in print (pp. xix–xxvi) of the problems involved in exact transcription (amply demonstrating that the process is not mechanical). Claude M. Simpson's edition of *The American Notebooks* of Nathaniel Hawthorne (Ohio State University Press, 1972), as is usual with CEAA volumes, makes some emendations in the text but records them, as well as authorial alterations of the manuscript, in lists at the end. And Mark Twain's *Notebooks & Journals* (University of California Press, 1975–   ), as edited by Frederick Anderson *et al.*, offers an

73. Such as closing parentheses and quotation marks. Although Cooper's use of a dash for a period is respected, sentences are nevertheless made to begin with capital letters.

74. Pochmann, as general editor of the Irving edition, was instrumental in formulating the policy for editing the journals; the volume editor for the first volume (1969) is Nathalia Wright and for the third (1970) Walter A. Reichart. William H. Gilman has said that the Irving editors "have spelled out their answers to problems [of journal editing] in more detail than any other conscientious and sophisticated editors I know of" (see his important review, cited in note 105 below).

excellent discussion of editorial procedures (pp. 575–84) and is a model of how to combine the emendation of certain obvious errors (always listed at the end, accompanied by "doubtful readings") with the preservation of "the texture of autograph documents" (which contain "irregularities, inconsistencies, errors, and cancellations").[75]

These are not the only praiseworthy editions of letter and journals in the 1960s and 1970s,[76] and a few others deserve mention not simply for their high standards of literal transcription but for the cogency of their statements justifying that approach. *Shelley and His Circle* (Harvard University Press, 1961–   ), edited from the holdings of the Carl H. Pforzheimer Library by Kenneth Neill Cameron (later by Donald H. Reiman),[77] surpasses all these other editions in its efforts to reproduce in type the features of manuscripts—printing careted material, for example, above the line and in smaller type. The aim is "the traditional one" of producing "a foundational text . . . from which other editors may depart as they wish," and the rationale is stated with great effectiveness:

75. Cancellations are thus included in the text, but there is also a list of "Details of Inscription" at the end, making clear the stages of revision at each point.

76. Harold Williams's edition of *The Correspondence of Jonathan Swift* (Clarendon Press, 1963–65) also prints the texts with "exact care," preserving "variants in spelling, capitalization, and punctuation" (p. xviii), including the period-dash combination at the ends of sentences; and Elvan Kintner's edition of *The Letters of Robert Browning and Elizabeth Barrett Barrett, 1845–1846* (Belknap Press of Harvard University Press, 1969) similarly presents a literal text, indicating insertions with arrows and allowing sentences to end with dashes and without periods. Some generally successful editions of these years do, however, include a small amount of modernization or normalizing. A. Rupert Hall and Marie Boas Hall's edition of *The Correspondence of Henry Oldenburg* (University of Wisconsin Press, 1965–   ) follows the spelling and punctuation of the original but expands some abbreviations. Chester L. Shaver's *The Early Years* (Clarendon Press, 1967) and Mary Moorman's *The Middle Years* (1969) in the revised edition of *The Letters of William and Dorothy Wordsworth* preserve the spelling and punctuation of the originals, but they inexplicably expand ampersands. Sentences are allowed to end with a dash and no period, but the "frequent ampersands have been changed to 'and' for the convenience of the reader" (Moorman, p. ix); it is difficult to see how ampersands constitute a sufficient inconvenience to warrant alteration in any case, but particularly when other potentially more troublesome practices are not altered. M. R. D. Foot and H. C. G. Matthew's edition of *The Gladstone Diaries* (Clarendon Press, 1968–   ) follows the original punctuation and spelling "as closely as can be" (p. xxxviii) but expands some abbreviations and alters dashes to periods or commas "as the sense requires." The policy of the second volume of the "Research Edition" of *The Yale Edition of The Private Papers of James Boswell* is to normalize capitals and periods for sentence openings and closings and to ignore insignificant deletions, but to report any alterations of punctuation to "relieve ambiguities" and any corrections of "patent inadvertencies" in spelling; see Marshall Waingrow's edition of *The Correspondence and Other Papers of James Boswell Relating to the Making of the "Life of Johnson"* (McGraw-Hill, 1969), pp. lxxix–lxxxiii. (Cf. Frederick A. Pottle, "The Yale Editions of the Private Papers of James Boswell," *Ventures*, 2 [Winter 1963], 11–15.)

77. See also Reiman's "Editing Shelley," in *Editing Texts of the Romantic Period*, ed. John D. Baird (1972), pp. 27–45.

There is, moreover, it seems to us, aside from the question of accuracy of representation a positive value in this traditional method which is insufficiently stressed. Changes, no matter how trivial, take the reader one remove from the author. An author's own punctuation, his cancellations and interlineations, even his misspellings, play a part in expressing mood or personality. Retained, they make a text no more difficult to read than an everyday letter from a friend. And even if an occasional passage could be made clearer by changing it, such exceptions are not, in our opinion, balanced by the total loss. (p. xxxiv)

Herbert M. Schueller and Robert L. Peters, in their edition of *The Letters of John Addington Symonds* (Wayne State University Press, 1967–69), give some additional reasons for offering a literal text:

We know that sometimes a quiet changing of manuscripts meets with approval; this practice, however, seems indefensible with respect to Symonds because, 1) the letters were not edited by *him* for publication, 2) they extend over his whole lifetime and show the influences of maturity on his personal expression, 3) the continuing characteristics are often Victorian practices rather than personal idiosyncrasies, and 4) to make deliberate changes in the originals is to go beyond the prerogatives even of editors. (p. 14)

In *The Journals and Letters of Fanny Burney* (Clarendon Press, 1972–), Joyce Hemlow[78] allows errors to stand "as the normal hazards of hasty or spontaneous writing" and believes that "the twentieth-century reader probably needs few such props" as modernization (p. lviii). Leslie A. Marchand, in his editorial introduction to *"In my hot youth": Byron's Letters and Journals* (Murray, 1973–   ), adds further to the strength of the case:

Byron's punctuation follows no rules of his own or others' making. He used dashes and commas freely, but for no apparent reason, other than possibly for natural pause between phrases, or sometimes for emphasis. He is guilty of the "comma splice", and one can seldom be sure where he intended to end a sentence, or whether he recognized the sentence as a unit of expression. . . . Byron himself recognized his lack of knowledge of the logic or the rules of punctuation. . . . It is not without reason then that most editors, including R. E. Prothero, have imposed sentences and paragraphs on him in line with their interpretation of his intended meaning. It is my feeling, however, that this detracts from the impression of Byronic spontaneity and the onrush of ideas in his letters, without a compensating gain in clarity. In fact, it may often arbitrarily impose a meaning or an emphasis not intended by the writer. I feel that there is less danger of distortion if the reader may see

78. See also her "Letters and Journals of Fanny Burney: Establishing the Text," in *Editing Eighteenth-Century Texts*, ed. D. I. B. Smith (1968), pp. 25–43.

exactly how he punctuated and then determine whether a phrase between commas or dashes belongs to one sentence or another. (p. 28)

Marchand, like most of the other advocates of this point of view, adds that the unmodernized text is not difficult to read; but the reasons for not modernizing, it is clear, are of sufficient weight that the question of whether the resulting text is somewhat difficult to read is of secondary importance.[79]

The statements quoted here, which make a number of different points and refer to a variety of periods and kinds of material, add up to an impressive argument and are no doubt sufficient in themselves as a criticism of the partially modernized and silently emended editions described earlier. Merely to juxtapose comments on editorial policy from the two kinds of edition is to show up the weaknesses of attempting to justify modernization and silent alterations in scholarly editions of historical documents. But it will perhaps be useful to try to sort out more clearly the issues involved, especially since there has been so little discussion of the matter, at least in connection with the editions of statesmen's papers. Although a voluminous literature has grown up around the NHPRC editions, it contains very little commentary on textual procedures, and what there is seldom touches on fundamental questions. The NHPRC editions have probably been more extensively reviewed than the CEAA editions; but in both fields it is difficult to find reviewers who can adequately analyze textual policies, and the reviews of NHPRC volumes in particular have almost consistently slighted—or ignored completely, except for a perfunctory word of praise—the textual aspects of the editions.[80] The historical significance of the contents of these edi-

79. Another example of the kind of significance which punctuation can have is offered by Desmond Pacey, in "On Editing the Letters of Frederick Philip Grove," in *Editing Canadian Texts*, ed. Francess G. Halpenny (1975), pp. 49–73; Grove placed slang words in quotation marks, and Pacey retains them "since they indicate something of his stiffness of character" (p. 72). (Pacey, however, favors silent emendation of spelling errors, expansion of abbreviations, and regular italicization of titles.)

80. Reiman (see note 77 above) comments on the "dearth of knowledge and standards of judgment of editing . . . among those who review such publications [editions] in learned journals" (p. 37). And L. H. Butterfield, in "Editing American Historical Documents" (see note 10 above), says, "It is in fact shocking to find how low the threshold of tolerance sometimes is for poorly edited materials among those who should know better" (p. 98). Examples of the praise bestowed on the editorial practices of some of the historical editions, without a serious analysis of those practices, are the following: the Jefferson edition is said to be provided "with every ingenuity of typographical suggestion of the state of the manuscripts" (*Times Literary Supplement*, 6 April 1951, p. 206); the Jefferson practices are called "so satisfactory as to require only minor modifications to adapt them to each later project" (*American Archivist*, 25 [1962], 449); the Clay edition reflects "the precision that has come to distinguish the science of historical editing at its mid-twentieth century peak of perfection" (*Journal of Southern History*, 26 [1960], 238); "Boyd and his fellow editors have per-

tions and the quality of the explanatory annotation—on which the reviews concentrate—are important matters, but the way in which the text has been established and presented is surely of first importance in evaluating an edition.

Considerable criticism has been directed at the NHPRC editions but for essentially irrelevant or trivial reasons. One objection, raised by Leonard W. Levy, for example, in his reviews of the Madison edition, is that the explanatory annotation is carried to excessive lengths.[81] Another criticism questions the choice of material to be edited. J. H. Plumb, among others, believes that too much attention is paid to unimportant documents,[82] and Jesse Lemisch argues that the pattern of figures chosen to be edited reflects a bias "in the direction of white male political leaders."[83] Whatever justice there may be to these opinions, they have nothing to do with the quality of the editions themselves. If the annotation is accurate and helpful, it will be of use, and there is little point in wishing there were less of it; and any document or figure is of some historical interest. Individual tastes regarding what material is worth spending time on, and judgments about priorities, will naturally vary; one may deplore another's choice of subject, but it is unrealistic to criticize accomplished work for having usurped time better spent on something else. Still another frequent complaint is that letterpress edi-

fected techniques of research, skills of analysis, and modes of presentation" (*Louisiana History*, 8 [1967], 282).

81. *Mississippi Valley Historical Review*, 49 (1962–63), 504–6; *Journal of American History*, 51 (1964–65), 299–301. The first refers to "the editorial imperialism and compulsiveness that characterize these volumes"; the second comments on "monumentally trifling footnotes" and "fantastically detailed annotations" and finds the editors "making the profession of editing look purely pedantic."

82. Writing on "Horace Walpole at Yale" in the *New York Review of Books*, 5, no. 4 (30 September 1965), 9–10, Plumb objects to publishing "every scrap of writing committed to paper by one man" (which demands "little more than industry and accuracy") and asserts that Wilmarth Lewis started "a new and dangerous form of historical activity" which has "spread among historical and literary scholars like measles among the Aztecs, and as disastrously." Similarly Esmond Wright, in "Making History," *Listener*, 68 (1962), 803–804, names five ways in which the editions threaten the historian; one of them is the scale of the editions, for all the facts "blur rather than reveal."

83. In "The American Revolution Bicentennial and the Papers of Great White Men: A Preliminary Critique of Current Documentary Publication Programs," *AHA Newsletter*, 9, no. 5 (November 1971), 7–21 (p. 9). "The present publications program," Lemisch believes, "should be seen in part as a vestige of the arrogant nationalism and elitism of the 'fifties" (p. 11), and he suggests other kinds of papers worthy of attention, such as the records of ordinary and "inarticulate" people which would provide materials for studying popular protest, racism, sexism, and so on. Some correspondence relating to his article appeared in the same journal in May 1972 (10, no. 3, 25–28). The article was later excerpted in the *Maryland Historian*, 6 (1975), 43–50, followed by a new article in which Lemisch states that little progress has been made since 1971 in editing the papers of undistinguished persons: "The Papers of a Few Great Black Men and a Few Great White Women," pp. 60–66.

tions are too expensive and time-consuming to produce and that microfilm publication of the documents would be cheaper, faster, and more appropriate.[84] Certainly the well-established microfilm publication programs of the NHPRC, the National Archives, the Library of Congress, and various state historical societies are to be praised;[85] but making photographic reproductions of document collections widely available is by no means a substitute for editing those documents,[86] as Julian Boyd and Lester Cappon, among others, have effectively pointed out.[87] The skilled editor, employing his critical intelligence and fund of historical detail, establishes a text which marks an advance in knowledge over the mere existence of the document itself. Microfilm editions of unedited documents do not obviate true editions; but editing takes time, and one is back at the earlier question of individual priorities for spending time.

These controversies are really peripheral to the main business of editing. Since individual priorities do differ, anyone may decide not to become an editor; but for those who elect to undertake editorial projects, surely the first priority is the text itself, its treatment and presentation. And when one considers the divergences of textual policy which

84. For example, Gerald Gunther, reviewing the Adams papers in the *Harvard Law Review*, 75 (1961–62), 1669–80, argues that "the present emphasis on multi-volume publication projects" is the "slowest and costliest" way to make manuscripts accessible; he believes that the NHPC has inadequately identified "the purposes of publishing manuscript collections," confusing publication with printing, and that more use should be made of microfilm (esp. pp. 1670–76). Steven R. Boyd, in "Form of Publication: A Key to the Widespread Availability of Documents," *AHA Newsletter*, 10, no. 4 (September 1972), 24–26, also favors microfilm, asserting that the NHPC letterpress program "is failing to make documentary sources generally available" and that "no new letterpress projects should be begun at this time." General discussions of alternatives are Charles E. Lee, "Documentary Reproduction: Letterpress Publication—Why? What? How?", *American Archivist*, 28 (1965), 351–365; and Robert L. Zangrando, "Alternatives to Publication," *Maryland Historian*, 7 (1976), 71–76 (which suggests that historians in general should give more consideration to forms of publication other than letterpress).

85. Some accounts of these programs can be found in Fred Shelley, "The Presidential Papers Program of the Library of Congress," *American Archivist*, 25 (1962), 429–433; Wayne C. Grover, "Toward Equal Opportunities for Scholarship," *Journal of American History*, 52 (1965–66), 715–724; L. H. Butterfield, "The Scholar's One World," *American Archivist*, 29 (1966), 343–361; Frank B. Evans, "American Personal Papers," *Quarterly Journal of the Library of Congress*, 24 (1967), 147–151; and Shelley, "The Choice of a Medium for Documentary Publication," *American Archivist*, 32 (1969), 363–368.

86. It should also be recognized that even photographic reproductions can distort the originals. Cf. note 36 above.

87. For example, see Boyd, "Some Animadversions" (see note 14 above), p. 51, and "'God's Altar . . .'" (see note 10 above), p. 21; Cappon, "The Historian as Editor," in *In Support of Clio: Essays in Memory of Herbert A. Kellar*, ed. William B. Hesseltine and Donald R. McNeil (1958), pp. 173–193, and "A Rationale" (see note 10 above), pp. 72–73. The debate over the role of the editor as an interpretive historian is further examined by Cappon in "Antecedents of the Rolls Series: Issues in Historical Editing," *Journal of the Society of Archivists*, 4 (1970–73), 358–369.

distinguish most NHPRC editions from the CEAA and CSE editions, the first question to ask is whether there is an essential difference between the materials of historical interest and those of literary interest that would necessitate differing treatments. Nathan Reingold, in a letter to the *American Scholar* (45 [1976], 319) commenting on Peter Shaw's article, suggests such an explanation, pointing out that the CEAA editors work with printed texts, whereas the historical editors for the most part deal with thousands of "scrappy and informal" bits of manuscript. It is true that the bulk of the CEAA and CSE editions are of works which have previously appeared in print,[88] but those editions do include numerous volumes of manuscript letters and journals, and of course in the literary field in general many editions of such material exist. It may also be true that letters predominate in editions of statesmen's papers, but the comprehensive editions do include speeches, reports, and other works of a public nature normally intended for distribution in printed form. Is a letter written by a literary figure in some way fundamentally different from a letter written by a statesman? Both are historical documents: literary history is still history, and all letters offer historical evidence. And either letter may be regarded as "literature": a statesman may produce masterly letters, and a literary figure may write pedestrian ones. Is a novel or a poem fundamentally different from a work which a statesman prepares for publication? At their extremes, imaginative literature and factual reporting seem to be different kinds of communication, but in between there is a large area in which they overlap. No clear line can be drawn between writing which is "literature" and writing which is not. Certainly the editor of an individual's whole corpus of papers is likely to encounter writings which can be regarded either way: some of Franklin's and Jefferson's best-known writings have often been classified and analyzed as literary works, whereas Hawthorne's *Life of Franklin Pierce* and Whitman's journalism are not always considered literature. There sometimes seems to be an assumption that close attention to textual nuances—and thus the need for recording textual details—is more vital to the study of literary works and other writings by literary figures.[89] Apparently that is part of Fred-

88. Even in these cases, however, a manuscript rather than a printed edition may be chosen as the proper copy-text.

89. Robert Halsband, editor of *The Complete Letters of Lady Mary Wortley Montagu* (Clarendon Press, 1965–67), remarks, "It seems paradoxical that political and social historians—who, one would think, are sticklers for exactness—should prefer normalized texts, whereas literary historians strive for exact transcription"; and he conjectures that to the former "the facts are paramount," whereas the latter are concerned also with "nuances of style" (pp. 30–31). See his discussion of "Editing the Letters of Letter-Writers," *SB*, 11 (1958), 25–37—a useful survey of the problems involved (although it favors partial normalization and selective recording of deletions). Another general survey is James Sutherland's

erick B. Tolles's point when he criticizes the "zeal" of the editor of George Mercer's papers for her "reverent handling" of the texts: "it seems important to remind ourselves," he says, "that they are not sacred codices of Holy Writ or variant quartos of *Hamlet*."[90] He also means, of course, that Mercer's papers are not as important as *Hamlet*. But neither the importance nor the literary quality of a piece of writing determines the amount of attention that must be paid to nuances of expression; if one seriously wishes to understand a text, whatever it is, no aspect of it can be slighted.[91] There is no fundamental distinction, then, from a textual point of view, between the materials edited by the historian and those edited by the literary scholar. Letters, journals, published works, and manuscripts of unpublished works fall into both fields; all of them are historical documents, and any of them can be "literary."[92]

A distinction does need to be made, but not between literary and historical materials. Rather, the important distinction is between two kinds of writings which both historians and literary scholars have to deal with: works intended for publication and private papers.[93] Works intended for publication are generally expected to conform to certain conventions not applicable to private documents. For example, a finished work is expected to incorporate the author's latest decisions about what word he wishes to stand at each spot; in a private notebook jotting, however, or even in a letter to a friend, he can suggest alternative words and is under no obligation to come to a decision among them.[94] Simi-

---

"Dealing with Correspondences," *Times Literary Supplement*, 26 January 1973, pp. 79–80 (in a special issue on "Letters as Literature").

90. In his review of Lois Mulkearn's edition of the *George Mercer Papers Relating to the Ohio Company of Virginia* (University of Pittsburgh Press, 1954), *Pennsylvania Magazine of History and Biography*, 74 (1955), 113–114. Cf. Julian Boyd's reply in "Some Animadversions" (see note 14 above), p. 50.

91. Reuben Gold Thwaites, early in the century, recognized the literary interest in essentially nonliterary materials in his edition of the *Original Journals of the Lewis and Clark Expedition, 1804–1806* (Dodd, Mead, 1904–5); he prints the texts of successive drafts because "in a publication of original records it appears advisable to exhibit the literary methods of the explorers" (p. lvii).

92. The 1951 and 1954 reports of the NHPC (see note 8 above) include the names of literary figures in the lists of papers which need to be edited; the 1963 report comments, "American literature also presents a picture of compelling need. With few exceptions, no scholarly and acceptable texts of the works of any national figure in the field of American letters are available" (p. 28), and adds that it is prepared to give to literary editions "such assistance and encouragement as may be within its power."

93. Reingold approaches this point in his letter to the *American Scholar* when he acknowledges that occasionally "historical editors may reprint publications or present the texts of unpublished writings intended for print."

94. One of the best assessments of the importance of this practice is made by Timothy L. S. Sprigge in his edition of *The Correspondence of Jeremy Bentham* (University of London Athlone Press, 1968–): "Special mention must be made of Bentham's habit, even in his letters, of writing alternative words and phrases above the line without deleting the

larly, he can spell and punctuate as he pleases in a private document, but he will have difficulty getting a work published if it does not conform, at least to some extent, to current standards. Whether or not a writer really wishes to have his manuscript altered by a publisher's editor or a printer to bring it into such conformity is a complex question of intention, and editorial debate on this issue is likely to continue. Some editors feel that a surviving completed manuscript of a published work is the proper choice for copy-text because it reflects the author's characteristics more accurately, while others feel that the published text should be the copy-text because the author expected his manuscript to be subjected to the normal routines of publishing. No doubt the answer will vary in different situations, but this is not the place to explore the question.[95] The point here is to contrast that situation with the very different one which exists for private documents. In the case of notebooks, diaries, letters, and the like, whatever state they are in constitutes their finished form, and the question of whether the writer "intended" something else is irrelevant. One still sometimes hears the argument that an editor must make alterations in such documents because the writer would have expected to make changes in them for publication. If the writer had in fact prepared them for publication, they would then no longer be private documents but works intended for the public; they would have passed through the usual steps leading to publication, as any other work would, and the author probably would have made alterations in them, since the original documents would be parallel with the rough or semifinal drafts of other kinds of works. But when the writer did not prepare his own letters or diaries for publication, they remain private papers. The scholarly editor who later wishes to make them public is not in the same position as the writer or the writer's contemporary publisher. Not only is it impossible for him to know what the writer or his publisher would have done to them; but if he presents them as anything more polished or finished than they were left by the writer, he is falsifying their nature. A journal, as a piece of writing for one's own use, is in its final form whenever one stops adding to it; a letter, as a communication to a private audience of one or two, is in its

---

original. In draft letters his intention was presumably to make a final choice at a later stage. But when writing to intimates he often left these alternatives standing; and this is at times a literary device of a distinctive character, the effect of which is that the sense of the passage arises from an amalgam of the two (or more) readings" (p. xxi). (After this admirable statement, it comes as a surprise to learn that Sprigge does not always print these alternative readings; to do so, he says, "would seriously imperil the readability of the text." And the ones he includes are marked in such a way as to be indistinguishable from interlinear insertions that replaced canceled matter.)

95. I have commented on this matter in "The Editorial Problem of Final Authorial Intention," *SB*, 29 (1976), 167–211 (esp. pp. 183–191); cf. *SB*, 28 (1975), 222–227.

final form whenever it is posted. The writer is under no constraint to conform to any particular convention in these writings, except to the extent that he hopes a letter will be comprehensible to its recipient. Any idiosyncrasies in them—however contrary to the standards for published works—are an essential part of their character.

These considerations lead to the conclusion that a scholarly edition of letters or journals should not contain a text which has editorially been corrected, made consistent, or otherwise smoothed out. Errors and inconsistencies are part of the total texture of the document and are part of the evidence which the document preserves relating to the writer's habits, temperament, and mood. Modernization, too, is obviously out of place. While it is not the same thing as the correction of errors or inconsistencies, the line between the two is often difficult to establish. Even in many published works the spelling, punctuation, and capitalization are inconsistent, and to assume that the writers or publishers intended them to be consistent or cared whether they were consistent or not is to read into the situation a point of view held by many people today but one that has apparently not always been held. Correcting errors is somewhat different, since by definition an error is not intended; but it is frequently difficult to avoid a modern bias in deciding what constitutes an error. Editors of published works are increasingly recognizing that to regularize or to make certain supposed corrections is to modernize.[96]

In the case of private documents, then, where errors and inconsistencies are an integral part of the text, the argument against modernization is doubly strong. Indeed, the position that the text of a *scholarly* edition of any material can ever be modernized is indefensible. Many editors of literary works have long understood this fact,[97] and it is difficult to explain why such a large number of editors of private documents have, during the same period, neglected it. They are not always cognizant of a distinction between correcting and modernizing; but to sub-

96. A cogent statement of this position is Hershel Parker's "Regularizing Accidentals: The Latest Form of Infidelity," *Proof*, 3 (1973), 1–20, which also contains an excellent summary of the arguments against "full" or "partial" modernization. See also Joseph Moldenhauer's comments in his edition of Thoreau's *The Maine Woods* (Princeton University Press, 1972), pp. 399–400.

97. See, for example, W. W. Greg's strong statement of the position in *The Editorial Problem in Shakespeare* (2nd ed., 1951), pp. l–liii; and Fredson Bowers, "Old-Spelling Editions of Dramatic Texts," in *Studies in Honor of T. W. Baldwin*, ed. D. C. Allen (1958), pp. 9–15 (reprinted in his *Essays in Bibliography, Text, and Editing* [1975], pp. 289–295 [esp. pp. 291–293]). A standard exposition of many of the arguments for and against modernization is found in two essays of 1960: John Russell Brown (favoring modernization), "The Rationale of Old-Spelling Editions of the Plays of Shakespeare and His Contemporaries," *SB*, 13 (1960), 49–67; and Arthur Brown (opposing modernization), ". . . A Rejoinder," *ibid.*, 69–76.

ject such documents to either is to violate their integrity. Ultimately the position of these editors rests on a failure to grasp the significance of punctuation, capitalization, and spelling as functional elements of written expression. They think, as a result, that they can make alterations "for clarity" and "for the reader's convenience" without affecting the content of the document in any important way. In most instances, they greatly exaggerate the difficulty of reading the original text, and it is hard to see how the reader's "convenience" is really served by changing a dash to a period, an ampersand to "and," or an upper-case letter to lower case.[98] What, in the end, do they accomplish, other than depriving the reader of the experience of reading the original text? Is the text "clearer" as a result of their labors? Frequently it is less clear, because documentary editors rarely modernize more than a few features, leaving the text with a confused and unhistorical mixture of elements that clash with each other.[99] What is intended as a help becomes a barrier between the reader and the text he is interested in reading. Anyone who has examined a number of the partially modernized editions of letters can only react with incredulity at the things which editors seem to think readers need to have done for them. The modernizing editor is both condescending and officious: he assumes that the reader is not serious enough to persevere in reading a work if the punctuation, capitalization, and spelling do not conform to present-day practice, and his belief in the necessity of making changes blinds him to the triviality and senselessness of many of his alterations.[100] Modernization, or partial modernization, is clearly incompatible with the goals of the scholarly editing

98. As Samuel Schoenbaum says, "Surely the illusion of quaintness fades very quickly as the reader settles down to the material at hand" (p. 23); see "Editing English Dramatic Texts," in *Editing Sixteenth Century Texts*, ed. R. J. Schoeck (1966), pp. 12–24. A curious fact is that the feature of manuscript letters most frequently discussed and altered by editors is a dash (with or without other punctuation) at the end of a sentence (or even within sentences). Changing the dash to a period (or, within sentences, to some other appropriate mark) is usually regarded not as modernization but as the correction of an error; any practice that has been so widespread in private writing over so many years, however, is more sensibly regarded as a standard custom than as an error. (Of course, even if it were an idiosyncrasy—"error"—of a particular writer, that fact would not be a reason to alter it.)

99. The case against partial modernization of a published work has been most effectively stated by Fredson Bowers (who calls it "basically useless and always inconsistent") in his review of the second volume (1963) of *The Yale Edition of the Works of Samuel Johnson*, which modernizes capitalization (and the italicization of quotations) but not spelling and punctuation; see "The Text of Johnson," *Modern Philology*, 61 (1964), 298–309, reprinted in his collected *Essays*, pp. 375–391 (esp. pp. 378–381). Hershel Parker (see note 96 above), surveying a number of comments, says that partial modernization "has been all but hooted out of textual circles" (p. 1).

100. The point has been succinctly put by Hershel Parker (see note 96 above): "Normalizing to satisfy an editor's instinct for tidiness or to make smooth the way of a reader is ultimately demeaning for the editor and insulting to the reader" (p. 19).

of private documents—a fact which points to the most tragic weakness of many of the NHPRC editions.

Once it is settled that letters and journals are not to be presented in a corrected or modernized text, there still remains the question of whether editorial symbols are to be employed within the text or whether the text is to be free of such symbols ("clear text"). Even though no corrections are made,[101] there will be occasions when the editor needs to introduce a comment, such as "word illegible," "edge of paper torn, eliminating several words," or "written in the margin." Whether these explanations are entered in brackets in the text or printed as appended notes is to some extent merely a mechanical matter. But there is a theoretical aspect to the question. It is often argued that novels, essays, poems, and other works intended for publication should be edited in clear text, because such works are finished products, and the intrusion of editorial apparatus into the text (recording emendations or variants, for example) would be alien to the spirit of the work. For this reason the CEAA editions of this kind of material are in clear text, with the textual data relegated to lists at the ends of the volumes.[102] Private documents are different, however, in that they are often characterized by not being smooth—by containing, that is, false starts, deletions, insertions, and so on. The problem of how to handle deletions gets to the heart of the matter. Simply to leave them out, as is often done (or done on a selective basis), is indefensible, since they are essential characteristics of private documents.[103] One solution would be to leave them out of the text and report them in notes. But to do so would make the text appear smoother than it is; no evidence would be lost, but the reader would have to reconstruct the text of the document, which is after all of primary interest. If, on the other hand, the deletion is kept in the text but clearly marked as a deletion (with angle brackets or some other device),

101. Some responsible editions, as noted earlier, do incorporate certain minor categories of correction—not modernization—into the text and indicate exactly what has been done in notes. If these categories are carefully defined, their presence in the text may not seriously interfere with the aim of maintaining the texture of the original. It is dangerous to argue, however, that nothing is lost just because all the evidence is available in the notes; there is an important difference in emphasis between a reading which is chosen to stand in the text and one which is relegated to a note or a list.

102. There are practical advantages to this system, also, in the case of works likely to be reproduced photographically for widespread distribution by commercial publishers. For further discussion, see G. T. Tanselle, "Some Principles for Editorial Apparatus," *SB*, 25 (1972), 41–88 (esp. pp. 45–49).

103. One of the reasons for their importance is suggested by Boyd when he refers to "those revealing deletions and first thoughts that so often unmask the writer's true feelings or motives" ("Some Animadversions" [see note 14 above], p. 52). Even when they are not revealing in this way, they are still part of the characterizing roughness of the document and are indicative of the writer's process of composition.

the nature of the original is more accurately rendered in print. In reading the original, one would see a phrase with a line through it, for instance, and then read the phrase which replaced it; by keeping the deleted matter in the text, the editor allows the reader to have the same experience. But when canceled matter is recorded, it is essential at the same time to indicate whether the replacement (if any) occurs on the same line or is inserted above the line, so that the reader can tell whether the revision was made in the process of writing the words or perhaps at a later time.[104] A number of the NHPRC editions devote some attention to cancellations, but their frequent failure to specify interlinear insertions makes it impossible for the reader to use properly the texts of the cancellations which they do provide. Some situations can become very complex and may require an editorial description of what has happened as well as editorial symbols. This description might well be placed in a note rather than in the text; but since the text will contain editorial symbols in any case, one could decide to include editorial comments—at least the brief ones, like "illegible"—within the text.[105] The crucial point is that if a private document is presented in clear text it loses part of its texture.[106]

The argument thus far has assumed that for any given text the evidence available to the editor is a single document in the hand of the author. In those cases the editor's goal is to reproduce in print as many of the characteristics of the document as he can. The goal is not, in other words, to produce a critical text, except to the extent that judgment is involved in determining precisely what is in the manuscript. And judgment is inevitably involved: the editor of *Shelley and His Circle* points out that if a word clearly intended to be "even" looks more like "ever" it is still transcribed as "even." Distinguishing between

104. Methods of transcribing manuscripts in clear text (with apparatus) or in descriptive form (with symbols in the text) are carefully described by Fredson Bowers in "Transcription of Manuscripts: The Record of Variants," *SB*, 29 (1976), 212–264.

105. Of course, a text with several kinds of brackets in it (and other symbols such as arrows) will be more awkward to quote in secondary works, and this practical consideration may, in the case of a few important texts likely to be widely quoted, cause the editor to choose clear text and record all deletions in notes; it is questionable, however, whether what is gained from a practical point of view really justifies the loss incurred. Generally, in any case, there is no more reason to regularize or modernize a quoted excerpt than the complete text itself. The problem of the quoter as his own editor, along with many other considerations affecting the extent of editorial intrusion in private documents, is taken up by William H. Gilman in an excellent and thorough discussion (occasioned by the appearance of the first volume of the Irving *Journals*), "How Should Journals Be Edited?", *Early American Literature*, 6 (1971), 73–83.

106. This point was not recognized by Lewis Mumford in his famous review of the Emerson *Journals*, "Emerson Behind Barbed Wire," *New York Review of Books*, 18 January 1968, pp. 3–5, which objects to the inclusion of cancellations and editorial symbols. (See also the related correspondence in the issues of 14 March, pp. 35–36, and 23 May, p. 43.)

an actual misspelling or slip of the pen and merely indistinct or hasty handwriting requires careful judgment. The editor, even in presenting an "exact" transcription of the text of a document, must keep the writer's habits and intention in mind, if he is to be successful in discovering what that text actually says at difficult spots. If, for instance, a manuscript clearly reads "seperate," there is no doubt that the author wrote the word with a middle "e"; whether or not the author intended to misspell is irrelevant, so long as one agrees that an author's errors in private documents are of interest and should be preserved. But if the word only looks like "seperate" because the author has been careless in forming an "a" in the second syllable, the editor who prints "seperate" is neither transcribing accurately nor respecting the author's intention. In a case like "even"/"ever," the intention as determined by the context plays a greater role: deciphering handwriting and understanding the content are inseparable.[107] It is frequently necessary, therefore, even in connection with a so-called "literal" transcription, for an editor to append notes recording editorial decisions, if the reader is to be fully apprised of the state of the manuscript. But these decisions, it should be clearly understood, result from the effort to determine what the text of the document actually says, not what the editor believes it ought to say.

The situation is different, however, when the textual evidence is not limited to a single holograph document; there may be several drafts, versions, or copies, and they may be in the hand of a copyist or in printed form. In such cases the editor has a fundamental decision to make about the nature of his edited text: is it still to be a transcription of the text of a single document (with evidence from related documents given in notes), or is it to be a critical text which attempts through emendation (based on a study of all the documents) to represent the writer's intentions more fully than any single surviving document can? This decision will rest on the nature of the surviving documents—on their relative authority and completeness. When there are various versions or drafts of a letter in the author's hand, the editor would normally choose the one actually posted, if it survives, or the retained copy or latest surviving draft if it does not, as the document to be edited; variant readings and canceled matter in the other documents might then be added in notes, but—in line with the reasoning suggested above—they would not be emended into the text itself. If, on the other hand, the extant version or versions of a text are not in the author's hand—as when a letter

107. Shaw (see note 17 above) objects to the "essentially subjective basis for editorial revisions" (p. 741) in the critical-text policies of the CEAA editions and regards the attempt to "recapture 'the author's intention'" as opening "the door to chaos" (p. 740). He fails to acknowledge the subjectivity and concern for "intention" which are a part of all editing, even the transcription of a single manuscript text.

survives only in several scribal copies or in print—the editor is faced
with the problem of distinguishing those features which reflect the author's intention from those which result from the habits and errors of
another person (the copyist, the compositor, the printer's or publisher's
reader, and so on). Since the interest is in the characteristics of the author's expression, not in those of a copyist or compositor, this problem
is worth solving. For if an editor presents the text of a nonholograph
document in an exact transcription, as he would that of a holograph
document, he is respecting equally its authorial and its nonauthorial
features; but if he attempts, so far as his evidence allows, to remove
some of the nonauthorial features, he comes that much closer to offering
what was present in the author's manuscript.

Editors of works which were intended to be made public commonly
have this problem to deal with. When confronted with a printed text
or texts, or with a printed text which differs from the author's manuscript, or with a scribal copy or copies, these editors frequently take it
as their responsibility to evaluate the evidence (on the basis of their
specialized knowledge of the author, his time, and the textual history
of the work) and then to choose and emend a copy-text so as to obtain
a maximum number of authorial readings and characteristics and a
minimum number of nonauthorial ones.[108] The CEAA editions of works
intended for publication have taken this approach, on the ground that
more is to be gained by encouraging a qualified editor to apply what
judgment and sensitivity he has to the problem of determining the author's intended text than by requiring him to reproduce the text present in a particular surviving document. Some mistakes are bound to
result, but in general a text produced in this way is likely to come
closer to what the author intended than a single documentary text
could possibly do. (An accompanying record of emendations and variant readings is naturally important, so that the reader can reconstruct
the copy-text and reconsider the evidence for emending it.) Editors of
letters and journals will perhaps less frequently encounter similar situations, but when they do they should remember that preparing a critical
text of nonholograph materials is not inconsistent with a policy of presenting a literal text of holograph manuscripts. Rather, it is an intelligent way of recognizing that a consistency of purpose may require different approaches for handling different situations. The aim of an edition
of a person's letters and journals is to make available an accurate text

108. This "eclectic" approach is thoroughly discussed in Fredson Bowers's "Remarks
on Eclectic Texts," *Proof*, 4 (1975), 31–76 (reprinted in his collected *Essays*, pp. 488–528).
See also the various writings on Greg's rationale of copy-text; many are mentioned by
G. T. Tanselle in *SB*, 28 (1975), 167–229.

of what he wrote; that goal cannot be achieved as fully for nonholograph documents as for holograph ones, but it is the editor's responsibility to come as close as he can in either case.[109]

When Peter Shaw claims that the NHPRC editions show more respect for historical fact than do the CEAA editions, he fails to recognize that an edition with a critical or "eclectic" text does not necessarily conceal historical facts and that an edition of a single documentary text does not necessarily reveal all relevant facts. Whether they do so or not depends on their policies for recording textual data.[110] CEAA editions are required to include textual apparatuses which contain records of all editorial emendations as well as several other categories of textual information;[111] most of the NHPRC editions, on the other hand, incorporate several kinds of silent emendations.[112] Readers of the former are able to reconstruct the original copy-texts and are in possession of much of the textual evidence which the editor had at his disposal; readers of the latter cannot reconstruct to the same degree the details of the original documents and are not provided with carefully defined categories of textual evidence on a systematic basis. The CEAA editors fulfill an essential editorial obligation: they inform their readers explicitly

109. A difficult category consists of semifinished manuscripts of the kinds of works normally intended for publication: the manuscripts of some of Emily Dickinson's poems and of Melville's *Billy Budd* are prominent examples. From one point of view they are private documents, and their nature can best be represented by a literal transcription showing cancellations and insertions in the text; from another point of view they are simply unfinished literary works and ought therefore to be printed in a critically established clear text, the form in which one normally expects to read poems and fiction. The solution which Harrison Hayford and Merton M. Sealts, Jr., reach in their edition of *Billy Budd* (University of Chicago Press, 1962) is to print a "genetic text" accompanied by a "reading text." For some comments on the general problem and on Dickinson's poems in particular, see Tanselle's "The Editorial Problem of Final Authorial Intention" (see note 95 above), esp. pp. 205–207.

110. Shaw says, "With an eclectic text, the problem of variants is solved at the expense of making them disappear from view" (p. 739)—as if there is something about an eclectic text which prohibits the recording of variant readings.

111. Including at least the substantive variants in post-copy-text editions and the treatment of ambiguous line-end hyphens, along with a textual essay and discussions of problematical readings. For further explanation of the CEAA requirements, see the CEAA *Statement of Editorial Principles and Procedures* (rev. ed., 1972).

112. Shaw's argument for the Freudian significance of errors (pp. 742–743) is actually a more telling criticism of most of the NHPRC editions than of the CEAA editions; when a CEAA editor does correct an error, he reports that fact in a list of emendations, whereas NHPRC editors often make corrections without notifying the reader where these corrections occur. Shaw objects to the CEAA editor who "rewrites usage, punctuation, spelling, capitalization, and hyphenation" (p. 741) and misleadingly implies that this practice is in contrast to that of NHPRC editors; actually, changes of this kind occur with greater frequency in the NHPRC editions—and are often not recorded in any way. At another point Shaw seems to take a different position on the question of errors: "It would be unfair to the author literally to transcribe his manuscript without correcting his obvious oversights" (p. 740).

of what textual information can and what cannot be found in their pages.[113] The truth is, therefore, that the CEAA editions are actually more respectful of documentary fact, and at the same time they recognize more fully that fidelity to a writer's intention demands, under certain circumstances, an eclectic approach to the documents. Comparing a CEAA edition of a novel with an NHPRC edition of letters creates a false opposition; but when CEAA and NHPRC editions of similar materials—two volumes of letters[114] or two volumes of works intended for publication—are compared, the CEAA volumes characteristically exhibit a more profound understanding of the problems involved in textual study and a greater responsibility in treating textual details. The NHPRC editors have undeniably been successful in the nontextual aspects of their work, and the CEAA editors could learn from them in regard to explanatory annotation. But in textual matters the CEAA editors are far in the lead.

This state of affairs is a depressing reminder of how little communication sometimes exists between fields with overlapping interests. In 1949, the year before the first volume of the Jefferson edition appeared, Fredson Bowers commented on the importance of textual study for all fields of endeavor:

No matter what the field of study, the basis lies in the analysis of the records in printed or in manuscript form, frequently the ill-ordered and incomplete records of the past. When factual or critical investigation is made of these records, there must be—it seems to me—the same care, no matter what the field, in establishing the purity and accuracy of the materials under exami-

113. One of the reasons the CEAA editions are not "definitive," Shaw says, is "the physical impossibility of comparing and recording all the variants as demanded by copy-text theory" (p. 748). Presumably any respectable theory would require an editor to compare texts and locate variants; the CEAA policy for recording variants, however, has nothing to do with theory—obviously a text edited according to Greg's theory of copy-text would remain so edited whether or not it were accompanied by any apparatus. It is true that CEAA editions do not always record all variants (neither do the NHPRC editions); but the important point is that CEAA editions clearly define what categories of variants are to be recorded and record all that fall within those categories, whereas NHPRC editions normally record variants selectively on the vague basis of "significance." Therefore, if the word "definitive" must be used, it would seem to fit CEAA apparatus but generally not NHPRC apparatus. The objection has been well put by Bowers, who says of the Johnson edition (see note 99 above) that the reader "has no way of knowing whether he is or is not accepting in ignorance any of the extensive editorial silent departures from the copy-text features" (p. 379).

114. Shaw is incorrect in saying that CEAA editions "include no plans to publish authors' letters" (p. 748). The opening of the same sentence is also incorrect: "Unlike the historical editions, most of them are selected, not complete, editions." It would be more accurate to say that most of the CEAA editions are planned to be complete, not selective, and that many of the NHPRC editions are in fact selective (leaving out the texts of certain less important documents and instead summarizing them or mentioning their existence in a calendar of manuscripts).

nation, which is perhaps just another way of saying that one must establish the text on which one's far-reaching analysis is to be based.[115]

In the twentieth century scholars of English literature—especially of Elizabethan drama—have taken over from the Biblical scholars and classicists as leaders in the development of textual theory and practice; and in the last generation the editing of nineteenth-century American literature has been a focal point in this continuing tradition. But the principles that have been emerging are not limited in their applicability to the field of literature. Students in all fields have occasion to work with written or printed documents, and they all need to have the habit of mind which inquires into the "purity and accuracy" of any document they consult. The NHPRC volumes have been singled out here because they constitute a prominent block of modern editions and can serve as an instructive example: the difference between the way American statesmen and American literary figures have recently been edited is a striking illustration of how two closely related fields can approach the basic scholarly task of establishing dependable texts in two very different ways, one of which seems superficial and naïve in comparison to the other. But history and literature are not the only fields that would mutually profit from a more encompassing discussion of textual problems; many editorial projects are now under way in philosophy and the sciences, and the fundamental questions which editors must ask are the same in those fields also. Editing is of course more than a matter of technique; a text can be satisfactorily edited only by a person with a thorough understanding of the content and historical and biographical setting of that text. Nevertheless, there is a common ground for discussion among editors in all fields. The time for closer communication of this kind is overdue; not only editors but all who study the written heritage of the past will benefit from it.

115. "Bibliography and the University," *University of Pennsylvania Library Chronicle*, 15 (1949), 37–51 (p. 37); reprinted in his collected *Essays*, pp. 3–14.

Classical, Biblical, and Medieval Textual Criticism and Modern Editing

MOST SCHOLARLY EDITORS, REGARDLESS OF THE NATURE OR DATE of the material they work with, recognize that they are participating in a tradition extending back to antiquity; they realize that the activity of "textual criticism," whether called by that name or not, was for centuries concerned with the establishment of the texts of ancient Greek and Roman writings and of the Old and New Testaments and that the development of their discipline is therefore tied to the history of those works. Even if they are not familiar with the details of that history, they know that Aristarchus and other librarians at Alexandria in the third and second centuries B.C. attempted to determine what was authentic and what was spurious in the texts of the manuscripts they assembled; that the Renaissance humanists (among them Poggio, Politian, Aldus, and Erasmus) were particularly concerned with locating, establishing, and disseminating texts in the ancient languages; that Richard Bentley in the early eighteenth century made contributions to the textual study of several Latin authors and proposed a text of the New Testament based on the earliest manuscripts; and that Karl Lachmann, a century later, provided the fullest exposition up to that time of the genealogical approach and is therefore sometimes regarded as the father of modern textual criticism. They probably also know that A.E. Housman had some sharp things to say about the editorial practices of many of his predecessors, comments that emerged from important methodological considerations.

But unless their own work involves classical or biblical or medieval texts, they have in all likelihood not followed closely the nineteenth- and twentieth-century history of textual study in these areas. The explanation is not simply the growing specialization of scholarship but the feeling that the textual criticism of manuscript texts produced centuries after their authors' deaths has little, if any, relevance to textual work on printed texts published during their authors' lifetimes. The foolishness of this view is evident to anyone who has read in the editorial literature concerning both ancient and modern texts, for the same issues keep turning up, and some writers seem to be rediscovering, with effort, what was thoroughly discussed in a different field years before. By not familiarizing themselves with the textual criticism of classical, biblical, and medieval literature, textual scholars of more recent literature are cutting themselves off from a voluminous body of theoretical discussion and the product of many generations of experience. And by not keeping up with developments in the editing of post-medieval writings, students of earlier works are depriving themselves of the knowledge of significant advances in editorial thinking. Whereas in the classical and biblical fields textual scholarship was at the forefront, both in prestige and in achievement, in the nineteenth and early twentieth centuries, the leadership in theoretical debate about textual matters has in more recent years passed to the field of Renaissance and later literature in English. If textual scholars of these later writings have never quite been accorded by their colleagues the same position of centrality that editors of the classics had long held in their field,[1] there can be no doubt that the extensive, and sometimes acrimonious, debate provoked by Greg's famous essay on copy-text,[2] and its extension by Fredson Bowers and then by the Center for Editions of American Authors,[3] have caused textual and editorial questions to be of serious concern to a larger portion of the

1. Robert R. Bolgar evocatively describes the situation in the last decades of the nineteenth century: "Textual criticism was the branch of Latin studies that enjoyed most esteem. . . . Successful editors, critics whose conjectures appeared in learned journals or in their *adversaria critica* were regarded as the leading scholars of their day. They had the stature of paladins in the eyes of their colleagues." See "Latin Literature: A Century of Interpretation," in *Les Études classiques aux XIXe et XXe siècles: leur place dans l'histoire des idées*, ed. Willem den Boer (1979), pp. 91–126 (quotation from p. 99).

2. W. W. Greg, "The Rationale of Copy-Text," *Studies in Bibliography*, 3 (1950–51), 19–36; reprinted in his *Collected Papers*, ed. J. C. Maxwell (1966), pp. 374–391.

3. I have attempted to provide a critical survey of these developments in "Greg's Theory of Copy-Text and the Editing of American Literature," *SB*, 28 (1975), 167–229 (reprinted in *Selected Studies in Bibliography* [1979], pp. 245–307), and in "Recent Editorial Discussion and the Central Questions of Editing," *SB*, 34 (1981), 23–65. Four publications of the Modern Language Association of America contain basic statements about editing that derive from Greg's rationale: *The Aims and Methods of Scholarship in Modern Languages and Literatures*, ed. James Thorpe (1963; rev. ed., 1970), which contains Fredson Bowers's "Textual Criticism" (pp. 29–54); Center for Editions of American Authors, *Statement of Editorial Principles and Procedures* (1967; rev. ed., 1972); *The Center for Scholarly Editions: An Introductory Statement* (1977; also printed in *PMLA*, 92 [1977], 586–597); *Introduction to Scholarship in Modern Languages and Literatures*, ed. Joseph Gibaldi (1981), which contains G. T. Tanselle's "Textual Scholarship" (pp. 29–52). (In the latter three I have suggested further related reading.) Two other general treatments in this tradition are Fredson Bowers, "Scholarship and Editing," *PBSA*, 70 (1976), 161–188, and G. T. Tanselle, "Literary Editing," in *Literary & Historical Editing*, ed. George L. Vogt and John Bush Jones (1981), pp. 35–56.

scholars in the field than they had ever been before. Although the phrase "modern editing" in my title of course refers elliptically to the editing of modern literature, there is some justice in taking it at the same time to mean, more literally, the latest developments in editing.

As a contribution toward what I hope will become increased communication among scholars in all these fields, I should like to offer in what follows a few reflections on the relations between textual work on early or medieval manuscripts and that on later printed texts. Although I do not propose a systematic survey of the history of classical, biblical, and medieval textual criticism,[4] I believe that some purpose is served by bringing together, in this context, references to a number of the significant discussions. What I trust will become clear in the process is that editors of ancient and modern materials have much more to learn from one another than they have generally recognized. Equally revealing, if rather depressing, is the fact that many of their areas of confusion are the same: some of the questions that have been endlessly and inconclusively debated—and often, it must be said, illogically argued as well—are identical in both fields. In either case, the essential point is the relevance each field has for the other.

I

It should not be surprising that all textual scholarship is related, for the same activities are involved, regardless of the diversity of the materials. One must decide whether to produce a diplomatic—that is, unaltered—text of a single document or a critical text, which is a new text that incorporates the results of editorial judgment regarding variant readings and errors. One must assemble the relevant or potentially relevant documents (handwritten, typed, or printed), then find out in what ways their texts differ by collating them, then attempt to determine the relationships among the texts, and finally, if the edition is to be critical, construct a new text by choosing among variant readings and by making conjectures where errors seem to be present in all texts. These stages are interrelated: the kind of thinking one brings to the task of determining relationships among texts, for example, will obviously have a bearing on the decisions made at the next stage. Although these two

4. Excellent accounts of the history of classical and biblical textual criticism can be found in Bruce M. Metzger, *The Text of the New Testament: Its Transmission, Corruption, and Restoration* (1964; 2nd ed., 1968); L. D. Reynolds and N. G. Wilson, *Scribes and Scholars: A Guide to the Transmission of Greek and Latin Literature* (1968; 2nd ed., 1974); and E. J. Kenney, *The Classical Text: Aspects of Editing in the Age of the Printed Book* (1974). For the Renaissance humanists, see also M. D. Feld, "The Early Evolution of the Authoritative Text," *Harvard Library Bulletin*, 26 (1978), 81–111. Some further studies of nineteenth- and twentieth-century developments are listed below in note 38.

stages are not entirely separable, textual discussions do, in practice, often emphasize one or the other; and I think it is fair to say that perhaps the principal distinction between the body of writing concerned with editing the classics and that dealing with editing modern literature is their differing emphases in this regard. Editors of the earlier material have access to no authorial manuscripts and must contend with copies an unknown number of steps removed (and often many centuries away) from those originals, and such copies sometimes exist in the hundreds, or even—as with the Greek New Testament—the thousands. The task of working out the relationships among the texts of these documents is indeed formidable, and it is natural that a great deal of the thought and writing about editing ancient texts[5] has concentrated on this stage of the editorial process. What has traditionally been called "textual criticism"—or, more recently, "textual analysis"—is this attempt to fix the relationship of the surviving documentary witnesses; and though many of the theories of textual criticism have entailed certain assumptions about how the editor's critical text should be constructed, the focus of attention has normally been not on the "editorial" phase (the actual selection or emendation of readings) but on the prior analysis of the texts that results in the assignment of relationships among them.[6]

Methodological writings about the editing of post-medieval literature, on the other hand, have reversed this emphasis. Although relationships among the texts from this period are by no means always clear-cut, the dimensions of the problem are often significantly different: manuscripts in the author's hand, copies made directly from them, printed editions set from such documents (and perhaps proofread by the author), and later editions during the author's lifetime (perhaps set from copies of the earlier editions annotated by the author) are the characteristic materials. Editorial theorists concerned with this period

5. When I speak of "ancient" (or "early") texts, I include medieval texts, which also normally depend on scribal copies a number of removes from the original (though generally not as many steps removed).

6. The term "textual analysis" has been used—particularly by Vinton A. Dearing (see note 11 below) and James Thorpe (note 39 below)—to refer specifically to the process of establishing the relationships among texts, which is only one of the operations that make up the larger undertaking of "textual criticism." Dearing's use of the term helps him to emphasize that what he is concerned with is the relationship of "messages," not their "transmitters"; but "textual criticism," in which one applies the abstractions of "textual analysis" to the specific instance of verbal texts, can also draw on "bibliographical analysis," the analysis of the physical documents transmitting the texts. I use these terms here with this distinction in mind, though I often employ the more general term where some might prefer the more specific. Whether "analysis" can be wholly objective and can be kept entirely distinct from the larger process of "criticism," in which subjective judgment plays a role, is a debatable question, and is taken up at several points later in this essay.

have therefore not been required to give as much thought to the question of establishing relationships among texts and instead have concentrated their attention on the choice and treatment of a "copy-text." Choosing a copy-text is of course dependent on knowing the relationships among the texts; the central problem, however, is not the process of establishing those relationships but of defining the authorial intention that is to be reflected in the critical text, since often more than one document exists that is directly associated with the author. The term "textual criticism" can be used broadly to designate the evaluation of textual witnesses for writings of any period; but its traditional, and more restricted, application to the study of ancient manuscripts is appropriate, for it refers to the kind of analysis that has bulked largest in textual work on those manuscripts.

In classical textual criticism, these basic operations have generally been referred to as *recensio* and *emendatio*, and the distinction between the two points up another contrast with textual scholarship of later literature. *Recensio* refers to the process of establishing the archetype, or the latest common ancestor of all surviving manuscripts, insofar as it can be established from the evidence in those manuscripts, which are the only witnesses to the tradition. The particular decisions made about individual variant readings in the construction of this archetype depend, at least in part, on the relationships that have been postulated among the manuscripts; the practice of stemmatics—of constructing genealogical trees to show manuscript relationships—is therefore also sometimes called "recensionism." And whether or not one aspires to a system that eliminates judgment in the construction and use of the stemmata, the fact is that ultimately judgment will have been involved in the attempt to choose the wording of the archetype from among the variant readings. Swings in scholarly fashion toward, and away from, the use of critical judgment—along with the associated tendency to favor, or disapprove of, eclecticism—must be looked at later; but the point here is not whether a single text is principally adhered to in producing the new recension but the fact that the recension is defined as being limited to readings present in the witnesses (or obvious corrections of them). It is the next stage, *emendatio*, in which the editor can engage in conjecture to rectify what appear to be errors in all preserved texts.[7] Editorial dis-

7. Paul Maas, in his celebrated essay "Textkritik" (note 44 below), as well as many other writers, specifies a step called *examinatio* between *recensio* and *emendatio* (or *divinatio*). But examining the recension to determine whether or not it can be regarded as furnishing what the author intended is a necessary first step in the process of deciding when to emend; it is simply a matter of definition whether or not one takes *emendatio* to comprehend the examination that leads to emendation, and in any case the two are intimately related. As E. J. Kenney concisely notes in his article on "Textual Criticism" in

cussion dealing with post-medieval works, in contrast, generally takes the term "emendation" to refer to any alterations introduced by the editor into a particular documentary text (the one chosen as "copy-text"), whether the source of those alterations are other texts or the editor's own ingenuity. It is perhaps natural that this usage should have prevailed among editors of modern works, since they often have an author's manuscript or a text only one or two steps from it to use as a copy-text, and all their alterations may then be seen as corrections to that single documentary text; editors in the earlier manuscript tradition, on the other hand, normally have no such text to choose, and the process of arriving at what might be regarded as the counterpart is a major undertaking in itself, to be accomplished before one can begin to think about how that text departs from what the author must have intended to say. In any event, however the difference in usage came about, it should be clear that both groups of editors are talking about the same categories of editorial intervention—alterations based on readings present in one or more of the documents and alterations emerging from the editor's own conjecture.

It should further be evident that any approach or vocabulary suggesting that the latter are more conjectural than the former is delusory. Of course, a reading adopted from one of the documents may be a striking reading that the editor would not have thought of or dared introduce independently, but the decision to consider it as worthy of acceptance into the critical text is still an act of conjecture, always entailing the potential danger that the reading is accorded too much credence by the mere fact of its existence in one of the documents. To regard the choice among variants as "recension," defined as establishing "what *must* or *may* be regarded as transmitted" (Maas), and then to label further editorial alteration as "emendation" or "conjectural emendation," would seem to overemphasize the objectivity of the first and to imply a greater distance between the two than in fact exists. The recension, after all, is a conclusion resulting from scholarly judgment or conjecture—except, of course, when only one text survives or (theoretically) when all surviving texts are identical. Even when the archetype appears to be the text of one of the extant manuscripts, judgment regarding individual variants is still involved in reaching that decision. To think of

the *Encyclopaedia Britannica*, 15th ed. (1974), the two activities are "in practice performed simultaneously." (He also recognizes that even recension "entails the application of criteria theoretically appropriate" to examination and emendation.) Maas in fact takes up *divinatio* in his section entitled "Examinatio." A similar point is implied by Robert Renehan, in *Greek Textual Criticism* (1969), which aims "to show the textual critic actually at work on a number of specific passages," when he says that his book deals with "*examinatio*, including both *selectio* between variants and *divinatio*" (p. 2).

"what *must* or *may* be regarded as transmitted" as a single text, when variant texts survive, is to engage in conjecture; and some of the "conjectural emendations" that an editor thinks of may attain to a higher degree of certainty than some of the choices that are made among variant readings in the documents. I do not believe that editors in any field would disagree with this point, despite the implications of the language sometimes used. The fact that the terminology employed by editors of classical and of modern texts diverges somewhat is not important, so long as both groups of editors recognize that they are dealing with the same fundamental questions and so long as they are not misled by the superficial suggestiveness of some of the terms.

As the division of the editorial process into *recensio* and *emendatio* makes clear, editors of ancient texts are normally concerned with producing critical editions—editions, that is, containing texts that are different, as a result of the editors' intervention, from any of the documentary texts now existing. Editors of printed texts from the last five hundred years have also been engaged for the most part with this kind of edition: the extensive discussion in the wake of Greg's "Rationale," for instance, has concentrated on critical editions. Yet in the exchange of views that has increasingly been taking place in recent years between editors of modern literature and editors of statesmen's papers, some of the so-called "historical" editors have questioned the value of critical texts, or at least of texts that are "eclectic" in incorporating readings from two or more documents. It is easy to see why a historian editing letters and journals in the hand of a particular statesman would think primarily of a diplomatic edition, and similarly understandable that an editor of an ancient Greek text surviving in much later manuscripts would probably wish to construct a new text attempting to restore the author's words. But the difference between the two situations does not really rest on the different nature of the materials: there are different goals involved, the aim in the former instance being the reproduction of the content of a given document and in the latter being the reconstruction of what the author of a text intended to say. Both approaches are applicable to any material: documents containing ancient Greek texts, for instance, can obviously be treated as entities in their own right, with texts to be exactly reproduced, as manifestations of particular moments in the history of the pieces of writing involved; or they can be regarded as evidence to be used in reconstructing a text nearer its author's intentions than any of the surviving texts manages to come. Historians may more often find themselves producing diplomatic texts of particular *documents* (the contents of which were often not intended for publication), and scholars of literature (both ancient and modern) may more often be engaged in constructing critical texts of *works* (ordinarily finished pieces of writing—whether "literary" or not—intended for public dissemination). But each group should recognize the value of both approaches and understand how they are related to one another.

This point would seem to be so elementary and obvious as not to need stating; but unfortunately some textual controversies have arisen through a failure to keep in mind the most basic distinctions and to appreciate the place each editorial undertaking occupies in the large framework that encompasses all textual work in all fields. One historical editor has gone so far recently as to make this statement: "To what uses literary critics may put bastard documents is for them to say, but the saying of the same will not likely change the historical discipline's rules of evidence and citation."[8] The narrowness and closed-mindedness of this position is astounding. In a more sophisticated form, however, this issue keeps turning up: the question of eclecticism has perennially been a point of controversy among editors of the classics as well as of modern works.[9] Some editors of modern literary works, who well understand the value of critical texts, have nevertheless argued against combining into a single text readings that reflect different stages of authorial revision. There is nothing wrong in principle, of course, with the position that authorially revised texts may at times be best handled by preparing separate critical editions of each version. But the mistake that sometimes follows is the belief that no variant from one version can be incorporated into another. That injunction would naturally be proper if one were producing a diplomatic edition of each version; but if a critical text of each version is the goal, then one must recognize that some of the variants among versions do not represent a particular stage of revision or rethinking but are precisely the kinds of corrections that the editor is already committed to inserting—without documentary authority. I make this point (which has been discussed more fully elsewhere)[10] in order to suggest, once again, that the distinction between

8. Wayne Cutler, "The 'Authentic' Witness: The Editor Speaks for the Document," *Newsletter of the Association for Documentary Editing*, 4, no. 1 (February 1982), 8–9. A notorious example of this view, arguing that historical editions exhibit a "respect for historical fact" lacking in literary editions, is Peter Shaw's "The American Heritage and Its Guardians," *American Scholar*, 45 (1975–76), 733–751 [i.e., 37–55]; his position has been commented on by G. T. Tanselle in "The Editing of Historical Documents," *SB*, 31 (1978), 1–56 (*Selected Studies*, pp. 451–506)— cf. *SB*, 32 (1979), 31–34 (*Selected Studies*, pp. 385–388).

9. For an authoritative statement on eclecticism in the editing of modern works, see Fredson Bowers, "Remarks on Eclectic Texts," *Proof*, 4 (1975), 13–58 (reprinted in his *Essays in Bibliography, Text, and Editing* [1975], pp. 488–528).

10. See G. T. Tanselle, "Problems and Accomplishments in the Editing of the Novel," *Studies in the Novel*, 7 (1975), 323–360 (esp. 329–331); see also *SB*, 34 (1981), 30–31, 55 n.65.

adopted variant readings and conjectural emendations needs to be thought about less mechanically than it often is and to show that editors would be well advised to keep abreast of textual debate in fields other than their own. Just as editors of statesmen's papers and of modern literature stand to benefit from knowing more about the editorial thinking underlying critical editions of ancient texts, so editors of the classics (and of statesmen's papers) will find that the discussions of authorial revisions, engaged in fully by editors of modern literature, raise questions relevant for them.

Further indication of these connections can be suggested by referring to three of the more recent manuals on textual criticism, published coincidentally at about the same time, James Willis's *Latin Textual Criticism* (1972), Martin L. West's *Textual Criticism and Editorial Technique Applicable to Greek and Latin Texts* (1973), and Vinton A. Dearing's *Principles and Practice of Textual Analysis* (1974).[11] These books offer several contrasts. Willis and West, classicists and editors, address their work, as the titles indicate, to other editors of classical texts; Dearing, a professor of English who is establishing the text for the California edition of Dryden and is also working on an edition of the Greek New Testament, intends for his book to be applicable to all editorial scholarship, indeed "to the transmission in any form of any idea or complex of ideas" (p. ix). Willis, whose writing is marred by unsuccessful sarcasm, is principally occupied with restating "the many ways in which scribes were accustomed to make mistakes" (p. ix), though he prefaces that account with a brief section on "Fundamentals"; West, who writes lucidly and concisely, would claim originality largely (though not entirely) for his way of stating certain complex questions and their conventional answers and for choosing passages to illustrate his points; Dearing, who writes at greater length and with some obscurity, covers what a manual must cover but uses the occasion to set forth his own proposal for the analysis of relationships among texts. Willis's book is the narrowest and least significant of the three, focusing on scribal errors and devoting considerable space to "trial passages," on which readers are invited to exercise their ingenuity by proposing emen-

---

11. An earlier, and much briefer, version of Dearing's book, entitled *A Manual of Textual Analysis*, appeared in 1959. Two manuals on medieval literature, which appeared later in the 1970s, are Charles Moorman's *Editing the Middle English Manuscript* (1975), a slight and very elementary book, and Alfred Foulet and Mary Blakely Speer's *On Editing Old French Texts* (1979), a much more useful and sophisticated treatment. A thorough and learned manual dealing with Italian literature of all periods is Franca Brambilla Ageno's *L'edizione critica dei testi volgare* (1975). A somewhat earlier manual that is full of common sense and wise observations is Ludwig Bieler's "The Grammarian's Craft: A Professional Talk," *Folia*, 2 (1947), 94–105; 3 (1948), 23–32, 47–58; 2nd ed., *Folia*, 10, no. 2 (1956), 3–42 (and as a separate).

dations (answers are provided). Dearing's experience with both ancient and modern texts (he is perhaps unique in working in both fields) and his view of textual analysis as "a completely general discipline of very wide specific applicability in the arts and social sciences" (p. 1) are encouraging signs, and one has good reason to expect his book to have broader significance than West's.[12] In my view, however, West's book is calmer, clearer, and more sensible and finally a better introduction for students from any discipline. Whether or not I am right, I hope that one point implicit in my opinion will be granted: that the interests of all who deal with texts are closely related and therefore that the sources of specific illustrations are of less moment than the basic statements and discussions of principles. A book that draws its examples from many periods and languages is not necessarily of more general applicability than one that takes all its illustrations from Greek and Latin texts; it may be, but the range of examples and even the immediate aims of the author are not the decisive tests.

One vital matter commented on in all three books—and one that editors of modern literature have a particular interest in—is the role of the analysis of physical evidence in textual decisions. What has come to be known as "analytical bibliography" is crucial to the editing of texts in printed books: in order to be in a position to understand textual anomalies in a printed text, one must first have extracted as much information as possible about the printing of the work from the evidence preserved in the printed sheets themselves. As a result of the efforts of McKerrow, Pollard, Greg, Bowers, and Hinman,[13] and of those that followed their lead, editors of printed texts must now deal with such matters as the identification of compositors' habits and of the order of formes through the press. Knowing as much as one can about what happened to a particular text in the printing shop or the publisher's office puts one in a better position to recognize those features of the text that did not come from the author (or at least were not present in the copy furnished to the printer); analytical bibliography has shown time and

12. He specifically mentions its use by "historians, cartographers, musicologists, iconographers, and so on," who will have to "translate from the more literary terminology and examples into their own" (pp. 1–2).

13. For an account of the development of analytical bibliography, see F. P. Wilson, "Shakespeare and the 'New Bibliography,'" in *The Bibliographical Society 1892–1942: Studies in Retrospect* (1945), pp. 76–135; it has been reprinted as a separate volume (1970), revised and edited by Helen Gardner. See also my "Physical Bibliography in the Twentieth Century," in *Books, Manuscripts, and the History of Medicine: Essays on the Fiftieth Anniversary of the Osler Library,* ed. Philip M. Teigen (1982). The central statements of the field are R. B. McKerrow, *An Introduction to Bibliography for Literary Students* (1927); Charlton Hinman, *The Printing and Proof-Reading of the First Folio of Shakespeare* (1963); and Fredson Bowers, *Bibliography and Textual Criticism* (1964).

again that much can be learned from physical evidence about the transmission of the text. The same principle obviously applies to manuscripts as well: in the case of manuscript texts not in their authors' hands, the scribe or copyist occupies the roles of publisher's editor, compositor, and pressman combined. Introductory manuals for editors of manuscripts have recognized this point to some extent in that they often contain fairly detailed comments classifying the kinds of errors that scribes were likely to make. Such "habits" are generalized ones, and less attention has been paid to uncovering the habits of particular scribes through physical evidence, including that which fixes the manuscript in time and place.

This whole question enters Dearing's book in the first sentence, where we are told that textual analysis "determines the genealogical relationships between different forms of the same message" but not "the relationships between the transmitters of the different forms"—or, as he puts it in the next paragraph, "the genealogy of the variant states of a text" but not "the genealogy of their records."[14] The distinction, indeed, Dearing regards as one of his central achievements: he believes that his book "carries out to the full" the differentiation set forth in the earlier version[15] between "the genealogy of manuscript and other books as physical objects and the genealogy of the ideas or complexes of ideas that these physical objects transmit" (p. ix). It is of course quite proper to begin with this basic point; editors of all materials from all periods must recognize that the chronology of texts does not necessarily match the chronology of their physical presentation. The point is perhaps not quite such a revelation as Dearing thinks. Nevertheless, it is always good to have fundamental distinctions set forth clearly at the outset of a discussion, and one would have no cause for complaint if Dearing had not carried the point to the opposite extreme, slighting the legitimate role of physical evidence in textual study. Writers in the past, he says, have "almost always" confused the physical document with the text it carries, and he admits that "it is extremely difficult to free oneself from the bibliographical spell"; but it is a "fundamental and important" matter, he insists, "to exclude bibliographical thinking from textual analysis"

14. He immediately proceeds to say that the goal of textual analysis is not "merely to provide a genealogy of the states of a text" but, if the state from which all the others descended is not known to be extant, "to reconstruct the latest state from which all the extant states have descended." This goal is proper, but one must remember that reconstructing a text is a very different activity from analyzing the relationships of those that exist.

15. In the 1959 *Manual* (note 11 above) he considers himself to be introducing this idea: "My method for the first time distinguishes the text conveyed by the manuscript— a mental phenomenon—from the manuscript conveying the text—a physical phenomenon" (p. ix).

(p. 15). That the valid distinction he began with could have led to this wrongheaded conclusion is unfortunate; but the problem might have been predicted from some remarks made along the way to illustrate the basic point that texts are different from their transmitters. To show that "the same record" may preserve "two or more states of a text," he cites as one illustration a poem appearing twice in an anthology (p. 14). But how is "record" being defined here? What is the physical unit? One may ask the same questions when he then says that different records may "transmit the same state of a text when they are produced by a mechanically perfect reproductive process, such as Xerox copying, and whenever it is deemed vital to preserve the text without change, as in statute books, state documents such as the Constitution of the United States, religious documents such as the Book of Common Prayer, and careful scholarly reprints of all sorts" (pp. 14–15). Xerox copying is not "mechanically perfect," if only because the size of the image is not identical with the original. Beyond that, it is no criticism of the Xerox process to say that it is not "mechanically perfect," since no system can be, if what is meant is that the reproduction is identical to the original. The reproduction is a different physical object, and therefore it is not the same thing; and most, if apparently not quite all, users of Xerox reproductions are aware of the dangers of assuming that what they see in the reproduction is precisely what they would see in the original. Furthermore, is Dearing suggesting that whenever "it is deemed vital to preserve the text without change" such preservation is achieved? Are there never errors in the reprintings of statutes, or prayer books, or "careful scholarly reprints"? Does not the acceptance of aim for fact question the need for textual scholarship at all (or any other effort to establish truth)?

The serious bibliographical problem raised by these statements becomes even more evident with Dearing's next sentence: "The many identical copies produced by printing from the same setting of type, however, provided they are uniformly bound and readied for sale as a single lot, are usually counted as one record." Analytical bibliographers have been demonstrating for three-quarters of a century that surviving copies from the same setting of type (i.e., from the same edition) are not necessarily "identical" in their text—indeed, that they are frequently (or, in some periods, usually) not identical. (Whether or not they are "uniformly bound" or "readied for sale as a single lot" has nothing to do with their text.) Differences can come about either intentionally or inadvertently, through stop-press corrections and alterations between printings or through accidents that damage the type (perhaps necessitating some resetting) and deterioration of type or plates through wear. The essential point is that different copies of an edition are different physical objects and are therefore separate pieces of evidence; it is unscholarly to assume, without investigation, that they are identical, and in fact such an assumption would very often be wrong, for books of any period, even the twentieth century. If one were to regard all copies of an edition as a single "record," one would have to define "record" in a special way, for there would frequently be textual variants among particular copies of the "record." It is difficult, for example, to say what "the" text of the Shakespeare First Folio is; one might say that it is the text in Charlton Hinman's *Norton Facsimile* (1968)—but that work assembles from various copies of the Folio the pages representing corrected formes. No one surviving copy contains all the corrected pages, and constructing such a copy in facsimile is a task requiring scholarly judgment. Some people who work only with manuscripts (and some who work with printed books as well) think of copies of printed editions as identical, in contrast to manuscripts, each of which is expected to be different. Undeniably manuscripts and printed books are produced in fundamentally different ways; but the fact that copies of an edition are mass-produced and intended to be identical does not mean that they are actually identical. Indeed, they cannot be identical, since no two physical objects are identical in every respect; and textual differences are among the kinds of variations that occur. Printed books resemble manuscripts more than many people seem to think. These are elementary points, and Dearing (who has done a great deal of work with seventeenth- and eighteenth-century English books) certainly understands them; why he fails to take them into account here is inexplicable.[16] The fact that their absence is more likely to be noticed by students of printed books than by students of the manuscript tradition is an indication of the distance that exists between the two groups—an unfortunate distance, since these points clearly have their implications for manuscript study as well and form one more illustration of the common issues facing all textual scholars.

We thus come back to Dearing's assertion that "bibliographical thinking" should be excluded from "textual analysis." It is no doubt true that some textual critics have been confused in their thinking and have not differentiated between a document and the text it contains; but it is an overstatement to say that "textual critics in the past almost always confused the two genealogies when they did not devote their attention exclusively to the genealogy of records" (p. 15). In any case,

16. He does later show his awareness of some of them, as when he cautions against using reproductions, which are "subject to all sorts of unexpected failures to perform their function" (p. 148). In his article on "Textual Criticism" in *Encyclopedia of Poetry and Poetics*, ed. Alex Preminger et al. (1965), he properly points out that "early books preserved in only a few copies may differ in every copy."

the solution to the problem is not to banish the allegedly overemphasized bibliographical approach, since it unquestionably plays a crucial role in the whole process. To be fair to Dearing's argument, one must remember that he distinguishes "textual analysis" from "textual criticism": the latter is the larger term, covering all the stages of textual work, whereas the former is one particular operation, concerned with working out the "genealogy of the states of a text" (p. 2) and reconstructing their latest common ancestor. It is from "textual analysis" that bibliographical thinking is to be excluded. Nevertheless, one can insist that even here bibliographical analysis is important without being guilty of equating texts with records, for the texts are tied to the records, and an understanding of the physical evidence is necessary for an informed interpretation of the textual evidence. Dating a document (manuscript or printed book), for example, is significant even if one recognizes that the state of the text is not necessarily of the same date. Dearing makes much of what he sees as different uses of manuscript dates for textual analysts and for bibliographers: he neatly pairs the successful copyist, who "produces a record that postdates the state of the text it records," with the successful editor, who "produces a state of the text which anedates his exemplar" (p. 39). But to contrast "successful" copyists and editors is to place the emphasis on what they intended to do. In actuality copyists do not always reproduce with fidelity the texts in front of them, and though the records they create certainly postdate the records they use, their texts may also postdate those of the earlier records. Similarly, editors do not always succeed (it must be assumed but cannot be proved) in reconstructing earlier forms of the texts, and the texts they do produce may be said to postdate the other extant states.

Without losing sight of the idea that the genealogy of texts is a different concept from the genealogy of documents, there is a real sense in which one may still claim that a text does date from the time it is inscribed or set in type. The changes introduced by a scribe or compositor, whether out of habitual practice or out of inadvertence, produce a new text;[17] and understanding as much as possible about the production of that text—the habits of the individual scribe, the characteristics of the period, and so on—helps one to know how certain readings occurred. If one rules out this knowledge, one makes textual analysis a rather fruitless exercise, for one may postulate relationships that are shown by

17. Even if no changes are introduced (a theoretical possibility), the text is still new —though this possibility illustrates what Dearing means by bibliographical thinking, since there is no difference between the two "messages" but only between their "records." Nevertheless, the fact that separately produced texts may happen at times to be identical does not alter the general point that physical details are relevant to textual analysis.

physical evidence to be incorrect. Purely as abstract statements about agreements and divergences among certain messages, they are not incorrect, and this is Dearing's point; but so long as textual analysts are concerned—as they ultimately must be—with direction of descent, with genealogical relationships, they cannot ignore any physical evidence that eliminates certain relationships from further consideration as factual possibilities. Dearing himself does discuss general categories of scribal error (pp. 44–54) in his treatment of directional variation. Recognizing the influence of the physical process of transmission on what the text says (that is, "bibliographical thinking") cannot therefore be divorced from the analysis of the relationships among texts and need not involve a confusion of texts and records. Dearing asserts that textual analysts describe "not what was but what is and therefore what all can agree upon" (p. 19). They describe "what is," however, only if their aim is to record variant readings, and even then it is by no means certain that all would agree on what the reading of each text is at every point. But if the textual analyst's work includes reconstructing "the latest state from which all the extant states have descended," a state that is "in most respects the closest we can approach to the author's original intention" (p. 2), the textual analyst does deal with "what was," just as the bibliographer does. Both are engaged in historical reconstruction, and their tasks are intimately linked. When Dearing speaks of "bibliographical thinking" he may be referring more to descriptive bibliography (the history of the physical forms in which a work has appeared) than to analytical bibliography (the analysis of the physical evidence present in those physical forms), but the latter is of course a tool used in the former; in any case Dearing's approach, in the course of emphasizing texts as "messages," neglects the inextricability of the "transmitter" and the "message" and therefore the role of physical evidence in the interpretation of textual evidence that the textual analyst must perform.[18]

In contrast, West's manual sets forth emphatically, if briefly, the role that the analysis of "external" evidence must play. He points out that the process of examining texts has refined "our understanding of the languages, metres, and styles of the Greeks and Romans," which in turn provides a background for examining further texts; we learn about "such matters as the proclivities of scribes" and "the processes governing the spread of texts at different periods" (p. 8) and need that knowledge (which, as he correctly says, is of interest in its own right) in evaluating particular texts. At other points he refers to the use of paleographical

18. Willis neglects the same fact, in his much less sophisticated way, when he claims that, whereas a paleographer is concerned with a manuscript as "a physical entity," to a textual critic "a manuscript is of interest only as a vehicle of readings" (p. 5).

evidence and watermarks in dating manuscripts (p. 30), along with information about "what is known of the general historical conditions that governed the transmission of classical texts at different times" and "more particular facts such as the movements of individual known scribes" (p. 31); and he speaks of eliminating from the text "those features which we know, from our general knowledge of the history of books and writing, to have been introduced since the time of the author" (p. 54). He recognizes, in other words, the relation of physical evidence to textual study, even if he does not go beyond the traditional statements of its role. Like most writers of textual manuals, he explains the categories of alteration that scribes are likely to be responsible for (pp. 18–29);[19] as usual, these characteristics are discussed as generalized possibilities, and little attention is given to procedures for establishing the habits of individual scribes or assessing the textual implications of physical features that may reveal information about the method of production of individual manuscripts. One misses the kind of detail now standard in the compositorial and physical analysis of printed books; more work is needed for manuscript studies along the lines of Farquhar's and Van Sickle's investigations of the physical characteristics of codices and book rolls and Colwell's focus on the characteristics of particular scribes.[20] But even if, to students of printed books, West's manual seems to slight the explicit treatment of techniques for analyzing physical evidence, they would nevertheless find his essential position congenial. His repeated, if general, comments on the necessity for investigating the processes of the production of manuscripts form a sounder basis on

19. Among the many other treatments of scribal error are Willis's (pp. 51–161) and Vinaver's (note 50 below); and Louis Havet, *Manuel de critique verbale appliquée aux textes latins* (1911). Two classic psychological studies of scribal alterations are Jakob Stoll, "Zur Psychologie der Schreibfehler," *Fortschritte der Psychologie und ihrer Anwendungen*, 2 (1913–14), 1–133; and Sebastiano Timpanaro, *Il lapsus freudiano: psicanalisi e critica testuale* (1974; translated into English by Kate Soper, 1976). In the latter, textual study is the basis for a criticism of Freud's theory in *The Psychopathology of Everyday Life*.

20. James Douglas Farquhar, "The Manuscript as a Book," in Sandra Hindman and J. D. Farquhar, *Pen to Press: Illustrated Manuscripts and Printed Books in the First Century of Printing* (1977), pp. 11–99; John Van Sickle, "The Book-Roll and Some Conventions of the Poetic Book," *Arethusa*, 13 (1980), 5–42, 115–127; Ernest C. Colwell, "Scribal Habits in Early Papyri: A Study in the Corruption of the Text," in *The Bible in Modern Scholarship*, ed. J. Philip Hyatt (1965), pp. 370–389 (reprinted as "Method in Evaluating Scribal Habits . . ." in Colwell's *Studies in Methodology in Textual Criticism of the New Testament* [1969], pp. 106–124). See also C. H. Roberts, "The Codex," *Proceedings of the British Academy*, 40 (1954), 169–204; and G. S. Ivy, "The Bibliography of the Manuscript-Book," in *The English Library before 1700: Studies in Its History*, ed. Francis Wormald and C. E. Wright (1958), pp. 32–65. (An example of an inept effort to base textual decisions on physical evidence is Albert C. Clark's argument, in *The Descent of Manuscripts* [1918] and other works, that many omissions result from scribes' skipping whole lines, since the lengths of omissions, he believed, often corresponded to multiples of the number of letters in a characteristic manuscript line.)

which to proceed than Dearing's well-grounded but inappropriately applied segregation of bibliographical and textual concerns.

West's inclusion of the results of paleographical analysis and watermark study among the types of "external" evidence points to the way in which terminology reflects point of view. To the analytical bibliographer such evidence would be thought of as internal, because it is part of the physical evidence of the document, as opposed to relevant information that comes from outside the document, such as that from publishers' archives or from one's knowledge of the book-making practices of the period (itself built up from internal evidence from other documents). West can place both watermark evidence and one's general knowledge of the period together as external evidence because they are both external to the text, even though one is not external to the document transmitting the text. Both usages—that of the analytical bibliographer and that of the textual critic—are proper: they simply result from different approaches to the material. Such differences in terminology should prove no obstacle to mutual comprehension so long as the operations being referred to are thoroughly understood and so long as the line between the approaches is not imagined to be firmer than it actually is. Some techniques of analytical bibliography—compositorial analysis, for instance—involve evidence drawn from the text itself; determining the habits of a compositor, or a scribe, depends on a close examination of practices within the text. One can say, and some have said, that this kind of examination takes the text only as additional physical evidence, regarding it simply as ink on paper. It is true that those inked shapes constituting the text are physical evidence; it is also true, however, that the analytical bibliographer must understand what the text says, in order to know which characteristics are worth studying as possibly attributable to compositorial or scribal practice. Determining whether this evidence is internal or external is not a very productive problem; what is important is to guard against equating "external" with "objective" and "internal" with "subjective." The terms unfortunately come to have these connotations in many discussions of the textual criticism of manuscripts. Sometimes "internal evidence" is used to refer to the kind of evidence adduced by an editor to support a conjectural emendation (largely evidence from context, which, in varying degrees, involves interpretation and is therefore subjective), and "external evidence" is taken to mean the relationship among manuscripts, which in turn leads (without the necessity of literary judgment) to the adoption of certain readings rather than others. West is too sensible to make this mistake: he describes "the more exact information derived from internal evidence" as "the interrelationships of the copies as inferred from comparison of their readings" (p. 31), recognizing that the establishment of a genealogy involves inferences and that the result is normally conjecture rather than established fact.

Nevertheless, his statement is not as clear as it might be. One assumes that "copies" refers to texts, for if it referred to the manuscripts themselves the statement would be guilty of the confusion, about which Dearing warns, between records and texts. Even so, there is a problem, for the sentence seems to make "the interrelationships of the copies" wholly dependent on a "comparison of their readings" and leaves one wondering how the "external" evidence previously described fits in. "The inquiry," West says, "proceeds on two fronts, from external and from internal evidence" (p. 30). The external evidence of provenance, paleography, "general historical conditions," and the like then becomes the "historical backcloth" (p. 31) against which to "project the more exact information derived from internal evidence." Stated in this way, it is hard to comprehend precisely what the function of the "backcloth" is in the whole process. West does understand that physical evidence plays a role in interpreting the readings present in a text, but his category of "external evidence" is here presented largely as having to do with the relationships of documents rather than of texts. What is lacking is explicit recognition that the comparison of readings, leading to inferences about the relationships of the texts, must involve analysis of physical evidence as well as literary analysis: examination of the physical features of a document is relevant not only to dating the document but also to evaluating the readings in the text contained in that document. Whether one is dealing with printed books or with manuscripts, understanding the physical evidence may set limits on the literary speculation that can be engaged in. I do not wish to dwell on what is only an infelicity in West's exposition, but it provides an occasion for underscoring a significant point. Distinguishing "external" and "internal" as they refer to evidence is finally not so important as recognizing the interrelatedness of all evidence. Neither kind of evidence has a monopoly on demonstrable conclusions; because generalizations based on inductive evidence are inevitably provisional, some historical "facts" may be more conjectural than emendations based on an editor's judgment. And if one wishes to think of the physical evidence of a document as external to the text, then one must think of degrees of externality, for such evidence is not in the same realm as the larger historical framework into which one hopes to place both the document and the text. If West, instead of asserting that "the interrelationships of the copies as inferred from comparison of their readings" should be projected onto a "historical backcloth," had said—turning his statement around—that the comparison of readings, taken together with physical evidence and the historical background, results in the tentative establishment of the relationships among the texts, his comment would not have required discussion. That he could state the matter as loosely—in effect, carelessly —as he did must reflect, at least to some extent, a general lack of awareness, among textual critics of manuscript material, of the contribution analytical bibliography has made to the editing of printed texts.

Some of the techniques of bibliographical analysis, such as some of those used to distinguish compositors, rely on characteristics of spelling and punctuation; and data about compositors' habits in these respects are important to the editor whose aim is to restore the author's spelling and punctuation as well as wording.[21] Most scholarly editors of post-medieval writing have such an aim: since spelling, punctuation, capitalization, and so on must be considered an integral part of texts, affecting their meaning, and since most of the extant documents containing these writings are relatively near to the authors' manuscripts (or include those manuscripts), editors dealing with these centuries have given a great deal of thought to the problem of authoritative spelling, punctuation, and capitalization (or "accidentals," as these features are sometimes called, in distinction to "substantives," or the words themselves). It is a common notion that the treatment of accidentals is one of the major respects in which the editing of ancient writing differs from the textual work on more recent material; because the spelling, punctuation, and system of abbreviations in the surviving texts of ancient works generally reflect the customs of scribes who lived long after the authors of the works, many people assume that even if these matters are of bibliographical significance they are not of textual importance and that editors of such texts would therefore find nothing relevant in the extensive discussion of recent decades concerning the accidentals in literature of the last five hundred years. At first glance there would seem to be good reason for this position, when one considers, among other points, that, although punctuation was in use from at least the fourth century B.C., the extent of its use is a matter of considerable debate; that in ancient times texts were normally written as a continuous series of letters, without spaces to separate words; and that in both Greek and Latin there was flexibility in spelling in certain periods.[22] Thus both the possibility of restoring to a classical text the spelling and punctuation of its author

21. Of course, knowledge of each compositor's habits and reliability is useful in evaluating substantive readings in the part of the text he set, not just in dealing with the spelling and punctuation.

22. For information about ancient punctuation, see the interesting discussions cited in Reynolds and Wilson, *Scribes and Scholars* (note 4 above), pp. 214–215, 216.

and the desirability of restoring certain features in use in the author's time (such as the lack of word-division) are seriously to be questioned. This conventional position is expressed by West in his manual when he says, "The critic is at liberty . . . to repunctuate, even if he has taken a vow never to depart from the paradosis" (p. 55).[23] Later he repeats, "Careful thought should be given to punctuation, which can be a great help or hindrance to following the author's train of ideas, and which is of course entirely a matter for the editor's discretion" (p. 69).

The issue is not as simple, however, as these statements, taken out of context, would suggest, and West's own discussion raises some of the considerations that link so-called accidentals with meaning and with the author. West recognizes that "in theory an accent or a breathing in a medieval copy of a post-Hellenistic writer might go back to the author's autograph"; but he goes on to say that in most cases "all such features of the tradition will represent some later person's interpretation of a text consisting of virtually nothing but a continuous sequence of letters" (pp. 54–55) and that the textual critic is also "at liberty" to "reinterpret" the text in this respect. The question of how, or whether, to divide a continuous text into separated words is one that editors of modern works do not have to face, and it has therefore not been included in those editors' discussions of accidentals. In one sense word-division does fall into the group of features sometimes classed as "accidentals," for it is a matter of spacing and not of what letters are present. But obviously there may be ambiguous spots in an undivided text, where the letters can be formed into more than one set of words that make sense in the context, and matters of wording are usually called "substantive." The point is not what label ought to be used but the fact that the distinction between substantives and accidentals involves form, not meaning.[24] West further underlines the connection between marks and meaning when he says that, in the case of a nonsense word, "accents etc. may be valuable clues to what lies behind it, since they must have been supplied when the text was in a more intelligible state" (p. 55). Words that are not nonsense, however, may still be wrong (as West recognizes elsewhere), and accents or punctuation may provide clues anywhere in the text, not just where the text fails to make sense. Similarly, scribal

23. "Paradosis" is "a rather imprecise but convenient term meaning 'the data furnished by the transmission, reduced to essentials' " (p. 53). Willis calls it "a pedantic synonym for 'transmitted reading' or for 'reading best attested' " (p. 228).

24. Greg, in his "Rationale" (note 2 above), says that the distinction is not "theoretical" or "philosophic" but "practical," separating two categories toward which scribes or compositors reacted differently; thus even if punctuation affects meaning, "still it remains properly a matter of presentation" (p. 376), for it would normally have been perceived so by scribes and compositors.

abbreviations in manuscripts are not always unambiguous; and though West is right to caution that "abbreviations are not actually misread as often as some ingenious emenders think" (p. 28), editors should remember that abbreviations do sometimes affect substance as well as form. The same points are also applicable to spelling. As West realizes, spelling variants "can be of use (though not by themselves) in working out the details of a stemma, and they are not uninstructive in themselves" (p. 66). This view is not always accepted, even by persons who emphasize the breadth of significant evidence; thus Willis claims that "any variant other than the purely orthographical *may* be significant, however trivial it may appear" (p. 36). For Dearing spellings, and the other accidentals as well, enter into bibliographical, but not textual, analysis: "the textual analyst," he says, classifies variations as "*substantive, quasi-substantive,* and *accidental* and ignores the latter class" (p. 34); later he says that an editor who concludes that scribes or compositors were following copy "even in accidentals" can "make a bibliographical analysis in which he includes accidental variations with the rest of his evidence" (p. 154). The idea that accidentals partake more of the nature of physical than of textual evidence fails to give them their due as elements of meaning in a text; indeed, the interpolation of a class of "quasi-substantives" between substantives and accidentals shows that accidentals are being thought of here as not involving meaning. However, they are indisputably part of the text and may affect the meaning of the text at any time; whether or not they do in a given instance[25] has no bearing on their classification as accidentals. I am not suggesting that scribal punctuation, abbreviations, and spelling necessarily ought to be preserved in a critical text, but they should certainly be taken seriously as part of the textual evidence present in manuscripts; they may point to how the text was understood at a particular time and may therefore—like the words themselves—be a link to a tradition and help to establish the author's meaning.

The attention one pays to accidentals, in other words, goes beyond the question of whether they reflect authorial or scribal practice. It is no doubt true that the accidentals in surviving manuscripts of classical texts exhibit more alterations by scribes than do the words, and equally true that editors have more basis for attempting to establish authors' wording than punctuation and spelling. Nevertheless, scribes do alter words as well as accidentals; the distinction is one of degree, and the texts one has to deal with contain both words and accidentals. If one decides in a given case that the accidentals of the manuscript tradition have no au-

25. In itself not a matter about which universal agreement can be expected.

thority, the decision results not from theory but from the circumstances of the individual situation. To agree with Greg that people involved in the transmission of a text have generally felt freer to alter accidentals than to alter substantives is not to say that accidentals in scribal copies are necessarily unauthoritative, though it does provide a basis, when the evidence warrants, for treating accidentals differently from substantives. The editor is finally responsible for establishing both substantives and accidentals, and to assume that scribal accidentals are too far removed from the author's practice to be worth preserving is to ignore the connections between accidentals and meaning. One may not in the end accept those accidentals, but the question of what accidentals to include in a critical text must be faced. Authorial accidentals in ancient texts may be more conjectural than in modern texts, but the attempt to approximate them is not necessarily to be rejected in favor of standardized spelling and modernized punctuation. West's discussion takes this point into account:

As a general rule it would seem most rational to impose consistently the spelling that the original author is most likely to have used (for which the manuscript tradition may not be the best evidence). It is true that he himself may have been inconsistent, and it may be argued that the best manuscript authority should be followed on each occasion. But this will be no reliable guide to his practice; we shall surely come nearer the truth by regularizing the spelling than by committing ourselves to the vagaries of the tradition. (p. 69)

Presumably this "regularizing" would be to the practice contemporary with the author, insofar as it is known. West also takes up briefly the question of variations in spelling in Greek and Latin: in contrast to early Greek, he says, "In Latin there is not the problem of different alphabetic systems, but notions of the correct way to spell things were more fluid until the first century of the Empire, and here again (though with less justification) the convention has been established of presenting authors at least of the late Republic in the orthography of a somewhat later period" (pp. 69–70). This matter is not pursued, but a doubt about the convention has been registered. The point he proceeds to make about still later texts in which "it is often impossible to distinguish between the barbarisms of copyists and those of the original" is illogical but instructive: "In this situation, rather than impose a consistent system which can only be chosen rather arbitrarily, it is better to follow the paradosis, not under the delusion that it is at all reliable, but as the most convenient way of exhibiting it" (p. 70). Of course, in a critical, as opposed to a diplomatic, text, exhibiting the paradosis within the text is not in itself a virtue, and the accidentals of the paradosis would properly be retained only if there is a chance of their reflecting authorial practice more accurately than another system. But West's concern for establishing accidentals contemporary with the author and possibly retaining the accidentals of the manuscript tradition is uncommon in this field; though his discussion is undeveloped, it implies a greater link than some have imagined with the approach to accidentals followed by many editors of post-medieval work. Indeed, one must ask whether for a work of any period there is ever a justification, from a scholarly point of view, of any aim regarding accidentals other than the reconstruction of the author's own practice; however imperfectly that aim may be realized in many instances, it is the only aim consistent with the view that accidentals are integral to a text and that modernization therefore has no place in scholarly editing. Without underestimating the differences between ancient and modern texts, one can see a common issue here; West's brief remarks would strike an editor of modern literature as bordering on familiar territory.[26]

These considerations have direct implications for the apparatus. Since accidentals can affect meaning and scribal practices in accidentals can constitute important textual evidence, a complete recording of such details, as well as of substantive variants, would seem to be desirable. Selectivity, of one kind or another, has been the rule, however, in apparatuses for early texts, though disagreement has existed about the principles of selection. Willis approvingly claims that it is "a matter of common consent that purely orthographical variants should be excluded" (p. 35). His statement is disproved by West, who finds it "advisable to record orthographical variants fairly systematically, at least for portions of the text," and who further implies their significance by holding that, if one decides not to record "certain orthographical trivialities," "the fact should be stated" (p. 66).[27] Of course, printing costs

26. For further discussion of the accidentals of manuscript texts, see Bieler (note 11 above), who is sensible on this subject as on much else: his basic point is that "we should always try even in externals [i.e., accidentals] to keep to the original as nearly as evidence warrants and the reader may be reasonably expected to follow" (p. 28), for "the editor should prefer to make his readers think rather than to save them the trouble" (pp. 29–30); it is not proper for editors to insert "the standard punctuation of their mother-tongue," and an editor must never "wish to be more consistent than his author" (p. 29). Similarly, S. Harrison Thompson on the classicizing of medieval Latin: "Medieval Latin writers had a right to spell as they wanted to, and we may not change their orthography and put it out under their names" ("Editing of Medieval Latin Texts in America," *Progress of Medieval and Renaissance Studies in the United States and Canada Bulletin*, 16 (1941), 37–49 (quotation from p. 47).

27. West's phrase "at least for portions of the text," however, indicates that the listing is being thought of more as a suggestive indication of the nature of the spelling variants than as a record of the evidence that was available to the editor and that may be relevant in understanding a particular passage or evaluating the editor's treatment of it.

sometimes dictate selectivity. Even some of the CEAA/CSE editions of nineteenth-century authors, which always contain complete lists of editorial alterations in the copy-texts, exclude accidentals from the lists of variants among other collated texts. But it is one thing to be selective as a result of believing that completeness is unimportant or even undesirable and quite another to recognize selectivity as a matter of expediency only—for in the former case one is likely to think that subjective notions of significance are sufficient for determining what to include, whereas in the latter one will wish to define the categories included or excluded as objectively as possible. Willis advocates (in addition to the elimination of spelling variants) the exclusion of certain manuscripts, but on grounds that grossly misunderstand the purposes of an apparatus: "An apparatus criticus," he maintains, "which tries to use too many manuscripts is liable not only to be obscure and hard to use (the problem of finding enough sigla is not the least), but to be inaccurate, since the task of collating accurately some thirty or forty manuscripts is enormous for one man, and to find and organize reliable helpers is scarcely less difficult than doing it all oneself" (p. 43). It seems hardly necessary to reply to these objections, for the difficulty of using a complex apparatus is of no importance to a person who values having the evidence recorded (the designation of sigla is surely a trivial matter), and the attainment of accuracy is always a challenge, regardless of the scope of the coverage (one wonders how scholarship would ever progress if this challenge were allowed to inhibit activity). Willis's statement that "About ten manuscripts should be enough to set up the text of a Latin author" (p. 42) may be accurate on the average (I am not questioning Willis's knowledge of his field), but it seems unwise to prescribe how much evidence will be significant. In justifying a selective approach, Willis enunciates the principle that it is preferable "to give all the readings of some than some of the readings of all" (p. 44). This particular point can be (and has been)[28] legitimately objected to, but the motivation behind it—to find an objective basis for selectivity—is one to be taken seriously. Dearing, thinking along the same lines, says, "The critic should define the interesting variations as precisely as possible so as to be consistent and accurate himself and to facilitate consistency and accuracy in the work of his staff or associates" (p. 147). There is no doubt that the number of

Years earlier MacEdward Leach had made a plea for constructing apparatus so that "the state of the manuscript in the smallest particular can be ascertained" (p. 150); regardless of the editorial alterations made in the text, these details should be available to the reader, because medieval capitalization may not have been haphazard and medieval punctuation "may be important and significant" (p. 147). See "Some Problems in Editing Middle English Manuscripts," *English Institute Annual*, 1939, pp. 130–151.

28. See R. J. Tarrant's review in *Phoenix*, 27 (1973), 295–300.

manuscripts available in some cases, especially in biblical studies, is so large as to make impractical the goal of recording everything in all of them (or even the examination of all of them). But whenever one finds it necessary to be selective—either in the texts to be covered or in the details from those texts to be recorded—one should remember that no amount of rationalization will conceal the fact that the resulting apparatus is a compromise and is less satisfactory than a complete record. In such cases one owes the reader the courtesy of an unambiguous definition of what is included (not just some such statement as "the most significant readings"), so that the reader will be in the position of knowing precisely what kinds of evidence must be looked for elsewhere.[29] These questions concerning the construction of an apparatus thus raise issues relevant to all textual scholarship, regardless of the period involved or the nature of the surviving textual witnesses—as indeed, I have tried to suggest, do many other questions relating to other aspects of the editorial process.

II

If discussion of the role of punctuation and spelling and of physical analysis in editing has been rather neglected in the theoretical writings devoted to early texts, the problem of how to determine the relationships among the surviving texts certainly has not been neglected. The great body of literature on the theory of the textual criticism of ancient and medieval writings has focused on what is after all at the heart of all critical editing: the question how to choose among variant readings, which in turn involves an assessment of the relationships among the witnesses and an evaluation of when a departure from all the variants would bring one closer to the author's intention. These matters have of course been debated at length by editors of modern works also, and the same central issues link all these discussions together. All of them in fact can be seen as variations on the theme of objectivity versus subjectivity. Some urge the desirability of as objective a system as pos-

29. Most manuals on manuscript editing of course discuss the form of apparatus; the treatment in the Foulet-Speer manual (note 11 above) emerges from a long tradition of published rules for the medieval French field (and aims to supersede those set forth by Mario Roques in *Romania*, 52 [1926], 243–249). The Leiden system—*Emploi des signes critiques: disposition de l'apparat dans les éditions savantes de textes grecs et latins* (1932, 1938)—is an official publication of the Union Académique Internationale and is intended to apply to all kinds of editions, not only those of epigraphical and papyrological interest; O. Stahlin's *Editionstechnik* (2nd ed., 1914) has long been regarded as standard for classical texts. Two treatments concerned with later materials, but raising some general considerations, are G. T. Tanselle, "Some Principles for Editorial Apparatus," *SB*, 25 (1972), 41–88 (reprinted in *Selected Studies*, pp. 403–450); and Fredson Bowers, "Transcription of Manuscripts: The Record of Variants," *SB*, 29 (1976), 212–264.

sible, in which the role of the scholar's own judgment is minimized; others argue for the superiority of taste and insight applied to individual cases over the attempt to follow a predetermined rule. One's position along this spectrum affects, directly or indirectly, how one will approach all other textual questions—such as how much authority one assigns to a "copy-text" or a "best text" and how much freedom one perceives to be justified in altering it (by drawing on other texts or on one's own conjectures). Fluctuations from one direction to the other have characterized editorial thinking in all fields; but the lack of interdisciplinary communication is reflected in the fact that the various fields have not fluctuated in unison.

Fredson Bowers, writing on "Textual Criticism" in the 1958 edition of the *Encyclopaedia Britannica*, illustrates this point by suggesting how the editing of modern texts has benefited from earlier work on the classics: "The acceptance of Housman's attitude and its extension, about the middle of the 20th century, to editing from printed texts constitutes one of the most interesting of modern developments in editorial theory." Bowers here takes Housman as the exponent of a movement away from the Lachmannian tradition of relying whenever possible on the archetype as established through genealogical reasoning. Although many have pointed out the fallacy of believing that a "best" text has the correct readings at points where it is not obviously in need of emendation, Housman's famous remark in the preface to his 1903 edition of the first book of the *Astronomicon* of Manilius must be regarded as the classic statement of it:

To believe that wherever a best MS. gives possible readings it gives true readings, and that only where it gives impossible readings does it give false readings, is to believe that an incompetent editor is the darling of Providence, which has given its angels charge over him lest at any time his sloth and folly should produce their natural results and incur their appropriate penalty. Chance and the common course of nature will not bring it to pass that the readings of a MS. are right wherever they are possible and impossible wherever they are wrong: that needs divine intervention; . . . .[30]

The reason that this fallacious approach (the "art of explaining corrupt passages instead of correcting them" [p. 41]) gained currency, according to Housman, is not only that "superstition" is more comfortable than truth but also that it was a reaction against an earlier age in which "conjecture was employed, and that by very eminent men, irrationally" (p. 43). Exactly the same sequence—but delayed by several decades—can be

---

30. Part of this preface is conveniently reprinted in Housman's *Selected Prose*, ed. John Carter (1961), pp. 23–44 (quotation from p. 36).

observed in the history of editorial approaches to printed texts. R. B. McKerrow's edition of Thomas Nashe (1904), though it appeared at almost the same time as Housman's Manilius, represented the kind of distrust of eclecticism that Housman was attacking. McKerrow was one of a group of scholars of English Renaissance drama whose work would revolutionize the study of printed texts by showing the interdependence of physical and textual evidence; the analytical techniques that resulted did at times enable McKerrow and his colleagues to settle a textual point conclusively, as a matter of demonstrable fact, and to that extent editing was legitimately put on a more "scientific" basis. But in most cases there was still a large area in which the facts were not conclusive, and here McKerrow took the position that involved the least exercise of editorial judgment, the decision to adhere to the text chosen as copy-text. In so doing he was reacting, at least in part, against the undisciplined eclecticism that had characterized the nineteenth-century editing in this field.[31] The event that Bowers refers to, in the mid-twentieth century, representing a reinstatement of editorial judgment—but, like Housman's, on a more responsible basis than previously—was W. W. Greg's "The Rationale of Copy-Text." Greg broke down the notion of a single authoritative text in two ways: the more novel way, which he was the first to suggest, was that the primary authority for accidentals might reside in a different text from that for substantives (generally an early text for the accidentals, a later one for the substantives); the less surprising way, in line with Housman's criticisms, was that an editor could judge individual readings on their own terms and did not have to accept all variants that were not manifestly impossible simply because they came from a text that was known to contain some authorial revisions.[32] Both Greg and Housman restore editorial judgment to a place of prominence; but that judgment is firmly directed toward the determination of what the author would have written, whereas the earlier proponents of eclecticism (against whom the immediate predecessors of Greg and Housman were rebelling) tended to be less scrupulous in distinguishing between what they themselves preferred and what the authors being edited would have preferred.

The hope of having a single text to rely on dies hard, however, and

31. See Fredson Bowers, "McKerrow's Editorial Principles for Shakespeare Reconsidered," *Shakespeare Quarterly*, 6 (1955), 309–324.

32. Greg's own evolution from a position similar to McKerrow's can in part be seen in "McKerrow's Prolegomena Reconsidered," *Review of English Studies*, 17 (1941), 139–149, and in the prefaces to the first two printings of his *The Editorial Problem in Shakespeare* (1942, 1951), as well as in what he sees as the relation of his own "Prolegomena" (pp. vii–lv) to McKerrow's *Prolegomena for the Oxford Shakespeare* (1939).

one mark of the wisdom of Greg's essay is that he recognized the danger that he labeled "the tyranny of the copy-text."[33] Although his rationale for selecting a copy-text entailed choosing a text that could justifiably be accorded presumptive authority in cases where the variants seemed completely equal (particularly, in practice, in regard to accidentals), he understood that there had always been a temptation to let the weight of copy-text authority extend to readings that did not deserve such support. Greg's rationale does not (though some of its critics seem to think it does) provide timid editors with the opportunity to shirk, in the respectable name of conservatism, difficult decisions. Of course, it can rightly be regarded as conservative, and sensibly so, to retain a copy-text reading, even if one personally does not prefer it, when one is not convinced that any of the alternatives are authorial; Greg's point is simply that one should not be deterred, by whatever authority attaches to the copy-text, from altering it when one is convinced (through critical insight, in the light of all available evidence) that another reading is, or comes nearer to, what the author intended.[34] Sometimes editors, both of classical and of modern works, argue that the most they are justified in doing is to attempt to purge the copy-text, or archetype, or paradosis, of errors—not to try to restore what the author wrote. But this argument cannot be praised for its respect of historical evidence; rather, it confuses two kinds of edition, both legitimate, neither of which, when done properly, disregards the evidence. If one is interested in a text as it appeared at a particular time to a particular audience, a diplomatic or facsimile edition of it serves the purpose best; correcting errors in it— editing it critically—would be out of place, for the errors, though unintended, were part of what the contemporary readers saw in the text in front of them. If, on the other hand, one wishes to correct errors—to try to repair the damage done to the text in transmission, however famous or influential its corrupt form may be—then one is producing a text that differs from any now extant (probably from any that ever existed), and

33. He attributes the term to Paul Maas, who used it—somewhat differently—in a review of Greg's *The Editorial Problem in Shakespeare*, in *Review of English Studies*, 19 (1943), 410–413; 20 (1944), 73–77. After praising the book as "a decisive step forward from McKerrow's orthodoxy towards the eclecticism which the character of the transmission requires" (p. 410) and congratulating Greg on his "courageous vindication of eclecticism" (p. 75), Maas objects to the idea of copy-text and expresses the hope that the "bibliographical school . . . will continue to move towards emancipation from the tyranny of the copy-text" (p. 76). Greg replied (20 [1944] 159–160) that a classicist would naturally object to copy-text, claiming that the concept "has no place in the editing of classical texts," where one is not concerned with preserving documentary accidentals. Cf. note 45 below.

34. Housman (in the Manilius) ridiculed the equation of conservatism with a thoughtless adherence to a single text: "assuredly there is no trade on earth, excepting textual criticism, in which the name of prudence would be given to that habit of mind which in ordinary human life is called credulity" (p. 43).

the aim of the alterations is obviously not the preservation of a documentary form of the text but the construction of a text as close as possible (as close, that is, as surviving evidence permits) to the one the author intended.[35]

Some confusion on this point has been exhibited in the debate among editors of modern works over whether to choose an author's final manuscript as copy-text in preference to the first printed edition set from it. Of course, any attempt to fix a general rule on this matter is misguided, since situations vary greatly, and in some cases an author's revisions in proof may have been so thorough as to make the printed edition the proper choice. Some editors, however, prefer the first edition not for such reasons, but because it is the product of a historical moment; even though some aspects of its text may be the result of changes made in the publishing office or pressures brought to bear on the author by the publisher or others, the author accepted these conditions, they say, as part of the whole publishing process, and the text of the first edition is the one that emerged from a specific set of historical forces and the one that the public first read. This argument, however, leads only to the production of a facsimile edition; it has no relevance to a critical edition, although it is sometimes offered as if it did have, through a failure to think clearly about what the two approaches mean. Editors of earlier material do not encounter the problem in quite this form, since they do not deal with authorial manuscripts or authorially supervised printed texts, but the general issues are familiar to them. One manifestation of the exaggerated respect accorded to individual printed texts is the problem of the *textus receptus* of ancient writings. The text of the New Testament, or of other writings, that reached print was not, of course, necessarily more authoritative than other texts; but the controversy that sometimes surrounds editorial decisions to depart from the *textus receptus* suggests the irrationality with which a favored text can be defended. Clearly there are many differences between this situation and the question, faced by editors of modern works, whether to turn from printed book to manuscript for copy-text. But there is an essential similarity as well: in both cases the scholar's responsibility is to examine all the evidence in an effort to come as close as possible to the text intended by the author,[36] however many or few steps removed

35. Of couse, it is possible to set some other goal for a critical edition; e.g., one could attempt to reconstruct the text of any particular document presumed to have existed but no longer extant. More often, however, the goal of critical editing is the restoration of what the author wished. This goal is still historical, even though the resulting text is not that of any surviving document, and the evidence from all those documents can be reported in the apparatus.

36. One cannot simply say "written by the author," since the author's manuscript may

such a text may be from the texts that survive. Deciding whether an author's intention includes acquiescence to changes made by the publisher is a problem of more immediate concern to editors of modern writings; even so, such an editor's decision to follow a first edition may look just as foolish as the hesitation to depart from the *textus receptus* on the part of an editor of earlier material.

Greg's rationale for selecting a copy-text was of course set forth in the first instance for editors of printed texts that are not far removed from authorial manuscripts; and near the beginning of his essay he distinguishes his approach (growing out of McKerrow's) from that appropriate for the classics. In the latter, he says, "it is the common practice, for fairly obvious reasons, to normalize the spelling," whereas in the editing of English texts "it is now usual to preserve the spelling of the earliest or it may be some other selected text":

Thus it will be seen that the conception of "copy-text" does not present itself to the classical and to the English editor in quite the same way; indeed, if I am right in the view I am about to put forward, the classical theory of the "best" or "most authoritative" manuscript, whether it be held in a reasonable or in an obviously fallacious form, has really nothing to do with the English theory of "copy-text" at all. (p. 375)

It is true that a concern for incorporating in an edition documentary punctuation and spelling led to Greg's perception that the text with authority for accidentals might not be the same as the one with authority for substantives and to his statement that "the copy-text should govern (generally) in the matter of accidentals" (p. 381). In fact, however, the distinction between substantives and accidentals, though it has its uses, is not crucial to the concept of copy-text that Greg calls "English," as the word "generally" in his sentence suggests. Editors following Greg's general line would in practice emend the copy-text with a later reading of any kind, a substantive or an accidental, that could convincingly be argued to be authorial; and in the cases where the variants seem evenly balanced, they would fall back on the copy-text reading. Thus what underlies this conception of copy-text is the idea of presumptive authority, a text to be relied on when one finds no basis for preferring one variant over another—an authority, it must be emphasized, that does not restrict one's freedom to choose variants from other texts when there is reason to do so. It may be that editors of modern writings will normally choose their copy-texts, as Greg was the first to point out explicitly, to serve primarily as the authority for accidentals; but it does not follow

---

have contained slips of the pen, and the critical editor is aiming for an ideal that may not ever have been realized in any document, even the author's own manuscript.

that a different understanding of copy-text is required for editors of earlier materials, even when they are not concerned with reproducing documentary accidentals.[37] The fact that editors dealing with different periods may have to take somewhat different positions regarding accidentals is a superficial matter that does not alter the fundamental questions they all have to face. The real issue that should be raised about the "English" conception of copy-text is whether the idea of a text of presumptive authority is appropriate to all patterns of textual descent—an issue relevant to modern as well as earlier texts. If we are not distracted by the problem, undeniably troublesome, of how to treat spelling and punctuation, we can see that Greg's essay takes its place in the larger tradition of textual theory: like the seminal pieces on the editing of classical, biblical, and medieval works, its dual theme is textual authority and editorial freedom. To state a rationale of copy-text is inevitably to take a position on how much weight should be given to the editor's critical judgment in establishing a text—that is to say, how much alteration should be permitted in any given documentary form of the text, on the basis of the editor's assessment of its status, of the variants in other texts, and of further conjectures. The principal approaches to this question that have been advanced over the years are well known, and have often been surveyed.[38] I propose to do no more here than specify some

37. That they should in some cases be more concerned with it than they have been is a separate issue. Even when there is legitimately no question of retaining the accidentals of the manuscript tradition, documentary accidentals may be significant (as I suggested earlier) in assessing the presence of certain substantives and may play a role in the thinking that leads to the choice of a copy-text.

38. In addition to the splendid surveys in Metzger, Reynolds-Wilson, and Kenney (mentioned in note 4 above), other helpful discussions are by Bieler (note 11 above); Edward B. Ham, "Textual Criticism and Common Sense," *Romance Philology*, 12 (1958–59), 198–215; E. J. Kenney in the *Encyclopaedia Britannica* (note 7 above); Pasquali (note 45 below); and Robert Marichal, "La Critique des textes," in *L'Histoire et ses méthodes*, ed. Charles Samaran (Encyclopédie de la Pleiade 11, 1961), pp. 1247–1366. A convenient survey, making particular reference to the Old French field, appears in the Foulet-Speer manual (note 11 above); two useful collections emphasizing medieval texts are Christopher Kleinhenz (ed.), *Medieval Manuscripts and Textual Criticism* (1976), containing reprinted essays (some translated for the first time), and A. G. Rigg (ed.), *Editing Medieval Texts, English, French, and Latin, Written in England* (1977), bringing together the papers from the 1976 Toronto editorial conference. For the biblical field, see also Bruce M. Metzger, *Chapters in the History of New Testament Textual Criticism* (1963), and "Recent Developments in the Textual Criticism of the New Testament," in his *Historical and Literary Studies: Pagan, Jewish, and Christian* (1968), pp. 145–162; Eldon Jay Epp, "The Twentieth Century Interlude in New Testament Textual Criticism," *Journal of Biblical Literature*, 93 (1974), 386–414; Frederic G. Kenyon, *The Text of the Greek Bible: A Students Handbook* (1937; 3rd ed., rev. A. W. Adams, 1975); D. Winton Thomas, "The Textual Criticism of the Old Testament," in *The Old Testament and Modern Study*, ed. H. H. Rowley (1951), pp. 238–263; and Harry M. Orlinsky, "The Textual Criticism of the Old Testament," in *The Bible and the Ancient Near East*, ed. G. Ernest Wright (1961), pp. 113–132.

main lines, so that Greg's rationale can be seen in relation to them. They have not usually been taken up in this context, but doing so shows, I think, that editorial discussion might be sharpened by greater awareness of the entire tradition.[39]

For this purpose it is not necessary to go back beyond the approach usually associated with Karl Lachmann. Although scholars have shown that Lachmann's own contributions to the development of the "genealogical" approach have been greatly exaggerated,[40] his editions of the New Testament (1831) and of Lucretius (1850) stand as monuments linking his name with this method. Historically the importance of this movement is that it represented a reaction against the unprincipled eclecticism that had prevailed in the previous century (of which Richard Bentley was the most important, and most notorious, exemplar) and marked a recognition of what a scholarly approach must entail, at a time when ancient documents were beginning to be more accessible. There can be no question that the general drift of the genealogical approach is correct: that scholars must examine all the extant documents, learn as much about them as possible, and attempt to establish the relationships among the texts they contain. This much we would now take for granted as part of what it means to be scholarly. The difficulty comes in choosing a means for working out those relationships and in deciding what use to make of the data thus postulated; and when people refer to "the genealogical method" they normally mean the particular recommendations on these matters associated with Lachmann and his followers. Taken in this sense, the genealogical method can certainly be criticized, and its defects have by now been enumerated many times.[41] The essence of the method is to classify texts into families by

39. One book that does look at the traditions of the textual criticism of early manuscript materials in the context of the study of post-medieval English and American literature is James Thorpe's *Principles of Textual Criticism* (1972; see "Textual Analysis," pp. 105–130). Thorpe says in his preface, "I believe that the same textual principles are true for all periods and for all literatures" (p. viii).

40. The fullest and most impressive treatment of this point is Sebastiano Timpanaro, *La genesi del metodo del Lachmann* (1963)—revised from its earlier appearance in *Studi italiani di filologia classica*, 31 (1959), 182–228; 32 (1960), 38–63. Particularly important forerunners of Lachmann in developing a genealogical approach were the eighteenth-century scholars J. A. Bengel and J. J. Griesbach.

41. E.g., briefly in Reynolds-Wilson (note 4 above), pp. 192–194, and more thoroughly by Ernest C. Colwell, "Genealogical Method: Its Achievements and Limitations,' *Journal of Biblical Literature*, 66 (1947), 109–133 (reprinted in his *Studies in Methodology* [note 20 above], pp. 63–83). See also Vinton A. Dearing, "Some Notes on Genealogical Methods in Textual Criticism," *Novum Testamentum*, 9 (1967), 278–297. E. Talbot Donaldson makes a strong plea for abandoning the Lachmann approach in "The Psychology of Editors of Middle English Texts," in *Speaking of Chaucer* (1970), pp. 102–118 (see also his complaint

examining "common errors," on the assumption that texts showing common errors have a common ancestor.[42] Despite the obvious fallacies of such an approach, it had an influential life of more than a century and is regarded as the classic method of textual criticism. Two landmarks in its history added to its stature but at the same time can be seen to have made its weaknesses evident. One is B. F. Westcott and F. J. A. Hort's great *Introduction* to their edition of the New Testament (1881), which brilliantly stated the rationale for the approach and improved it methodologically (e.g., by focusing on agreements in correct or possibly correct readings rather than agreements in errors); they conclusively showed the illogic of relying on the *textus receptus*. However, as Ernest Colwell has carefully explained, Westcott and Hort in practice did not strictly adhere to the method, recognizing that editorial judgment in assessing the general credibility of individual manuscripts and the intrinsic merits of individual readings must remain central, even in an approach that emphasizes objectivity.[43] The second classic statement of the genealogical method is Paul Maas's famous essay, "Textkritik" (1927), best known to English readers in Barbara Flower's translation (not published until 1958).[44] It is a highly abstract distillation of the basic principles, showing their logic and soundness under certain conditions; but unfortunately those stated conditions (p. 3)—that each scribe copied from a single exemplar, not "contaminating" the tradition by drawing readings from two or more exemplars, and that each scribe also

---

about the amount of energy that has been devoted to trying to devise a "scientific system," p. 129). Most of the older standard introductions contain an exposition of Lachmann's method and some criticism of it; among them are Kirsopp Lake, *The Text of the New Testament* (1900; 6th ed., 1928); R. C. Jebb in *A Companion to Greek Studies*, ed. Leonard Whibley (1905; 4th ed., 1931); J. P. Postgate in *A Companion to Latin Studies*, ed. J. E. Sandys (1910, 1913, 1921), and in the *Encyclopaedia Britannica*, 11th ed. (1911); F. W. Hall, *A Companion to Classical Texts* (1913); and Hermann Kantorowicz, *Einführung in die Textkritik* (1921).

42. On the place of "common error" in Lachmann's own work, see Kenney (note 4 above), p. 135 n. 1.

43. Colwell, after saying that Westcott and Hort did not actually apply the genealogical method to New Testament manuscripts, adds, "Moreover, sixty years of study since Westcott and Hort indicate that it is doubtful if it can be applied to New Testament manuscripts in such a way as to advance our knowledge of the original text of the New Testament" (*Studies in Methodology* [note 20 above], p. 63). Colwell believes that the method is useful only for closely related families of manuscripts "narrowly limited in time and space" (p. 82).

44. *Einleitung in die Altertumswissenschaft*, 1 (3rd ed.), part 7 (1927), 18 pp.; separate editions appeared in 1950 and 1957. The 1958 English edition (*Textual Criticism*) includes a translation of Maas's "Leitfehler und stemmatische Typen," *Byzantinische Zeitschrift*, 37 (1937), 289–294. (For the Italian translation, *Critica del testo*, see note 49 below. Some comments on the influence of Maas in Italy and France appear in Luciano Canfora, "Critica textualis in caelum revocata," *Belfagor*, 23 [1968], 361–364.)

made distinctive departures, consciously or unconsciously, from that exemplar—are unlikely to have obtained in real situations.[45]

The force of these weaknesses is obvious, as is their relevance to the textual analysis of later material. Another of the often-discussed limitations of the method deserves to be underscored here: the fact that it does not make allowance for authorial revisions, for the possibility that variant readings result from the author's second thoughts as well as from scribes' errors and alterations. This oversight is not unique to the genealogical method but in fact exists, in greater or less degree, in all the approaches to textual criticism, regardless of the date of the works being considered. It springs from wishful thinking, for however difficult it is to choose among variants, it is easier to proceed on the basis that one is right and the others wrong than to recognize that several may be "right" or at least represent the author's preference at different times. Even among editors of modern works, where many authorial revisions can be documented, there is a reluctance to conceive of a text as containing multiple possibilities; and though an editor's goal is indeed to "establish" a text, editors—of works from all periods—should not forget that a "work" comprehends all the authorial readings within its several texts.

Another common criticism of the genealogical method—that one must revert to one's own judgment when the choice is, to quote Maas, "between different traditions of equal 'stemmatical' value" (p. 1)—calls attention to what may be a more serious problem: the tendency to think that the method generally minimizes the role of subjective judgment. The Lachmannian system is responsible for the standard division of editorial activity into recension and emendation and is therefore conducive to an attitude, as I suggested earlier, that takes the first of these procedures to be more objective than it is (or can be). There is superficially an appropriateness in distinguishing readings thought of by the

45. It is likely, of course, that a scribe would depart from his exemplar, but not that his departures would be such that no other scribe might hit on them independently. Maas, because his name is linked with the abstract and theoretical statement of stemmatics, is sometimes—but wrongly—thought to represent rigidity and an opposition to individual judgment. The truth is altogether different, as illustrated by his review of Greg (note 33 above), which includes the remark, "Misuse of conjecture is not more probable than misuse of conservatism, and is perhaps less dangerous" (p. 76). Giorgio Pasquali's long review of Maas in *Gnomon*, 5 (1929), 417–435, 498–521, was the predecessor of his great book, *Storia della tradizione e critica del testo* (1934; 2nd ed., with a new preface and appendixes, 1952). Pasquali's position (along with that of Michele Barbi, *La Nuova Filologia e l'edizione dei nostri scrittori da Dante al Manzoni*, 1938) in the Italian school of "new philology" is concisely described by Mary B. Speer in a review of two other books in *Romance Philology*, 32 (1978–79), 335–344; she notes their reaction against the rigidity of Maas's stemmatics and their emphasis on critical judgment as a scholarly and responsible procedure.

editor from those present in at least one of the surviving documents; indeed, from the point of view of documentary evidence, one is bound to regard any proposed reading not in the documents as falling into a distinctly separate category. But from the point of view of what are likely to be the authorial readings, this distinction is of no significance, for an editorial "conjecture" may be more certainly what the author wrote than any of the alternative readings at a point of variation. The very term "conjecture," or "conjectural emendation," prejudices the case; readings in the manuscripts are less conjectural only in the sense that they actually appear in documents, but they are not necessarily for that reason more certain. One is conjecturing in deciding that one of them is more likely to be authorial than another, just as one conjectures in rejecting all the variants at a given point in favor of still another reading. The process of conjecture begins as soon as one combines readings from two documents,[46] and every decision about what is an "error" in a document rests on the editor's judgment. Unquestionably the attempt to establish first a transmitted text is a more responsible procedure than to engage at once in speculation, before surveying the range of documentary evidence; but one must then resist the temptation to regard that text as an objective fact. Colwell states this point well in a comment on Hort:

His prudent rejection of almost all readings which have no manuscript support has given the words "conjectural emendation" a meaning too narrow to be realistic. In the last generation we have depreciated external evidence of documents and have appreciated the internal evidence of readings; but we have blithely assumed that we were rejecting "conjectural emendation" if our conjectures were supported by some manuscripts. We need to recognize that the editing of an eclectic text rests upon conjectures. (p. 107)

This problem is equally of concern to editors of modern works. Although their tendency to use "emendation" to mean any editorial change in the copy-text, including readings drawn from other documents, is more realistic, they are inclined to think that they are being cautious if they choose a documentary reading over one newly proposed by an editor. Such is not necessarily true, of course: the quality of the reading is everything, finally, and the editorial tact necessary to recognize that quality is at the heart of the whole process. The system associated with Lachmann's name cannot be held entirely responsible for editors' misunderstanding of this point, but it does seem to make the point harder to see by imputing to certain kinds of editorial decisions a greater objectivity than can usually exist.

46. Sometimes it begins sooner, if one has difficulty determining some of the readings present in a particular document.

Some of the people who have criticized the "Lachmann method" have set forth alternative approaches that have themselves become the subject of considerable discussion. One such person is Joseph Bédier, whose work, particularly influential in the medieval field, can serve to represent another general approach to editing. The introduction to his second edition (1913) of Jean Renart's *Le Lai de l'Ombre*, which has become the point of departure for the twentieth-century criticism of Lachmann,[47] concentrates on the two-branched stemma as evidence of the weakness of the genealogical method. The fact that most stemmata turn out to be dichotomous is regarded suspiciously as indicating more about the operation of the system than about the actual relationships among the manuscripts. What Bédier recommends instead is to choose a single good manuscript and to reprint it exactly except for any alterations that the editor finds imperative. This approach has been called "a return to the method of the humanists of the Renaissance";[48] certainly it is a move in the opposite direction from Housman's criticism of Lachmann at nearly the same time. When Giorgio Pasquali, ridiculing this best-manuscript approach, linked the English Shakespeare scholars with the medievalists in following it,[49] he was essentially correct in regard to the period before Greg's "Rationale." There is no question that, in spite of Housman's incontrovertible logic, the best-text theory —whether or not directly influenced by Bédier in every case—held sway over a great deal of editing in the first half of the twentieth century. An instructive paradox of the commentary on Bédier is that his position has been regarded both as extremely conservative, restricting the role of editorial judgment, and as extremely subjective, emphasizing the editor's own critical decisions. The strict adherence to a single text does suggest an attempt to minimize subjectivity; but the leeway then allowed the editor in deciding what readings are not possible and must be replaced sets very few restrictions on subjectivity. The point in the edi-

47. Bédier extended his discussion in "La Tradition manuscrite du Lai de l'Ombre: reflexions sur l'art d'editer les anciens textes," *Romania*, 54 (1928), 161–196, 321–356; and in "De l'Édition princeps de la *Chanson de Roland* aux éditions les plus récentes: nouvelles remarques sur l'art d'établir les anciens textes," *Romania*, 63 (1937), 433–469; 64 (1938), 145–244, 489–521. For an example of the voluminous later commentary on Bédier, see Frederick Whitehead and Cedric E. Pickford, "The Introduction to the *Lai de l'Ombre*: Sixty Years Later," *Romania*, 94 (1973), 145–156 (also published in Kleinhenz [note 38 above], pp. 103–116). Whitehead and Pickford find that textual criticism in the Old French field has "moved decisively away from the phase of extreme conservatism" (p. 156) associated with Bédier and has returned "to procedures familiar to textual critics in the classical field but completely lost to sight by editors of French medieval texts at the turn of the century" (p. 155).
48. By William P. Shepard (note 58 below), p. 140.
49. In his introduction to Nello Martinelli's translation (1952, 1958), of Maas's *Text-kritik*.

torial procedure where subjectivity enters may seem to have been shifted, but its extent has not been reduced. And in fact it is present from the beginning in both approaches—both in the selection of a "best" text and in the decisions involved in *recensio*.

Followers of Bédier and of Lachmann have been adept at suppressing recognition of the role of critical judgment at certain stages of the processes they favor, and they have failed to see that their apparently quite different approaches have much in common. The narrowness and confusion exhibited by such partisans can be illustrated in the work of a distinguished medievalist, Eugène Vinaver.[50] Admiring Bédier's criticism of Lachmann, he makes sweeping claims for the newer system:

> Recent studies in textual criticism mark the end of an age-long tradition. The ingenious technique of editing evolved by the great masters of the nineteenth century has become as obsolete as Newton's physics, and the work of generations of critics has lost a good deal of its value. It is no longer possible to classify manuscripts on the basis of "common errors"; genealogical "stemmata" have fallen into discredit, and with them has vanished our faith in composite critical texts. (p. 351)

The real issue of course is whether objective rules or individual judgment will bring us closer to the author's text, and this fact is nowhere better shown than in the conclusion Vinaver draws from these observations (that "composite critical texts" are discredited) or in the statement he proceeds to make: "nothing has done more to raise textual criticism to the position of a science than the realisation of the inadequacy of the old methods of editing." Housman, for instance, would have agreed in general with most of Vinaver's paragraph but would have come to the opposite conclusion: that we must put more faith in critical texts and not aim to place editing in "the position of a science."[51] Vinaver realizes that Bédier's position, which he essentially approves, does not eliminate subjectivity, and his own effort toward injecting more objectivity into it is to explain six kinds of errors that arise from scribal transcription.[52]

50. "Principles of Textual Emendation," in *Studies in French Language and Mediaeval Literature Presented to Professor Mildred K. Pope* (1939), pp. 351–369 (reprinted in Kleinhenz [note 38 above], pp. 139–159).

51. Vinaver argues ineffectually with Housman later in the essay, twisting Housman's point in order to claim that it "*is* right to preserve a reading as long as it is *possible* that it comes from the original" (p. 368).

52. Vinaver is criticized by Henry John Chaytor, in "The Medieval Reader and Textual Criticism," *Bulletin of the John Rylands Library*, 26 (1941–42), 49–56, for assuming that scribes had "visual memory" rather than "auditory memory"—a difference that would affect the kinds of errors they made. Another effective criticism of Vinaver is provided by T. B. W. Reid, in "On the Text of the *Tristran* of Béroul," in *Medieval Miscellany Presented to Eugène Vinaver by Pupils, Colleagues and Friends*, ed. Frederick Whitehead, A. H. Diverres, and F. E. Sutcliffe (1965), pp. 263–288 (esp. pp. 269–272); reprinted in Kleinhenz (note 38 above) pp. 245–271 (esp. pp. 252–254). (On scribal errors, see note 19

Knowledge of them, he believes, will "widen the scope of 'mechanical' emendation" and "narrow the limits of 'rational' editing" (p 365).[53] Vinaver is one of those editors who, in their eagerness to find objective criteria for editorial decisions, exaggerate the distinction between correcting an error and making a conjectural emendation. Vinaver's attention to scribal error stems from his belief that an editor should aim at "lessening the damage done by the copyists," not at reconstructing the original. To do the latter, he thinks, would be to "indulge in a disguised collaboration with the author" (p. 368). He does not seem to see that attempting to restore what the author wrote is different from altering the text to what, in one's own opinion, the author should have written. Like Bédier and other advocates of the best-text approach, he is not willing to say that the former is important enough to be worth risking along the way a few instances of the latter. Yet in defining the editor's role as that of "a referee in the strictly mechanical conflict between the author and the scribe" (p. 368), he does not eliminate the problem; he is not, after all, ruling out every editorial departure from the chosen text, and he leaves unsolved the question how one can satisfactorily distinguish safe and unsafe categories of critical activity. His effort to assist Bédier proves no assistance in the end, for he overestimates, along with Bédier, the difference between their approach and Lachmann's. It is interesting to learn that the predominance of the dichotomous stemma is mathematically not such an oddity as Bédier thought;[54] but that fact does not make Lachmann right and Bédier wrong. The approaches associated with both their names are in fact subject to the same criticisms, for they both cover up much of the uncertainty and subjectivity in the detection of error and therefore entail a misunderstanding of the nature and scope of conjectural emendation.

It was inevitable that the desire for objectivity in textual analysis would lead to the use of quasi-mathematical or quasi-statistical ap-

---

above.) See also George Kane's defense of emendation, in opposition to Vinaver and Bédier, in "Conjectural Emendation," in *Medieval Literature and Civilization: Studies in Memory of G. N. Garmonsway*, ed. D. A. Pearsall and R. A. Waldron (1969), pp. 155–169 (reprinted in Kleinhenz [note 38 above], pp. 211–225); and in his editions of the A and B versions of *Piers Plowman* (1960, 1975, the latter with E. Talbot Donaldson).

53. What it really does, however, is to provide the editor with information that may be of assistance in making a critical judgment. Knowing that a category of error exists may help the editor to recognize an instance of it, but one cannot assume that all possible instances of it are in fact errors. The editor must still decide whether a particular reading, in a particular context, is best explained as falling into one of those categories, or whether it need not be regarded as an error at all.

54. See Frederick Whitehead and Cedric E. Pickford, "The Two-Branch Stemma," *Bulletin bibliographique de la Société internationale arthurienne*, 3 (1951), 83–90. Cf. Jean Fourquet, "Le Paradoxe de Bédier," *Mélanges 1945* (Strasbourg, 1946), 2:1–16; and "Fautes communes ou innovations communes," *Romania*, 70 (1948–49), 85–95.

proaches. Nine years after Bédier's famous introduction, Henri Quentin, in his *Mémoire sur l'etablissement du texte de la Vulgate* (1922), announced a system that proved to be the first of a long line of twentieth-century attempts to make textual analysis something akin to formal logic.[55] The heart of Quentin's system is the rule that, in any group of three manuscripts, the intermediary between the other two will sometimes agree with one or both of them, but they will never agree against it. Quentin's system is thus to build a stemma by taking up manuscripts (and their families) in groups of three, following this rule. In the process of comparison no attempt is made to recognize "errors"; variants are simply variants, without a direction of descent implied. The concept of the intermediary therefore encompasses three possibilities: the intermediary could be (a) the archetype from which the other two manuscripts are independently descended, (b) the descendant of one of them and the ancestor of the other, or (c) the descendant, through conflation, of both of them. In order to determine which of these possibilities is actually true, Quentin resorts to so-called "internal" evidence—that is, to subjective judgments about the nature of the variants. He envisions his system as an attempt to reconstruct the archetype—the latest ancestor of all the surviving texts—rather than the author's original; in Lachmannian terms, he is concerned only with *recensio*. And certain central difficulties in Lachmann are present in Quentin also: the definiteness Quentin imputes to his method does not seem fully to recognize the amount of subjectivity that is finally relied upon; nor does the suggestion that there is something more objective in attempting to reconstruct the archetype than in trying to approach the author's original acknowledge adequately how indistinct the line is between the two, at least from the point of view of the nature and certainty of the conjectures involved.[56] Although the same cannot be said of W. W. Greg's effort five years later (*The Calculus of Variants*, 1927)—for Greg more openly admits the limitations of his "calculus"—the problems with his work are essentially the same. The details of his procedure are of course different (in a quasi-algebraic operation, he factors his formulaic representations of complex variants so that he can focus on two variants at a time), but it reaches an impasse, as Quentin's does, beyond which one cannot proceed without the introduction of subjective judgments regarding genetic

55. Further elaborated in his *Essais de critique textualle (ecdotique)* (1926).

56. For more detailed criticism of Quentin, see E. K. Rand, "Dom Quentin's Memoir on the Text of the Vulgate," *Harvard Theological Review*, 17 (1924), 197–264; and J. Burke Severs, "Quentin's Theory of Textual Criticism," *English Institute Annual*, 1941, pp. 65–93. Bédier's 1928 criticism is cited above (note 47). The Quentin-Bédier controversy is treated in a number of well-known books, such as Paul Collomp, *La Critique des textes* (1931) and Arrigo Castellani, *Bédier avait-il raison?* (1957).

relationships. As a mental exercise (and as a demonstration of the keenness of Greg's analytic mind), the *Calculus* is a fascinating work; but as a contribution to editorial theory it does not have the significance of his "The Rationale of Copy-Text" a generation later.[57] Not long after the publication of Quentin's and Greg's proposals, William P. Shepard performed the interesting experiment of applying both to a number of medieval works, some of which had previously been studied by other textual scholars. Invariably the two methods produced different stemmata, both from each other and from those proposed by earlier editors. Shepard's experiments, as he stressed, are not conclusive, but they lend weight to his doubt whether the human activity of copying can be given a "mechanistic explanation."[58]

He recognized, however, that "we are bound to seek such an explanation if we can"; and the dream that "some day a law or a formula will be discovered which we can apply to the reconstruction of a text as easily and as safely as the chemists now apply laws of analysis or synthesis" (p. 141) continues to intrigue us, as evidenced by the scholars—such as Archibald Hill, Antonín Hrubý, and Vinton A. Dearing—who have followed in the tradition of Quentin and Greg.[59] Hill, Hrubý, and Dearing all attempt to work out problems left unsettled by Greg, and all recognize the importance, first seen clearly by Quentin, of examining distributional before genealogical evidence (i.e., studying the record of

57. The importance of the *Calculus* as a starting point for further thinking about objective methods of analysis, however, is recognized in the work of Dearing and Hrubý, commented on briefly below, and in F. M. Salter's critical but balanced review of Greg's edition (1935) of *The Play of Antichrist* in *Review of English Studies*, 13 (1937), 341–352 (to which Greg replied at 13 [1937], 352–354, and 14 [1938], 79–80).

58. "Recent Theories of Textual Criticism," *Modern Philology*, 28 (1930–31), 129–141. Greg replied to Shepard's criticisms (28 [1930–31], 401–404), emphasizing the distinction between the "mechanism of transmission," with which he was dealing, and the reconstruction of texts, which he acknowledges cannot be mechanical.

59. Hill, "Some Postulates for Distributional Study of Texts," *SB*, 3 (1950–51), 63–95; Hrubý, "Statistical Methods in Textual Criticism," *General Linguistics*, 5 (1961–62), 77–138; Hrubý, "A Quantitative Solution of the Ambiguity of Three Texts," *SB*, 18 (1965), 147–182 (the opening pages of which offer a good survey of the statistical tradition); Dearing, *Principles and Practice of Textual Analysis* (1974; see part I above and note 11). Other quantitative approaches involving the tabulation of agreements are represented by Ernest C. Colwell (e.g., several of the papers collected in his *Studies in Methodology* [see note 20 above]), Paul R. McReynolds (e.g., "The Value and Limitation of the Claremont Profile Method," in the 1972 volume of the Society of Biblical Literature seminar papers), and John G. Griffith (e.g., papers on "numerical taxonomy" in *Museum Helveticum*, 25 [1968], 101–138, and *Journal of Theological Studies*, n.s., 20 [1969], 389–406); brief comments on Colwell appear in Metzger (see note 4 above), pp. 180–181, and Dearing, pp. 120–121, and on Griffith in West, pp. 46–47 (West's own approach, pp. 38–39, though simpler, is related). For comments on the use of computers in textual analysis, see Dearing, pp. 215–236; Jacques Froger, *La Critique des textes et son automatisation* (1968); and the works listed in the Center for Scholarly Editions statement (note 3 above), p. 9.

variant readings for evidence of relationships before attempting to assess which descended from which). Hill proposes a principle of "simplicity" as a mechanical means for choosing among alternative stemmata: one scores two points for each line connecting a hypothetical intermediary and one point for the other lines and then selects the diagram yielding the smallest total. Hrubý tries to use probability calculus applied to individual readings in texts in order to solve what Greg called "the ambiguity of three texts"—to distinguish, in other words, between states of a text resulting from independent descent and those resulting from successive descent. Dearing's work is an extension of Greg, taking into account and adapting Quentin's idea of intermediaries and Hill's of simplicity; like Greg, he offers a "calculus" that involves the rewriting of variations, and he sets forth in detail the formal logic that underlies it. Because a primary deficiency of earlier approaches was their inability to deal with situations in which a scribe conflated the texts of two or more manuscripts,[60] Dearing's handling of this problem is of particular interest. For him, a logical consequence of his distinction between bibliographical and textual analysis is that in the latter conflation simply does not exist. A scribe using two manuscripts, he says, would not think of himself as conflating them but as attempting to produce a more accurate text (a text nearer the archetype) than either of them; to say that he had "manufacturered one state of the message out of two others" would be "to confuse means and ends" (p. 17). The bibliographer, who is concerned with the physical means of textual transmission, can say that a record has been produced out of two others; but the textual analyst will see it simply as a message that may at times have affinities with other texts. Although this observation is presented as a remarkable revelation ("The light of truth blinded Saint Paul. New insights are not always easy to understand, much less to accept when understood"), one may wonder whether it is not in fact commonly understood and taken for granted. Clarity of thought does demand that some such distinction be recognized, and one cannot quarrel with Dearing for attempting to make it explicit; but whether it materially affects one's dealing with "conflation" is another matter. If, from the textual point of view, there can be no "conflation," one has eliminated the word as an appropriate way of describing the situation; but one has not eliminated the situation itself or the problem it poses for textual analysis. Dearing speaks instead of "rings" in genealogical trees and devotes considerable space to tech-

60. Sometimes "contamination" is distinguished from "conflation," the former resulting from the use of now one and now another manuscript, the latter from the combining of elements from two or more manuscripts. In a looser usage, they can be employed interchangeably to refer to the results of a scribe's use of two or more manuscripts.

niques for rewriting trees so as to eliminate rings, either by inferring states or by breaking the weakest connection in a ring. One breaks the weakest, rather than some other, link in deference to the "principle of parsimony": "The fewest possible readings are treated as something different from what they really are" (p. 88). As with the other systems, the nature of the concessions required to make the system work causes one to question the validity of the results.[61] Dearing's effort to encompass conflation within his system is laudable, but his confidence that his book "for the first time formulates the axioms of textual analysis and demonstrates their inevitability" (p. x) would seem to be excessive.[62] In the half century since Shepard discussed Quentin and Greg a great deal of effort has been expended on statistical approaches to textual analysis, but there seems little reason for a more optimistic verdict than his.

Different as these various methods—from Lachmann to Dearing—are, they all have the same problem: the questions of conflation and the direction of descent prove to be the stumbling block for systems that attempt to achieve objectivity, and those systems either rely on subjective decisions, covertly or openly, or else set up conditions that limit their relevance to actual situations. This is not to say that one or another of the procedures developed in these systems will not be helpful to editors—of modern as well as earlier material—on certain occasions,[63] and editors can profit from the discussion of theoretical issues that the exposition of these systems has produced. But the impulse to minimize the role of human judgment (the view, in Dearing's words, that "textual analysis, having absolute rules, is not an art" [p. 83]) has not led to any satisfactory comprehensive system. In this context, it is useful to look again at the approach suggested by Greg in "The Rationale of Copy-Text," for it places no restrictions on individual judgment—that is, informed judgment, taking all relevant evidence into account and directed toward the scholarly goal of establishing the text as the author wished it. The idea that all alterations made by an editor in the selected copy-text are emendations—whether they come from other documentary texts or from the editor's (or some editor's) inspiration—gives rise to a fundamentally different outlook from that which often has prevailed in the

61. The considerable amount of labor entailed by all these systems, often cited as a criticism, would not be a serious objection, of course, if the results were conclusive.

62. More detailed criticism of Dearing can be found in M. P. Weitzman's trenchant review in *Vetus Testamentum*, 27 (1977), 225–235. Dearing makes some comments on this review in "Textual Analysis: A Consideration of Some Questions Raised by M. P. Weitzman," *Vetus Testamentum*, 29 (1979), 355–359. His 1959 book is discussed by David M. Vieth in *Journal of English and Germanic Philology*, 59 (1960), 553–559 (cf. *Harvard Library Bulletin*, 24 [1976], 210 n. 14).

63. Among the notable features of Bieler's essay (note 11 above) is his discussion suggesting situations in which various of these approaches might be appropriate.

textual criticism of earlier material. It leads to a franker acceptance of the centrality of critical judgment because it calls attention to the similarity, rather than the difference, between adopting a reading from another text and adopting a reading that is one's own conjecture. Both result in a form of the text unlike that in any known document and therefore represent editorial judgment in departing from documentary evidence. Some documentary readings are—or seem—obviously wrong, but obviousness is itself subjective, and correcting even the most obvious error is an act of judgment; and attempting to work out the relationships among variant documentary readings involves judgment, or at least, as we have seen, evaluation of the varying results of different systems for establishing those relationships. This approach recognizes that what is transmitted is a series of texts and that to think of a single text, made up of readings from the documentary texts, as "what is transmitted" is to confuse a product of judgment based on the documentary evidence with the documentary evidence itself. But the choice of one of the extant texts as a copy-text in the sense that emerges from Greg's rationale is not at all the same as taking a "best-text" approach (whether Bédier's or some other variety), for one has no obligation to favor the copy-text whenever one has reason to believe that another reading is nearer to what the author intended. Indeed, if one has a rational basis for selecting one reading over another at all points of variation, there is no need for one text to be designated as "copy-text" at all. In this conception, therefore, copy-text is a text more likely than any other—insofar as one can judge from all available evidence—to contain authorial readings at points where one has no other basis for deciding. The usual deterioration of a text as it is recopied suggests that normally the text nearest the author's manuscript is the best choice for copy-text—except, of course, when the circumstances of a particular case point to a different text as the more appropriate choice.

All available evidence should be considered by the editor in making these decisions—evidence from the physical analysis of the documents and from the textual analysis of their contents as well as from the editor's own judgment as to what, under the circumstances, the author is likely to have written. Although Greg's proposal is specific, dealing with the printed dramas of the English Renaissance, the spirit of his rationale can, I think, be legitimately extended in this way, providing a comprehensive approach that encompasses other more limited approaches. It allows one to go wherever one's judgment leads, armed with the knowledge of what evidence is available and what systems of analysis have been proposed; and it provides one with a mechanical means of deciding among variants only when all else fails, a means that is still rationally based. One must postulate a relationship among the texts, of course, before one can select and emend a copy-text, and Greg does not suggest in his essay on copy-text how to work out that relationship. His emphasis is different from that of most of the writers on the textual criticism of earlier materials, and in this sense his work is not directly comparable to theirs. But many of them have also talked about the construction of a critical text and have revealed in the process that the two activities cannot always be kept entirely separate. Since the analysis of textual relationships involves judgment at some point, the examination of variants for that purpose is intimately linked with the consideration of variants for emendation. It is not arguing in a circle to decide (having used subjective judgment to some extent) on a particular tree as representing the relationship among the texts, and then to cite that relationship as one factor in the choice among variant readings; the latter is simply a concomitant of the former, for the process of evaluation employed in working out the relationship between the two readings overlaps that used in making a choice between them. Ideally the relationship among the texts should be a matter of fact, which can then be taken as a given in the critical process of deciding what the author wrote. But historical "facts" vary in their degree of certainty; and the more judgment is involved in establishing the "fact" of textual relationship the more such a process will coincide with that of evaluating readings to produce a critical text. The traditional division between recension and emendation is an illustration of this point, though it often has served as a way of concealing it. The open reliance on critical judgment in Greg's rationale and the lack of dogmatism manifested there can appropriately be extended to the prior task of dealing with genealogical relationships. It would seem reasonable to maintain an openness to all approaches that might be of assistance both in evaluating variants and in pointing to relationships. A statistical analysis might prove suggestive, for example, but should be used in conjunction with other data, such as physical evidence. Bibliographical and textual evidence, though undeniably distinct, must be weighed together, since physical details sometimes explain textual variants.

Because Greg spoke specifically of copy-texts that were chosen for the relative authority of their accidentals, editors of earlier works—of which the preserved documents are not likely to contain authoritative accidentals—have concluded that his approach is relevant only for works preserved in authorial manuscripts or in printed editions based on them. Such a view does not take into account the natural extension of Greg's position that I have mentioned: the idea of copy-text as presumptive authority, which one accepts (for both accidentals and substantives) whenever there is no other basis for choosing among the variants. This concept of copy-text is relevant for materials of any period, for it is not tied to the retention of accidentals: any feature of the copy-text that one has good reason for emending can be emended without affecting the status of the copy-text as the text one falls back on at points where no such reason exists to dictate the choice among variants. Dearing takes too narrow a view of the matter, therefore, when he says that one chooses a particular text as copy-text if one concludes that the scribes "tended to follow copy even in accidentals" (p. 154). Furthermore, the point is not whether they followed copy; it is simply that the text located at the smallest number of steps from the original is likely to be the best choice to use where the variants are otherwise indifferent, because that text can be presumed, in the absence of contrary evidence, to have deteriorated least, even if the scribes were not careful in following copy.[64] When there are two or more lines of descent, an editor may conclude in a given case that a text in one line, though it is probably more steps removed from the original than a text in another line, is nevertheless more careful and more representative of the original; one would then select it as copy-text, for the point of this approach is that one turns to the text nearest the original only when there is no other evidence for deciding.

This procedure, derived from Greg, would seem to be appropriate for all instances in which—if the choice of copy-text is not clear on other grounds—one can decide that a particular text is fewer steps removed from the original than any other known text. It is not helpful, however, in those instances in which two or more texts are an equal, or possibly equal, number of steps from the original. These situations are taken up by Fredson Bowers in an important essay on "Multiple Authority,"[65] which is the logical complement to Greg's "Rationale." What is par-

---

64. Dearing says, "In fact, Greg's rule implies that scribes and compositors tend to follow copy in accidentals. If the evidence is clear that they did not, then any extant text may be the most like the author in the matter of accidentals, and the bibliographical tree does not limit the editor's choice of copy-text" (p. 155). It would be more accurate to say that Greg assumes deterioration as one text is copied from another and believes, when no other evidence is available, that more of the author's practices are likely to show through in the earliest copy. As Dearing implies, it would be possible for a later copyist, being unfaithful to the deteriorated text he is copying from, to happen to reintroduce a number of authorial practices. But they would carry no more authority than the editor's own decision to introduce them—unless, of course, there were reason to believe that the copyist had drawn on a more authoritative document, in which case the editor would have good cause to select the text containing them as copy-text. Greg would agree that "the bibliographical tree does not limit the editor's choice of copy-text," for he never argued for following a mechanical rule if the evidence, as one sees it, points another way.

65. "Multiple Authority: New Problems and Concepts of Copy-Text," *Library*, 5th ser., 27 (1972), 81–115; reprinted in his *Essays in Bibliography, Text, and Editing* (1975), pp. 447–487.

ticularly interesting about Bowers's essay is that, although it deals with a problem especially relevant to earlier material, it is occasioned by work on modern literature, specifically Stephen Crane's stories that were published through a newspaper syndicate.[66] In the absence of any of the presumably duplicate copies of the text sent out by the syndicate office, what the editor has are the appearances of the text in the various newspapers that belonged to the syndicate. These are all apparently removed from the syndicate's master proof, and from the author's original, to exactly the same extent; and unless one has other evidence to suggest that one of the newspapers is likely to be more accurate than the others, there is no way to choose one of these texts as carrying presumptive authority. In such cases, therefore, Bowers recognizes that "critical tests (guided by bibliographical probabilities) must be substituted for the test of genealogical relationship" (p. 467). Statistical analysis is important, but, as Bowers says, "quantitative evidence is not always enough" and "qualitative evidence, the real nature of the variant, needs to be considered" (p. 468). What Bowers implies, but does not quite say, is that in such cases there is no copy-text at all, since no text can be elevated over the others and assigned presumptive authority; the critical text is constructed by choosing among readings, at all points of variation, on critical and bibliographical grounds.[67] If one finds two readings evenly matched, there is no copy-text authority to fall back on, and one must settle the dilemma some other way (such as by a statistical analysis to determine which text has apparently been correct most often). This approach to radiating texts, taken in conjunction with the idea of a copy-text of presumptive authority, when the situation warrants, provides a comprehensive plan for dealing with variants. The point that should be stressed is that neither part of this plan is limited to material of a certain type or period.[68]

66. Bowers also speaks of carbon copies from typewriting—another modern phenomenon that can produce radiating texts.

67. I have explored this point, and its implications for the recording of variants, in "Editorial Apparatus for Radiating Texts," *Library*, 5th ser., 29 (1974), 330–337. Dearing —both in *Principles and Practice of Textual Analysis* (p. 154) and in "Concepts of Copy-Text Old and New," *Library*, 5th ser., 28 (1973), 281–293 (p. 291)—continues (as does Bowers) to use the term "copy-text" in these situations, but he confuses the concepts of "copy-text" and "printer's copy," as when he says (in the article) that "if we can completely reconstruct the archetype, any copy-text is as good as any other and we need only choose the one we must change the least to bring it into conformity with the archetype." What is being chosen in such a case is not a copy-text but a text that can conveniently serve as the basis for printer's copy; indeed, at the beginning of the article Dearing defines "copy-text" as "what a scholar-editor sends to the press." The necessity for maintaining a distinction between "copy-text" and "printer's copy" is shown, I hope, in my "The Meaning of Copy-Text: A Further Note," *SB*, 23 (1970), 191–196.

68. Another point that should perhaps be repeated to avoid misunderstanding: what

My comments in the preceding pages aim to be nothing more than a series of reflections arising from an effort to think about what connections there are between the textual criticism of ancient writings and the editorial scholarship devoted to modern works. I do not claim to have proposed a new "method"; but I do hope that I have exhibited a coherent line of thinking applicable to all editorial scholarship. The issues will always be debated, and there will always be champions of various approaches. But no approach can survive in the long run that does not recognize the basic role of human judgment, accept it as something positive, and build on it. Welcoming critical judgment is not incompatible with insisting on the use of all possible means for establishing demonstrable facts. Scholarly editors are, after all, historians as well as literary critics, and they must understand the subjective element in the reconstruction of any event from the past. Establishing texts from specific times in the past, including the texts intended by their authors, is a crucial part of this large enterprise of historical reconstruction and cultural understanding. It seems obvious that textual scholars dealing with modern works can benefit from examining the ways in which editors of earlier materials have dealt with complicated problems of transmission and from studying the theories underlying those treatments; I think it equally clear that editors of earlier writings will find relevant what students of later texts have said about authors' revisions and the choice and treatment of a copy-text. One of the textual scholars who have emphasized the importance of cooperation among specialists in different areas is Bruce Metzger. He has urged New Testament scholars, through his own impressive example, to explore textual work in the Septuagint and the Homeric and Indian epics and to "break through the provincialism . . . of restricting one's attention only or chiefly to what has been published in German, French, and English." As he says, "An ever present danger besets the specialist in any field; it is the temptation to neglect taking into account trends of research in other fields. Confining one's attention to a limited area of investigation may result in the impoverishment rather than the enrichment of scholarship." [69] It is to be hoped that many more textual scholars will pursue their work with this same breadth of vision and will welcome the "cross-fertilization of ideas and

I have said here does not purport to summarize Greg and Bowers but tries to extend their ideas in a direction suggested by their essays.

69. *Chapters* (see note 38 above), pp. ix and 142 respectively. This statement would in fact serve well as the motto for the Society for Textual Scholarship, founded by David Greetham in 1979; some remarks of mine along the same lines appear at the beginning of the first volume of *Text* (1981), the Society's publication. Forty years ago R. W. Chapman indicated some connections between the editing of ancient and of modern works, in "A Problem in Editorial Method," *Essays and Studies*, 27 (1941), 41–51.

methods" that results. Editing ancient texts and editing modern ones are not simply related fields; they are essentially the same field. The differences between them are in details; the similarities are in fundamentals.

Epilogue

Textual Study and
Literary Judgment

BIBLIOGRAPHERS HAVE BEEN REMINDED ON MANY OCCASIONS THAT THEIR field is not an exact science. Repeatedly over the years writers on textual criticism, after outlining various procedures for minimizing the role of subjective judgment in the analysis of variant readings, have been forced to admit that certain issues cannot be decided without the exercise of judgment. Greg, for example, in *The Calculus of Variants* (1927), provided a brilliant example of an algebraic analysis of variants; but in the end he concluded that the limitation imposed upon this calculus by what he called the "ambiguity of three texts" could be overcome only by moving outside the calculus and using individual judgment to determine the direction or order of the variations.[1] Similarly, Archibald Hill, in his discussion of the distributional study of variants, pointed out that after distributional, "genealogical," and external evidence has been exhausted one must turn to literary or stylistic evidence.[2] Recently D. F. McKenzie, in evaluating the methods by which analytical bibliographers reconstruct the detailed printing history of a text as an aid to editorial decisions, has emphasized the inherent weaknesses of the inductive method and has suggested that "bibliography might grow the more securely if we retained a stronger assurance of its hypothetical nature."[3]

1. W. W. Greg, *The Calculus of Variants* (1927), esp. pp. 43–54 ("Method and Limitations of the Calculus"). Cf. Antonín Hrubý, "A Quantitative Solution of the Ambiguity of Three Texts," *Studies in Bibliography*, 18 (1965), 147–182.

2. Hill, "Some Postulates for Distributional Study of Texts," *SB*, 3 (1950–51), 63–95.

3. McKenzie, "Printers of the Mind: Some Notes on Bibliographical Theories and Printing-House Practices," *SB*, 22 (1969), 1–75 (quotation from p. 61); see pp. 2–3 for his citation of other statements recognizing the limitations of bibliography as an exact science. Another recent essay which surveys the "scientific" tradition in modern bibliography and expresses doubt about textual criticism as a "scientific discipline" is James Thorpe's "The Ideal of Textual Criticism," in *The Task of the Editor: Papers Read at a Clark Library Seminar, February 8, 1969* (1969), pp. 1–32.

Despite the general recognition in statements such as these—and there have been many others[4]—that bibliographical and editorial work cannot be scientific in the same sense that research in the natural sciences is, there has remained a widespread belief, both among certain bibliographers themselves as well as among persons outside the field, that bibliographical and textual research is in some vague way more "scientific" than "humanistic." It is true that, in the twentieth century, many bibliographers and textual critics have felt impelled to construct methods of procedure which tend toward the elimination of individual judgment—hence the search for ways of handling textual variants in terms of mathematics and symbolic logic or in terms of the physical evidence afforded by the processes of textual transmission. Bibliographers who have engaged in such activities have not necessarily been under any misapprehension as to the nature of bibliographical and textual research; rather, they have often been motivated by a desire to counteract the practice, common with some nineteenth-century editors, of choosing among variant readings in a wholly unsystematic way according to the whims of personal taste. Fredson Bowers has observed that McKerrow's rigidity in his recommendations for emending a copy-text probably stemmed from his overreacting against the tradition of subjective eclecticism and from his desire to emphasize the need for order and method in editorial procedure.[5] Since McKerrow's time the pendulum has swung back from his position of extreme conservatism to a middle position which gives literary judgment, when carefully applied, its proper place in editorial decisions. In "The Rationale of Copy-Text" (which has provided editors of the last two decades with their central statement of procedure), Greg asserted, "The judgement of an editor, fallible as it must necessarily be, is likely to bring us closer to what the author wrote than the enforcement of an arbitrary rule."[6] And more recently William Gibson has called attention to the importance, in an editor, of "a kind of instinct that is acquired only after long immersion in the thought and feeling and

4. Two of the most important are R. C. Bald, "Evidence and Inference in Bibliography," *English Institute Annual 1941* (1942), pp. 159–183; and Madeleine Doran, "An Evaluation of Evidence in Shakespearean Textual Criticism," *English Institute Annual 1941* (1942), pp. 95–114.

5. Bowers, "McKerrow's Editorial Principles for Shakespeare Reconsidered," *Shakespeare Quarterly*, 6 (1955), 309–324. Cf. W. W. Greg, "McKerrow's Prolegomena Reconsidered," *Review of English Studies*, 17 (1941), 139–149.

6. Greg, *Collected Papers*, ed. J. C. Maxwell (1966), p. 381. The essay originally appeared in *SB*, 3 (1950–51), 19–36. Cf. Fredson Bowers, "Current Theories of Copy-Text with an Illustration from Dryden," *Modern Philology*, 68 (1950), 12–20. An application of Greg's theory to a later period is Bowers's "Some Principles for Scholarly Editions of Nineteenth-Century American Authors," *SB*, 17 (1964), 223–228.

style of his author."[7] No bibliographer or editor who has given the matter serious thought can disagree.

Nevertheless, many persons not directly connected with bibliographical and editorial work—including a number of literary scholars who should know better—have observed the increasing employment in this field of mechanical devices (such as computers and Hinman Collators) and have drawn the conclusion that this kind of research does not, after all, require any literary sensitivity or critical judgment. Those who take this point of view may be misguided and misinformed, but they cannot be held entirely to blame for their misconception, since some bibliographers and editors themselves have been guilty of exaggerating the scientific nature of the subject. The urge on the part of certain scholars in the humanities to make their work appear to be more closely akin to the physical sciences than it actually is may be regarded simply as harmless pretentiousness in most cases. But when that urge takes the form of such persuasive expression or such publicized equipment that people begin to believe that there is some substance to the viewpoint, it is not always harmless—for it can cause the conclusions reached to be accorded a higher level of certainty than they deserve and can thus affect any further thinking based on those conclusions.

All that "scientific" can mean when applied to bibliographical analysis and textual study is "systematic," "methodical," and "scholarly." The eclectic editing that McKerrow objected to was unscientific because it was both uninformed and whimsical: there was often no systematic effort made to ascertain the history and nature of the variant readings, and the resulting decisions stemmed from no coherent rationale. But to object to the unscientific nature of this procedure is not to suggest that editing and bibliography can ever be exact sciences. Although the bibliographer inevitably finds himself dealing with certain elementary physical laws (such as the fact that a particular piece of type cannot be in two places at the same time), he is principally concerned with human behavior, and he can never predict with certainty what an author, a scribe, a compositor, a pressman, or a proofreader can be expected to do at any given moment. The physical evidence embodied in manuscripts and printed books, because of the immense variety of human variables lying behind it, does not furnish a basis for inductive generalizations on the same level of probability as does the evidence of natural phenomena. To call bibliography and textual study "scientific" is not to suggest an analogy with the

7. Gibson, "The Center for Editions of American Authors," *Scholarly Books in America*, 10 (January 1969), 8. A similar statement is E. L. McAdam's "The Textual Approach to Meaning," *English Institute Essays 1946* (1947), pp. 191–201.

natural and physical sciences in any sense except their rigor of systematic investigation. In D. F. McKenzie's words, "scientific" refers simply to "an honesty of method"[8]—one which bibliographical studies share with all other scholarly pursuits.

It may seem superfluous to repeat at such length observations which must be regarded as truisms by anyone who has turned his attention to the matter. My point in doing so is to suggest that, however axiomatic these statements are granted to be, bibliographers and editors have not always in practice seemed to be fully aware of their implications. That is to say, there is sometimes a discrepancy between the authority which a bibliographer claims for his work (in his zeal to assert the objectivity and definiteness of his conclusions) and what he knows, upon sober reflection, to be its tentative and subjective nature. If there has been a healthy tendency in recent years, as reflected in Greg's "Rationale," to reinstate critical judgments as one of the editor's important resources, there still remains—following McKerrow's over-emphasis on mechanical rules—a lingering reluctance to admit the extent and value of its contribution to editorial decisions.

The whole area of the relationship between literary judgment and textual study can be looked at from two directions: one is the effect which the findings of bibliographical and textual research have on the ultimate meaning of the work of literature as evaluated by the critic; the other is the role which critical judgment plays in producing those findings in the first place. Of these, the first requires less discussion than the second. That the establishment of texts is the basic task of literary scholarhip, a prerequisite to further critical study; that emendations which result from textual research can significantly affect the critical interpretation of a work; and that detailed collation and bibliographical analysis are necessary activities for the establishment of every text, even if only to prove that no variants exist or that the variants are inconsequential—all these propositions are, to the scholarly mind, self-evident, and they have all been buttressed by numerous concrete examples in recent years.[9] I do not, therefore, propose to explore them further but

8. McKenzie, p. 2; McKenzie's excellent discussion of the nature of bibliographical investigation is on pp. 2–6.

9. See, for example, Fredson Bowers, "Textual Criticism and the Literary Critic," in his *Textual and Literary Criticism* (1959), pp. 1–34; Bruce Harkness, "Bibliography and the Novelistic Fallacy," *SB*, 12 (1959), 59–73; and Bowers, "Textual Criticism," in *The Aims and Methods of Scholarship in Modern Languages and Literatures*, ed. James Thorpe (1963), pp. 23–24 and *passim*. Bowers points out that "the complacency with which critics quote from corrupt texts in any sort of reprint edition, whether English or American, is shocking," in "Old Wine in New Bottles: Problems of Machine Printing," in *Editing Nineteenth Century Texts*, ed. John M. Robson (1967), p. 35. Some examples, drawn from the editing of

instead to comment on the less-discussed question of the importance of critical powers in editorial procedure—of the way in which a critical *edition* is, in itself and of necessity, also a critical *study*.

To begin with, it must be admitted that the kind of undisciplined eclecticism which often prevailed in editorial work before the present century does have its merits. A person of taste and sensitivity, choosing among variant readings on the basis of his own preference and making additional emendations of his own, can be expected to produce a text that is aesthetically satisfying and effective. Whether or not it is what the author wrote is another matter; but editing which does not have as its goal the recovery of the author's words is not necessarily illegitimate—it is creative, rather than scholarly, but not therefore unthinkable. The scholarly study of literature is historical, and the aim of scholarly editing must be the reconstruction of the exact words which a particular author used. But it is an obvious absurdity to suppose that the "best" reading, from an artistic point of view, is always the author's; and it is equally obvious that an editor could conceivably produce a version of a work aesthetically superior to the original. In such a case the editor would in effect become a collaborator of the author,[10] in the way that publishers' editors or literary executors sometimes are. So long as one is concerned only with individual aesthetic objects, there can be no objection to the procedure; but if one is interested in a work as part of an author's total career, one must insist on having the words which that author actually wrote. The scholarly editor, though he may be equally as capable of producing a superior work as the creative editor, puts his critical abilities to the service of understanding what the author (given his turn of mind and his habits of expression) would have preferred at any particular point. I belabor this distinction in order to emphasize the fact that "scholarly" or "scientific" editing does not preclude literary judgment; rather, it relies on such judgment—but, for the scholarly editor as well as the scholarly critic, the judgment is effective to the extent that it reflects an insight into the author's thought and expression.

In scholarly editing the role of literary judgment is vital to all decisions—

Hawthorne, of the ways in which bibliographical evidence can "yield conclusions of literary significance" are provided by Claude M. Simpson, Jr., in "The Practice of Textual Criticism," in *The Task of the Editor* (see note 3 above), pp. 33-52.

10. James Thorpe, in his important essay on "The Aesthetics of Textual Criticism," *PMLA*, 80 (1965), 465-482, says, "The work of art is thus always tending toward a collaborative status, and the task of the textual critic is always to recover and preserve its integrity at that point where the authorial intentions seem to have been fulfilled" (p. 481)—but he is speaking, of course, of the scholarly or historical study of the text. For further comment on the distinction between scholarly and creative editing, see G. T. Tanselle, "The Editorial Problem of Final Authorial Intention," forthcoming in *Bibliographia*.

those concerning accidentals as well as those concerning substantives. However, the degree to which literary judgment comes into play in any given instance is not a constant and varies according to the situation. Professor Bowers, in discussing the different orders of certainty which can be achieved in the interpretation of bibliographical (i.e., physical) evidence, has conveniently set up three general classes: the demonstrable, the probable, and the possible.[11] In a similar way, one can adduce certain categories of emendations which are suggestive of the shifting—but rarely negligible—role of literary evaluation in editorial procedure. To do so is, in a sense, to look at Bowers's continuum from a different direction, for as the conclusiveness of physical evidence increases, the role of individual judgment must necessarily decrease. Yet the point is precisely that the cases in which absolute certainty is demonstrable on mechanical grounds are relatively few, leaving a large number of instances for the operation of critical thinking.

First, in regard to substantives, an example from Melville's *Typee* (1846) may serve to illustrate the place of literary judgment in cases which fall near the "demonstrable" end of the spectrum. Some copies of the 1846 revised printing have the word "groves" (the reading in the first printing) and others "grove" (the reading in all subsequent printings) in a sentence which makes sense with either the singular or the plural.[12] Collation shows that the "grove" copies have two entire pages and a fraction of a third page reset, but the only other changes on these pages aside from "grove" involve two hyphens and one misspelling; furthermore, in the portion of the third page which was not reset, both the "grove" and the "groves" copies have the word "bloody" where the original American printing has "booby." From these facts an editor can conclude, without the assistance of literary judgment, that "grove" is not an authorial revision: the resetting cannot have been for the purpose of altering "groves" to "grove," since this change would not have necessitated the resetting of two pages; and the general revision of the text had previously been incorporated in the plates of these pages, as evidenced by the presence of the word "bloody" in both states. The editor can reasonably classify "grove" as a compositorial error made in the course of resetting this passage.

The case is not entirely demonstrable from the physical evidence, how-

11. Bowers, *Bibliography and Textual Criticism* (1964), p. 77 and *passim*.

12. See the Northwestern-Newberry Edition of *Typee*, ed. Harrison Hayford, Hershel Parker, and G. T. Tanselle (1968), p. 91, line 37; further discussion of this variant is on pp. 310–311.

ever, for the conclusion rests either on an assumption of normality in the compositor's habits or on an assumption that an unlikely coincidence did not in fact take place. That is, it assumes that no compositor would reset two pages for the purpose of altering one word; or, alternatively, it assumes that no new authorial revisions (either overlooked before or newly communicated by the author) were introduced simultaneously with the resetting of those pages (along one side of the forme) which had been damaged in some way. In terms of probability, either of these assumptions is safe enough; but the contrary conditions in each case are not impossible. As it turns out, the plural reading is also supported on literary grounds: though either word makes sense in the sentence, the plural fits the larger context better since "groves" had been mentioned three paragraphs earlier. Suppose, for the sake of argument, that the situation were reversed and that the singular reading had been replaced by the plural at the time of the resetting. Would the improbability that the later reading is authorial (on the basis of the physical evidence) cause the editor to reject what, in literary terms, seems to be the reading the author must have intended? It need not, either because the physical evidence is not compelling or because he regards the emendation as one he would have been obliged to make in any case, whether it had appeared as a variant or not. Whenever the physical evidence is not absolutely incontrovertible, one is frequently inclined to rationalize, in bibliographical terms, the choice of reading which one has actually determined on literary grounds. To do so is to perform a disservice to the cause both of bibliography and of editing. Bibliographical analysis has served its purpose when it settles a question with demonstrable certainty; when it cannot do so much, the editor must face the decision with the tools of his critical intelligence. He should not hesitate to use them nor feel that his conclusions will appear somehow more authoritative if couched in bibliographical language.

Another class of examples in *Typee* represents a position somewhat farther from the "demonstrable" end of the scale. The so-called "revised edition" of *Typee* was printed from the plates used for the first printing, extensively altered to eliminate religious and sexual comments. Melville made the revisions himself, but at the request of his publisher. An editor may with good reason reject these revisions, even though the author acquiesced in them, since they were thrust upon him; but the editor is still confronted with many small alterations seemingly unrelated to religious and sexual matters. Are they evidence that the author took advantage of the enforced opportunity for revision to make additional changes of his own? Or are they further alterations requested by the publisher? Or simply compositors' errors? When these occur in passages not otherwise reset, an editor is probably justified in regarding them as authorial without resorting to any literary analysis whatever. The argument would be, first, that the resetting of only one word (as "this" for "the" in Chapter 11)[13] in a given plate can hardly have been performed unintentionally (whereas a variant reading in a longer reset passage could be the result of compositorial error in the course of the resetting); and, second, that the publisher would have been unlikely to have requested such a trivial change, particularly in view of the time and effort involved in altering a plate. In all *probability*, therefore, such changes reflect the author's own intention—but the case must remain, after all, one of probability, not certainty, since this argument rests on a presumption of normality in human behavior which need not necessarily operate in any particular instance. Besides, a change which seems trivial or indifferent to an editor may not have seemed so to the publisher; thus one underlying assumption of the argument is itself a matter of subjective judgment. Even though the changes in this category are probably authorial, an editor is not bound to accept them all as authorial if he has strong stylistic evidence for believing that the altered wording is uncharacteristic of Melville. The fact that physical evidence suggests them to be probably Melville's is not strong enough assurance to counteract unusually convincing literary evidence. Of course, if the literary evidence were less strong, the probable conclusion based on physical evidence might be correspondingly more persuasive. But judgment is involved in either case.

Still another similar instance occurs in *Omoo* (1847). At one point in Chapter 76 the American edition reads "whalers," where the English (set from proof sheets of the American) reads "whalemen."[14] An editor's problem is to decide whether the English reading is an authorial revision of the American, or whether the American is actually the later reading, having been changed after the proofs had been sent to England. The fact that the American edition shows peculiarly large spaces before and after the following word in the line would seem to support the idea that the American reading is later and that originally the longer word "whalemen" stood in this line. There can scarcely be any question but that "whalers" is the preferable reading in the context, since it avoids the awkwardness of describing a whaling ship in

13. See *Typee*, p. 86, line 24, and the note on p. 329.
14. See the Northwestern-Newberry Edition of *Omoo*, p. 290, line 10; further discussion of this variant is on pp. 355, 366.

feminine terms after referring to such ships as "whalemen"; and an editor is happy to have the physical evidence of the wide spaces to strengthen his argument for the reading which he already believes, on stylistic grounds, to be authorial. Presumably it would be a rare coincidence for unusually wide spaces to have been present in the American edition all along at precisely the point where, in the English edition, a word was later altered; but such an occurrence is not impossible, and the wide spaces are not conclusive evidence that another word was once set in type at that location. If the English reading had been superior, an editor might well have disregarded the unlikelihood of the coincidence in order to adopt that better reading. Once again, critical judgment carries the controlling share of the responsibility for an editorial decision.

All these examples have been instances in which physical evidence provided varying degrees of probability, though never quite demonstrable certainty. But there are many other instances, nearer the opposite end of the editorial spectrum, in which no physical evidence is available and the editor's decision must rest entirely on his literary judgment. In Chapter 27 of *Typee*, for example, the opening sentence of the third paragraph of the original version is drastically altered in the revised version,[15] and the change reflects the kind of care that may reasonably be attributed to an author, since it eliminates what might be regarded as an awkward repetition; on the other hand, one could argue that it is not beyond the abilities of a publisher's reader. One of the great merits of Greg's theory of copy-text is that it provides a systematic way for an editor to extricate himself from such an impasse: when there is no other means for deciding, he selects the reading of the copy-text (in this case the original version), on the grounds that by following this procedure he is maximizing the chances of choosing the author's wording more times than not. However, whether or not there is no other means for deciding is itself a matter of individual judgment. A particularly conservative editor may in this instance decide that the case for the revised reading is not convincing enough to warrant emending the copy-text; another editor may consider the likelihood overwhelming that no one but Melville was responsible for this change and may therefore feel justified in making the emendation.[16] The fact that two editors—neither of them irresponsible—can come up

15. See *Typee*, p. 201, lnes 27–29, and the note on p. 332.

16. In cases involving arguments as to the kinds of changes more characteristic of an author than of someone at the publisher's or printer's, the nature of the changes throughout a text needs to be taken into account. There are several variants in the English edition of

with opposite decisions is no indication that their procedures are unscientific; but it does demonstrate that editing is not a science.

A related category in which emendations are wholly dependent on literary judgment consists of those readings introduced by an editor to correct what he considers erroneous readings in all extant authoritative texts. At one point in the English edition of *Typee* the phrase "Lacedemonian nations" occurs, and in the American the same phrase in the singular;[17] but neither "nations" nor "nation" makes much sense in the context, and an editor is obligated to try to discover a word meaning "women"—as called for by the sense—which yet could have been misread in Melville's handwriting as "nations." Hershel Parker's solution, "matrons," is one of those emendations which fits all the conditions so perfectly that it must be the word originally written (or intended) by the author. The degree of certainty which attaches to it is surely much higher than that associated with many emendations for which a considerable amount of bibliographical evidence is available. But the basis for the emendation is an individual editor's immersion in the author he is editing, his familiarity with the author's language and handwriting. An important and demanding part of an editor's task is to locate and emend such errors, even when they are not drawn to his attention by the existence of variant readings. Yet in most cases there will be no bibliographical evidence to analyze, and his only preparation will be his intimate knowledge of and sensitivity to the author's thought and style.

Turning briefly to accidentals, one may first note that examples of emendations in accidentals can be found which correspond to all these types of emendations in substantives. In the majority of cases, however, following Greg's theory, the punctuation and spelling of the copy-text are retained, for more often than with substantives one has no other means of deciding. Bibliographical evidence that provides demonstrable certainty occurs no more frequently in connection with accidentals than with substantives, and one generally has less means for judging critically the authority of accidentals. Nevertheless, certain crucial critical questions lie at the heart of any editorial policy for treating accidentals. If an editor is preparing an old-spelling critical edition, then modernization of accidentals is out of the question, but what about correction of them in conformity with the standard of the author's

---

Mardi (1849), for example, which can be more reasonably explained as the sort of revision an author would do than as the sort anyone else would be likely to engage in; on the other hand, the small number of such variants in relation to the large size of the book weakens one's belief that they resulted from authorial revision.

17. See *Typee*, p. 215, line 10, and the note on p. 332. Cf. Hershel Parker, "Species of 'Soiled Fish,'" *CEAA Newsletter*, No. 1 (March 1968), pp. 11–12.

times? If the copy-text is a printed book, an editor will be extremely cautious in altering accidentals because in general they must represent what was tolerated at the time and bring one closer to the author's intention than an editorial reconstruction could usually do. For this reason it is often sounder practice to allow inconsistencies to stand, since an imposed consistency may have the result of eliminating the author's preferred usage; but obviously in certain cases an editor will feel that he has strong enough evidence to justify his alteration of anomalous usages. If the copy-text is a manuscript, an editor must decide, on the basis of his knowledge of the author's practice, whether it contains the spelling and punctuation intended as final by the author or whether the author would have expected it to be put into final form at the printer's or publisher's. In other words, when bibliographical evidence is not conclusive, an editor's decisions about accidentals ultimately rest on his individual judgment, informed by his understanding not only of the author but of the author's times as well.

One of the particularly difficult decisions about accidentals which an editor must make concerns the spelling of proper names. For ordinary words contemporary dictionaries and the works of other authors offer guides to the acceptable range of usage, but for proper names no similar guide is normally available to help establish a dividing line between allowable variants and outright errors. An editor may be willing to endorse several different spellings of "Shakespeare"—each one supported by a long tradition—but can he allow "Davy Crocket" to stand in the text of *Mardi* (1849) with only one *t* or "Captain Marryatt" in *Typee* with two *t*'s?[18] Even if Melville had habitually spelled the names in this fashion, and even if other writers at the time had done so, the number of occurrences would be no indication that the spellings were not errors. Presumably correctness in a personal name is an arbitrary matter not governed by general usage, though the attitude toward spelling at the time when the person lived and the familiarity which a particular spelling has achieved over an extended period of time must be regarded as factors that limit the arbitrariness with which an editor can alter personal names. Another factor involves a critical judgment about the nature of the work: are different standards applicable to works of fiction and works of history? In *Mardi*, Melville refers to a painter named "Sebastioni."[19] Should an editor who finds no trace of the existence of such a painter emend the word to "Sebastiano" on the presumption that Melville was alluding to

18. See the Northwestern-Newberry Edition of *Mardi* (1970), p. 105, line 30; *Typee*, p. 21, line 25.

19. See *Mardi*, p. 447, line 10, and the note on p. 700.

Sebastiano del Piombo? Or should he let the spelling stand on the ground that *Mardi* is a creative work and that this name may be, like a number of others, a literary invention of Melville's? The decision in cases of this kind will rest not only on the nature of the work and the immediate context but also, to some extent, on the general familiarity of the name to Western readers. A misplaced or incorrect letter in Rembrandt's name can be rectified by an editor with considerable certainty that he is doing no injustice to the author's intention; but the lesser fame of Sebastiano makes an editor correspondingly less sure of the intended reference. Such decisions as these, fundamental to any editorial policy, require literary sensitivity and historical knowledge; and Greg's theory of copy-text does not—nor did Greg suggest that it should—relieve an editor of the responsibility for making them in regard to accidentals any more than it does in regard to substantives.

In going over once again what is by now familiar ground, I am not trying to minimize the role of bibliography in editing or to encourage wild subjectivism. Thanks to the work of Greg and Bowers and their followers, we have happily moved beyond the point where any serious question can be raised about the necessity of beginning each textual study with rigorous bibliographical analysis of the physical evidence. Similarly, there can be no quarrel with Bowers's assertion that, "when bibliography in its pure state *can* operate at the level of demonstration, and bibliographical and critical judgement clash . . . , the critic must accept the bibliographical findings and somehow come to terms with them."[20] All I am saying could perhaps be regarded as the converse of this statement. For when bibliographical analysis provides anything less than demonstrable certainty, literary judgment must necessarily take over; and since demonstrable certainty is—in this field as in any other—a less common commodity than one might wish, literary judgment must dominate a good deal of the time. Certain conclusions suggested by bibliographical analysis with varying degrees of probability and possibility may of course furnish valuable assistance, taken in conjunction with literary evidence, for reaching a final decision[21]—but the evaluation of relative degrees

20. Bowers, *Bibliography and Textual Criticism*, pp. 155–156. See also another of his important treatments of this subject, "Some Relations of Bibliography to Editorial Problems," *SB*, 3 (1950–51), 37–62, which contains the statement that "textual criticism cannot controvert accurate bibliography in its findings when the subject is one on which bibliography can properly operate." For Greg's earlier examination of the relationship, see "Bibliography —An Apologia," *Library*, 4th ser., 13 (1932–33), 113–143, reprinted in *Collected Papers*, pp. 239–266.

21. As Bowers has recently said, "The chief function of analytical bibliography is to guide and to set the limits within which the critical judgment must operate in the final

of probability is in itself a subjective matter. It follows, therefore, that an edition may conceivably be "definitive" in terms of its scholarly method and of the material assembled in it; but—except perhaps in the most simple cases—"definitive" is not an adjective which can meaningfully be applied to the actual text of an edition, since decisions about an author's final intention are more often matters of judgment than matters of fact.

The ultimate dependence of textual study on literary judgment has never been better expressed than by Housman in his famous address to the Classical Association in 1921. Textual criticism, he said, deals with "the frailties and aberrations of the human mind, and of its insubordinate servants, the human fingers. It therefore is not susceptible of hard-and-fast rules." And then he added, "It would be much easier if it were; and that is why people try to pretend that it is, or at least behave as if they thought so."[22] I am merely trying to emphasize the fact that, in an age of computers, his point is as valid as ever. Editing is not simply a prerequisite to scholarly literary criticism; it is a part of that criticism.

---

selection of readings." See his "Practical Texts and Definitive Editions," in Charlton Hinman and Fredson Bowers, *Two Lectures on Editing* (1969), p. 55.

22. A. E. Housman, "The Application of Thought to Textual Criticism," in *Selected Prose*, ed. John Carter (1961), p. 132.

Index

Index

Abernethy, Cecil, 214
Accidentals: editorial treatment of, 20, 28, 94–97, 109, 199–201, 203, 218–73 *passim*, 292–98, 317–18, 334–36; recording of, 164, 169–73
Adams, A. W., 304
Adams, Charles Francis, Jr., 239
Adams, John, 219
Adams family papers, 243–44, 247, 261
Adaptations, 52–53
Aiken, Henry David, 40
Aldus (Manutius), 274
Alexandrian library, 274
Alfred (king), 81
Allen, Don Cameron, 125
Allusions. *See* Quotations
Alston, William P., 34
American Fiction Series, 214–15
American Historical Association, 224
American Philosophical Society, 224
Analytical bibliography. *See* Bibliography, analytical
Anderson, Charles R., 214
Anderson, Frederick, 13, 121, 190, 256–57
Anderson, Sherwood, 43–44, 46–47, 216
Anderson, W. E. K., 103
Anglo-American Historical Committee, 239
Annotation. *See* Editorial apparatus
Anscombe, G. E. M., 30
Apparatus. *See* Editorial apparatus
Appleton, D., & Co. *See* D. Appleton & Co.
Aristarchus, 274
Arlen, Michael J., 100

Arnold, Matthew, 93
Aschenbrenner, Karl, 37
Association for Documentary Editing, xiii
Atlantic Monthly, 195–96, 197
Auden, W. H., 62–63
Austen, Jane, 214
Austin, J. L., 33, 34, 35, 37, 39

Bacon, Francis, 84
Bacon, Nathaniel, 238
Baender, Paul, 48, 69–70
Bailyn, Bernard, 218–19
Bain, Alexander, 108
Baird, John D., 255, 257
Balboa, Vasco Nuñez de, 72–73, 117
Baldwin, T. W., 125
Bally, Charles, 92
Balzac, Honoré de, 106, 184–85
Banta, Martha, 197
Barbi, Michele, 307
Barker, Nicolas, 221
Barnes, Warner, 179
Barr, Robert, 195
Barrett, Elizabeth B., 257. *See also* Browning, Elizabeth B.
Baskin, Wade, 92
Basler, Roy P., 255
Bateson, F. W., 122
Battestin, Martin C., 21, 122, 201–3, 204, 211
Beach, Joseph Warren, 62–63
Beale, Thomas, 77, 100–101
Beard, James Franklin, 255–56
Beardsley, Monroe C., 30–31, 36, 38, 39, 41

Beaumont, Francis, 122, 132, 144, 148, 164, 166
Bebb, Bruce, 201
Becker, Robert, 249
Beckford, William, 215
Bédier, Joseph, 309–10, 311, 312, 316
Beinecke Library, 208
Bell, Whitfield J., Jr., 220, 222, 240
Bellow, Saul, 99
Bemis, Samuel Flagg, 243
Bengel, J. A., 305
Bennet, George, 85, 96
Bennett, Frederick Debell, 78, 85
Bennett, Scott, 197, 198
Bentham, Jeremy, 263–64
Bentley, G. E., Jr., 84
Bentley, Richard, 40, 274, 305
Bentley's Miscellany, 204–5
Bergeron, Paul H., 223
Béroul, 310
Besterman, Theodore, 250–51
Bible, 304, 312; Job, 77; King James, 238; New Testament, 274, 277, 282, 302, 305, 306, 320; Psalms, 84
Bibliographical evidence. *See* Documents, physical evidence in
Bibliography, analytical, 21–22, 45, 283–93, 336–37
Bieler, Ludwig, 282, 296, 315
Black, Max, 34
Blackstone, William, 78
Blair, Walter, 121
Bobbs-Merrill Library of Literature, 106, 215
Boer, Willem den, 275
Bolgar, Robert R., 275
Boni & Liveright, 47
Bonnard, G. A., 180
Booth, Bradford, 216
Booth, E. T., 43, 46–47
Boswell, James, 85, 257
Bourget, Paul, 108
Bowers, Fredson, xiii, 77, 120, 320; on analytical bibliography, 45, 283, 330, 336–37; on apparatus, 122, 124, 125, 175, 268, 298; on copy-text, 27, 191, 326; on Dewey, 107, 121, 166; on Dickens, 205; on eclectic texts, 270, 281; on Greg, 20, 28, 217, 275, 326; on intention, 28; on Johnson,

266, 272; on line-end hyphens, 153; on McKerrow, 27, 300, 326; on modernization, 265, 266; on multiple authority, 318–19; on "practical editions," 124, 180; on radiating texts, 46, 167–71, 176; on revision, 52; on textual criticism, 191, 272–73, 275, 299, 328
—, as editor of Beaumont and Fletcher, 122, 144, 148, 166; of Crane, 21, 46, 59–61, 121, 139, 144, 163, 166, 167, 170–72, 190, 195, 199; of Dekker, 21, 121, 122, 126, 130, 131, 135, 144, 145, 163, 166; of Dryden, 21; of Fielding, 21, 45, 122, 144, 166, 201–3; of Hawthorne, 21, 95, 121, 153, 166, 194, 221; of William James, 4, 110, 112, 220; of Whitman, 60, 61, 126, 141
Boyd, Julian P., 220, 222, 259–60, 261, 263, 267; on Adams edition, 243; as editor of Jefferson, 218, 221, 223, 225–31, 235, 236, 239, 240, 242, 247, 249, 252
Boyd, Steven R., 261
Boydston, Jo Ann, 21, 107–9, 121, 220
Brack, O M, Jr., 179
Brackenridge, Hugh Henry, 215
Bradley, F. H., 108
Brady, Frank, 36
Brambilla Ageno, Franca, 282
Brant, Joseph (Thayendanegea), 102
Brontë, Charlotte, 210–11
Brontë, Emily, 216
Brown, Arthur, 239, 265
Brown, Charles Brockden, 214
Brown, John Russell, 265
Brown, Merle E., 31
Brown, William Hill, 151, 190
Browne, J. Ross, 81
Browne, Thomas, 79
Browning, Elizabeth B., 11, 257
Browning, Robert, 11, 257
Brubaker, Robert L., 222
Bruccoli, Matthew J., 121, 127, 131, 189
Bunyan, John, 79, 81–82, 89, 214
Burke, Edmund, 251
Burkhardt, Frederick, 4
Burnet, William, 95
Burney, Fanny, 258

Burns, Robert, 116
Burrows, David, 193
Butler, William, 102
Butt, John, 179–80, 204
Butterfield, Lyman H., 219, 221, 250, 259, 261; as editor of Adams papers, 243–44; on W. C. Ford, 222; on Jefferson edition, 225
Byron, George Gordon, 6th baron, 11, 258–59

Cady, Edwin H., 21, 122, 190, 222
Calhoun, John C., 240, 242
Cameron, Kenneth Neill, 8, 257–58
Canfora, Luciano, 306
Capitan, William H., 31, 38
Capote, Truman, 100
Cappon, Lester J., 222, 223, 261
Capps, Jack L., 47
Cardwell, Margaret, 207–9
Carrithers, Gale H., Jr., 31
Carter, Clarence E., 221; editorial practices of, 10, 231–34, 235, 239, 240, 254
Carter, Everett, 216
Carter, John, 299, 337
Castellani, Arrigo, 312
Center for Editions of American Authors, 48, 217, 275, 327; editions of, 6, 121–22, 127, 154–55, 180, 190–201, 203, 213, 218–24, 252, 256, 259, 262, 267, 269, 270, 271–72, 297; statement of, 27, 122, 154, 191, 221, 231, 271, 275
Center for Scholarly Editions: editions of, 6, 218, 220, 252, 262, 297; statement of, 6, 21, 224, 275, 313
Century Magazine, 198
Channing, Edward T., 113–14
Chapman, R. W., 11, 72, 214, 254, 255, 320
Chase, Owen, 88, 96
Chatman, Seymour, 36
Chaytor, Henry John, 310
Cheever, Henry T., 81, 88–89
Church, Benjamin, 102
Cioffi, Frank, 31, 40
Clarendon Editions, 201–11
Clark, Albert C., 289
Clark, Harry Hayden, 214

Clark, William, 245, 263
Clay, Henry, 240, 242–43, 259
Clayton, Thomas, 56, 122
Clemens, Samuel L., 11, 181; Iowa-California edition of, 13, 121, 130, 132, 141, 145, 154, 190, 193, 256–57
Coburn, Kathleen, 254–55
Coleridge, Samuel Taylor, 254–55
Coley, W. B., 21, 122, 201
Collaboration, 50–51
Collomp, Paul, 312
Colnett, James, 85
Colwell, Ernest C., 289, 305, 306, 308, 313
Consistency, 74–75, 94–97, 199–201, 265–67, 335
Cook, Don L., 181, 222; as editor of Howells, 21, 74, 122, 190, 198
Cook, James, 85
Cooke, Jacob E., 244
Coomaraswamy, Ananda K., 30, 39
Cooper, James Fenimore, 255–56
Copeland, Thomas W., 251
Copyright, 196, 197–98
Copy-text: bases for choice of, 19–21, 48–50, 120–22, 147–50, 164, 167–76, 191, 204–5, 207–13, 277–78, 300–305, 315–19, 333; manuscript as, instead of printed edition, 193–95, 302–3, 335
Cortez, Hernando, 72–73, 117
Cowley, Malcolm, 61, 89
Cowper, William, 78
Crain, William Leeper, 184
Crane, Stephen: George's Mother, 196; "A Grey Sleeve," 170–72; Maggie, 59–61, 144, 199; newspaper sketches, 45–46, 139, 163, 167, 170–72, 319; The O'Ruddy, 195; The Red Badge of Courage, 180–81, 192, 195; Virginia edition of, as a whole, 21, 121, 127–28, 132, 133, 139, 145, 154, 156, 163, 166, 170–72, 190, 194, 200
Critical editing. See Editing, scholarly
Crockett, David, 335
Crowley, J. Donald, 95
Cushman, Robert E., 249
Cutler, Manasseh, 222
Cutler, Wayne, 281

D. Appleton & Co., 59, 199
Daniel, Pete, 248
Darwin, Charles, 4, 84, 88
Dates, 94, 112
Davenant, William, 84
Davis, Herbert, 215
Davis, Jefferson, 247
Davis, Merrell R., 12, 256
Dearing, Vinton A., 305, 318, 319; on
    "textual analysis," 277, 282, 283,
    284–88, 290, 294, 297, 313–15
De Beer, E. S., 251
Defoe, Daniel, 215
Dekker, Thomas: Cambridge edition of,
    21, 121, 122, 126, 130, 131, 132, 135,
    144, 145, 163, 164, 166
Demetz, Peter, 31
Deventer, Heinrich van, 83
Dewey, John: Southern Illinois edition
    of, 21, 107–9, 110, 114, 121, 127–28,
    129, 130, 132, 133, 134, 145, 154,
    156, 159, 166, 220
Diaries. See Documents, private
Dickens, Charles, 204–10, 213, 216
Dickie, George, 31
Dickinson, Emily, 11, 66–68, 69, 255, 271
Diplomatics, 280, 281. See also Tran-
    scription
Discrepancies. See Consistency
Diverres, A. H., 310
Documentary History of the First Fed-
    eral Elections, The, 249
Documentary History of the Ratifica-
    tion of the Constitution, The, 249
Documents: physical evidence in, 16,
    21–22, 283–93; private, 5–13, 16,
    64–65, 103–4, 218–73; public, 5–6,
    13–23, 103–5, 125, 179–217, 270–71;
    texts of, distinguished from texts of
    works, xiv, 14, 16–17, 19, 22–23, 104,
    280–81, 284–88; visual attributes of,
    7–9, 16
Donald, David, 243
Donaldson, E. Talbot, 305, 311
Douglas, David, 197–98
Drama, 14, 181. See also Works, verbal
Dryden, John, 21, 126, 238, 282, 326
Duneka, Frederick A., 193
Dunlap, Leslie W., 222, 223
Dyson, A. E., 214, 216

Eaton, Marcia Muelder, 32, 34, 36–37,
    41
Eaves, T. C. Duncan, 182, 183, 255
Eckermann, Johann Peter, 85
Eclecticism, 268–72, 278, 280, 281, 300.
    See also Editing, scholarly, and
    critical judgment
Edel, Leon, 252
Editing, scholarly: and annotation, 119–
    76; "best-text" approach to, 309–
    11, 316; of classical, biblical, and
    medieval writings, 274–75, 278–79,
    282–98, 305–15; for classroom, 215–
    17; and critical judgment, x, xiv,
    11–15, 18–21, 29, 32–33, 39–43, 60–
    61, 73–74, 92, 103–7, 110, 112, 114–
    15, 118, 188–89, 199, 278, 280, 298–
    321, 325–37; of fiction, 179–217;
    genealogical approach to, 305–10;
    of philosophy, 3, 107–10; of private
    writings, 6–13, 16, 64–65, 103–4,
    124–25, 218–73; quasi-mathemati-
    cal approaches to, 311–15; of texts
    of historical documents, xiv, 74,
    218–73; and treatment of facts, 72–
    118; of works in different genres,
    3–6; of writings intended for pub-
    lication, 13–23, 103–5, 125, 179–
    217, 270–71. See also Intention
Editorial apparatus, xiii, 5, 12–13, 14–
    15, 19, 22, 119–76, 191–93; arrange-
    ment and location of, 123–34; his-
    torical record of variants in, 159–
    66, 169–70, 192–93, 205–7, 296–98;
    list of emendations in, 142–53, 170–
    73, 192; list of line-end hyphena-
    tion in, 153–59, 175–76, 192, 207;
    notes in, 125–27, 141–42; for radi-
    ating texts, 167–76; symbols in,
    134–41, 171, 267–68
Edwards, Jonathan, 111–12
Efron, Arthur, 31
Eliot, George, 251
Eliot, T. S., 50–51
Eliot, Valerie, 50
Elliott, James P., 198
Emendation: bases for, 14–16, 19–21, 53,
    116–17, 278–79, 315–16; recording
    of, 142–53. See also Editing, schol-
    arly; Editorial apparatus

Emerson, Ralph Waldo: Harvard edition of journals of, 13, 65, 122, 127, 141, 256, 268; letters of, 11, 253
Epp, Eldon Jay, 304
Erasmus, Desiderius, 274
Errors. *See* Consistency; Emendation; Facts
Erskine, Albert, 47
Essays. *See* Works, verbal
Evans, Frank B., 261
Evans, Mary Ann (George Eliot), 251
Evelyn, John, 251
Extracts. *See* Quotations

Facsimiles. *See* Reproduction
Facts: in literature, 4, 72–118
Farquhar, James Douglas, 289
Faulkner, William, 47, 189
Feld, M. D., 276
Feltskog, E. N., 112
Ferguson, E. James, 248
Fiction, 14, 179–217; American, 190–201; British, 201–13; and fact, 4, 72–118. *See also* Works, verbal
Fiedler, Leslie, 31
Fielding, Henry: Wesleyan edition of, 21, 45, 122, 133, 134, 137, 144, 145, 154, 156, 166, 201–4, 205, 206, 211
Fildes, Luke, 208
Firth, Edith G., 240
Fishel, Leslie, H., Jr., 222
Fisher, John H., 222
Fisher, Ruth Anna, 221
Fitzgerald, F. Scott, 127, 131, 189
Fletcher, John, 122, 132, 144, 148, 164, 166
Flower, Barbara, 306
Foot, M. R. D., 257
Footnotes. *See* Editorial apparatus
Ford, George, 216
Ford, Worthington Chauncey, 222
Foster, Elizabeth S., 214
Foulet, Alfred, 282, 298, 304
Fourquet, Jean, 311
Fox, William Lloyd, 221
Frank, Waldo, 44
Franklin, Benjamin, 220, 240–42, 243, 262
Franklin, R. W., 67–68
Frazer, James George, 4

Frederic, Harold, 216
Freidel, Frank, 234
Frémont, John Charles, 245
Freud, Sigmund, 4, 102, 271, 289
Froger, Jacques, 313
Fuller, Margaret, 85
Fuller, Thomas, 82–83
Furness, Horace Howard, 120, 127, 163

Gage, Thomas, 254
Gang, T. M., 33, 34, 43
Gardner, Helen, 283
Garibaldi, Giuseppe, 97
Garmonsway, G. N., 311
Garrett, Wendell D., 243
Garrett Press, 216
Gaskell, Philip, 48, 50, 210
Gendin, Sidney, 38
General Services Administration, 222
Gerber, John C., 181
Gibbon, Edward, 106
Gibson, William M., 11, 121, 193, 222, 255, 268
Gillies, Robert P., 88
Gilman, William H., 12, 13, 65, 122, 256, 326–27
Gimbel, Richard, 208
Gladstone, William Ewart, 257
Goethe, Johann Wolfgang von, 85
Golden, Arthur, 141
Gottesman, Ronald, 21, 122, 190, 193, 195, 197
Graf, LeRoy P., 247
Grant, Ulysses S., 247
Gray, Thomas, 11, 253
Greene, Thomas, 31
Greetham, David, 320
Greever, Garland, 214
Greg, W. W., 320; and analytical bibliography, 283, 336; *Calculus of Variants*, 312–13, 314, 325; on copytext, 19–21, 27–29, 48, 61, 120, 160, 167, 168, 174, 176, 190–91, 200, 201, 204, 208, 209, 212, 213, 214, 217, 223, 270, 272, 275, 280, 293, 295, 300–301, 303–5, 309, 313, 315–19, 326, 328, 333, 334, 336; on editorial judgment, 71, 300; on emendation, 39–40, 54; on intention, 35, 48; on McKerrow, 300, 326; on moderni-

Greg (cont.)
    zation, 265; reviewed by Maas, 307;
    on superscript index numbers, 151
Gregg Press, 216
Grice, H. P., 34, 37
Griesbach, J. J., 305
Griffith, John G., 313
Griggs, Earl Leslie, 255
Grove, Frederick Philip, 259
Grover, Wayne C., 261
Guilds, John Caldwell, 122, 190
Gunther, Gerald, 261
Guthkelch, A. C., 214

Hacke, William, 89
Haight, Gordon S., 251
Hakluyt, Richard, 96, 116
Hall, A. Rupert, 257
Hall, F. W., 306
Hall, Marie Boas, 257
Halpenny, Francess G., 189, 259
Halsband, Robert, 64, 262
Hamer, Philip May, 218, 221, 246
Hamilton, Alexander, 244–45
Hancher, Michael, 31, 34–36, 39, 41, 42,
    49
Handlin, Oscar, 234
Hardy, J. P., 109
Harkness, Bruce, 179, 180, 189, 190, 328
Harlan, Louis R., 248
Harper & Brothers, 77
Harper's Monthly, 197
Harper's Weekly, 97
Harris, John, 85, 96
Hart-Davis, Rupert, 251–52
Harvard Guide to American History,
    234–39, 240, 241, 242, 246, 252
Harvard (John) Library, 216
Haskins, Ralph W., 247
Havet, Louis, 289
Hawthorne, Nathaniel, 195; The Ameri-
    can Notebooks, 256; The Blithedale
    Romance, 95, 165, 194–95, 197;
    Fanshawe, 95, 145, 196; The House
    of the Seven Gables, 141, 156, 192,
    194; Life of Franklin Pierce, 262;
    The Marble Faun, 156, 165, 194;
    The Scarlet Letter, 130, 149, 153,
    165, 192, 196; The Snow-Image, 95,
    96; Twice-Told Tales, 95; Ohio

State edition of, as a whole, 21, 121,
    127–28, 132, 133, 137, 151, 154, 156,
    164–65, 166, 190, 200, 206, 221
Hayford, Harrison: as editor of Billy
    Budd, 16, 102–5, 106, 125, 141, 271;
    of Northwestern-Newberry edition
    of Melville, 21, 54, 77, 122, 190, 330;
    of Norton Moby-Dick, 216; of Sig-
    net Typee, 125
Hazard, Ebenezer, 222
Hazlitt, William, 77, 109
Heflin, Wilson, 87
Hemlow, Joyce, 258
Hemphill, W. Edwin, 242
Henry, Joseph, 247–48
Henry, Robert, 81
Hesseltine, William B., 261
Higginson, Thomas Wentworth, 68
Hilen, Andrew, 252
Hill, Archibald A., 92, 313–14, 325
Hindman, Sandra, 289
Hinman, Charlton, 45, 180, 283, 286,
    337
Hirsch, E. D., Jr., 31, 37, 38–39, 40, 41,
    93
History: documents of, 218–73; facts of,
    in literature, 4, 72–118; pursuit of,
    x, 5, 10, 320, 329; works of, 4, 14
Hobbes, Thomas, 88
Hodgart, M. J. C., 93, 116
Hogg, James, 112
Holland, Philemon, 85
Holman, C. Hugh, 214
Holmes, Oliver W., 218, 224
Homer, 72, 320
Honigmann, E. A. J., 66
Hopkins, Gerard Manly, 35
Hopkins, James F., 242
Horne, Colin J., 109
Horsford, Howard, 255
Horsman, Alan, 209–10
Hort, F. J. A., 306, 308
Housman, A. E., 274, 300, 309; on edi-
    torial judgment, 299, 301, 310, 337
Howard, William J., 47, 65, 69
Howarth, William L., 21
Howells, William Dean: The Altrurian
    Romances, 197; April Hopes, 74–
    75, 198; A Chance Acquaintance,
    197; A Hazard of New Fortunes,

Howells (*cont.*)

97–99; *Indian Summer*, 198; letters, 11; *The Rise of Silas Lapham*, 44–45, 181, 198; *The Shadow of a Dream*, 197–98; *The Son of Royal Langbrith*, 193–94, 195, 200; *Their Wedding Journey*, 21, 195-96; *Through the Eye of the Needle*, 197; *A Traveller from Altruria*, 197; Indiana edition of, as a whole, 21, 121, 122, 132, 133, 134, 137, 138, 142, 146, 154, 160, 190

Hrubý, Antonín, 313–14, 325

Hungerland, Isabel C., 39

Hunter, John, 81

Huntley, John, 31

Hussey, Cyrus, 85, 88

Hutchinson, William T., 245

Hyatt, J. Philip, 289

Hyman, Stanley Edgar, 4, 106

Hyphenation, line-end, 153–59. *See also* Editorial apparatus

Idzerda, Stanley, 223

Intention: active, 34–36, 42–43, 51; of authors of verbal works, x, xii, 17–19, 27–71, 181, 198–99, 200, 264–65, 272, 298, 316, 329; changes of, 18–19, 51–63, 307; distinguished from acquiescence, 53; distinguished from expectation, 46–51; final, 18–19, 51–67, 70–71; kinds of, 33–37; in nonfiction works, 106–17; to keep a piece of writing private, 5–13, 263–67; to make a piece of writing public, 5–6, 13–23

Irving, Washington: Wisconsin edition of, 11, 112, 113, 114, 121, 122, 132, 133, 134, 138, 141, 146, 154, 160, 256, 268

Ivy, G. S., 289

Jack, Ian, 210

Jack, Jane, 210

Jackson, Donald, 245–46

James, Henry, 189; letters, 252; New York Edition, 18, 56, 58, 59, 61, 187

James, William, 3, 109, 110, 112, 114, 220

Jameson, J. Franklin, 221, 222, 223

Jebb, R. C., 306

Jefferson, Thomas, 85, 89, 94, 262; Princeton edition of, 218, 221, 225–31, 243, 244, 247, 252, 253, 259, 272

Jenkinson, Hilary, 240

Jensen, Merrill, 243, 249

Johnson, Andrew, 247

Johnson, Herbert A., 248–49

Johnson, Richard Colles, 77, 122

Johnson, Samuel, 11, 109, 254, 255, 257

Johnson, Thomas H., 11, 66, 255

Jones, H. G., 222

Jones, Huw Morris, 40

Jones, John Bush, xi, 275

Jonson, Ben, 60

Journals. *See* Documents, private

Judgment, editorial. *See* Editing, scholarly, and critical judgment

Kable, William S., 151, 190

Kane, George, 311

Kantorowicz, Hermann, 306

Katz, Joseph, 180–81

Kaufman, Stuart, 248

Keats, John, 11, 72–73, 117, 255

Kellar, Herbert A., 261

Kemp, John, 34, 61

Kennedy, John F., 222

Kenney, E. J., 276, 278–79, 304, 306

Kenyon, Frederic G., 304

Kewer, Eleanor D., 65

Kimpel, Ben D., 182, 183

Kinkead-Weekes, M., 183

Kinsley, James, 215

Kintner, Elvan, 11, 257

Kleinhenz, Christopher, 304, 309, 310, 311

Koch, Adrienne, 222

Kolb, Harold H., Jr., 98

Kuhns, Richard, 34, 58

Labaree, Leonard W., 220, 240–42

Lachmann, Karl, 274, 299, 305–10, 311, 312, 315

Lake, Kirsopp, 306

Lang, Cecil Y., 251

Langland, William, 311

Language: as medium of literature, xi, 36–37. *See also* Literature; Works, verbal

Lanham, Jon, 116
Lanier, Sidney, 214
Laurens, Henry, 246
Lawrence, D. H., 251
Lay, William, 85, 88
Leach, MacEdward, 297
Lee, Charles E., 261
Leiden system of transcription, 298
Leland, Waldo G., 221
Lemay, J. A. Leo, 242
Lemisch, Jesse, 260
Letters. See Documents, private
Levy, Leonard W., 260
Lewis, Meriwether, 245, 263
Lewis, Wilmarth S., 249–50, 260
Lincoln, Abraham, 255
Lingelbach, William E., 240
Link, Arthur S., 246–47
Literary criticism: in relation to textual criticism, xi, 67–71
Literary figures: private papers of, 249–59
Literature: in relation to other verbal works, 3–6, 106–7, 262–63. See also Works, verbal
Litz, A. Walton, 69
Locke, John, 220
Longfellow, Henry Wadsworth, 252
Lonsdale, Roger, 215
Lottinville, Savoie, 5
Lovelace, Richard, 56
Lowell, Amy, 72, 117
Lucian, 77
Lucretius, 305
Lyas, Colin A., 36

Maas, Paul, 278–79, 301, 306–7, 309
McAdam, E. L., 327
Macaulay, Thomas Babington, 106
McCulloch, John Ramsay, 86
Mace, C. A., 42
McElroy, John Harmon, 99
McIntosh, James T., 247
McKenzie, D. F., 325, 328
McKerrow, R. B.: and analytical bibliography, 283, 300; as editor of Nashe, 120–21, 300; editorial principles of, in Prolegomena, 121, 135–36, 139, 162, 163, 300, 301, 303, 326, 327, 328

McNeil, Donald R., 261
McReynolds, Paul R., 313
Madison, James, 245, 260
Maier, Rosemarie, 31, 32
Mailloux, Steven, 82
Malone, Dumas, 222
Manilius, 299, 300, 301
Mansfield, Luther S., 214
Manuscripts. See Copy-text, manuscript as; Documents, private
Manutius, Aldus, 274
Marchand, Ernest, 214
Marchand, Leslie A., 11, 258–59
Marichal, Robert, 304
Marryat, Frederick, 335
Marshall, John, 248–49
Martinelli, Nello, 309
Marx, Karl, 4
Marx, Leo, 223
Mason, George, 247
Matthew, H. C. G., 257
Matthiessen, F. O., 115–16
Maxwell, J. C., 27, 120, 167, 191, 326
Meaning. See Intention
Meiland, Jack W., 30
Melville, Elizabeth Shaw, 59
Melville, Herman, 49; Billy Budd, 16–17, 102–5, 125, 141, 271; The Confidence Man, 214; journals, 255; letters, 12, 256; Mardi, 165, 196, 334, 335–36; Moby-Dick, xii, 45, 74–75, 76–91, 96, 99, 100–102, 116, 181, 214, 216; Omoo, 196, 332–33; Pierre, 196, 214; Redburn, 196; Typee, 53–55, 59, 60, 125, 144, 145, 165, 198–99, 330–32, 333–34, 335; White-Jacket, 115–16, 164, 165, 196–97; Hendricks House edition of, as a whole, 214; Northwestern-Newberry edition of, as a whole, 121, 122, 132, 133, 134, 141, 143, 151, 154, 156, 160, 163, 164, 190, 200
Mercer, George, 263
Meriwether, James B., 122, 189–90
Meriwether, Robert L., 242
Meserve, Walter J., 45, 198
Metzger, Bruce M., 276, 304, 313, 320
Milton, John, 69, 78

Modern Language Association, 27, 121, 220, 222–23, 275
Modernizing, 10–11, 201, 203, 237–39, 250, 252, 259, 265–67, 296. *See also* Accidentals
Moldenhauer, Joseph J., 112, 114, 265
Monod, Sylvère, 216
Monroe, Haskell M., Jr., 222, 247
Montagu, Lady Mary Wortley, 262
Montaigne, Michel de, 77
Montgomery, James, 88, 89
Moore, Harry T., 251
Moorman, Charles, 282
Moorman, Mary, 257
Morgan, Edmund S., 219
Morison, Elting E., 253–54
Morison, Samuel Eliot, 234–39
Morris, Richard B., 222
Morris, Robert, 248
Moser, Edwin, 112, 114
Mulkearn, Lois, 263
Mumford, Lewis, 268
Murphy, Arthur, 201
Murray, Henry A., 214
Murray, John, 54

Names, proper, 94–97. *See also* Accidentals
Nashe, Thomas, 120–21, 300
National Endowment for the Humanities, 223
National Historical Publications and Records Commission: editions sponsored by, 6, 218–24, 231, 243, 249, 250, 252, 255, 259, 260, 261, 262, 263, 268, 271, 272, 273
National Historical Publications Commission. *See preceding entry*
Nelson, Lowry, Jr., 31
New, Melvyn, 83–84
New Testament. *See* Bible
Newcomer, Lee Nathaniel, 222
Newlin, Claude M., 215
Newton, Isaac, 310
Nichol, John W., 115
Nidditch, Peter H., 220
Noggle, Burl, 246
Nonfiction, 14, 106–15, 181. *See also* Works, verbal

Nordloh, David J.: as editor of Howells, 21, 45, 98, 122, 190, 193, 197, 198
Normalizing. *See* Accidentals; Regularizing
North American Review, 193
Norton, David L., 222
Norton Critical Editions, 215–16
Notebooks. *See* Documents, private
Notes. *See* Editorial apparatus
Nowell-Smith, Simon, 47, 64

Octher, 81
Odell, Alfred Taylor, 255
Odyssey Series in Literature, 214
Ohmann, Richard, 36
Oldenberg, Henry, 257
Oliphant, Mary C. Simms, 255
Orlinsky, Harry M., 304
Oxford English Novels, 211, 215

Pacey, Desmond, 259
Paine, Albert Bigelow, 193
Paley, William, 81
Palmer, John, 36
Paraphrases. *See* Quotations
Parker, Hershel: on CEAA, 201; on editions of *Moby-Dick*, 181; as editor of Melville, 21, 54, 122, 190, 216, 330, 334; on intention, 55; on regularizing, 201, 265, 266
Pasquali, Giorgio, 304, 307, 309
Passmore, John, 3
Pater, Walter, 93
Payzant, Geoffrey, 37
Pearsall, D. A., 311
Peckham, Morse, 31, 33, 34, 38, 39, 69–70
Penguin English Library, 215
Pepys, Samuel, 6
Perkins, Maxwell, 69
Peters, Robert L., 11, 258
Philbrick, Francis S., 240
Philosophy, 3–5, 107–10
Phips, William, 95
Pickford, Cedric E., 309, 311
Pierce, Franklin, 262
Pierson, Robert Craig, 182
Pike, Zebulon M., 245
Plumb, J. H., 260
Plutarch, 85

Pochmann, Henry A., 11, 109, 112, 113, 122, 256
Poetry, 14, 181. *See also* Works, verbal
Poggio Bracciolini, Giovanni, 274
Politian (Angelo Poliziano), 274
Polk, James K., 246
Pollard, A. W., 283
Pope, Alexander, 78, 109
Pope, Mildred K., 310
Postgate, J. P., 306
Pottle, Frederick A., 257
Pound, Ezra, 50–51
Preminger, Alex, 286
Price, Martin, 36
Pringle-Pattison, A. S., 112
Printed books. *See* Documents
Printing and publishing practices, 21, 49–50, 196, 198, 199, 330–31
Prothero, R. E., 258
Publishers' editors. *See* Revision, by persons other than the author
Publishing practices. *See* Printing and publishing practices
Punctuation. *See* Accidentals
Purchas, Samuel, 116

Quentin, Henri, 312–13, 314, 315
Quotations, 75–91, 93–94, 107–12

Rachal, William M. E., 245
Radiating texts, 167–76, 318–19
Raleigh, Walter, 112
Ramsey, Paul, 111, 112
Rand, E. K., 312
Ray, Gordon N., 11, 179, 253
Readers, convenience of, 9–10, 237–39, 266
Redpath, Theodore, 42
Reeves, John K., 195
Regularizing, 10–11, 199–201, 203, 206. *See also* Accidentals
Reichart, Walter A., 256
Reid, T. B. W., 310
Reidlinger, Albert, 92
Reiman, Donald H., 8, 257, 259
Reingold, Nathan, 247–48, 262, 263
Rembrandt Harmensz van Rijn, 336
Renart, Jean, 309
Renehan, Robert, 279

Reproduction: of documents, 8, 16, 22, 239, 302. *See also* Transcription
Revision: kinds of, 52–67; motivations for, 18, 49, 52–67; by persons other than the author, 45, 46–51, 68–70, 193, 194, 202; in private writings, 7, 10, 16, 64–67, 229–30, 245, 267–68; in writings intended for publication, 16–19, 43–63, 65–67, 204–5, 207–13, 307. *See also* Editorial apparatus; Textual variants
Reynolds, L. D., 276, 292, 304, 305
Richardson, Charles, 96
Richardson, Samuel, 182–84, 187, 189
Ricks, Christopher, 93
Rideout, Walter B., 44
Rigg, A. G., 304
Ringler, Richard N., 90
Riverside Editions, 215
Roberts, C. H., 289
Roberts, Jeanne A., 22
Robson, John M., 184, 328
Rockas, Leo, 31
Rogers, George C., Jr., 246
Rollins, Hyder Edward, 11, 255
Roma, Emilio, III, 31
Roosevelt, Theodore, 253–54
Roques, Mario, 298
Rosenfeld, Paul, 43–44
Rowley, H. H., 304
Rundell, Walter, Jr., 222, 223, 250
Runge, William H., 245
Rush, Benjamin, 250
Rusk, Ralph Leslie, 11, 253
Rutland, Robert A., 245, 247

Sachs, Viola, 76
Sale, William M., Jr., 216
Salter, F. M., 313
Samaran, Charles, 304
Sandys, J. E., 306
Saussure, Ferdinand de, 37, 92, 93
Savile, Anthony, 30, 42, 69
Schoeck, R. J., 266
Schoenbaum, Samuel, 266
Scholarly editing. *See* Editing, scholarly
Scholes, Robert, 31
Schouten, Willem Cornelis, 85
Schueller, Herbert M., 11, 258

Science: in bibliography and textual criticism, 325–28; works of, 14

Scoresby, William, 77, 101

Scott, Walter, 103

Scribners, 69

Sealts, Merton M., Jr.: as editor of *Billy Budd*, 16, 82, 102–5, 106, 125, 141, 271

Searle, John R., 34

Sebastiano del Piombo, 336

Sechehaye, Albert, 92

Severs, J. Burke, 312

Shakespeare, William, 179, 238, 263, 335; characteristics of early texts of, 21, 45; editing of, 120–21, 127, 134–35, 163, 309; Norton facsimile, 286; *The Tempest*, 22

Sharrock, Roger, 214

Shaver, Chester L., 257

Shaw, Peter: on CEAA editions, 102–5, 224–25, 262, 269, 271, 272, 281

Shelley, Fred, 222, 223, 261

Shelley, Percy Bysshe, 8, 69, 257–58, 268

Shepard, William P., 309, 313, 315

Shillingsburg, Peter L., 213

Shipley, Joseph T., 30

Sibbald, Robert, 84

Simms, William Gilmore: letters, 255; South Carolina edition of, 121, 122, 132, 133, 134, 154, 156, 157, 190, 197

Simon, John Y., 247

Simpson, Claude M., Jr., 256, 329

Skinner, Quentin, 33, 34, 37, 38

Smith, D. I. B., 250, 258

Smith, D. Nichol, 214

Smith, Elizabeth Oakes, 79–80

Smith, Henry Nash, 11, 255

Smith, John E., 111

Smith, Margaret, 210–11

Smith, R. Jack, 31

Smock, Raymond W., 248

Smollett, Tobias, 95, 215

Somers, 105

Soper, Kate, 289

Sources, 80–83, 88–89, 100–101

Sparks, Jared, 222

Speer, Mary Blakely, 282, 298, 304, 307

Spelling: of proper names, 94–97. *See also* Accidentals

Spence, Joseph, 109

Spence, Mary Lee, 245

Spenser, Edmund, 80, 83

Sprigge, Timothy L. S., 263–64

Stafford, Richard, 85, 89

Stahlin, O., 298

Starr, G. A., 215

Statesmen's papers: editions of, 240–49

Stedman, Arthur, 59

Stendhal (Marie Henri Beyle), 108

Stern, Milton, 106

Sterne, Laurence, 83–84, 211–12, 214

Stevens, Jane, 213

Stoll, Jakob, 289

Stout, Gardner, 211–12

Stow, John, 85

Strawson, P. F., 37

Substantives, 20, 28, 164, 169–73, 330–34

Sutcliffe, F. E., 310

Sutherland, James, 262–63

Swift, Jonathan, 214, 257

Swinburne, Algernon Charles, 251

Symonds, John Addington, 11, 258

Syrett, Harold C., 244–45

Tanselle, G. Thomas: on analytical bibliography, 283; on Anderson edition, 43, 216; on Brown edition, 190; on copy-text, 147, 319; on Crane edition, 61; on editing historical documents, 13, 103, 281; on editing fiction, 281; as editor of Melville, 21, 54, 122, 190, 330; on editorial apparatus, 65, 168, 191, 267, 298, 319; on editorial judgment, 29, 97, 124; on Hawthorne edition, 61; on intention, 4, 82, 92, 106, 124, 188, 264, 271, 329; on Melville, 197; *A Rationale of Textual Criticism*, ix, xi; *Textual Criticism since Greg* (and constituent essays), ix, xi, xii, xiii, 20, 27, 50, 191, 223, 264, 270, 275; on textual scholarship 275; on type damage, 149

Tarrant, R. J., 297

Taylor, Edward, 238

Tebbel, John, 222

Teigen, Philip M., 283

Tennyson, Alfred, 1st baron, 69
Texts: distinguished from works, xiv,
    14, 16–17, 19, 22–23, 104, 280–81,
    284–88
Textual criticism: of classical, biblical,
    and medieval writings, 274–75, 278–
    79, 282–98, 305–15; defined, xiv,
    277, 278; and literary criticism, xi,
    xiv. See also Editing, scholarly
Textual variants: in printed editions,
    21, 44–46, 149–50, 164, 285–86. See
    also Editorial apparatus; Revision
Thackeray, William Makepeace, 11,
    212–13, 253
Thomas, D. Winton, 304
Thomas, Jonathan, 197
Thompson, S. Harrison, 296
Thoreau, Henry David, 21, 112, 113–14,
    265
Thorp, Willard, 216, 222
Thorpe, Clarence DeWitt, 72
Thorpe, James: as editor of MLA
    pamphlet, 28, 52, 122, 191, 275,
    328; Principles of Textual Criti-
    cism (and constituent essays), 48–
    50, 68, 277, 305, 325, 329
Thwaites, Reuben Gold, 263
Tillotson, Geoffrey, 212–13
Tillotson, Kathleen, 179, 204–7, 212–13
Timpanaro, Sebastiano, 289, 305
Titian (Tiziano Vecellio), 72
Todd, Mabel Loomis, 68
Tolles, Frederick B., 262–63
Tompkins, E. Berkeley, 222
Tooke, William, 77
Toynbee, Paget, 11, 253
Transcription, 8–9, 12, 16, 225–40, 298
Troil, Uno von, 78, 86, 90–91
Trollope, Anthony, 216
Truman, Harry S, 221
Twain, Mark. See Clemens, Samuel L.
Tyerman, Daniel, 85
Type damage, 149–50
Typography, 203

Ulloa, Antonio de, 86
Urmson, J. O., 34

Van Marter, Shirley, 182–84, 185
Van Sickle, John, 289

Vandersee, Charles, 56
Variants, textual. See Textual variants
Versions: distinguished from works, 18–
    19, 52–63, 185–88
Vieth, David M., 315
Vinaver, Eugène, 310–11
Vincent, Howard P., 214
Vivas, Eliseo, 31
Vogt, George L., xi, 275
Voltaire (François Marie Arouet), 250–
    51

Wade, Allan, 251
Waingrow, Marshall, 257
Waldron, R. A., 311
Waller, Edmund, 77, 80, 81–82, 83
Walpole, Horace, 249–50, 252–53, 260
Warren, Austin, 38
Washington, Booker T., 248
Washington, George, 246
Watt, Ian, 201, 214
Weaver, Herbert, 246
Webster, Daniel, 249
Weinberg, Bernard, 184–85, 186
Weitz, Morris, 37
Weitzman, M. P., 315
Wellek, René, 38, 106
West, Martin L., 282, 283, 288–97, 313
Westbury, Barry, 216
Westcott, B. F., 306
Whalley, George, 34
Wharey, James B., 214
Whibley, Leonard, 11, 253, 306
White, Ray Lewis, 43, 47, 216
Whitehead, Frederick, 309, 310, 311
Whitehill, Walter Muir, 243
Whitman, Walt, 18, 60, 61, 62, 262
Wilde, Oscar, 251–52
Wiley & Putnam, 53
Wilkes, Charles, 79
Williams, Harold, 257
Willis, James, 282–83, 288, 289, 293, 296,
    297
Wilson, Angus, 208
Wilson, Edmund, 122
Wilson, F. P., 283
Wilson, N. G., 276, 292, 304, 305
Wilson, Woodrow, 246–47
Wiltse, Charles M., 249
Wimsatt, W. K., 30–31, 36, 37

Wolf, Edwin, 2nd, 220
Woodbridge, F. J. E., 108
Wordsworth, Dorothy, 257
Wordsworth, William, 38, 60, 257
Work, James A., 214
Works, verbal: distinguished from texts, xiv, 14, 16–17, 19, 22–23, 104, 280–81, 284–88; distinguished from versions, 18–19, 52–63, 185–88; form and content in, 5; genres of, 3–6; intended for private purposes, 5–13, 16, 64–65, 103–4, 218–73; intended for public distribution, 5–6, 13–23, 103–5, 125, 179–217, 270–71

Wormald, Francis, 289
Wright, C. E., 289
Wright, Esmond, 219, 260
Wright, G. Ernest, 304
Wright, Nathalia, 256
Wright, William Aldis, 120, 134–35

Yeats, William Butler, 116, 251

Zall, P. M., 220, 241
Zangrando, Robert L., 261
Zeller, Hans, 39–40, 48–49, 57, 69, 186–88